The Attention Economy

Karen Nelson-Field

The Attention Economy

A Category Blueprint

Karen Nelson-Field
Amplified Intelligence
Adelaide, SA, Australia

ISBN 978-981-97-0083-7   ISBN 978-981-97-0084-4   (eBook)
https://doi.org/10.1007/978-981-97-0084-4

This Palgrave Macmillan imprint is published by the registered company Springer Nature Singapore Pte Ltd.
The registered company address is: 152 Beach Road, #21-01/04 Gateway East, Singapore 189721, Singapore

If disposing of this product, please recycle the paper.

Foreword

It has been over five years since Karen first embarked on the exploration of human attention measurement in advertising, and the journey has been nothing short of transformative. As we dig deeper into the follow-up to her groundbreaking first book, it's remarkable to witness that the foundational knowledge laid out in the initial exploration has not only stood the test of time but has become the cornerstone upon which an entire category has been erected—an intricate edifice of insights, learnings, and paradigm shifts.

In the world we inhabit today, the noise has not diminished; if anything, it has become more intricate, demanding a level of sophistication in our approach to capturing and retaining the precious commodity of human attention. Karen's pioneering work has been a guiding light for marketers navigating the dynamic landscape of data abundance and attention scarcity.

This second installment looks deeper into the now-established domain of human attention measurement in advertising. Karen invites us to explore the ramifications of rapidly changing technology on businesses striving to thrive in the attention economy. In a world where misinformation can eclipse truth, her voice emerges as a beacon—steadfast in its dedication to objective theory grounded in scientific measurement and methodological rigor.

The pages that follow are a testament to Karen's unwavering commitment to uncovering the truths that lie at the intersection of data-driven insights and human-centric perspectives. Her work provides not just answers but evidence-based revelations that distill the complexities of modern media challenges into simple, yet powerful truths.

This book is not just a sequel; it is a testament to the enduring relevance of Karen's contributions in a landscape where the pursuit of attention is both an art and a science. As we consider the findings that she has illuminated, we are reminded that the quest for attention is not just about capturing moments but about understanding the very essence of what captivates us all.

Brussels, Belgium   Laurent Larguinat
February 2024

Preface—An Adventurer's Log

We're very simple people at Apple.
We focus on making the world's best products and enriching people's lives.
Tim Cook, CEO Apple

Mapping the Past and Charting the Future

It has been four years since the release of the first Attention Economy book, where we explored pivotal moments that transformed our industry, like the advent of hyperscaling and the 'Like' button, as well as the arrival of programmatic trading. A period that I said brought chaos to the CMO like no other time in marketing history. Well dear friends, I stand corrected. The last few years has seen a reckoning of ad fraud, the imminent collapse of third-party cookies, a movement towards sustainability plus our entire currency constitution called to account with industry bodies driving advanced plans for transparency and change. And if that's not enough, a period that (due to many things notwithstanding the pandemic) has brought chaos up the food chain to the CEO, who is currently interrogating down the food chain to the

CMO on the discrepancy of increased advertising costs yet diminished results for the bottom line. A period where a whole marketing industry swooped on attention economics seizing it as an opportunity to address the questions posed by their CEO.

This book serves as a comprehensive guide, chronicling the lessons learned since the first book's release and providing a clear blueprint and point-of-view for initiating change now and outlining the changes required for the future. It aims to provide coherence to a domain that previously lacked it, covering topics such as the birth of the category, the value and monetization of attention, with updated research and stories to illustrate key concepts. It discusses rogue reach and rogue measurement, category generation and the generation of outcomes, ethical practices and practicing change. As well as relationship breakdowns and makeups, unlearning and relearning, the perfect storm and the perfect response.

To make the reading experience a bit more enjoyable and informative, the book includes breakouts with quick tips for practical use, explanations of complex concepts, amusing industry anecdotes and more, these include:

- **TAKE IT TO WORK** (quick tips for the readers to use attention in practice)
- **QUICK EXPLAINER** (where a concept needs more explanation but not to interrupt the main copy flow)
- **RAPID RECAP** (where the concept needed to be included but had already been written about in the first book)
- **MEANWHILE IN THE REAL WORLD** (funny stories about somewhat relevant situations in industry)
- **EXPERT INSIGHT** (serious stories from serious industry legends that add value to the context)

These pages are supposed to be both fun and serious at the same time, so you might encounter a diverse cast of characters that help tell the attention story including Kim Kardashian, Moira Rose, a professional thief, Han Solo, a Harvard Professor, a famous tech entrepreneur, an Emmy Award winner and a bit of 70's glam.

But above all this book is designed to get your attention so you can understand attention.

On the Shoulders of Others

But this book isn't just my story; it celebrates industry giants who embraced innovative thinking and pushed boundaries to drive progress. These pioneers recognized the potential of innovation and played a pivotal role in the historical change in measurement. So, much like a blueprint, this book offers different views and perspectives on attention measurement and economics from multiple angles, showcasing their trials, tribulations and their invaluable contributions to the most significant shift in measurement in 30 years.

Though I owe a debt of gratitude to many more, this book spotlights these exceptional individuals (full bios at the end of each chapter).

The Promise

So dear readers, as you step into this journey with me, I promise to bring you scientific facts and provide you with memorable benchmarks that will guide your work. Above all else I promise to simplify the complex, to bring calm to your chaos, to bring rigor to the laxity and to bring a dash of humor to an otherwise boring subject.

Together, we'll explore The Attention Economy in both its inception and its development, and emerge on the other side with a clearer blueprint for restoring equilibrium to an industry lost.

Happy reading.

Adelaide, SA, Australia   Karen Nelson-Field

Acknowledgements

For my Family

Boys. When I wrote my first book you were tiny, when I wrote my second you were teenagers. And now here I am thanking you again with you as young adults. Life goes so fast. Now you cook me dinner, while I am stuck in the office finishing yet another book. I know you still don't actually know what your mum does for a living, except now you think it is cool that I work with some of your favorite media brands.

Pete. Your husband skills are, without a doubt, best in class. Thankyou for being so supportive while I lived in this office for months to get this book done. And thankyou for trying to coax me out of the office on occasion to ensure I don't miss the entire Australian summer. Oh and thankyou for letting me get a cat.

Thank you family, much love to you.

For the Amplified Team

Team. As I pen this final acknowledgement, I'm reminded of the remarkable team we've become. We are such a diverse group with varying expertise, yet our unique blend is pure gold, consistently delivering outstanding work. Our rapid progress and global recognition fill me with pride. Every Town Hall meeting I am in shock how much progress we make. Equally, the fun we have in the office, the moments of uncontrollable laughter, are sources of joy. Fun is an essential ingredient of our success, and an essential ingredient in happiness.

I am profoundly grateful to each of you.

For Laurent Larguinat, the writer of the Foreword

Laurent Larguinat is VP Mars Horizon for Mars Inc. Mars Horizon lives at the intersection of Sciences, Technology and Business. This intersection is where the magic happens. We collaborate with world-class academic partners, research organizations and start-ups to incubate, develop and deploy solutions to Mars' marketing and sales challenges.

For our Customers

Attention Advocates. You have written this book with me. Without you there would be no second edition. You have not merely been spectators, you have been active participants in the research and innovation that has literally brought change to an industry. Your willingness to step out of the ordinary has played a pivotal role in shaping the content of this book. So this book is a testament to you and the commitment you have all made to innovation.

Thank you for thinking differently.

Contents

List of Figures

List of Tables

1

The First Episode

Children, keep an eye on these bags. Apparently in hell, there's no bellman!
Moira Rose. Schitts Creek. Season 1, Episode 1 (2015)

Every story, much like the debut episode of a multi season Netflix series, needs initial context. While the first episode may not be quite as funny or lovable as found in later episodes, and sometimes it needs greater attention to understand the context, it serves a crucial purpose—the stage needs to be set, the key characters introduced and laying the foundation for the plot. This is the reason for this chapter—we need some plot setting.

In the first chapter of the first Attention Economy book, we went on a tour through two transformative decades—a pivotal 20-year span marked by technological upheaval, chaos, and societal adaptation. These were the years that forever altered our media landscape, gave us the Like button, programmatic and virality, and in turn reshaped our relationship with advertising forever. In these plot setting pages you will find less about the moments that mattered in media, rather the moments that mattered to seeking, researching and defining attention. These moments are important in a category blueprint.

Rest assured though, just because this chapter is plot setting it doesn't mean it's boring. Sure there is a bit of research theory in here, but it is sprinkled

© The Author(s), under exclusive license to Springer Nature
Singapore Pte Ltd. 2024
K. Nelson-Field, *The Attention Economy*, https://doi.org/10.1007/978-981-97-0084-4_1

with memorable fails, flying Teslas, elephants and even the Kardashians make an appearance.

So in echoing the wisdom of Moira Rose, who once aptly declared, "One must become their own champion and declare, 'I am prepared for this!'"—should you choose to dig into this chapter, rest assured that the ultimate reward will be even more satisfying (plus the rest of the book will make more sense).

1.1   A Journey Through Advertising's Attention-Seeking History

Happy Birthday Google

On September 27, 2023, Google marked its 25th anniversary, commemorating a quarter-century of transformative changes in the media landscape. Gone are the days when brand managers had to rely on phone calls to local newspapers and radio stations, competing for limited advertising space or airtime to convey geographically restricted, one-dimensional messages.

Today, brand managers enjoy an array of tools for creating personalized narratives and capturing global attention. Brands can effectively stand out in the crowded digital space, connecting with a broader audience than ever before. Google, and other online publishers, has opened up exceptional opportunities for audience engagement, allowing brands to build deeper connections and enhance brand recognition.

Or do they?

Amidst this seemingly limitless potential, a darker issue looms—the prevalence of unclear and unreliable measurement. Ironically, contemporary measurement methods provide little insight into human engagement or the true effectiveness of brand visibility. This leads to the question: How does this lack of transparency affect the realization of brand goals? Does this unreliability hinder or facilitate a brand's ability to attract attention in the first place? And what impact does this have on brand recognition?

But before we dive into this Pandora's box, let's take a look at the historical journey of attention research across decades, and how the changing nature of inquiry has sparked fresh questions and ushered in new phases.

The History of Attention Experiments

To spare you from a lengthy and potentially dull account of the entire history of attention research, this section offers a concise compilation of some of the most influential and seminal papers in the field of attention research up to this point. It aims to emphasize the evolving focus of attention inquiry, transitioning from traditional media to digital, from basic to advanced research methodologies, and spanning industries from advertising to computer science.

While there are many more noteworthy papers that could be included, these selections have been chosen due to their widespread recognition within academic and research circles, their frequent citations, their lasting relevance, and their historical significance in shaping the field of advertising effectiveness. The following list serves as a foundation for the rest of the book.

If you're interested in a more comprehensive review of attention literature and case evidence, you may want to delve into the 2023 ARF Attention Validation Initiative, which includes a detailed literature review.

1. 1960s–1970s—Early Exploration of Attention to Print Advertising and Setting the Foundation

In the 1960s and 1970s, academic research marked the inception of attention study and set the groundwork for its connection with consumer behavior. This period yielded substantial insights into measuring and forecasting advertising effectiveness, forming the basis for comprehending attention in advertising. The study of attention was undeniably initiated by David Broadbent during this era.

a. Perception and communication (1958) by Broadbent, D.

Main Contribution: Broadbent is credited with pioneering the modern study of attention by consolidating various experiments in information theory and psychology. His groundbreaking work introduced the concept that attention functions as a filter, enabling the selection of certain information for deeper processing while filtering the rest out. Additionally, he was also the first to apply this to learning theory, specifically implicit and explicit learning.

b. A Model for Predictive Measurements of Advertising Effectiveness (1961) by Lavidge, R & Steiner, G.

Main Contribution: These authors introduced the Hierarchy of Effects model, which underscores the sequential stages that consumers typically experience when exposed to advertising: Awareness, Knowledge,

Liking, Preference, Conviction, and Purchase. Their model established the foundation for forecasting and assessing advertising effectiveness.

c. Visual Imaging Ability As a Mediator of Advertising Response (1978) by Rossiter, J & Percy, L.

Main Contribution: Rossiter introduced the groundbreaking concept of "visual imaging ability" as a pivotal factor in advertising response. This concept highlights an individual's capability to mentally create images from visual stimuli, emphasizing its significant impact on their reactions to advertising messages. It asserts that visual imaging ability plays a vital role in shaping the link between exposure to advertising and subsequent consumer responses.

2. 1980s–1990's Transition to Television Attention

During the late 1980s and throughout the 1990s, academic research witnessed a significant shift towards the examination of attention, particularly in the context of television advertising. These studies placed a considerable emphasis on assessing advertising effectiveness and the ability to predict viewer responses.

a. Television and Its Audience (1988) by Barwise, T & Ehrenberg, A.

Main Contribution: Barwise and Ehrenberg delivered a substantial contribution by questioning conventional assumptions about TV audiences and advertising. It offers valuable insights into audience behavior, uncovering that viewers are not as deeply engaged as previously believed. Many viewers engage in multitasking or channel surfing during commercials, challenging the notion of a captive and highly attentive audience.

b. Attention, Attitude, and Action: How Commercials Affect Television Viewers (1991) by Heath, R.

Main Contribution: In this paper, Robert Heath looks into the intricate relationship between television commercials, viewer attention, and their subsequent influence on attitudes and behaviors. The study explores how commercials succeed in both capturing and sustaining the attention of television viewers. It emphasizes that the effectiveness of advertising is not solely determined by reach but also by its capacity to engage the audience's attention.

3. 2000s—Rise of Attention Studies in Digital Advertising

The 2000s marked the rise of digital advertising, catalyzing a shift in academic research towards the examination of attention in online environments. This period represented a pivotal stage in evaluating the effectiveness and fairness of the expanding array of online formats. It was also a time when the initial inquiries into advertising fraud began to surface.

a. High-Cost Banner Blindness: Ads Increase Perceived Workload, Hinder Visual Search, and Are Forgotten (2005) by Burke et al.

Main Contribution: The study investigates the influence of banner advertisements on visual search and cognitive workload. It aims to resolve the apparent contradiction between "banner blindness," where users tend to overlook banner ads, and users' complaints about distracting advertisements.

b. First attention then intention: Insights from computational neuroscience of vision (2008) Milosavljevic, M & Cerf, M.

Main Contribution: The paper underscores the importance of considering attention as a two-component construct, involving both bottom-up and top-down processes, to gain a better understanding of how attention operates. Additionally, it highlights the significance of investigating attention within the intersecting fields of marketing and neuroscience, introducing computational neuroscience to the marketing discipline.

c. An Empirical Analysis of Search Engine Advertising (2009) by Ghose, A & Yang, S.

Main Contribution: This study examines sponsored search advertising, with a specific focus on metrics such as click-through rates, conversion rates, cost per click, and ad rankings. Notably, it is one of the early studies to challenge the prevailing assumption of equal value among different ad formats, highlighting the inequities that exist.

4. 2010s—Neuroscientific Methods Arrive

The 2010s witnessed a notable shift in the exploration of advertising attention. Academic research began incorporating neuroscientific approaches to delve into the physiological aspects of attention concerning responses to advertising stimuli.

a. Predicting advertising effectiveness by facial expressions in response to amusing persuasive stimuli (2014) by Lewinski, P., et al.

Main Contribution: Lewinski makes a substantial contribution to marketing research by showcasing the connection between facial expressions of happiness and viewers' attitudes and perceptions of advertisements. It provides insights into the role of specific emotions in advertising effectiveness. Additionally, it bolsters the credibility and reliability of computer science methodologies in contrast to traditional self-reported methods.

b. Predicting Advertising Success Beyond Traditional Measures: New Insights from Neurophysiological Methods and Market Response Modeling (2015) by Venkatraman, V. et al.

Main Contribution: Venkatraman and colleagues employed neuroscientific techniques, such as fMRI and skin conductance, to explore the cognitive and emotional dimensions of consumer attention when exposed to advertising stimuli. Their research unveiled the activation of distinct brain regions in response to different advertising elements, providing valuable insights into the neural processes governing consumer attention, emotional responses, memorability, and desirability.

5. 2020s—Attention Research and Advanced Methods

In the contemporary era, researchers started to more deeply consider the impact of attentional switching in media on memory and everyday life. This period has also witnessed a blurring of boundaries between the social sciences and computer sciences, facilitating greater interdisciplinary collaboration, particularly in the field of computational neuroscience.

a. Memory failure predicted by attention lapsing and media multitasking (2020) by Madore, K. P., et al.

Main Contribution: This paper explores the connection between attention lapses and memory within the context of the contemporary digital age. It specifically investigates how instances of inattention, whether spontaneous lapses or as a consequence of media multitasking, are inversely related to an individual's capacity to remember. Their findings indicated that increased engagement in media multitasking is linked to a higher likelihood of experiencing attention lapses and subsequently forgetting information.

b. Attention in Psychology, Neuroscience, and Machine Learning (2020) by Lindsay, G.

Main Contribution: Lindsay's research highlights the pivotal role of attention in shaping the content of memory, thereby influencing the learning process. Moreover, attention and learning are closely interconnected; attention serves as a guide for acquiring knowledge about the external world, and these internal world models, in turn, direct attention. The research shows that while conscious attention is essential for acquiring complex skills, like mastering a musical instrument, once fully learned, these processes can eventually become automatic.

MEANWHILE IN THE REAL WORLD
Apparently opening Pandora's Box is good for sustainability.

Pandora's Box is a phrase derived from Greek mythology often used as a metaphor to describe a situation where a seemingly innocent or simple action leads to a 'no turning back' moment filled with unexpected and harmful consequences. In the myth, Pandora was given a box and instructed not to open it. However, her curiosity got the better of her, and she opened the box, releasing all 'the evils', diseases, and troubles of the world (funnily enough according to some mythology literature, the target of all the evils were men). On a brighter side, the one item left in the box was 'hope'. Hope remained in the box as a gift to help those targeted by the evils during hardships and challenges that were now part of their existence.

A set of researchers in Germany wrote a paper in the Journal of Psychology of Sustainability and Sustainable Development titled; Why We Should Empty Pandora's Box to Create a Sustainable Future. According to the authors, motivation for action for climate change practices is inhibited largely by the perception of it being 'insufficiently probable'. In other words, humans are not motivated to act more sustainably in their daily lives due to lack of hope that their efforts are worth it. The authors studied the construct of 'hope' in more than 2500 people and found that indeed hope is a key ingredient for making positive changes in our world, especially when it comes to actioning sustainable development. Without it people become cynical and take on a passive stance.

This is good news for all men who are both targeted with the evils and live under the effects of climate change.

AIDA was the Kardashian Moment

When there is contention for attention, those who seek it turn to the most reliable attention getters: sex, hierarchy, calamity, and so forth. (Thomas H. Davenport & John C. Beck, 2001)

The Kardashian name has become synonymous with the art of attracting and commanding attention. If you could pinpoint a pivotal (family friendly) moment that launched them into the mainstream, it would be the premiere of their reality TV series 'Keeping Up with the Kardashians' airing in October 2007. Over the years, the family's fame grew meteorically, and they became influential figures in the world of entertainment and popular culture.

Now, let's rephrase that in the context of attention economics. When did professionals begin to recognize the significance of capturing attention in advertising, marking the pivotal moment that popularized attention attraction as a crucial phase in the marketing process? This pivotal moment can be attributed to the evolution of the Hierarchy of Effects model, known as AIDA.

AIDA, as likely 99% of you know, stands for Attention (creating awareness), Interest (generating interest), Desire (stimulating desire or want for the product), and Action (promoting a purchase or other response).

First developed by Elmo Lewis in the late nineteenth century, the 'Hierarchy of Effects Model' in advertising is a theoretical framework to explain how advertising can impact a consumer's choice to buy, or not buy, a product or service. It outlines sequential 'stages' or 'steps of learning' that consumers reportedly go through in the lead up to a sale. The theory is that when advertisers understand these stages they can build structured advertising messages around the user stages to improve the odds of action.

In a nutshell the Hierarchy of Effects Model attempts to explain how advertising works.

Though it originated in the early 1900s, more than a century later, these models continue to undergo refinement and adaptation. This ongoing evolution closely aligns with the natural progression of technology and shifts in the media landscape, as well as how people engage in communication and social interactions in the post-connectivity era. The table below (Table 1.1) shows a timeline of the critical papers in the field, and highlights the evolutionary modifications.

What is the shared characteristic among these models? Attention.

Among the papers listed, approximately 65% either include the term "attention" in their titles or incorporate stages related to attention in their

Table 1.1   A summary of the incremental development of hierarchy of effects models

Date	Model	Stages	Author	Modification
1898	AID	Attention, Interest, Desire	E. St Elmo Lewis	**Original** guide for salesmen to be successful in moving a prospect to buy
1900	AIDA	Attention, Interest, Desire, Action	E. St Elmo Lewis	Added the **Action** stage to complete the selling process
1911	AIDAS	Attention, Interest, Desire, Action, Satisfaction	Arthur F. Sheldon	Added **'Favorable Attention'** and **'Permanent Satisfaction'** as a necessary part of the persuasive selling process
1921	AIDCA	Attention, Interest, Desire, Caution, Action	Robert E. Ramsay	Introduced **Caution** to contend direct response advertising push back
1921	AIDCA	Attention, Interest, Desire, Conviction, Action	Harry D. Kitson	Introduced **Conviction** as related to how the mind of the buyer works
1922	AIJA	Attention, Interest, Judgement, Action	Alexander Osborn	Introduced **Judgment** as a component of the creative process
1938	(AID(W)C(S)PS)	Attention, Interest, Desire (Want), Conviction (Solution), Purchase, Satisfaction	Edward K. Strong, Jr	Introduces **three different stages of Attention** and interest before 'want' can occur
1956	AIDMA	Attention, Interest, Desire, Memory, Action	Merrill DeVoe	Referred to the importance of **Memory** in constructing advertisements
1961	ACCA	Awareness, Comprehension, Conviction, Action	Russell H. Colley	First consideration of **Comprehension** as it relates to advertising goals. Introduced DAGMAR related to goals.
1961	CAN	Cognitive, Affective, Conative	Robert Lavidge and Gary Steiner	Introduced **'Realm of Cognition'** being important to successful advertising
1961	EPC(K)C(A)A	Exposure, Perception, Communication (Knowledge), Communication (Attitude), Action	Advertising Research Foundation	First supported model **for Practitioners**
1962	AIETA	Awareness, Interest, Evaluation, Trial, Adoption	Everett M. Rogers	First to report **Trial** as an important part of the process

(continued)

Table 1.1 (continued)

Date	Model	Stages	Author	Modification
1969	PACYRB	Presentation, Attention, Comprehension, Yielding, Retention, Behavior	William J. McGuire	The first to attach conditional probabilities to the sequence, suggesting message **Retention** is conditional on likelihood of success
1971	ACALTA	Awareness, Comprehension, Attitude, Legitimization, Trial, Adoption	Thomas S. Robertson	The first to suggest that **Legitimization** (relates to cognition)
1974	ATR	Awareness, Trial, Reinforcement	Andrew S.C. Ehrenberg	The first to suggest a hierarchy model should not be **Linear/Sequential**
1975	APMAI	Attention, Perception, Memory, Attitude, Intention	Morris B. Holbrook	This model acknowledges the **Experiential Elements** i.e. how a consumer perceives the act of consumption as it relates to symbolic, pleasurable, and aesthetic aspects
1982	The Association Model	25 stages ranging from Distribution Exposure-Product Perception- Trial-Adoption-Evaluation	Ivan L. Preston	First to introduce **Search** behaviors
1982	CAC	Cognition, Affect, Commitment	Robert E. Smith and William R. Swinyard	First to point out that the learning hierarchy may not be appropriate for **Low Involvement** purchase situations
2011	AISDALSLove	Attention, Interest, Search, Desire, Action, Like/dislike, Share, Love/hate	Bambang S. Wijaya	First to shift from product-oriented to **Consumer-Oriented strategies** reflecting the evolving dynamics of consumer engagement and public influence in the digital age

(continued)

Table 1.1 (continued)

Date	Model	Stages	Author	Modification
2017	Three response sequences	Ad Processing Sequence, Brand Communication Effects Sequence, Buyer Stage Sequence	J. R. Rossiter and L. Percy	First to suggest that three **Simultaneous Response Sequences** should be considered. Attention is the first component of the model
2022	ARF Media Model	Vehicle Distribution, Vehicle Exposure, Advertising Exposure, Advertising Attentiveness, Advertising Communication, Advertising Persuasion, Advertising Response, Sales Response	Advertising Research Foundation	An update of the 1961 model to reflect changes in advertising theory and practice and the consideration of new media. The first model to have a **Greater Focus on Media Performance**. The stages are not necessarily sequential

models, underscoring its crucial role as an initial phase in understanding consumer behavior. The remaining papers utilize terms like cognition, exposure, and awareness, which are closely associated with attention.

Although AIDA and its various iterations have achieved widespread adoption, they have faced criticism over the years. As time has passed, several criticisms have emerged, including the following:

- the sequential stages are wrong (i.e. not all buying processes are linear),
- the current models don't account for a divided-attention situation (i.e. both active and passive attention play a role),
- attitude change is not a mandatory precursor to purchase (i.e. desire might not be in the right order).

In 2022, The Advertising Research Foundation (ARF) tackled contemporary concerns by introducing an updated, 21st-century iteration of the AIDA model that aptly mirrors the customer's journey in today's era of internet connectivity. The ARF unveiled 'Making Better Media Decisions,' a paper outlining a novel framework for gauging advertising effectiveness. The distinguished committee initiated the paper with the following introduction:

The way advertisers think about media has changed in the last forty years. Direct Response advertising, The Internet and Interactive TV have expanded media's job from simply exposing a message to include encouraging and facilitating a response. The concept of recency has focused marketers on advertising's contribution to making the next sale. And more and more, it is on response that media are being judged. We believe that media measurement has no choice but to follow media's newly expanded purposes.

In the paper, they introduced an updated version of their 2002 model that includes eight levels for assessing and measuring media performance to help practitioners plan and measure advertising campaigns (see Fig. 1.1). Each level is assigned a unique number and color, with increasing order of advertising relevance, this is not about order of importance or order of sequence, rather to depict the relative number of people they expect need to be involved at each level. This is an important distinction.

This is the example they use: The number of people who buy the advertised product (Sales Response, segment 8, colored red) is smaller than the number persuaded by the advertising (segment 6), which is smaller than the number attentive to the advertising (segment 4) and so on.

Here is a brief description of each level, more detail can be found on their website:

1. **Vehicle Distribution:** This measures the number of physical units through which advertising is distributed and is purely a media effect.
2. **Vehicle Exposure:** It counts the people exposed to the media vehicle with open eyes or ears and is a pure media effect.
3. **Advertising Exposure:** This counts people exposed to the media vehicle who also see its advertising. It's the highest level of measurement as a

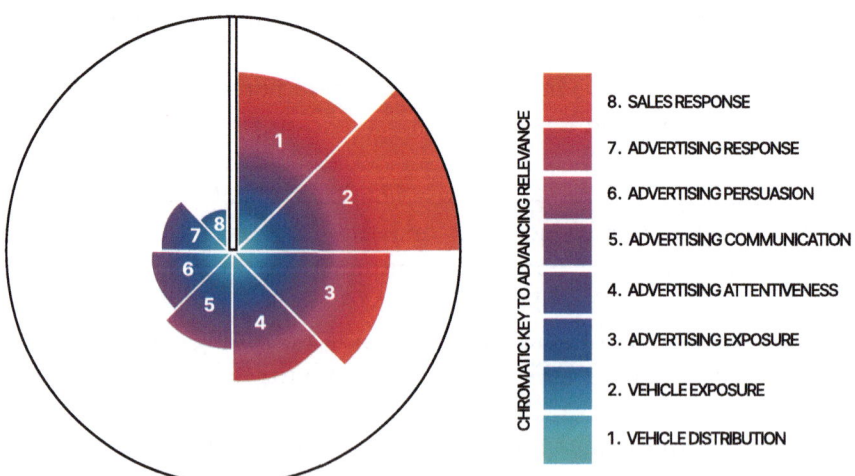

Fig. 1.1   The ARF new media helix (*Source* ARF Making Better Media Decisions 2022)

pure media effect and includes ratings, page-exposure studies, and ad-view counts.

4. **Advertising Attentiveness:** This assesses the degree to which viewers focus on advertising, with effects of creative coming into play.

5. **Advertising Communication:** It measures the information retained by consumers after exposure to the message, involving advertising and brand awareness tracking and recall studies.

6. **Advertising Persuasion:** This measures the impact of Advertising Communication on intentions, focusing on making the message credible and persuasive.

7. **Advertising Response:** It evaluates consumer actions short of sales, such as showroom visits, toll-free calls, or online ad clicks.

8. **Sales Response:** This is the purchase of the advertised product or service and is most relevant to advertisers.

In summary, as various models have evolved to accommodate changes in media and consumer behavior over the years, they consistently acknowledge the crucial role of attention in achieving advertising success. From the early 1900s to the present day, all hierarchy of effects models and broader advertising effectiveness models view attention as either a preliminary step or an integral part of the path towards a sales response. Attention plays a fundamental role in maintaining retention, fostering customer commitment, forming memories, promoting adoption, enhancing message comprehension, and addressing various other use cases within these models.

This is why AIDA was the Kardashian moment for attention.

MEANWHILE IN THE REAL WORLD

Here is a list of attention seeking stunts the Kardashian's wish they'd dreamt up (and the ones they are glad they didn't). The first 3 are attention grabbing stunts by brands that actually worked, and just for fun, these are followed by 3 that failed abysmally. The core themes of highly successful attention getting stunts: good media placement, strong branding, high intensity emotion and **GOOD** timing. The core themes of attention getting stunts that failed: good media placement, strong branding, high intensity emotion and **BAD** timing.

1. Win with Oral-B drone deliveries pandemic publicity stunt (2020)

Oral-B's innovative response to the pandemic involved using drones and robots to safely deliver their new high-tech toothbrushes to influencers and the press. This contactless delivery method was an ingenious response to social distancing measures, providing a glimpse of hope during the pandemic.

2. Win with Tesla in space (2018)

In 2018, Tesla and SpaceX made headlines by launching a Tesla Roadster into outer space using their Falcon Heavy rocket. This audacious concept generated a global buzz, providing substantial media coverage and reinforcing their status as pioneering companies.

3. Win with Virgin versus British Air (1999)

Virgin has always been in fierce rivalry with British Airways. In the late 90's when British Airways faced construction challenges with the London Eye, Virgin orchestrated a clever stunt by deploying a branded airship carrying a naughty message about BA's struggles to 'erect' the structure. Not a high tech stunt, but certainly has had a long lasting impact (no pun intended).

4. Fail with LifeLock's CEO stolen identity (2006)

LifeLock CEO Todd Davis boldly displayed his social security number across various media to promote his company's identity theft protection service. However, his own product didn't work and a few years later it was revealed that his identity had been stolen 13 times, with 87 failed attempts. Though Davis claimed this showcased the effectiveness of LifeLock, the Federal Trade Commission disagreed and fined the company $12 million for deceptive advertising in March 2010.

5. Fail with The South Australian Government 'big fish dead fish' debacle (2011)

The South Australian government approved a publicity stunt in 2011 in which 55 goldfish were sent out to media executives to promote a tour of the region by Advantage SA. The fish bowls were inscribed with the message: "Be a big fish in a small pond and come and test the water." However in spite of providing enough food to last each fish 6 months, most of the fish that arrived were already dead. The Australian newspaper reported "South Australia does have a reputation for the worst water in Australia but this is going too far."

6. Fail with The Cartoon Network 'glow in the dark' bombing (2007)

In an effort to promote the "Aqua Teen Hunger Force" film, Cartoon Network concealed illuminated metallic LED signs featuring the show's characters throughout large urban areas. However, once residents of Boston spotted these devices hidden across the city, they alerted the authorities, mistaking them for improvised explosive devices. As a result, Turner Broadcasting and the marketing firm Interference Inc. had to compensate $2 million in damages for the marketing stunt.

A Rising Star

In 2023, the International Journal of Advertising (IJA) celebrated its 40th anniversary by releasing a Special Issue, which marked a significant event recognizing its extensive history of pioneering research in marketing communications. This special release comprised thirty articles contributed by renowned authors who collectively reflected on four decades of advertising research, spanning from 1980 to 2020. The content covered a wide array of advertising topics and research methodologies, including influencer marketing, CSR marketing, electronic word of mouth, celebrity endorsements, sustainability, gender stereotypes, and more.

One particular paper, titled 'The evolution of advertising research through four decades' by Marla Stafford et al., held particular relevance to our own research timeline outlined earlier. This paper conducted a comprehensive meta-analysis of 6084 papers, revealing the prevalence and progression of research themes and trends in the field of advertising.

The authors initially employed topic modeling, an unsupervised machine learning technique for analyzing textual content, to construct a network of topics. Subsequently, they categorized the 70 topics, which encompassed approximately 500 unique words, into four overarching themes: (1) Advertising Effects (represented in blue, constituting 45% of the topics), (2) The Advertising Industry (in red, comprising 32% of the topics), (3) The Audience (in green, making up 12% of the topics), and (4) Commentary (in gray, accounting for 5% of the topics). It's important to note that the authors didn't include outliers, so these percentages do not sum to 100%.

This method produced an undirected network with weighted connections. This network provides insights into the closeness of topics, the strength of their connections, and the prominence of topics within each of the identified themes, as depicted in (Fig. 1.2).

The primary theme that emerges from this analysis centers around 'Advertising Effects' (highlighted in blue, constituting 45% of the topics). This theme encompasses various aspects related to how consumers react to advertisements, often influenced by consumer and content characteristics. Within this theme, attention is presented as an aspect that 'assesses whether an ad can capture and maintain a consumer's interest.' The network diagram illustrates the connections between attention and other related topics, such as neuromarketing and emotions, and to a lesser extent, message testing, narrative marketing, and product placement. These connections involve methodologies like eye tracking, galvanic skin response, and facial recognition, which are utilized to comprehend message effects and decision-making processes.

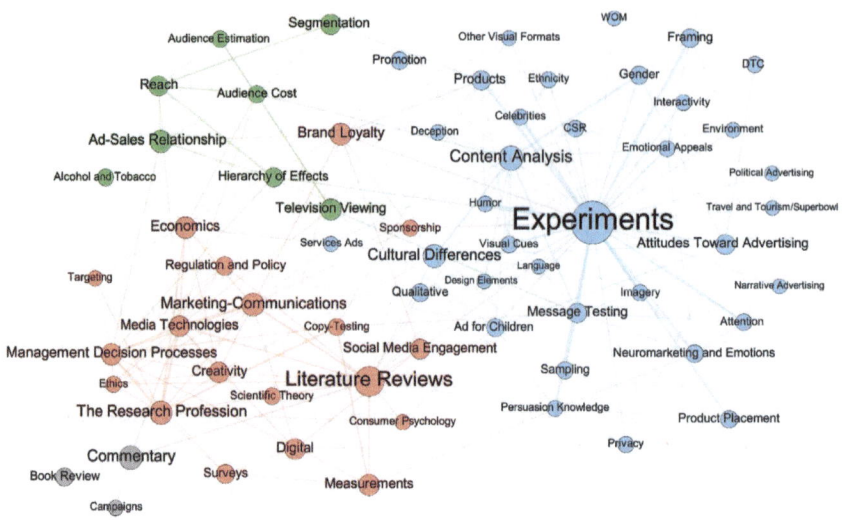

Fig. 1.2 The Stafford advertising research topic model network

In a nutshell, aligning with our own attention research timeline and the increasing trend in computational neuroscience, this study reveals that advanced methodologies, particularly concerning attention in advertising, have gained significant traction among researchers in recent years, with a notable surge starting from 2020. This suggests an evolution and maturation in advertising research, accompanied by a growing interest in more rigorous and robust research, largely driven by industry disruptors.

Fame Doesn't Mean Talent

Being famous is great, but does attention possess talent? Throughout our initial four years of deep diving into the complexities of attention economics, one question resounded consistently: "Is paying attention to advertising crucial for advertising outcomes?".

To help answer this question, here is a collection of nine seminal papers that unequivocally illustrate the significance of attention in achieving advertising success. These papers have played a pivotal role in comprehending the concept of attention and its subsequent influence on advertising outcomes.

In recent years, this question has grown quieter, signifying the industry's evolution. So whether you skim this section, skip it, or temporarily avoid it, this section serves as a valuable resource for revisiting when your CMO, CEO, or client seeks confirmation that attention is a valuable asset, not a fleeting trend.

How to navigate this list: The primary contribution is presented first, followed by the paper details below the text.

1. Product Choice

a. Increases in relative visual attention time (fixations) increase the probability of choosing items, and the opposite is true for aversive items.

This paper enriches our comprehension of how attention influences decision-making and underscores the adaptability of decision processes through attention manipulation. The study reveals that altering the time individuals fixate their visual attention can have a substantial impact on straightforward choices. When attention is directed towards a specific option, individuals are more inclined to select that option, emphasizing the significance of focused attention in the decision-making process.

Paper 1: Biasing simple choices by manipulating relative visual attention (2008) by Armel, K. et al.

b. The level of attention paid is directly linked to the likelihood of choosing products and this is mediated by brand size.

This paper explores the relationship between consumer attention and outcomes in the context of in-store marketing and point-of-purchase behavior. It demonstrates that while improved attention through in-store marketing activities can influence consumer behavior at the point of purchase, this influence is not absolute, as brand equity mediates the outcome. It suggests that low-market-share brands tend to be more responsive to increases in attention than high-market-share brands.

Paper 2: Does In-Store Marketing Work? Effects of the Number and Position of Shelf Facings on Brand Attention and Evaluation at the Point of Purchase (2009) by Chandon, P et al.

c. There is a clear relationship between attention and product choice, beyond the product offer.

This research introduces a new concept in preference formation, highlighting the role of selective attention and inattention. It challenges the traditional belief that product preference relies solely on its benefits. The study's key contribution is demonstrating that allocating or neglecting attention to a product in one context can significantly influence later choices related to that product. This has implications for understanding how attention and perception shape consumer decisions in visually complex environments and how stimulus-based choices can have lasting effects.

Paper 3: The Influence of Selective Attention and Inattention to Products on Subsequent Choice (2013) by Janiszewski, C., et al.

2. Memory

a. Limited attention can negatively influence the outcome of working memory capacity and processes in both early and later stages of processing.

This study enhances our understanding of the connection between attention and working memory. It investigates their interactions, uncovering that attention acts as a gatekeeper, deciding which items are granted access to the limited workspace within working memory.

Paper 4: Interactions between attention and working memory (2006) by Awh, E., Vogel, EK., & Oh, S.

b. Visual attention is a fundamental prerequisite for perception and memory emphasizing its critical role in identification and memory processes relevant to consumer behavior.

This paper revisits the classic work of Broadbent, emphasizing the importance of attention in the identification process. It reaffirms that attention remains a fundamental prerequisite for perception and memory. Furthermore, it introduces a revised version of selective filter theory, taking into account recent research findings.

Paper 5: Forty-Five Years After Broadbent 1958: Still No Identification Without Attention (2004) by Lachter, J., Forster, K., & Ruthruff, E.

c. Visual attention can predict how well a brand will be remembered, but fixation on the branded moment has a mediating influence on the outcome.

This seminal study offers valuable insights into the relationship between attention and memory. It uncovers the pivotal role of visual attention in advertising for memory formation. Additionally, it holds the distinction of being the first study to underscore the significance of eye fixations, specifically on the brand element.

Paper 6: Eye Fixations on Advertisements and Memory for Brands: A Model and Findings (2000) by Wedel, M., & Pieters, R.

3. Decision Making

a. Consumer attention and decision outcomes are directly related but the economics of the brand and the dynamics of the competition can profoundly affect the outcomes.

The paper investigates the competition for attention within the economic context, emphasizing that the attention garnered by a firm's strategy or product attributes is influenced by both competition with other firms and previous market outcomes. Additionally, it underscores the significance of brand salience in determining the outcomes associated with attention.

Paper 7: Competition for Attention (2016) by Bordalo, P., Gennaioli, N., & Shleifer, A.

b. Low attention processing can still lead to favorable emotional responses and may not always result in immediate recall.

The paper explores the measurement of affective advertising, emphasizing the significance of low attention processing in determining advertising effectiveness. It enhances our understanding of how advertising can emotionally impact consumers, offering valuable insights into measuring affective responses, even when attention is scarce.

Paper 8: Measuring Affective Advertising: Implications of Low Attention Processing on Recall (2005) by Heath, R., & Nairn, A.

4. Sales

a. Attention duration is related to sales and market share but this is mediated by ad characteristics including ad structure and placement.

The authors leverage data from eye-tracking tests, which they correlate with sales data. Their study uncovers that the duration of consumer attention on an advertisement has a substantial impact on product sales, extending beyond the mere presence of the ad. Nevertheless, various factors mediate this relationship, including ad structure and placement.

Paper 9: Sales Effects of Attention to Feature Advertisements: A Bayesian Mediation Analysis (2009) by Zhang, J., Wedel, M. & Pieters, R.

TAKE IT TO WORK

The core themes of highly successful attention getting stunts are exactly the same as successful attention getting ads i.e. good media placement, strong branding, high intensity emotion and good timing (aka relevance).

1.2   Attention Economics 101

In this section, we provide a summary of three distinguished figures in the field of behavioral economics concerning human attention. While their works are related, they are distinct from each other. Together they are often casually blended into the term 'The Attention Economy'.

- Donald Broadbent focused on understanding the 'cause' of inattention, its 'consequences' within social systems and strategies for 'correction'. This is 'the study of attention economics' (1958).
- Herbert Simon focused on the study of human decision making and how information overload influences how humans make choices and manage information. His work eventually flows into attention deficit, but it continues to focus on information management and human decision making. This is 'the study of behavioral economics' (1947, 1971).
- Thomas Davenport brings in a less theoretical view and focuses on the application of attention operating as a currency within an organization marketplace. This is the 'concept of the attention economy' (2001).

Donald Broadbent

Donald Broadbent is the indisputable father of the study of **attention economics.** He revolutionized the study of attention by amalgamating diverse research in information theory and early computational modeling, bringing much-needed coherence to this field. He demonstrated that it was possible to study attention rigorously, outside of the traditional psychology discipline, and explain it simply using information-processing constructs.

An influential British experimental psychologist, his earliest navy-funded work looked at the consequences of ambient noise to attention and the impact of performance on plane detection latency in air traffic control rooms. This agenda came from a strong fascination for aviation, after serving in the RAF as a youth, he observed that communication challenges predominantly stemmed from psychological factors, such as inefficient attention, perception, and memory, rather than technical malfunctions (Fig. 1.3).

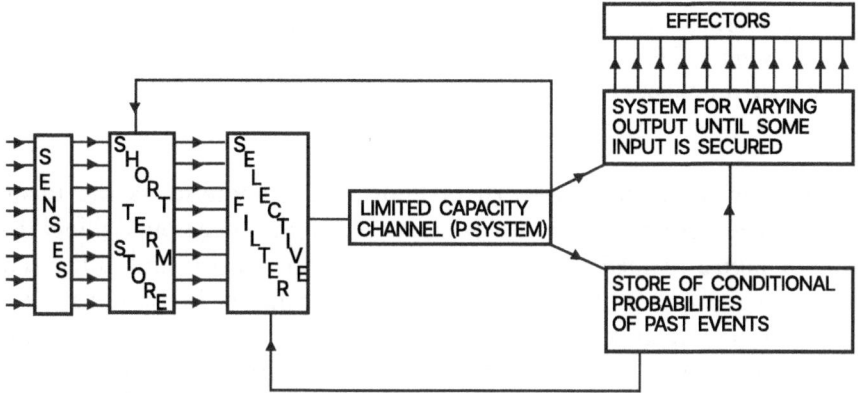

Fig. 1.3 Broadbent's information flow diagram from perception and communication, 1958 (p. 297)

Most notable firsts:

- **Filter Model of Attention:** Humans are incapable of processing the large amount of information we are confronted with so we only pay attention to some of it and filter the rest out (mind you the selection process is not random).
- **Explicit and Implicit Learning:** Learning is implicit when we acquire new information without intending to do so, in contrast to explicit learning, where people acquire knowledge in a more conscious and intentional way. So implicit is associated with incidental while explicit is intentional.

Herbert Simon

Herbert Simon is the indisputable father of the study of **human decision making**. He focused on understanding the mechanisms behind how individuals arrive at rational choices, particularly within the context of organizational structure and administrative behavior. He was awarded the Nobel Prize in Economics in 1978 for his pioneering research into the decision-making process within economic organizations. His research ranged across the fields of cognitive psychology, computer science, public administration, economics, management, philosophy of science and sociology and he earned the A.M. Turing Award in computer science in 1975.

What information consumes is rather obvious: it consumes the attention of its consumers. Hence a wealth of information creates a poverty of attention and a need to allocate that attention efficiently among the overabundance of information sources that might consume it. (Simon, 1971)

Simon is most famous for what is known to economists as the theory of 'bounded rationality'; a theory about economic decision-making that Simon famously coined 'satisficing', a combination of satisfy and suffice. The theory suggests the rationality of actual human behavior is always partial or 'bounded' by human limitations. These limitations come from three contributions: available information (too much), the limited processing power of the human mind, and the finite amount of time humans have to make a decision. Simon suggests that the combination of these components push decision-making to be done in haste due to the 'need of the hour'. Therefore the human mind, in many different situations, necessarily restricts itself and seeks something that is 'good enough', something that is satisfactory but not always best.

In his later years (1970s) he revolutionized the modern study of attention by bringing together the mass of diverse work on information theory and early computational modeling, providing much needed coherence to the discipline. He argued that attention, along with time, is a valuable and limited resource that individuals and organizations must manage in an information-rich world, drawing the connection between information and attention. He was the first to find that wealth of information creates a poverty of attention, an early hint as to what was to become the attention economy.

Most notable firsts:

- **Bounded Rationality**: Humans have cognitive limitations that prevent them from making perfectly rational decisions.
- **Satisficing**: To cope with information overload, and the limited time we have, we take decision shortcuts to simplify complex choices.
- **Poverty of Attention**: There is a simple but fundamental relationship between information and attention. Having abundant information creates a scarcity of something else: a deficit in what that data consumes: attention. In other words, having ample information makes it challenging to concentrate, so there's a need to manage attention wisely among the many information sources vying for it.

Thomas Davenport

Thomas Davenport is the indisputable father of the term **the Attention Economy.** While Simon's work laid the theoretical foundation for the concept of an attention economy, Davenport brought it to life by studying the attention poverty in organizational marketplaces. Thomas H. Davenport is a well-known author, speaker, consultant and academic who is recognised for his thought leadership in the fields of data analytics, business process management, and competitive strategy. Some of his notable books include "Competing on Analytics: The New Science of Winning," "The Attention Economy," and "Only Humans Need Apply: Winners and Losers in the Age of Smart Machines.

His studies explored attention markets within and outside organizations. He likens human attention to a currency due to its monetary attributes. Similar to successful marketplaces, human attention is characterized by scarcity, demand from sellers of goods, the unlikelihood of inflation (an unexpected surplus of attention), and the possibility to and through traditional media. This concept gave rise to the term "The Attention Economy."

> Human attention is in short supply, information is in oversupply but no one will be informed by it, learn from it, or act on it unless they've got some free attention to devote to the information. Welcome to the attention economy. (Davenport, 2001)

Most notable firsts:

- **Organizational Attention Deficit Disorder:** Organizations with attention deficit disorder have an increased likelihood of missing key information when making decisions which carry opportunity costs for individuals and organizations. Failure of attention management is responsible for many business problems.
- **Attention as a currency:** Attention acts as a currency operating in the context of a traditional marketplace.

In summary, Broadbent invented the modern study of attention and founded the concept of information filtering. Simon extended this to show that we filter information because we have limited time and cognitive capacity to process such vast information. To manage this we fill in the information gaps where we have to. Davenport recognized that the common traits in previous research align to traditional economies and coined the term the Attention Economy.

RAPID RECAP

Think about if Herbert Simon met Andrew Ehrenberg.

Herbert Simon's satisficing theory completely aligns with how Andrew Ehrenberg's theory of consumer behavior suggests consumers buy today. Buying is not rational and we don't have time to think alot about brands. We buy more by habit, with little thought, from a small repertoire of brands favoring one over the others. Occasionally we might try new things but we do not, week to week, seek a better taste, more practical packaging, improved ethical sourcing, a higher proportion of Omega-3 fatty acids, regardless of what the ad tells us we should do. We stick to the products we have bought before because it is easy and we are time poor.

This shows how polygamous loyal we are to our favorite brand, but only because it's bigger than the others, not because it's much different. For goods that we don't buy habitually we might aspire to find something optimal but when we come across an item that meets our level of 'good enough', and we need it to be delivered in time for the weekend, we go for it.

With all this said, in Chapter 5 Sofia Pires talks about the concept of 'AI Generated Attention', which challenges Simon's notion of "a wealth of information creates a poverty of attention", suggesting when it comes to generative AI it's the opposite that is true: *more information can lead to greater attention.*

TAKE IT TO WORK

We are overloaded and take decision shortcuts. This 'satisficing' means that our level of attention to advertising is far short of the undivided version most marketers idealize and chase.

Choose Your Own Definition

The final section of this chapter examines the definition of attention. Currently, there isn't a single universally accepted definition due to the rapid evolution of this field. Many in the commercial sector, such as vendors, publishers, and industry bodies, may not have easy access to the necessary literature to form their own views. The encouraging news is that most attention definitions used in industry documents closely align with those put forth by well-respected authors.

To assist you in selecting the most suitable definition for your attention strategy presentations in client or stakeholder meetings, we've compiled a list of 'verified' definitions for you to choose from. To determine 'verified,' we adopted a straightforward approach designed to minimize bias, simplify the process, and reduce semantic debates. First, we identified the most influential scholars in the field of attention, affectionately dubbed 'Attention Royalty.' These individuals have not only exerted a significant impact on the field but have also earned respect within academic and research communities, amassing a high number of citations for their primary attention-related publications. While many of these scholars haven't formally presented a single 'definition' of attention, each has contributed significantly to our comprehension of how human attention functions and its underlying intricacies. As of 2023, this group collectively boasts over 150,000 citations for their principal attention-related works (considerably more when considering their entire careers). The table below (Table 1.2) provides details about the Attention Royalty and their main contributions.

Next, we compiled a list of keywords extracted from the conclusions and primary findings in their groundbreaking papers. During this process, we excluded irrelevant words like conjunctions and pronouns that held no relevance to the core findings. Subsequently, we created a straightforward word

Table 1.2 List of attention royalty and their main contribution

Author	Year	Main paper	# Citations for main paper only	Main contribution
J. Williams	1890	The principles of psychology	60,699	Possession of the mind
H. Simon	1947	Administrative Behavior, A study of decision making processes in administrative organizations	40,477	Information Processing Model
D. Broadbent	1958	Perception and communication	13,726	Filter Model of Attention
D. Kahneman	1973	Attention and effort	18,271	Capacity Theory
A. Treisman	1980	A feature-integration theory of attention	16,361	Feature-Integration Theory
M. Posner	1980	Attention and the detection of signals	5025	Attention Network Theory

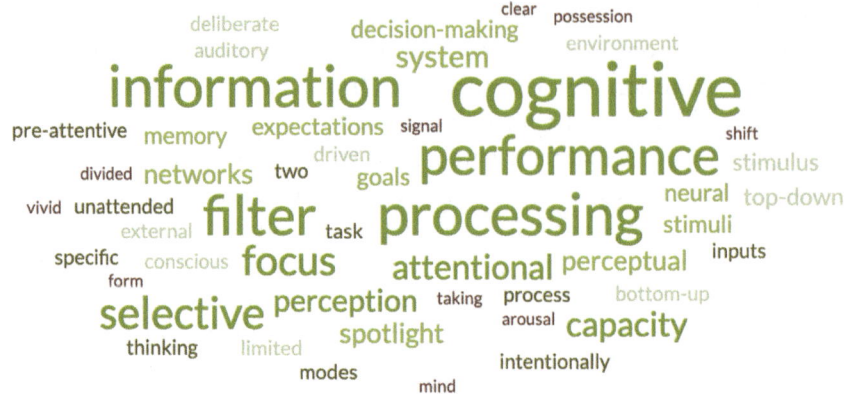

Fig. 1.4 Attention royalty word cloud

cloud based on the frequency of these keywords throughout the papers. This visual representation effectively encapsulates the key discoveries in the field of attention research spanning a century (Fig. 1.4).

Now for the exciting part—it's your turn to select your preferred definition.

The authors listed below (Table 1.3) have each put forth a definition of attention within the last decade. In most instances, these definitions are not entirely original to the authors but are synthesized from their comprehensive literature reviews of foundational work by others.

What's even more promising is that all of these definitions closely align with our 'Attention Royalty Word Cloud' and exhibit striking similarities. You might wonder why this alignment is crucial. It's essential because the definition you present to your stakeholders and clients shouldn't be viewed as mere words from a vendor or a biased source. Instead, it should be seen as a representation of a century of collective effort in understanding how attention works. This alignment lends confidence to the definition you choose to present.

Here are our top seven Attention Definitions, listed in alphabetical order, along with their respective citations. Feel free to choose the one that best suits your needs.

Table 1.3 Best in class definitions of attention

American Research Foundation (2023). Attention Validation Literature Review	*"The degree to which those exposed to the advertising are focused on it— ranging from a very brief exposure (or "scan") that is likely to leave very little memory trace, to intense focus with cognitive and emotional engagement that can lead to enduring recall and impact attitudes and behavior—both positively and negatively."*
American Psychological Association. APA Dictionary of Psychology, Attention	*"A state in which cognitive resources are focused on certain aspects of the environment rather than on others and the central nervous system is in a state of readiness to respond to stimuli."*
Eysenck, M. W., & Keane, M. T. (2015). Learning, memory and forgetting. Cognitive psychology: a Student's handbook, 239–295	*"A process of heightened mental activity and focus on discrete stimuli for the purpose of mental evaluation."*
Greenberg, A. (2012). The role of visual attention in internet advertising. Journal of Advertising Research, 52(4), 400–404	*"Attention can be 'captured' by the features of a stimulus or it can be 'directed' toward an item by some goals of the individual."*
Nelson-Field, K. (2020). The attention economy and how media works. Springer Nature	*"Concentrated awareness (even if fleeting) towards a reduced number of stimuli in our environment, while ignoring other stimuli."*
Posner, M. I., & Rothbart, M. K. (2007). Research on attention networks as a model for the integration of psychological science. Annu. Rev. Psychol., 58, 1–23	*"Attention is characterized by linking common neural networks with individual differences in their efficient utilization."*
Teixeira, T.S. (2014). The Rising Cost of Consumer Attention: Why You Should Care, and What You Can Do about It. Harvard Business School	*"Attention is the allocation of mental resources, visual or cognitive, to visible or conceptual objects."*

1.3   The Wrap Up: The Unconventional Dinner Party

In this chapter, we've explored the birth, study, definition, value, and mone-tization of attention. Along the way, we've met a colorful cast of characters who deserve our attention, including Moira Rose, Kim Kardashian, Andrew Ehrenberg, Donald Broadbent, and Thomas Davenport. Now, just imagine them all in the same room, sitting down for dinner. What would their conversation be like? (Fig. 1.5).

Fig. 1.5   The unconventional dinner party

References

Acar, A. (2007). Testing the Effects of Incidental Advertising Exposure in Online Gaming Environment. *Journal of Interactive Advertising, 8*(1), 45–56.

American Psychological Association. (2023, October). APA Dictionary of Psychology, Attention. https://doi.org/10.1017/S1930297500000413

American Research Foundation (2023). *Attention Validation Literature Review.* https://dictionary.apa.org/attention

Armel, K. C., Beaumel, A., & Rangel, A. (2008). Biasing Simple Choices by Manipulating Relative Visual Attention. *Judgment and Decision Making, 3*(5), 396–403.

Awh, E., Vogel, E. K., & Oh, S. H. (2006, April 28). Interactions Between Attention and Working Memory. *Neuroscience, 139*(1), 201–208.https://doi.org/10.1016/j.neuroscience.2005.08.023. Epub 2005 December 1. PMID: 16324792.

Baddeley, A., Lewis, V., Eldridge, M., & Thomson, N. (1984). Attention and Retrieval from Long-term Memory. *Journal of Experimental Psychology: General, 113*(4), 518–540.

Barry, T. E., & Howard, D. J. (1990). A Review and Critique of The Hierarchy of Effects in Advertising. *International Journal of Advertising, 9*(2), 98–111.

Barwise T. P., & Ehrenberg A. S. C. (1988). *Television and its Audience*. Sage Publications, Inc.

Berry, D. (2002, August). Donald Broadbent. *The Psychologist, 15*(8), 402–405. Retrieved October 20, 2008.

Broadbent. (1958). *Perception and Communication*. Pergamon Press.

Bordalo, P., Gennaioli, N., & Shleifer, A. (2016). Competition for Attention. *The Review of Economic Studies, 83*(2), 481–513.

Burke, M., Hornof, A., Nilsen, E., & Gorman, N. (2005). High-cost Banner Blindness: Ads Increase Perceived Workload, Hinder Visual Search, and are Forgotten. *ACM Transactions Computer-Human Interaction, 12*(4), 423–445. https://doi.org/10.1145/1121112.1121116.

Chakravarty, R., & Sarma, N. N. (2022). Evolutionary Framework of Hierarchy of Effects Models: Exploring Relevance in the Shifting of Customer Path. *Vilakshan—XIMB Journal of Management, 19*(1), 59–68.

Chandon, P., Hutchinson, J. W., & Young, S. H. (2002). Unseen is Unsold. *Journal of Marketing Research, 39*(2), 168–183.

Davenport, T. H., & Beck, J. C. (2001). *The Attention Economy: Understanding the New Currency of Business*. Harvard Business School Press.

de Souza Almeida, R., Faria Jr., A., & Klein, R. M. (2021). On the origins and evolution of the Attention Network Tests. *Neuroscience and Biobehavioral Reviews, 126*, 560–572. https://doi.org/10.1016/j.neubiorev.2021.02.028

Ehrenberg, A. S. C. (1974). Repetitive Advertising and the Consumer. *Journal of Advertising Research, 14*(2), 25–34.

Ehrenberg, A., Barnard, N., Kennedy, R., & Bloom, H. (2002). Brand Advertising as Creative Publicity. *Journal of Advertising Research, 42*(4), 7–18.

Eysenck, M. W., & Keane, M. T. (2015). Learning, Memory and Forgetting. *Cognitive Psychology: A Student's Handbook* (pp. 239–295).

Ghose, A., & Yang, S. (2009). An Empirical Analysis of Search Engine Advertising: Sponsored Search in Electronic Markets. *Management Science, 55*(10), 1605–1622. http://www.jstor.org/stable/40539228

Goodrich, K. (2011). Anarchy of Effects? Exploring Attention to Online Advertising and Multiple Outcomes. *Psychology & Marketing, 28*(4).

Graydon, J., & Eysenck, M. W. (1989). Distraction and Cognitive Performance. *European Journal of Cognitive Psychology, 1*(2), 161–179. https://doi.org/10.1080/09541448908403078

Greenberg, A. (2012). The Role of Visual Attention in Internet Advertising. *Journal of Advertising Research, 52*(4), 400–404.

Greenwald, A. G., & Leavitt, C. (1984). Audience Involvement in Advertising: Four Levels. *Journal of Consumer Research, 11*(1), 581–592. https://doi.org/10.1086/208994

Grund, J., & Brock, A. (2019). Why We Should Empty Pandora's Box to Create a Sustainable Future: Hope, Sustainability and Its Implications for Education. *Sustainability, 11*(3), 893. https://doi.org/10.3390/su11030893

Heath, R., & Feldwick, P. (2008). Fifty Years Using the Wrong Model of Advertising. *International Journal of Market Research, 50*(1), 29–59.

Hoffer, E. (2006). *The Ordeal of Change.* Hopewell Publications. ISBN 9781933435107 (First published January 1, 1963).

Hoffman, D. L., Moreau, C. P., Stremersch, S., & Wedel, M. (2022). The Rise of New Technologies in Marketing: A Framework and Outlook. *Journal of Marketing, 86*(1), 1–6. https://doi.org/10.1177/00222429211061636

James, W. (1890). *The Principles of Psychology* (Vol. 1). Henry Holt and Co. https://doi.org/10.1037/10538-000

Janiszewski, C., Kuo, A., & Tavassoli, N. T. (2013). The Influence of Selective Attention and Inattention to Products on Subsequent Choice. *Journal of Consumer Research, 39*(6), 1258–1274.

Kahneman, D. (1973). *Attention and Effort* (Vol. 1063, pp. 218–226). Englewood Cliffs, NJ: Prentice-Hall.

Katsuki, F., & Constantinidis, C. (2014). Bottom-up and Top-down Attention: Different Processes and Overlapping Neural Systems. *Frontiers in Systems Neuroscience, 8*, 138. https://doi.org/10.3389/fnsys.2014.00138

Lachter, J., Forster, K. I., & Ruthruff, E. (2004). Forty-five Years After Broadbent (1958): Still No Identification Without Attention. *Psychological Review, 111*(4), 880–913.

Lavidge, R. J., & Steiner, G. A. (1961). A Model for Predictive Measurements of Advertising Effectiveness. *Journal of Marketing, 25*(6).

Lewinski, P., Fransen, M. L., & Tan, E. S. H. (2014). Predicting Advertising Effectiveness by Facial Expressions in Response to Amusing Persuasive Stimuli. *Journal of Neuroscience, Psychology, and Economics, 7*(1), 1–14.

Lindsay, G. W. (2020). Attention in Psychology, Neuroscience, and Machine Learning. *Frontiers in Computational Neuroscience, 14*, 29–29.

Madore, K. P., Khazenzon, A. M., Backes, C. W., Jiang, J., Uncapher, M. R., Norcia, A. M., & Wagner, A. D. (2020). Memory Failure Predicted by Attention Lapsing and Media Multitasking. *Nature, 587*(7832), 87–91.

Malthouse, E., & Copulsky, J. (2023). Artificial Intelligence Ecosystems for Marketing Communications. *International Journal of Advertising, 42*(1), 128–140. https://doi.org/10.1080/02650487.2022.2122249

Milosavljevic, M., & Cerf, M. (2008). First Attention Then Intention. *International Journal of Advertising, 27*(3), 381–398. https://doi.org/10.2501/S02650487080 80037

Mole, C., Smithies, D., & Wu, W. (Eds.). (2011). *Attention : Philosophical and Psychological Essays*. Oxford University Press.

Percy, L., & Rossiter, J. R. (1978). A Model for Predictive Measurements of Advertising Effectiveness. *Journal of Advertising Research, 18*.

Pieters, R., Warlop, L., & Wedel, M. (2002). Breaking Through the Clutter: Benefits of Advertisement Originality and Familiarity for Brand Attention and Memory. *Management Science, 48*(6), 765–781.

Posner, M. I., & Rothbart, M. K. (2007). Research on Attention Networks as a Model for the Integration of Psychological Science. *Annual Review of Psychology, 58*, 1–23.

Posner, M. I., Snyder, C. R., & Davidson, B. J. (1980). Attention and the Detection of Signals. *Journal of Experimental Psychology: General, 109*(2), 160–174. https://doi.org/10.1037/0096-3445.109.2.160

Rizzolatti, G., Riggio, L., & Sheliga, B. M. (1994). Space and Selective Attention. In C. Umilta & M. Moscovitch (Eds.), *Attention and Performance XV* (pp. 231–265).

Robinson, P. (1995, January 15). Attention, Memory, and the "Noticing" Hypothesis'. *Language Learning, 45*(2), 283–331.

Rossiter, J., & Percy, L. (1978). Visual Imaging Ability as a Mediator of Advertising Response. In Kent Hunt & Ann Abor (Eds.), *NA—Advances in Consumer Research* (Vol. 5, pp. 621–629). Association for Consumer Research.

Rossiter, J., & Percy, L. (2017). Methodological Guidelines for Advertising Research. *Journal of Advertising, 46*(1), 71–82. https://doi.org/10.1080/00913367.2016.1182088

Russo, J. E. (1978). Eye Fixations Can Save the World: A Critical Evaluation and a Comparison Between Eye Fixations and Other Information Processing Methodologies. In Kent Hunt & Ann Abor (Eds.), *NA—Advances in Consumer Research* (Vol. 5, pp. 561–570). Association for Consumer Research.

Shankar, V., & Krishnamurthi, L. (1996). Relating Price Sensitivity to Retailer Promotional Variables and Pricing Policy: An Empirical Analysis. *Journal of Retailing, 72*(3), 249–272.

Simon, H. (1947). *Administrative Behavior: A Study of Decision Making Processes in Administrative Organizations*. Macmillan.

Simon, H. (1971). Designing Organizations for an Information-rich World. *Computers, Communications, and the Public Interest, 72*, 37.

Stafford, M., Himelboim, I., Walter, D., & Ophir, Y. (2023). The Evolution of Advertising Research Through Four Decades: A Computational Analysis of Themes, Topics and Methods. *International Journal of Advertising, 42*(1), 18–41. https://doi.org/10.1080/02650487.2022.2128005

Teixeira, T. (2014). *The Rising Cost of Consumer Attention: Why You Should Care, and What You Can Do about It*. Harvard Business School.

Treisman, A., & Gelade, G. (1980). A Feature-integration Theory of Attention. *Cognitive Psychology, 12*(1), 97–136. https://doi.org/10.1016/0010-0285(80)900 05-5

Treisman, A., & Gormican, S. (1988). Feature Analysis in Early Vision: Evidence from Search Asymmetries. *Psychological Review, 95*, 15–48.

Venkatraman, V., Dimoka, A., Pavlou, P. A., Vo, K., Hampton, W., Bollinger, B., Hershfield, H. E., Ishihara, M., & Winer, R. S. (2015). Predicting Advertising Success Beyond Traditional Measures: New Insights from Neurophysiological Methods and Market Response Modeling. *Journal of Marketing Research, 52*(4), 436–452.

Wedel, M., & Pieters, R. (2000). Eye Fixations on Advertisements and Memory for Brands: A Model and Findings. *Marketing Science, 19*(4), 297–312.

Wedel, M., & Pieters, R. (2008). A Review of Eye-Tracking Research in Marketing. In N. K. Malhotra (Ed.), *Review of Marketing Research* (Vol. 4, pp. 123–147). Emerald Group Publishing Limited. https://doi.org/10.1108/S1548-6435(200 8)0000004009

Wijaya, B. (2015). The Development of Hierarchy of Effects Model in Advertising. *International Research Journal of Business Studies, 5*(1). https://doi.org/10.21632/ irjbs.5.1.98

Wu, W. (2015). Attention. *Australasian Journal of Philosophy, 93*(3), 630–631. https://doi.org/10.1080/00048402.2015.1012090

Wu, W. (2023). *Movements of the Mind: A Theory of Attention, Intention and Action.* Oxford University Press.

Zhang, J., Wedel, M., & Pieters, R. (2009). Sales Effects of Attention to Feature Advertisements: A Bayesian Mediation Analysis. *Journal of Marketing Research, 45*(5), 669–681.

2

Big Little Learnings

You've got to think about 'big things' while you're doing small things, so that
all the small things go in the right direction.
Alvin Toffler, Futurist and Author (1980)

'Big little learnings' may not actually be a real phrase, but it perfectly describes the concept of this chapter.

BIG learnings are considered significant insights, knowledge or lessons that have had a profound effect on our understanding and perspective on the attention economy. These have been fundamental concepts or/and repeatable patterns that have substantially shaped both our thinking and the course of action needed to fix the problems the media and advertising effectiveness industry are dealing with today. Big learnings are transformative, and are the things that give us the standards on which to build practical applications that work. Big learnings offer the greatest peace of mind to those who look to the value of scientific evidence when making change.

On the other hand, little learnings often refer to smaller, more specific pieces of knowledge or insights. While they may not carry the same level of impact as big learnings, they are still valuable in their own right. These minor observations or findings may be accumulative, adding up to a broader understanding, or they can enhance certain ideas. Little learnings play a

K. Nelson-Field, *The Attention Economy*, https://doi.org/10.1007/978-981-97-0084-4_2

crucial role in filling in the gaps and providing nuanced layers and details that complement the overall picture created by big learnings.

By fusing these two concepts, we arrive at the term 'big little learnings', which acknowledges the importance of both profound, transformative revelations and smaller, incremental insights. This phrase emphasizes that growth and learning entail a holistic approach, embracing major breakthroughs alongside the valuable support provided by minor discoveries.

This phrase perfectly describes the last 4 years of our work in the attention economy. This chapter is all about the big little learnings we have discovered since the last book. All the small pieces of the puzzle that have taught us how attention works, and doesn't work, for advertisers and publishers and the implications for a future measurement category.

2.1   The Pernicious Cause

In homage to Donald Broadbent, the undisputed pioneer of the study of attention economics, this section dives into our four years of extensive research aimed at unraveling the root cause of inattention within the advertising industry. Throughout this section, you won't encounter any instances of natural causality. The central issue stems from deliberate decisions to modify media measurement metrics, which have gradually eroded the effectiveness of advertising over time. It's worth noting that these changes were not driven by malicious intent but nonetheless, set off a series of events from which our industry has struggled to recover. While this may come across as disheartening, its intention is purely to present facts—no negativity intended.

The Day Media Measurement Died

The day that measurement died was in the mid 90's when the concept of impression measurement began with the emergence of digital advertising on the World Wide Web. This marked the moment when basic web server logs were initially used to track how many times a web page was viewed, providing a rudimentary form of impression measurement. This was the critical moment when we transitioned from measuring humans directly to making assumptions about human behavior through data signals. To clarify this distinction, consider human data as 'outward-facing,' gathering information directly from individuals, while 'inward-facing' data collects information from devices.

All measurement consistency was indeed lost that day, as digital measurement diverged entirely from the established practices of legacy media. While legacy media continued its outward-facing efforts like newspaper subscriber counts and TV Gross Rating Points (GRPs) even if they were limited to rudimentary surveys and people meters, the digital realm forged its own path focusing on inward-facing measurements for a much larger scale.

No one really thought to consider the flow-on effects of this change.

But wait, if measurement wasn't 'dead' enough, it took another few hits over the next couple of decades. In the late 90s, with the rise of banner advertising, more advanced tracking methods were developed to not only simply count impressions served but to also gauge the duration users spent on webpages. It was during this era that the click-through metric (CTR) was introduced. And perhaps the final death knell occurred in the late 2000s to early 2010s with the introduction of real-time bidding.

What we know now, that we didn't know at the time of writing the first book, is that these critical moments in time started a chain reaction of events. A chain reaction that has advertisers struggling with achieving advertising value, hindering profitability and brand growth.

History has taught us that sometimes the flow-on effects from a discovery are far more powerful and pervasive than the original event. When nuclear fission was discovered in 1938 by Germans, Otto Hahn and Fritz Strassmann, they couldn't have foreseen its far-reaching implications. It wasn't until 1952 that the United States tested its first nuclear weapon, and today, nine countries possess around 15,000 nuclear weapons.

While not on the same negative scale as nuclear developments, the transformation in measurement is of immense magnitude and its flow-on effects bestow a far greater critical moment in media than its initial development. The cumulative impact has had a profound and lasting impact on all brands in the industry.

EXPERT INSIGHT: The Key to Change is Design Thinking and Proving Business Results by Moomal Shaikh

We often think about the immediate consequences of our decisions and actions, whether they will be beneficial, harmful, or neutral in their impact. Taking this a step further is where the real insight lies: Second Order Thinking. Here is a list of the components of this thinking.

Second Order Thinking Definition: Anticipating the consequences of those consequences.

1. Storytime. The Cobra Effect.

During the British colonial rule in the Subcontinent, the government wanted to tackle the growing problem of venomous cobra snakes in the city. They came up with a plan to offer a bounty for dead cobras. This led to many dead cobras being claimed for rewards, and a noticeable decrease in the number of cobras around the city. Nice. Soon after, there was a steep and continued rise in the number of dead cobras being presented for rewards. Suspicious. Turns out, a group of enterprising individuals started breeding cobras to cash in on the opportunity. The government realized this had created this unintended consequence, and terminated the program. The breeders, now left with all these unsellable cobras, simply released them into the city—making the initial cobra problem way worse. Yikes.

While it's unclear whether this is a real or fabricated story, it does illustrate the importance of second order thinking.

2. Attention in Advertising & Democratization of Content.

The digital marketing ecosystem has come together to figure out the best signals to measure "attention" across online ads. This is an important discussion—not just because the global digital ad spend is projected to reach $679B in 2023—but also because the implications of advertising are far reaching.

Advertising helps sustain the ecosystem of storytelling and journalism. This is a positive consequence. Yet, in this same economic structure, when advertisers found themselves spending money on ads that were never seen on screen by a human, the industry adopted standards of viewability as a transaction metric.

While well-intended, this strategy missed the mark on considering the complexity of behavioral economics (think: incentives), removed the consumer from the center of the solution (think: poor experience online), and predictably led to some negative unintended consequences.

Not an exhaustive list, but here are two important layers of consequences that followed.

3. The Rise of MFA sites.

Gaming the system. Similar to breeding cobras for bounty, MFA (Made for Advertising) sites are designed to have just enough contextually relevant content to bring a user to the site but are essentially cluttered with ads that meet the threshold to get paid. MFA traffic mostly comes from clickbait links and redirects from other sites, and MFA sites don't really need the audience on the page for longer than that 1-sec anyway to get paid. How big is this problem? $13B big. In other words, that's $13B of revenue lost for publishers doing the important work of investigating, reporting, and keeping society informed. With publishers under pressure for revenue, the user experience of reading content became a frustrating one. It also wasn't uncommon to see some publishers misrepresent, embellish, and compromise the overall accuracy of facts in pursuit of ad dollars.

It doesn't stop at MFAs.

4. Trust Deficit and Brand Equity.

Release the cobras: Trust erosion. Overall, this led to a trust deficit of what consumers read online. This is indicated by consumers shifting their content consumption to platforms such as Reddit, TikTok, X (previously Twitter), podcasts, newsletters, and other independent sources in search for authenticity, accuracy, truth, and a better content experience. It damages the brand equity of established publishers, adversely impacting the Halo effect of positive relationships with advertising. The erosion of trust also creates gaps that allow for newcomers, which is not necessarily a negative, but can bring forth the risk of breeding grounds for misinformation or accidental misinformation going unchecked. This can be especially problematic as newbies navigate the fact-checking maze. While this has been a concern for centuries, the speed and scale at which information can be shared online today can lead to faster reactions and decisions based on that information.

Ultimately, advertisers can't effectively reach their audiences, publishers lose revenue which hurts journalism and storytelling, and consumers and society overall loses out on quality content and information.

Now what?

Despite this observation sounding like doom & gloom, it simply means there are opportunities to learn, and course correct. Advertising experts are collaborating to revamp signals and measures of attention, with academics and scientists contributing their insights and cognitive frameworks. Visionaries are innovating content consumption platforms and channels, and leveraging AI to tackle misinformation and bias at scale for a more ethically sound media environment. Marketers are looking to implement attention measures into models to enhance the overall effectiveness of their ad spend.

It's impossible to predict all potential consequences. Analysis paralysis and fear of failure can immobilize one from taking action. The goal is to be thoughtful and thorough. We all have a stake in this problem. This is about advertising, and this is not about advertising.

Recalibrating our approach to attention measurement has the potential to bring consumers back to the center of the solution, and drive us closer to the collective mission of a better internet.

References

1. Global Digital Ad Spend is expected to reach $679B in 2023 https://www.statista.com/outlook/dmo/digital-advertising/worldwide

2. ANA Programmatic Media Supply Chain Transparency Study. https://www.ana.net/miccontent/show/id/rr-2023-06-ana-programmatic-transparency-first-look

3. Center of Humane Technology: Exploring the negative effectives of persuasive advertising and impact of social media. https://www.humanetech.com/

RAPID RECAP

Let's recap on the other critical media moments in time.

In the first book we talked about other critical monuments in digital media history (from 2003) that changed the course of advertising effectiveness. Here is a list of those included:

1. Blitzscaling and the accidental media companies.

Websites out of the pioneering Silicon Valley that went from zero customers to a gazillion in record time. And the value of these customers' eyeballs was quickly realized. Creating a commercial online media platform became the new business model, even when the original plan may not have been. Think FashMash (now Meta) and Amazon.

2. Free reach and going viral.

The term "viral" has been used in medicine for centuries to describe the rapid spread of a virus during an epidemic. In marketing, it refers to content that spreads quickly, but it's often vaguely defined and measured. To truly go viral, a video's view-to-share ratio should show more shares than views, meaning one viewer leads to many shares. Some believe that viral content will bring free reach, but this assumption doesn't always hold, and investing in reach may still be necessary.

3. Instant measurement appeared in an instant.

We saw a rise of short-termism. Marketers have become addicted to instant measurement and switched focus from investing in and measuring, longer term brand impacts to fleeting campaigns that see immediate spikes in sales and have easily accessible ROI metrics. Heavy buyers typically respond to short-term campaigns and are more likely to engage in liking/sharing/commenting in brand communities. Engagement from these customers is expected and tells us nothing about brand growth potential.

4. The programmatic machines arrived.

The purchase of DoubleClick by Google ignited an era of programmatic trading. Suddenly the manual processing of buying media was taken away from humans and given to much smarter computers to automate which ads to buy and how much to pay for them. Programmatic started as a way of using up remnant digital inventory but it has evolved to become the very soul of real-time online targeting. At this time, the assignment of power to a few main players in digital. Those who own the data, own the world.

5. Hyper-personalization (aka 'web of one').

From a place of good intention, real-time targeting went from technology that could find groups of target customers for the purpose of marketing efficiency, to hyper-personalization algorithms that monitor you on and offline 24/7. Your phone, IoT devices, and smart TV know every single thing about you and your friends, for the sole purpose of predicting your next move. All in the name of marketing efficiency. Targeting got weird.

We can now safely add the transition from measuring 'outward' to measuring 'inward' to this mantel.

The Achilles Heel of Modern Measurement

Within every challenge lies the Achilles' heel, the vulnerable point waiting to be discovered. Finding this weakness can transform obstacles into triumphs. Well, we have found it.

At the very heart of the issues plaguing digital advertising measurement today, we find a critical flaw in the concept of Time-in-View—a measure introduced back in the 1990s to transcend simple impression counts. Its purpose was to provide insight into how long humans engage with ads, and it became a key input variable for the MRC Viewability standard in 2014.

As we entered the late 2010s, the chorus calling for improvements in measurement data quality grew louder (refer to Chapter 4 for further details). During this period, measurement companies began asserting that viewability alone was insufficient to capture attention and deliver results. They argued that Time-in-View, not just viewability, more accurately represented whether an ad was truly 'seen' not merely 'served'.

Soon enough, Time-in-View became the default 'seen' measure, said to truly represent human attention.

On the surface, this measure appeared to align perfectly with its purpose—a counter designed to record and display the passage of time a human spent with the ad. However, a closer examination reveals that it failed to fulfill its intended function.

This is where our story takes a turn for the worse.

As per the time of this writing, Time-in-View has become the most critical independent variable of modern media measurement and is used most commonly as the lynchpin for attention measurement. But it fundamentally fails to tell us whether a human has, in fact, paid attention.

Let's look at some data for verification.

The diagram below (Fig. 2.1) depicts findings produced after analyzing a once-off random sample of human attention to around 70,000 typical online ads. It shows that across the first 10 seconds in the life of an ad, arguably the most critical seconds, less than a third of its Time-in-View can be accounted for by human attention. Interestingly, this pattern worsens as more Time-in-View is accumulated, which stands in stark contrast to the success metrics based on 'anything per completion.'

In keeping with the principles of good science, of which are set out in more detail in Chapter 3, we validated our findings by conducting the test

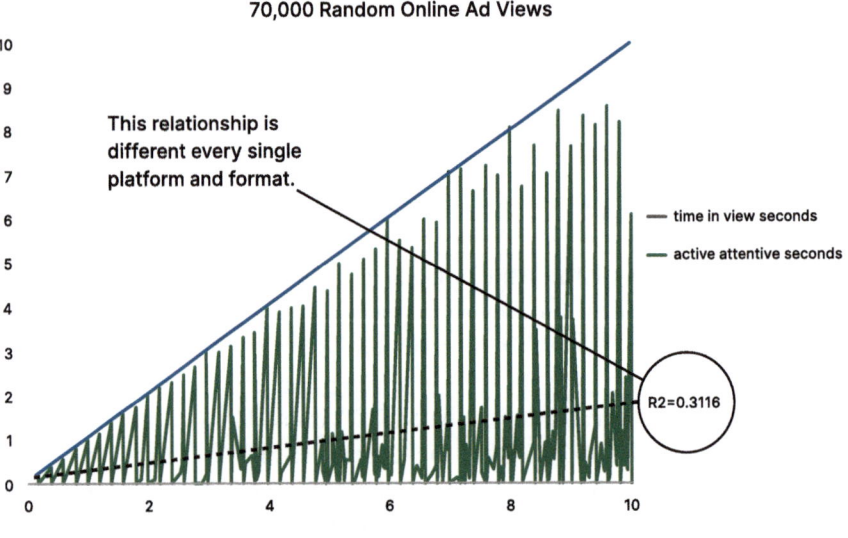

Fig. 2.1 The relationship between human attention and time-in-view (showing 10 seconds time-in-view)

an additional 28 times using a more extensive dataset before sharing these results in 2022/2023. We looked at the new data with multiple combinations of: Time-in-View, Active Attention plus long and short-term brand outcomes (i.e. STAS and Mental Availability).

The findings are quite striking:

1. The data shows that there is approximately a one in three chance that, at any given moment, a human will be looking at the ad while it is on the screen (r = 0.31, sig < 0.001).
2. This relationship between Time-in-View and human attention varies significantly across different platforms and ad formats.
3. Time-in-View does not serve as a reliable predictor for both short and long-term outcomes.
4. On the other hand, human active attention does prove to be a valuable predictor for both short and long-term outcomes.

In summary, while Time-in-View remains a central component of modern media measurement, its inability to accurately predict what it has been touted to measure, which is attention, is often overlooked in the digital landscape. And it's often overlooked because the vendors who use it for attention either don't have (enough) human attention data to validate against, or don't want to (refer to Chapter 4 for details on this topic including factor weighting for modeling purposes).

This shortcoming can have far-reaching implications for any relationship, model, or metrics that rely on it as a lynchpin. Notably, this relationship provides, at best, a one in three chance of accuracy and is further heavily influenced by platform and format variations.

It raises the important question of whether, in any other context, one would consider incorporating metrics into critical organizational processes knowing they could yield error rates of over 70%. The subsequent sections delve into the cascading consequences of these findings.

TAKE IT TO WORK

The inability of Time-in-View to predict human engagement is scary given it is central to so many of our media practices. Whenever this metric is used in the context of your job function, challenge its value.

> **QUICK EXPLAINER**
> There was a (very long) path to an online viewability standard.
>
> In 2011, recognizing the pressing need for greater transparency and account-ability in the advertising industry, key players in the United States came together to chart a course toward a standardized currency for counting online ad impressions. The primary stakeholders in this initiative were the Interactive Advertising Bureau (IAB), the National Association of Advertisers (ANA), and the American Association of Advertising Agencies (4As). Together, they formed a collaborative effort known as "Making Measurement Make Sense" (3Ms).
>
> The consensus among these industry leaders was that the concept of "viewability" should lie at the core of this new metric. This was based on a straightforward and sensible premise: if an ad cannot be seen by the intended audience, it can't possibly have any impact or influence. This pivotal shift towards emphasizing viewability marked a crucial step in enhancing the effectiveness and efficiency of online advertising.
>
> By 2014, online ad viewability standards were set and the US Media Rating Council (MRC) published Version 1.0 (Final) of its Viewable Ad Impression Measurement Guidelines, stating that all MRC-accredited researchers and analytics vendors were to begin counting only viewable ad impressions. For online video, it was determined that at least 50% of the video must be visible for at least 2 seconds to be counted as a chargeable view. While these standards are minimalist by design, they are meant to measure an opportunity to see (OTS) that is comparable to more traditional media impressions like TV.
>
> This viewability metric gave rise to a whole host of companies that proffered from its common sense notion, that an ad needed to be served to be seen. Additionally, since its inception, viewability has become a media currency unto itself (see the concept of complementary currency in Chapter 4).

Distracted Focus

The reason why Time-in-View often falls short of fulfilling its intended purpose primarily stems from its continuous counting nature. Human attention tends to wander and is highly susceptible to distractions, especially when faced with tasks that hold little personal relevance, such as viewing ads. We don't stop and engage with advertising in any sustained or focused manner. Instead, we switch frequently between attention and in-attention across the entire course of the ad being on screen. We dual screen, check messages, talk to our colleagues or look at the feed, anything but fixating on the ad for extended periods of time. We do not stop and pay concentrated and sustained attention over the course of any ad view, let alone a 30 second one.

While most advertisers intuitively understand and accept this reality, they often fail to consider the implications of this natural behavior on a measure like Time-in-View. Consequently, when a viewer shifts their gaze away from the ad, but the Time-in-View counter continues to count, this creates gaps in the time scale that Time-in-View fails to acknowledge. This inherent discrepancy explains why the correlation between human attention and Time-in-View tends to be weak.

This phenomenon can be attributed to what is known in literature as divided attention, a well-established concept in cognitive psychology. Measuring divided attention essentially explores the construct of attention focus. For instance, attention time quantifies the duration a person devotes (in seconds or fractions of seconds) to concentrating their attention on a specific task, area of interest, content, or object. In contrast, attention focus assesses the extent of fixation, the direction of gaze, or the consistency of viewing over time when engaged with a particular task, content, or object. Attention focus provides a deeper understanding of conscious awareness and mental processing than attention time alone. This distinction underscores the need for a more nuanced approach to measuring viewer engagement (more on active, passive and inattention in this chapter, plus more on the measure of attention in Chapter 4).

The figure below (Fig. 2.2) demonstrates the point. It shows an example of attention switching behavior across a threshold of attention and inattention. It is also important to note that the degree of attention switching significantly varies across different platforms and ad formats. And perhaps no surprise, lower attention formats typically register a higher 'switching rate per ad second', than higher attention platforms do. And this is all related to the user experience as you will see in the section in this Chapter called 'Hooked'.

TAKE IT TO WORK

Divided focus is normal human behavior so measuring it is vital. Measurement methods over the last two decades don't offer us this granularity (which is in part why we are in this mess).

But for now, let's refer to an absolute 'must read' book on this topic, but with a broader remit than advertising, called 'Stolen Focus', by Johann Hari. It talks about the reasons why we 'can't' pay attention, the consequences

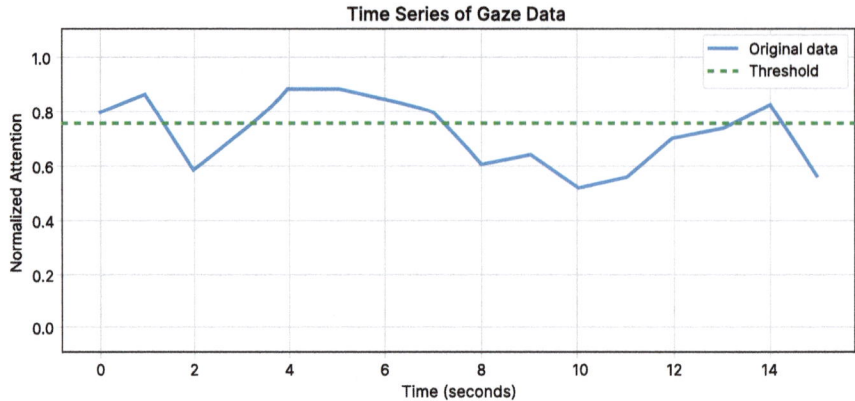

Fig. 2.2 Example attention switching behavior

in our society, and ultimately the pathway to course correct (which in this context is to switch off digital, do one thing at a time and sleep more). Moreover, in the aptly named Chapter: The Increase in Speed, Switching and Filtering, a summary of the research regarding the four main consequences of switching between tasks can be found, these include:

1. The Switch Cost Effect

When your brain switches tasks, i.e. from reading to checking your phone, you get slower because your brain has to reconfigure when it goes from one task to another. You have to remember what you were doing before, and that takes time. The literature suggests that the effects of this are surprisingly large including impairment equivalent to a 10 point drop in IQ.

2. The Screw Up Effect

When your brain switches tasks, you make more mistakes that wouldn't have happened otherwise. Because your brain has to reconfigure after switching, glitches can occur and accurate reconfiguration might fail. This is because your 'thinking' is superficial instead of deep.

3. The Creativity Drain

New thoughts and innovation come from your brain shaping new connections out of what you have seen, heard and learned. This happens at the subconscious level and when undistracted, thoughts that might have seemed previously unconnected, will become connected and innovation or ideas are born. When distracted and switching tasks your brain spends more time 'error-correcting' than it does building associative links for the purpose of original thinking and creative ideas. This consequence is less felt in the immediate like the others, and felt more in the medium to longer term.

4. The Diminished Memory Effect

When you switch between tasks you remember less than those who switch less. This is because it takes mental space and energy to convert your experiences to memories, so if you are spending your time on switching, you will remember and learn less.

In a broader societal context, and particularly concerning the impact on our youth, this situation is undeniably concerning. While less devastating for the human race, switching behavior should be of major concern for brands. The repercussions highlighted in Johann Hari's book closely mirror the trends we observe when examining the correlation between brand outcomes and switching behaviors.

In 2023, as part of our efforts to validate a 1000-person panel designed to explore attention dynamics in relation to brands, we constructed a robust logistic regression model. This model, based on a dataset comprising 41,801 human observations spanning 41 product categories and 2,155 unique brands, allowed us to thoroughly analyze interaction effects on various outcomes, including brand presence, brand size (market share), switching behaviors (attention focus), and audience demographics. It was built to cross validate the smaller sample. For those interested, our accuracy assessments include Cross-Validation (CV) Accuracy at 0.705 ± 0.002 and Test Dataset Accuracy at 0.707, with the dependent variable being 'brand choice.'

As anticipated, our findings confirm that both attention time AND attention focus is related to the chance of 'choosing' a brand. We found the more distracted we are, the more attention switching we do (which is obvious), subsequently the less likely we will choose the brand. It is worth re-emphasizing that how humans view, not simply how long they view, significantly impacts outcomes. All relationships identified in our study are statistically significant ($p < 0.000$).

However, the implications extend beyond brand selection alone. In the following sections, we will examine the implications for memory formation and error correction. All of our research aligns closely with the constructs described by the author of "Stolen Focus," highlighting the consequences of frequent switching and inattention to single tasks.

TAKE IT TO WORK

The more distracted we are, the more attention switching we do (which is obvious), subsequently the less likely we will choose the brand (and the more likely we will have diminished memory and spend more time error-correcting).

QUICK EXPLAINER

Let's do a quick explainer on methodology for context. There is a considerable amount of original research in this book, and while each section and chapter tries to explain how operationally each study works, here is a super quick overview of methodology used for the bulk of the studies discussed in this book.

The data used in this original work is collected via biometric and visual methods (i.e. eye tracking and facial detection using a customized app). There are a total of 110,000 panelists, more than 860 million human data points from 17 countries in the data sets across Mobile, TV, Desktop, Cinema, CTV, General Web, Socials, Gaming and more. The data is collected via device cameras in natural environments (no labs) and in the panelists own (real) platforms. In addition the app collects data signals via JavaScript tags that sit behind the view including ad placement and user device information such as scroll speed etc.

We pay for the panelists' time and we are grateful for their support in these studies. All participants give us informed permission on multiple occasions for us to collect this data. We are compliant with rules around data storage, transit and all other GDPR rules. The measure of attention you will see in any original research in this book will include 3 models: Active Attention: looking directly at the ad or content. Passive Attention: looking nearby, but not directly at the ad or content. In-Attention: not looking on or nearby the ad or content.

Both active and passive attention have their roles in visual information processing. Active attention involves a deliberate and focused mental processing of stimuli but cannot be sustained for extended periods. Passive attention, on the other hand, involves enhanced peripheral focus, where the brain processes non-central stimuli without intentional focus allowing us to process information without deep reflection.

Both levels of attention influence how consumers process advertising but are used in different contexts.

Active attention is more closely related to the creation of explicit, analytical forms of memory and choice because of active learning processes. Active learning makes use of working memory to analyze, reinterpret and then store information in long-term memory. However sustained Active Attention is uncommon.

Passive attention is related to less taxing action tasks as it relies more on implicit memory, making it suitable for situations where sustained mental effort is not necessary. Ads that capture passive attention, through unexpectedness or emotional appeal, and feature strong distinctive branding, can contribute to the formation of consideration sets and general recall. While the impact on brand choice and explicit memory is lower compared to active attention, it is more common and is a valuable aspect of advertising strategy.

More methodological detail can be found in each of the studies as they are reported.

Viewability is Not the Bad Guy

Over the course of the rise of attention measurement and metrics, viewability has certainly received a bad wrap. It has gone from being a proverbial golden child to a troublemaker who doesn't conform. On the surface this makes sense as to why, and our research may have started the finger pointing.

In 2016, when we first conducted research on attention, while we recognized the importance of establishing Viewable Ad Impression Measurement Guidelines, we also raised concerns about the limited utility of these standards, particularly from a brand's standpoint, given their relatively low thresholds (50% pixels and 2 seconds). The question arose: Why not require 100% pixels in view and for a longer duration, wouldn't this be more favorable to brand growth? However, this work also raised awareness (and more questions) about why media owners might resist adopting more favorable standards for brands anyway.

The answer showed up in the data when we considered what would happen to chargeable inventory if viewing standards changed. Here is a modified extract from the first Attention Economy book where the 2017 and 2019 data were reported.

The Battle Between Viewable and Chargeable

The ongoing viewability tug-of-war between advertisers and media owners isn't surprising at all. Advertisers naturally want their ads to be seen more, while many online platforms struggle to even meet the current standards of 50% pixel in view and a 2-second minimum exposure (measured by Time-in-View), let alone considering raising those standards. We would expect that increasing these criteria would impact the platforms' ability to commercialize both in terms of the ability to deliver vast levels of inventory under stricter criteria, and the subsequent impact on their CPMs.

This is important because in March 2019 the MRC released a call for research in an effort to review the current viewability standards including, but not limited to, consideration of increasing the standard to 100% pixels. In the MRC call for research document, they too discuss the implications to certain media types if the pixel standard were to be increased. They suggest that mobile newsfeed type platforms with vertical scroll would be hit the hardest as a change to 100% pixel requirement would represent a material reduction in reported viewable impressions.

In the first Attention Economy book we published viewability data across four countries and two formats (Facebook In-feed and YouTube Pre-Roll) in 2017 and 2019 (approximately 3000 ad views). Table 2.1 represents the reality of the proportion of impressions that meet the MRC standard, as well as the number that would meet a modified PIXELS standard. While Table 2.2 represents the reality of the proportion of impressions that meet the MRC standard, as well as the number that would meet a modified SECONDS standard. Both of the tables have all three time series data.

1. You can see across 2017–2019 there has been an improvement in higher pixel delivery on all counts. A result of both Facebook and YouTube being awarded with MRC Minimum Standards for Media Rating Accreditation in 2017 (so the 2019 numbers are improved in that more inventory now delivers more visibility for brands due to changes in the user experience including the first ever video eCommerce and Retail style ads on Facebook, while YouTube made significant changes to the ad delivery algorithms after what was called the ad apocalypse relating to brand safety and trustworthiness).
2. The data shows that formats offering high scroll in-feed advertising deliver very different levels of pixels for their advertisers compared with those offering non-scrolling pre-roll advertising.

Table 2.1 Proportion (%) of views reaching standard on mobile (varying PIXELS) 2017–2019

	In-feed video (2017)	In-feed video (2019)	Pre-roll video (2017)	Pre-roll video (2019)
10% pixels for 2 seconds	89	84	87	95
20% pixels for 2 seconds	83	83	85	95
30% pixels for 2 seconds	70	80	84	95
40% pixels for 2 seconds	63	75	81	95
50% pixels for 2 seconds	**56**	**69**	**78**	**95**
60% pixels for 2 seconds	50	61	76	94
70% pixels for 2 seconds	44	51	73	94
80% pixels for 2 seconds	37	41	68	92
90% pixels for 2 seconds	28	30	66	90
100% pixels for 2 seconds	21	19	48	88

3. Perhaps most importantly, we can see quite clearly from this table what happens to chargeable inventory if the MRC standard were to be increased on pixels alone.

   a. Cast your eyes to the bottom data row on Table 2.1. If the standard was increased to 100% pixels from 50% pixels holding the 2-second timeframe constant, the in-feed format (in 2019) would lose around 72% of chargeable inventory (pre-roll only 7%).

   b. Now cast your eyes to data row 2 of Table 2.2. If the standard for Time-in-View was increased from 2 seconds to 10, the loss would be significantly greater for both formats (in 2019) (the in-feed format would lose around 84% of chargeable inventory, pre-roll 55%). Let's be more conservative here. If the standard was increased from only 2 to 5 seconds (the in-feed format would lose around 60% of chargeable inventory, pre-roll 17%).

Table 2.2 Proportion (%) of views reaching standard on mobile (varying SECONDS) 2017–2019

	In-feed video (2017)	In-feed video (2019)	Pre-roll video (2017)	Pre-roll video (2019)
50% pixels for 1 second	66	89	78	97
50% pixels for 2 seconds	**56**	**69**	**78**	**95**
50% pixels for 5 seconds	30	28	76	79
50% pixels for 10 seconds	16	11	59	43
50% pixels for 15 seconds	8	6	46	37
50% pixels for 20 seconds	3	4	27	23
50% pixels for 25 seconds	2	3	23	16
50% pixels for 30 seconds	1	2	10	15

Firstly, the MRC was correct. In their current structure, and at that point in time, in-feed social platforms would suffer quite significantly from a material reduction in chargeable inventory over their non-scrollable competitors if 100% pixels became the standard.

Secondly, this analysis demonstrates why media owners might resist more stringent standards. Although interestingly, the data show that the average rate of loss of inventory is greater with increased units of time (seconds), than increased units of size (pixels) across both formats. In other words, increasing the pixel threshold would still be problematic for these media owners (moreso for the scrollable format) an increase in the Time-in-View threshold would be significantly more devastating on their rate of chargeable inventory.

This might tell us why online platform owners continue to tout that (very) short ads can still deliver advertising impact, perhaps to teach the industry that short duration is ok in order to keep the calls for reform away from time. Luckily for these publishers, to date the call for more stringent standards has only been for the consideration of pixels.

TAKE IT TO WORK
Question a media owner who touts that very short ads add significant value. Perhaps this claim is more about available inventory than truth.

The Battle Between Viewable and Attention

The early work on viewability only led to more questions. But this time the focus shifted from merely chargeable inventory to the relationship between viewability and attention.

We wanted to know whether viewability could truly serve as a suitable substitute for attention, considering that Time-In-View is a critical input variable to the metric, despite having little to no correlation with actual human viewing. To put it another way: can we equate "served" with "seen"?

Our initial study, conducted in early 2022, encompassed a snapshot of 20,000 ad impressions spanning four countries and involving seven popular platforms, including a mix of social and general web data. This study has since been repeated hundreds of times with the identical results.

The initial part is not breaking news: when looking at the big picture, 70% of all impressions served adhere to MRC compliance standards. This is a well-documented and expected baseline and tells us this data is 'normal'.

However, what is far more disconcerting lies in the second part. It's only natural to assume that this 70% ensures genuine human engagement with your advertisements. Nevertheless, here are the undeniable facts:

Of all impressions you are served:

- 44% are MRC compliant but get insignificant active attention (avg. half second).
- 9% are MRC compliant but get zero attention.
- 17% are both MRC compliant and get active attention for at least 2 seconds.

Thinking about it a different way; among the impressions you have technically paid for, based on MRC standards:

- 63% get insignificant active attention (< half second).
- 13% get zero attention.
- 24% get active attention for at least 2 seconds.

In simple terms, this means that approximately 75% of the ads you've invested in, following the currency you trust, fail to deliver the expected value. This glaring disparity between what's viewable and what's actually viewed underscores the failure of this currency originally designed around the concept of human engagement. It also calls into account any models or systems relying on this data, to meet the expectations of advertisers (Fig. 2.3).

Furthermore, when you consider this by platform and format, this disparity (or the ratio between what's viewable and what's actually seen) varies significantly across different platforms and formats. See Fig. 2.4. This tells us a number of alarming things:

1. Attention and viewability are not the same, if they were the metrics would move together, they don't.
2. Attention and viewability are not the same, if they were the ratio between viewable and viewed would be systematic across platforms and formats, it isn't.
3. Viewability is not a universal metric (which is the intention of a currency, see Chapter 4), because the underlying attentive return differs so drastically by platform and format.
4. Viewability analytics can't tell you how much attention has been paid, they can tell you whether an ad has been served.
5. Attention is a consumer output (which can be then correlated to outputs that matter to advertisers), viewability is a media owner output.

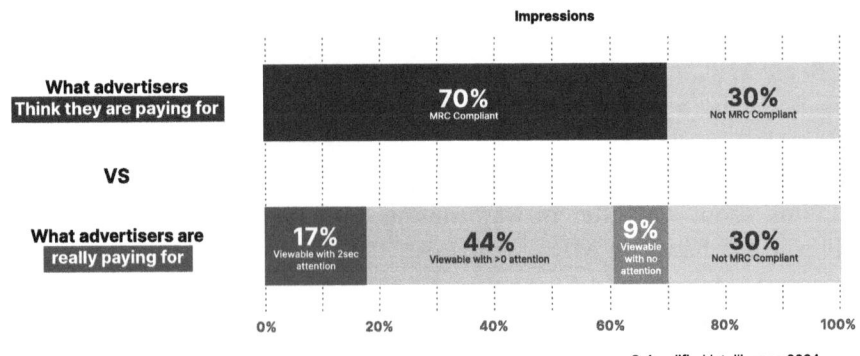

Fig. 2.3 The gap between 'viewable' with attention and 'viewable' with no attention

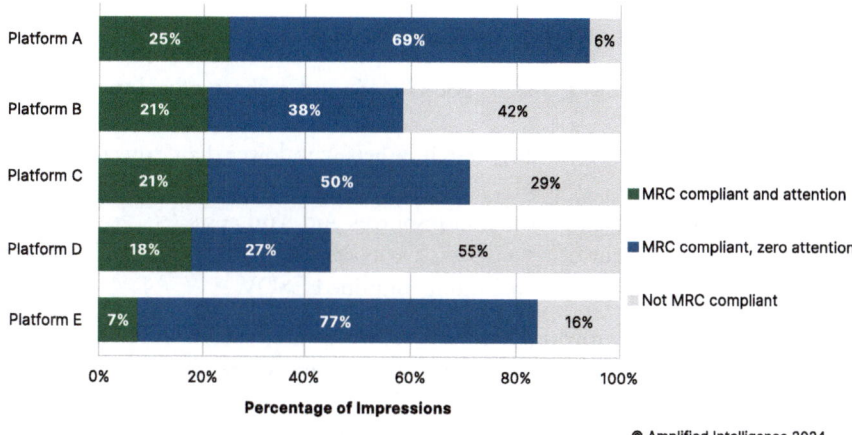

Fig. 2.4 The gap between viewable with attention varies by platform and format

MEANWHILE IN THE REAL WORLD

What is 'Meaty Proof'? It's code for 'outcomes that matter to CFOs and CEOs'.

At the ARF Audience x Science conference in March 2023, it became clear that attention measurement has advanced beyond vendors and agencies advocating attention's value. Advertising industry bodies are actively formalizing attention metrics for brands and agencies, marking a positive shift. A few years ago, the industry relied on imperfect measurement tools. However, reported case evidence still lacks depth. Until now, most use cases relied on post-campaign surveys to assess metrics like recall, purchase intent, and brand perception.

While these brand metrics are valuable indicators of campaign success, there's room to go further than survey-level insights. As more brands and agencies integrate attention data into media planning, we're now seeing stronger evidence of its impact on profitability and processes. Brand effects show how well people remember information which CMOs love, while business effects help CFOs gauge financial or strategic impacts which CEO's love.

What we need is 'Meaty Proof.' This term, borrowed from legal contexts, signifies substantial, compelling evidence that strongly supports a claim or case. It adds weight and credibility, making it difficult to dispute. For CFOs and procurement professionals, the bottom line is crucial. The good news is that we're now witnessing substantive evidence of positive impact, reinforcing the value of using visual attention data in existing workflows. Here are a few examples from our customers.

Some examples of Meaty Proof points from previous case studies:

1. More sales at a lower cost of goods sold, and a share of voice edge on competitors.
2. Faster achievement of sizable stretch targets with lower than expected cost-per-acquisition.
3. Significant savings in production resources and hard costs.
4. Faster establishment of new distinctive assets, at a cost saving.
5. Improved business results including amplified ESOV.

These cases show a growing trend towards improved business performance at reduced costs, a welcome development in an era where efficiency is under close scrutiny, especially for CFOs. Furthermore, these cases highlight how integrating "time-based" visual attention metrics into existing workflows can enhance the value of time-related ad measurements, like time-in-view and ad duration in seconds. It's evident that the industry requires more compelling evidence like this to persuade CFOs and procurement teams that cost-effective media can still deliver efficiency. When we prioritize business outcomes and align with CFOs' objectives, the entire industry stands to gain.

See all cases at WARC Attention Applied: 'Meaty Proof' in the field of attention measurement, Karen Nelson-Field (2023) https://www.warc.com/newsandopinion/opinion/attention-applied-meaty-proof-in-the-field-of-attention-measurement

Dirty Code

Viewability is not the villain here, it's rather a casualty of an unfortunate partnership.

Let's establish a fundamental distinction: viewability is a metric, not a direct measure. Measures are individual data points or pieces of information that are direct measurements of a specific attribute or aspect of something. Measures are the raw data or components that are used to calculate metrics. Metrics on the other hand are often composed of multiple measures and are used to track, evaluate, or compare performance, often against specific goals or benchmarks. A measure is essentially a numerical value, whereas a metric quantifies the relationship between numerical values. Measures precede metrics, providing significance to the data (for more in-depth information). The dilemma arises when inaccurate measures lead to metrics that fail to accurately reflect the true state of the system or process being assessed. This can result in misleading conclusions and decisions based on flawed data.

This is exactly what transpired with the viewability metric. The MRC designated viewability as the standard bearer, yet one of the measures within this partnership doesn't fulfill its intended purpose (truly representing human engagement).

TAKE IT TO WORK

Viewability is not the villain here, it's rather a casualty of an unfortunate partnership.

In a manner of speaking, it resembles the repercussions of 'dirty code' or a 'dirty variable.'

'Dirty code' is a term used in software development to describe problematic source code that is poorly written and full of problems. It often has errors and bugs that can make the program act strangely, crash, or become vulnerable to security issues. Consequently, the program it was introduced into doesn't function correctly.

Likewise a 'dirty variable' typically refers to a specific data attribute or column within a research dataset that contains issues or flaws that make it less reliable or accurate for analysis. These issues can include missing values, outliers, inaccuracies or inconsistencies within that particular variable. Consequently, the analysis it was meant to yield becomes unreliable and unrepeatable (see Chapter 3 on Good Science).

The second half of this 'two measures marriage' encounters its own set of problems in its capacity to genuinely reflect human engagement.

In the previous Attention Economy book we shared some early findings regarding the value of increased pixels on brand choice outcomes. We demonstrated that as the percentage of pixels on the screen rises, the more likely attention is paid and the more likely a sale will result. While this correlation remains valid, it runs deeper than we initially realized, there are more pieces to the puzzle (Fig. 2.5).

Our initial investigation was confined to the examination of just two social platforms. These platforms were in their early stages, characterized by basic formats, and operated within an emerging market. Over the years, as we accumulated more data concerning the influence of pixels on sales and other variables, including screen coverage, it has become evident that the percentage of pixels, as an indicator of human engagement, is influenced by a multitude of factors. To illustrate this concept simply, consider a 9:16 ad unit displayed on a website like Vogue in comparison to an MFA site. Do you believe it would receive the same level of attention in both scenarios? The answer is a

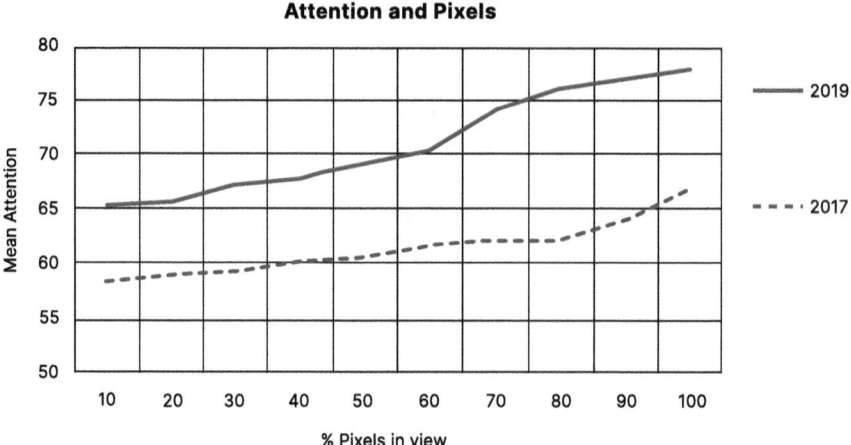

Fig. 2.5 Relationship between attention and pixels, 2017–2019 (Sourced from The attention economy and how media works 2019)

resounding no, and this discrepancy can be directly attributed to the context provided by the platform.

In our early research, the measure of pixel percentage appeared to behave predictably when all other variables were held constant. However, after five years of intensive research, we've come to realize that forecasting human behavior is anything but straightforward and constant (see Chapter 4 on A Human Informed Hybrid). As our research has progressed, we've identified the existence of an 'attention hierarchy,' in which numerous factors collectively mediate the impact of attention, and do so in a systematic way. Without a comprehensive grasp of this hierarchy, the measures employed in metrics resemble dirty code, leading to a host of errors.

A 2022 article by Helge Tennø in Medium sums up this type of dysfunctional marriage in metrics. His article talks about the need for better decisions, versus more metrics:

> One thing I've learned from the best data scientist I've met is that they are ruthlessly precise when it comes to what is being measured and not measured. In marketing we've become a bit more sloppy. We want to measure something complex, but only have the time, resources and/or imagination to measure something simple. So we pretend the measure is for something it isn't — and we market it as such to our colleagues. If your car breaks down what broke? It's usually not the whole car that fell apart, but something somewhere inside it. If our goal is to improve things we need to know where to make improvements. A discussion about metrics should not start with what can be measured. It

should start with: what are the most important decisions we could make? And then figure out what combination of metrics can lead to those decisions.

A summary of the advice offered as to how to move past bad metrics:

- Avoid Over-Marketing Metrics: Metrics should be precise and directly related to what is being measured. Avoid using metrics that are disconnected from their context or are simplified versions of a complex reality.
- Understand the System: When trying to improve something, it's important to identify where improvements are needed within a complex system. Measuring something too far removed from the goal may ignore other influential factors. Use a chain of measures to assess the impact of an event on the desired goal.
- Focus on Decisions: Start a discussion about metrics by identifying the most important decisions that need to be made. Then, select metrics that can help inform and support those decisions. This outcome-driven approach is more effective than simply collecting metrics without a clear purpose.

In closing this long, but important, section the simple truth is this: viewability was and still is a good viable solution for assessing 'ad served' but it was never designed to be a good solution for 'ad seen'. Viewability is not the villain in this scenario.

> **TAKE IT TO WORK**
>
> Any metric, old or new, which includes measures that don't do what they claim will end in pain. Just like a dysfunctional marriage.

A Slow and Steady Fable

When you step back from the years of research on viewability, chargeable inventory, Time-in-View and attention measurement obvious patterns emerge.

And as before mentioned, from these patterns, big things grow. One of the interconnected 'bigger little learnings' is attention decay.

But before we talk about the data let's talk about a tortoise and a hare.

The 'Tortoise and the Hare' is a fable that tells a valuable story of a boastful hare who challenges a slow-moving tortoise to a race. The hare, confident in his speed, takes an early lead but becomes overconfident and decides to take a nap midway through the race, underestimating the tortoise's determination and steady progress. While the hare sleeps, the tortoise continues plodding along and ultimately wins the race because of his perseverance. The moral of the story is "slow and steady wins the race," emphasizing the value of consistency and determination over arrogance and overconfidence.

This fable is an amusing, and somewhat related, introduction to the concept of fast versus slow decay, where a format that initially appears to be the fastest or most skilled, is ultimately defeated by a format that takes a slower but more consistent approach with its viewing behavior.

In the last section we discussed the impact on the chargeable inventory if changes were made to the number of seconds in the viewability standard. You can see clearly from eyeballing these tables that (a) the number of seconds humans view for is limited, (b) the dropoff in viewing is fast, and (c) the rate of dropoff in number of people viewing decreases at different rates by format. Putting a line in the sand, the decrease in the number of people viewing is 'faster' on the scrollable formats, and 'slower' on the non-scrollable formats.

This is the underlying formation of attention decay.

Attention decay is the individual level (human) viewing distribution that sits under each ad format. What we know is that some formats produce FAST attention decay distributions, while others produce SLOW attention decay distributions. Fast attention decay is when many people pay attention early then drop out fast. These are formats that are typically scrollable or skippable (but not always). Slow attention decay is when attention is largely stable across the entire course of the view. These are formats that are typically non-scrollable or non-skippable (but not always). The figure below (Fig. 2.6) demonstrates the distribution types.

Back to our fable, fast decay formats are the hare: they are typically high reaching, so they present well on the surface, yet under the surface the duration and focus of attention is not great. Slow decay formats are the opposite and are the tortoise: they are often lower reaching (not always), but are typically better in earning attention duration and focus (which ultimately benefits brands).

The examples on the previous page are simply a line in the sand. Fast versus Slow. But underneath the hood there are literally tens of thousands of these distributions. Fast, faster, fastest, hybrid (meaning a combination of fast and slow), slow, slower, slowest and everything in between.

What you can see here is that each format, within each platform, on each device has two different distribution components: a different attention decay gradient AND a different degree of attention volume. Attention decay is

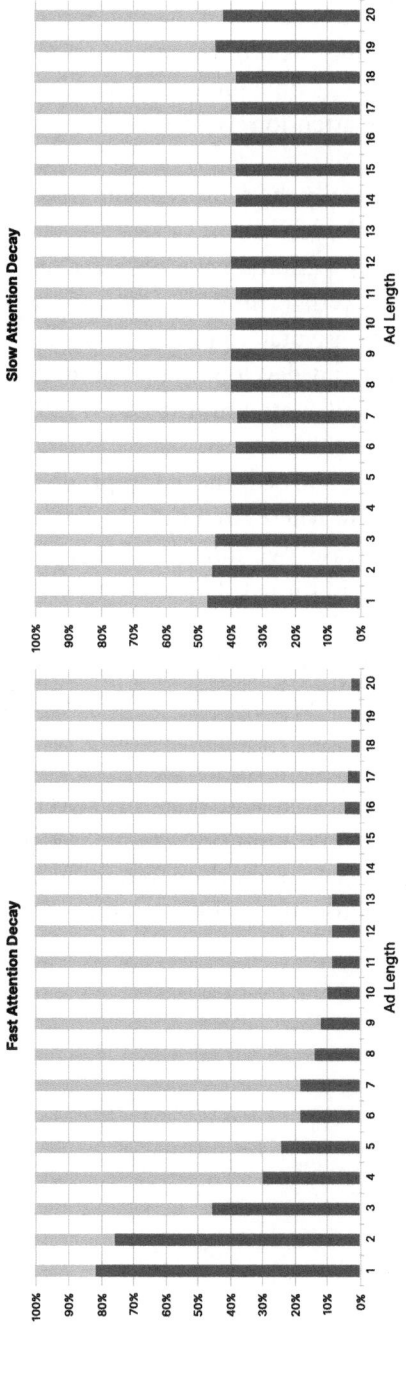

Fig. 2.6 Fast and slow attention decay example

about the shape of viewing, attention volume is about the impact to reach. Both of these components have different yet interconnected consequences, and the significance of the consequences of these attention distributions (both shape and volume) on planning workflows, attention prediction models and any systems or concepts that rely on equitable impressions, are grossly underestimated by industry and attention vendors. The next few sections and chapters discuss these.

These distributions are literally the source of why not all reach is equal and they are the source for the solution too.

Early hints of these decay patterns were observed in the first Attention Economy book, although at that time, it was too early in the research program to fully grasp the pivotal significance of these distributions in predicting human attention and developing planning and creative strategies to address the consequences of inattention (refer to Chapter 5, A Guide to Now and Next).

In the initial book, we discussed the concept of an "attention sweet spot," representing the point where attention begins to wane, and STAS or outcomes, begins to decrease. We discovered that this sweet spot varied depending on the platform and format. For instance, attention to advertising dipped earlier for in-feed social compared to pre-roll, and both dipped earlier than for TV. It led us to question whether these declines were solely due to a shift away from traditional long-form ads or whether there was something else driving this.

Our findings revealed that there were underlying contextual factors that affect the time course of attention and that this sweet spot is the natural point at which viewer attention diminishes serving as a genuine reflection of the platform experience (such as, content/programming served) and/or modal differences (such as, viewability and usability), rather than any reflection of ad length.

While we didnt know it at the time, this early exploration of attention decay had implications for ad length (as discussed in the next section, 'The Ad Length Affair'), attention volume in media planning (as covered in the next section on 'Reach-Based Planning'), and the impact of platform functionality on attention.

TAKE IT TO WORK

Why not all reach is equal can quite literally be attributed to the viewing distributions that sit under every platform and format. Reach can only be equal if humans watched in the same manner cross-media, but we don't. When reach was built for TV in the 50's this wasn't a problem then.

Hooked

Our devices don't have feelings (yet!) — if they did, they would be equivalent to the needy narcissistic partner for whom no amount of attention is ever enough. They superficially appear to care about you, give you just enough positive feedback to keep you interested in them, but never genuinely ask how you feel about your relationship. You doubt that you should get more serious, but it's too easy to stay.

Thatcher Wine, The Twelve Monotasks: Do One Thing at a Time to Do Everything Better.

Many individuals firmly believe they possess full control over their own attention while engaging with social media or video platforms. However, this perception often does not align with reality. Several enlightening books, such as Johann Hari's "Stolen Focus" and Adam Alter's "Irresistible: The Rise of Addictive Technology and the Business of Keeping Us Hooked," shed light on how influential technology manipulates individuals into addiction through their user interfaces. They do this by continually fine-tuning their products, making them increasingly harder to resist. These books emphasize a critical point: our ability to control our own attention is eroding, not due to personal shortcomings but is a direct consequence of the nature of the user experience itself.

Put another way, people use these platforms the way the platform trains them to.

With this in mind, it shouldn't come as a shock that the dynamics of viewing ads are quite similar. The capacity to capture more attention is intricately linked to the user experience of the platform. It's not as straightforward as merely creating excellent creative content and expecting attention; there exist underlying systematic patterns that dictate how individuals engage with or ignore ads. It is the user experience that is the primary determinant of how much attention ads receive, and this phenomenon is not isolated to social; it extends across all platforms and formats including non-digital such as Linear TV.

Let's consider two extreme scenarios for illustration. In the case of cinema, viewers are there by choice, it goes dark, content gets loud, communication with friends is discouraged, mobile phone usage is met with annoyance from fellow patrons and there are no distractions nearby.

In this environment, the natural focal point becomes the screen where advertising is displayed and they settle in for the show.

Conversely, MFA (Made For Ads) sites typically offer minimal valuable content, viewers are often there involuntarily, they are offensively cluttered with highly distracting filler content and clickbait style ads.

In this environment, it is natural for viewers to actively avoid the screen and exit the experience as soon as possible.

So all the prompts for sharing, liking, commenting, pushing or playing, and all the opportunities to connect, chat, message or poke others, and all the opportunities to scroll, skip, turn it down, swipe, leave the room or dual screen are all things that determine how much attention you will pay to ads.

Put another way people watch the ads the way the platform trains them to.

These user interface functionalities can vary significantly depending on the type of platform, highlighting the importance of human data as a baseline, allowing us to identify systematic patterns in how individuals pay attention to or disregard ads. Chapter 4 talks about factor weighting and ground truth, highlighting how the ability to capture and retain user attention hinges on these things. And unfortunately building compelling creative is not enough to change this (refer to the section below The Closure of the Chicken and Egg Debate).

This concept is not new; researchers have long deliberated the impact of spatial characteristics in traditional media like print. For instance, seminal research conducted by Rizzolatti et al. dates as far back as 1994, revealing how the spatial layout and overall design of printed materials can influence how readers engage with advertisements. Three decades later the theory remains valid, but the level of distraction, clutter and spatial features thrown at us is supercharged.

The irony of the irony is this; our attention is largely shaped by the user experience offered by the platform yet it is that very user experience that can hinder our attention to the ads that the platforms rely on for commercialization.

TAKE IT TO WORK

People watch the ads the way the platform trains them to. It is as simple as that. This has implications to how you plan your media and how your creative can work.

Here is some direct evidence of this.

Remember that earlier we discussed 'The Battle Between Viewable and Chargeable' where we looked at what would happen to chargeable inventory if the viewability threshold was to change. We also discussed briefly how changes to either the front or back end of the platforms can make sizable differences to how users pay attention i.e. in 2019 Facebook's video eCommerce and Retail style ads and YouTube's ad delivery algorithms changed how humans scrolled or skipped which ultimately changed the degree of chargeable inventory by MRC standards.

Here is some new data which includes the same formats across 7 countries and 56,817 human ad views. The last two columns to the right of Tables 2.3 and 2.4 show the newer data.

Overall, since the initial analysis 4 years ago, this new data shows:

1. Platforms offering high scroll in-feed advertising STILL deliver very different levels of pixels for their advertisers compared with those offering 'low to no scroll' pre-roll advertising.
2. If the standard for Time-in-View was increased from 2 seconds to 10, the loss would STILL be significantly greater for both formats than increasing the pixel threshold. The in-feed format would lose around 84% of chargeable inventory (was 84%), pre-roll 45% (was 55%).
3. Again being more conservative, if the standard for Time-in-View was increased from 2 seconds to 5, the loss would STILL be significantly greater for both formats than increasing the pixel threshold. The in-feed format would lose around 60% of chargeable inventory (was 60%), pre-roll 5% (was 17%).

Table 2.3 Version of Proportion (%) of views reaching standard on mobile (varying PIXELS)

	In-feed video (2017)	In-feed video (2019)	Pre-roll video (2017)	Pre-roll video (2019)	New data in-feed video (2023)	New data pre-roll video (2023)
10% pixels for 2 seconds	89	84	87	95	84	95.4
20% pixels for 2 seconds	83	83	85	95	79	95
30% pixels for 2 seconds	70	80	84	95	72	95
40% pixels for 2 seconds	63	75	81	95	65	95
50% pixels for 2 seconds	**56**	**69**	**78**	**95**	**56**	**95**
60% pixels for 2 seconds	50	61	76	94	48	95
70% pixels for 2 seconds	44	51	73	94	41	95
80% pixels for 2 seconds	37	41	68	92	34	95
90% pixels for 2 seconds	28	30	66	90	28	95
100% pixels for 2 seconds	21	19	48	88	22	95.2

Table 2.4 2023 version of proportion (%) of views reaching standard on mobile (varying SECONDS)

	In-feed video (2017)	In-feed video (2019)	Pre-roll video (2017)	Pre-roll video (2019)	New data in-feed video (2023)	New data pre-roll video (2023)
50% pixels for 1 second	66	89	78	97	89	97
50% pixels for 2 seconds	**56**	**69**	**78**	**95**	**56**	**95**
50% pixels for 5 seconds	30	28	76	79	23	90
50% pixels for 10 seconds	16	11	59	43	9	52
50% pixels for 15 seconds	8	6	46	37	5	38
50% pixels for 20 seconds	3	4	27	23	3	15
50% pixels for 25 seconds	2	3	23	16	2	6
50% pixels for 30 seconds	1	2	10	15	1	5

But if you look deeper, an interesting pattern emerges, particularly in the in-feed video format, and this relates to how the user experience 'trains' humans to view.

While the percentage decreases appear similar across time, the absolute number of chargeable inventory has significantly decreased in most cases. To illustrate this with a clear example of the In-feed format: In 2019, the proportion of '50% pixels and 2 seconds' inventory was 78%; in 2023, it's down to 56%. Similarly, the proportion of '50% pixels and 5 seconds' inventory was 28%, but it has since dropped to 23%. This highlights how the relative differences have remained the same, yet the overall inventory numbers have decreased. For Facebook in-feed video, 90% of the cases in these tables below (Tables 2.3 and 2.4) show there is a decrease in the proportion of inventory across the varying changes to pixels or time. Only 6% of the cases a decrease in the proportion of inventory from 2019 to 2023 is evident in the YouTube pre-roll format.

Why is this important? The significance of this lies in its ability to reveal how a shift in user experience can greatly impact human attention levels. In 2019, both Facebook's in-feed and YouTube Pre-roll ads underwent noteworthy alterations.

Google took a major step by extending the use of non-skippable 15-second video ads to mobile devices, allowing all advertisers on Google Ads, display, and video 360 participating in auctions to utilize them. Facebook, on the other hand, made its in-feed ad units larger by altering the aspect ratio from 2:3 to 4:5, reducing the amount of displayed text and providing more visibility for the video ad. Again one was a change to the algorithm the other was a change to the ad 'box' or aspect ratio.

What's interesting is that in 2019, we observed that increasing the ad size had a positive impact on the attention received by Facebook ads. However despite the ad unit remaining the same size, over the past few years our data show this attention is declining, which is also reflected in this data.

Please take a look at Figs. 2.7 and 2.8 below, which visually represent the data related to the in-feed format. The visualization specifically focuses on Facebook in-feed data, as there hasn't been any significant change in YouTube pre-roll data from 2019 to 2023. Figure 2.7 represents changes in available inventory as PIXELS change, while 2.8 represents changes in available inventory as TIME changes.

These illustrate that when Facebook increased the size of its ad unit in 2017, the proportion of pixels on the screen for a longer duration also increased. This was beneficial for advertisers and subsequently improved attention. However, when examining the 2023 figures, you'll notice that the proportion of pixels on screen and the time the ad remains in view have reverted to 2017 levels, despite the larger ad aspect ratio. This suggests that, for a brief period, the ad size did affect how people interacted with it, but over time, people learned to avoid them. This also suggests that bigger ads, under these conditions, (device, platform and format), now drive lower levels of human interaction (and attention) than before.

In-feed Video and Pixel Threshold (2017, 2019, 2023)

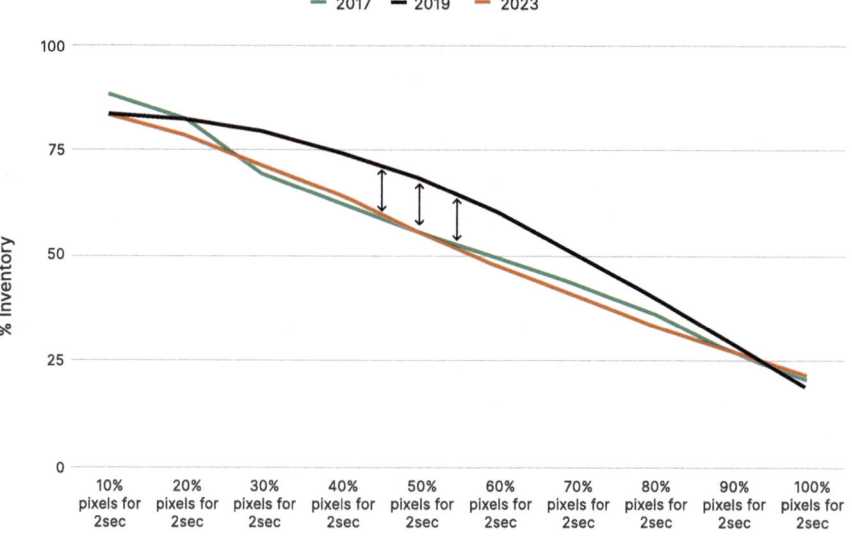

Fig. 2.7 Proportion (%) of views reaching standard on mobile (varying PIXELS) 2017–2019–2023

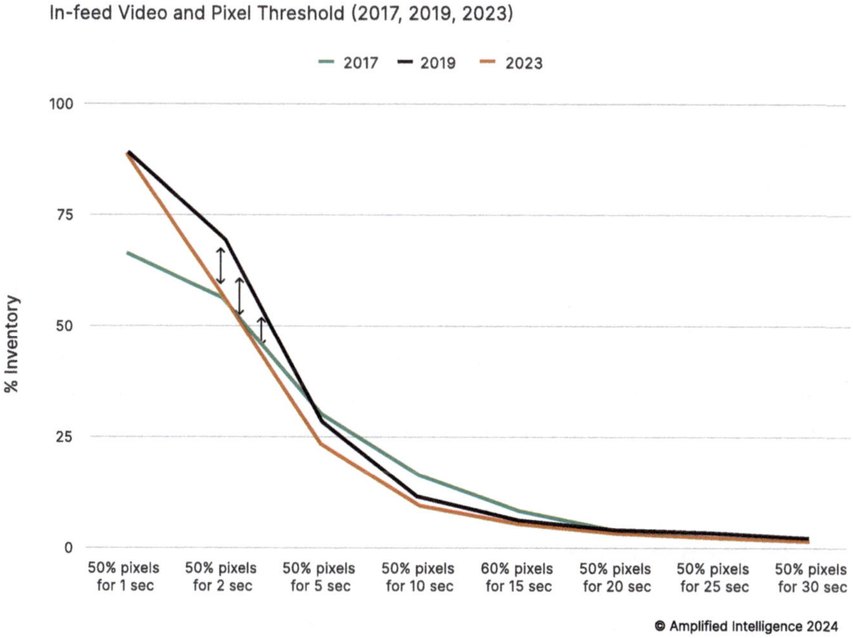

In-feed Video and Pixel Threshold (2017, 2019, 2023)

Fig. 2.8 Proportion (%) of views reaching standard on mobile (varying TIME) 2017–2019–2023

In summary, changes in the user experience indeed influence how a person engages with an advertisement, but it cannot always be assumed that this behavior will remain consistent over time. Humans tend to adapt and learn to avoid ads, which underscores the limitation of relying solely on the aspect ratio or "ad box" size for predicting attention.

This brings us back to the paradox of ad experiences: our attention is largely influenced by the user experience provided by the platform, yet it's that very user experience that can impede our attention to the ads the platforms rely on for monetization.

Before we move onto the next section let's take a positive pause.

While the current state of affairs may seem disheartening for advertisers, there is hope. Surviving and thriving as a brand operating within this landscape hinges on a fundamental understanding of what can be changed and what remains beyond our control. Subsequent chapters will provide some guidance in this regard. Once you understand this, navigating the attention economy becomes easier, we promise. We just need to do some unlearning first.

2.2   The Ill Considered Consequences

We have now progressed beyond dissecting the root cause(s) of inattention; now, we can begin to examine the repercussions.

Stepping back to our 'Tortoise and the Hare' fable we now understand attention decay, and stepping back to our 'Hooked' section we now understand why this happens. These next few sections are all interconnected and discuss the implications of both components: attention decay gradient AND attention volume. So there is a bit of jumping around and referring back and forwards, but they all related to the significant ill considered consequences from the day media measurement died.

Perhaps we should rename this section the 'cobra effect'. If only the measurement giants had given due consideration to second-order thinking, perhaps we wouldn't be recounting this tale today. However, regrettably, we are.

The Ad Length Affair

While we all know intuitively that attention towards advertising is limited and switching is normal, what most don't know is that the shape of these distributions have a marked impact on ad length (amongst other things).

Putting a line down the middle as we have previously (remembering there are thousands of variations to these decay patterns), putting longer ads on fast decay platforms will NOT deliver you longer attention, but longer ads on slow decay platforms WILL.

Let's begin with some data. Looking at Fig. 2.9, there are five different formats. Formats A to C are slow decay (which is flatter) while formats D to E are fast decay formats (which is exponential). Looking at the slow decay example (A to C), you can see that launching a 6 second ad might get 3 seconds of attention (which equates to 50% active attention % to ad length), then if you then launch a 15 second version of that ad on the same format, your ad would achieve double the active attention (the active attention % to ad length remains at 50%). This is usually consistent the whole way up to 30s and at 40 seconds, i.e. launch a 30 second ad you could expect to gain 15 seconds of attention or thereabouts (the pattern starts to break down at around the 40 second mark, incremental attention is gained over 30s, but not in line with the increase in ad length). Now look at the fast decay examples (D to E). There is no increase in attention seconds as the ad length increases, it remains largely the same. So for example you will likely achieve 2 seconds of attention regardless of how long the ad length is.

You might be wondering which formats are slow and which ones are fast?

Let's revisit the extreme scenarios we discussed in the previous section. Remember we discussed, in the case of cinema, viewers are there by choice, it goes dark, it gets loud, there are no distractions nearby and their natural focal point becomes the screen—this is slow decay, where the same volume of viewers are watching at the beginning of the ad and the end. On the other hand, MFA (Made For Ads) sites typically offer minimal valuable content, viewers are often there involuntarily, they are offensively cluttered and viewers try to actively avoid and exit as soon as possible—this is fast decay, where typically many viewers pay attention initially but then drop off rapidly. It's important to note that not all digital formats are inherently fast, and not all non-digital formats are inherently slow. The speed of decay depends on the user experience of each format.

In Fig. 2.9, you can also observe the impact of attention volume. Keep in mind that each format, on each platform, and across various devices has two distinct components: a different attention decay gradient (how attention declines over time) and a different degree of attention volume (the total amount of attention generated). Both of these factors influence the total attention seconds the ad unit receives. It's essential to consider both aspects because simply aggregating attention without taking these distributions into account provides limited insights.

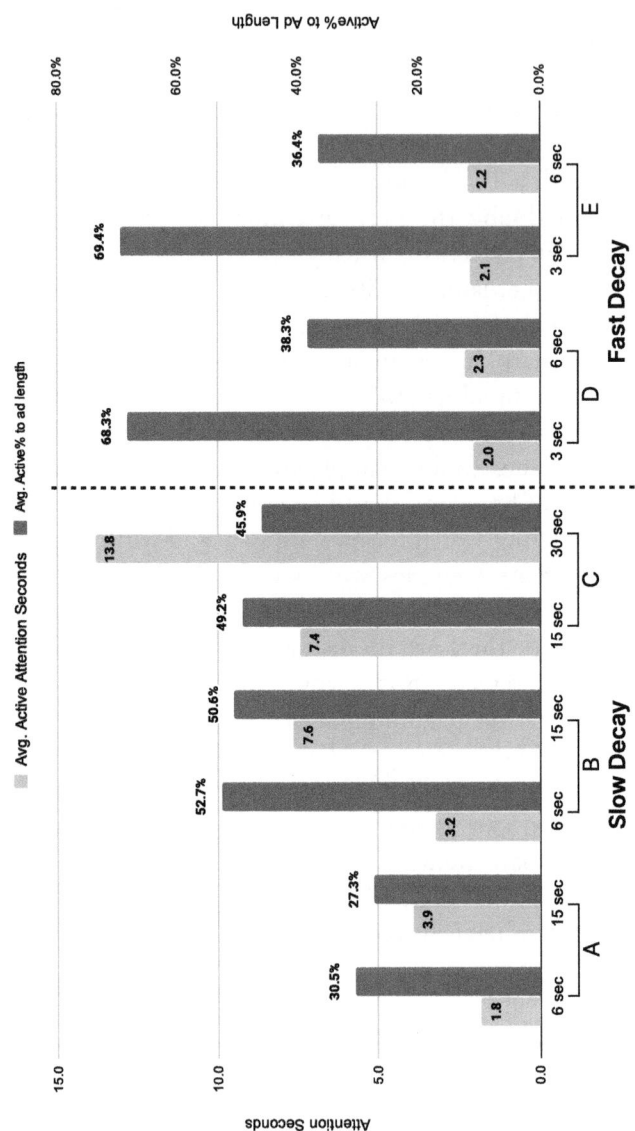

Fig. 2.9 Ad length and attention decay

Looking at the graph on the previous page (Fig. 2.9), you'll notice that formats A and C share the same distribution shape (slow/flat), reflecting a similar pattern across ad length. However, they have achieved different levels of active attention seconds. For instance, a 15-second ad of format A garnered 3.9 active seconds of attention, whereas a 15-second ad of format C obtained 7.6 active seconds of attention, despite having a highly similar viewing distribution shape. This variation is influenced by two factors: a) the creative content does play a role (although its impact may not be as significant as you might think, certainly not at this degree of sample size), and as discussed, b) attention volume.

Remember each format, within each platform, on each device has two different distribution components: a different attention decay gradient AND a different degree of attention volume. Attention decay is about the shape of viewing, attention volume is about the impact to reach for example how many eyeballs are actually watching in the target group (which also has an impact on the overall number of attention seconds it achieves). What we know is that decay is predicated on user experience of the platform, while attention volume is often about the content or watchability or enjoyability of the content that the ad sits within (different from the ad itself). Take a look at Fig. 2.10. These are two of the same types of ad formats, within the same type of media platform, on the same type of device and the same ad length. Yet one achieves a lower % attention to ad length and subsequently a lower overall average number of active attention seconds.

This is not about the creative there are hundreds of different creatives under these averages, this is about the content that the viewer stumbled across or decided to actively watch. In the Hierarchy of Attention (Chapter 3 'Science of Attention'), this is what we call context. Most people think of context to be ads related to the content or ads related to the position in the purchase funnel you are in (i.e. close to the purchase occasion), but it can be broader than that. Context is about YOU, the viewer. For example, context might be related ads in content, related ads close to the purchase occasion, or content you are interested in where ads, related or not, appeared. Figure 2.10 shows two different types of content quality, all of the other variables are the same (platform, ad format, ad length, creative, viewer sample size and device), the only difference is one of these sits within highly emotive content while the other doesn't. So more people watch A for longer with less switching, than B. Content quality can be anything from genre to production quality to journalistic quality.

The most significant implications of attention decay on ad length relates to creative storytelling which is ultimately connected to building memory

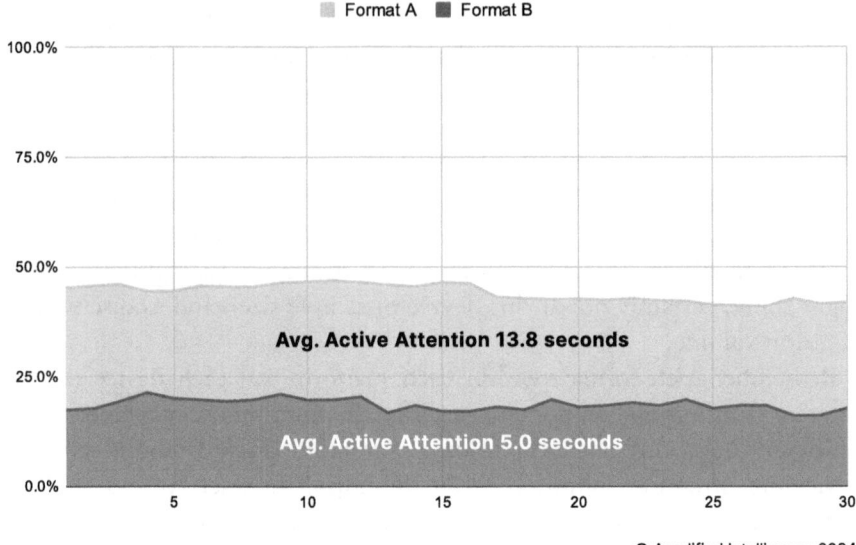

Fig. 2.10 Ad length and attention volume

structures and mental availability (refer to the Chapter 3 'Attention in Jeopardy'). If an ad has to be shorter to work within the format distribution, storytelling and brand building needs to be considered in a very different way. For example for brands that have a new product or a complex one, this makes life difficult because your ability to get the message across in shorter formats is highly restrictive. It has massive implications to your brand being seen at all quite frankly. We discuss more on this in Chapter 5 'A Guide to Now and Next'.

Now at this point you are likely thinking, that's ok, we will simply build better, more engaging creative, that should drive more attention. Sadly no, building compelling creative is valuable, but is not enough to change these systematic and generalizable viewing patterns (again refer to the section below The Closure of the Chicken and Egg Debate).

To recap:

- Slow decay means attention duration increases with increased ad length, while attention % to ad length remains stable.
- Fast decay means attention duration remains stable with increased ad length while attention % to ad length decreases.

Why is all of this important?

1. Resource Allocation: Putting resources into longer ads on fast decay plat-forms will mean that resources are wasted on both creative and media efforts. Advertisers need to understand what is possible to achieve in each platform and media type to effectively plan and buy for their specific business objectives.
2. Reach Based Planning: Just because the decay is slow doesn't always mean it is valuable. Reach based planning needs consideration of both attention decay and attention volume.
3. Aggregation Handicap: These distributions, and their interconnecting consequences, highlights the critical need for transparency in attention metrics. Failing to consider these underlying factors can lead to metrics that distort the true nature of their reported outcomes, much like what occurs with Time-in-View and Viewability.

TAKE IT TO WORK

What this means is longer ads, by default, don't deliver you more attention, it just gives you more wastage (looking nearby but not on the ad).

QUICK EXPLAINER

Aggregation can be a handicap in measurement.

When it comes to data analysis and decision-making, the choice between aggregation and granularity is a critical one, as it significantly influences the insights and outcomes derived from the data. While aggregated data offers a simplified overview that is often easier to understand, it can sometimes obscure crucial details that have significant implications for the accuracy of the predictions based on that data.

Here are a few important considerations when dealing with aggregated data:

1. Misrepresentation.

Aggregated data can sometimes misrepresent the underlying distribution of the data. For example, a high-level aggregate like an average or categor-ical labeling may not accurately reflect the true center of a skewed data distribution. This misrepresentation can lead to incorrect conclusions or decisions.

2. Lack of Nuance.

Aggregated data often lacks context, making it challenging to understand the underlying causes or relationships. Without proper context, it can be difficult to draw meaningful insights or make informed decisions. Understanding the nuances of the data is crucial for accurate analysis.

3. Incomplete Information.

Aggregated data may not include all relevant mediating variables or dimensions. If important factors are omitted during aggregation, it can lead to incomplete analyses, potentially missing critical aspects that influence the outcomes.

4. Oversimplification.

Aggregated data tends to simplify complex relationships. This simplification can be problematic when dealing with intricate systems or datasets where the interactions between variables are not straightforward. Oversimplification can lead to misguided conclusions.

5. Difficulty in Hypothesis Testing.

Aggregated data may not be suitable for certain types of statistical hypothesis testing or causal inference, as it may not capture the variability needed for robust analysis. Using aggregated data for such purposes can result in unreliable or biased results.

In light of these potential pitfalls, it's essential to approach aggregated data with caution. Always ask your attention data provider to explain the distributions, standard error, or other statistical details beneath their averages, units, scores, or any other simplified outputs. If they cannot or will not provide this information, it raises concerns about the accuracy and reliability of the data for making informed decisions.

Crossing the Attention Memory Threshold

So while it is true that not all digital formats are fast decay, many of them are. Particularly in general web. We undertook an exercise to demonstrate the significance of fast decay in its ability to earn attention on a random sample of around 130,000 ad views across a wide range of online formats and platforms (some social but not all). Our findings show (and continue to show with more data sets), around 85% get 2.5 seconds of attention or less (refer Fig. 2.11). We call this the 'attention-memory threshold'. A 'line in the sand' number that we repeatedly see as a threshold of longer term memory retention. There are nuances around this, but this number consistently shows up in our studies indicating that a threshold of sorts does exist. This is not to say that under 2.5 seconds is a complete waste, this simply says longer term measures of brand strength register change at this point. Let's begin by briefly discussing the two types of memory (explicit and implicit), and the methods used to measure these (short term advertising strength and mental availability)—before looking into a series of studies that investigate the relationship between memory and attention further.

Explicit memory and implicit memory are two different memory systems that work in distinct ways and have unique purposes.

Explicit memory, also called declarative memory, is all about consciously recalling facts, events, and experiences. It's the kind of memory where you intentionally bring up information that you can put into words. This includes things like general knowledge, facts, and ideas about the world, as well as specific personal experiences that happened at a particular time and place. Explicit memory plays a crucial role in how we learn and remember new information.

On the other hand, **implicit memory,** also known as non-declarative memory, is about the unconscious or automatic influence of past experiences on your current behavior, even if you're not aware of the original event. It involves skills, habits, and priming effects that you pick up through repetition or practice. Implicit memory also comes into play when you're exposed to something, like a word, which makes it easier for you to recognize or respond to a related stimulus later on, even if you're not consciously aware of it. For example, seeing the word 'yellow' might make it quicker for you to identify the word 'banana' in a later task.

The primary distinction between explicit and implicit memory hinges on conscious awareness and retrieval processes. Explicit memory involves the deliberate recall of facts and experiences, while implicit memory involves unconscious, automatic influences from past experiences on behavior, such as skills and priming effects. This is important when considering the measures and metrics to use in understanding how attention is related. A quick refresher on the two types of measures and metrics used in these studies:

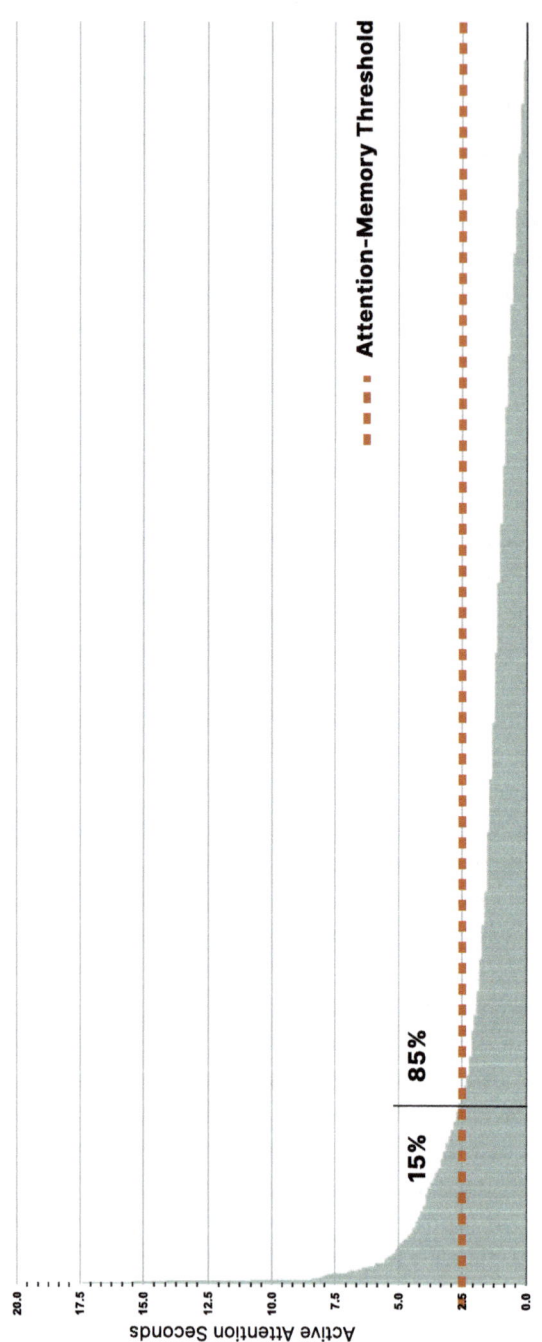

Fig. 2.11 The attention-memory threshold

1. Short Term Advertising Strength (for implicit memory tests)

Definition: The likelihood of your brand being *spontaneously* considered at a purchase occasion.

Measurement: Determined by comparing the buying behavior of two groups: those who were not exposed to brand advertising (the control group) and those who were exposed to the same brand advertising (the test group) within a specific category of buyers.

Metric: Index of #People who Did Buy and Exposed / #People who Did Buy and Not Exposed. A STAS score of 100 serves as a baseline, indicating that advertising had no noticeable impact. In other words, those exposed to the advertising were equally likely to make a purchase as those who were not exposed. Scores exceeding 100 suggest that advertising had a significant additional effect on sales. By examining purchasing data from the non-exposed control group, we can differentiate between the genuine effects of advertising and the influence of brand reputation or size on purchasing decisions.

Use Case: STAS serves as a measure of familiarity and spontaneous choice, emphasizing that it doesn't rely on explicit memory retrieval. Consequently, it can account for both active and passive attention. This is particularly advantageous since the majority of attention given to advertising occurs at lower levels of processing, a realm that this metric is well-equipped to assess.

2. Mental Availability (for explicit memory tests)

Definition: The likelihood of your brand being *deliberately* considered at the purchase occasion.

Measurement: Determined by comparing the mental market share of two groups: those who were not exposed to brand advertising (the control group) and those who were exposed to the same brand advertising (the test group).

Metric: Mental Availability (MA) is determined by multiplying the number of associations (entry points within a category) by the number of people associated with each brand within the competitor set. This figure is then expressed as a proportion of the mental market share in comparison to competitors. We calculate the change in the number of associations and the number of people associated with the brand between those Exposed and those Not Exposed, resulting in an index or percentage point increase/decrease. Analyzing MA data from the non-exposed control group allows us to distinguish the genuine effects of advertising from the influence of brand reputation or size on the ability to create associations.

Use Case: MA is a Holy Grail measure of brand strength and is directly related to market share change. The quantity of attributes linked to a particular brand strongly correlates with future buyer behavior and, consequently, market share changes. MA is also known to be a direct reflection of awareness, perception, consideration and retention. It directly measures the retrieval of brand cues from memory, making it a valuable tool for evaluating brand impact.

Test #1 Advertising Decay (short term measures, implicit memory)

1. Objective

Our aim was to investigate whether the relationship between attention and outcomes extends to memory retention. To do this, we wanted to understand how the rate of advertising decay might vary depending upon the exposure/viewing experience of the audience (i.e. the number of exposures, the platform, format or device on which the exposures occur, etc.). To achieve this, we examined differences in advertising impact decay rates across various media platforms.

Advertising decay is different from attention decay. Attention decay is the individual level viewing distribution that sits under each ad format (viewing). While advertising decay is the rate at which advertising impact decays over time (memory). While these are different they are related terms.

These studies encompassed data collection across 3 countries and 20 Tier 1 IAB categories including (not exhaustive) Technology & Computing, Food & Drink, Personal Finance, Automotive, Style & Fashion, Shopping, Travel, Pets, Home and Garden, Arts & Entertainment, Travel and others.

2. How it Worked

We collected attention data via gaze tracking and facial detection across various platforms, both those with slow decay and fast decay characteristics. These platforms included different formats and were experienced on multiple device types, including mobile, desktop, television screens, and cinema screens.

Following their viewing sessions, our panelists participated in a discrete choice survey conducted within a virtual store environment. This survey was indexed against a baseline to assess brand uplift using the STAS metric. We use STAS under these circumstances because we are not asking the exposed group to engage in conscious thinking, to recall or to remember explicitly. We wanted to test implicit memory within the framework of priming and/or familiarity, and this is the best measure for this.

To consider advertising decay, we then re-engaged the same individuals without exposing them to the ad again. They completed the same discrete choice survey at two additional points in time: 14 days and 28 days after the initial contact. From this we can plot the reduction in STAS after first exposure, from the same people, over time. This approach allowed us to examine changes in the STAS metric over both short and longer terms, facilitating a comprehensive longitudinal analysis of advertising impact.

In the context of priming, implicit memory operates in a way that affects your behavior and perception without conscious awareness, drawing from past experiences. Priming itself is when exposure to one stimulus influences your response to a related stimulus that follows. For instance, if you've encountered a brand's logo or jingle frequently in the past, your implicit memory can hold associations tied to that brand, even if you aren't consciously aware of them. This process entails the activation of mental associations linked to specific brands, subtly guiding your subsequent reactions and choices without you consciously realizing it.

3. Results

An example of some of the results, with a few formats only, are shown in Fig. 2.12. It shows both the first impression impact and the point at which the impact of decay erodes to zero. This demonstrates that an inverse exponential distribution provides a good description for how advertising impact declines over time regardless of the circumstances for exposure as it fits of this model is over $R^2 = 0.75$ in every group tested (for device, platform and all other iterations and tests of potential influencing variables in the analyses that follow).

What we found is that different media types do differ in their initial STAS impact, and that the initial impact causes a compound effect on the slope of the advertising decay. We also found that memory and number of active attention seconds is related ($r = 0.76$, $p = \; < 0.05$). Seeing that different devices, platforms and formats behave differently under these conditions was another early sign of an attention hierarchy forming (see Chapter 3).

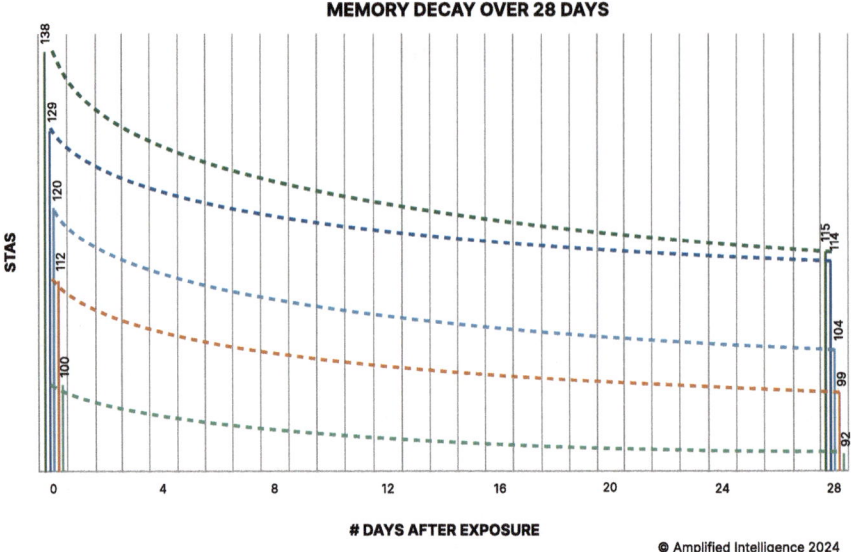

Fig. 2.12 Decay of advertising impact over time

4. Key Take Out

Advertising Impact is greatest immediately after exposure but then it declines as time passes. Attention is related to this phenomenon. We found, and continue to find, the rate at which advertising impact (memory) decays over time is directly related to how many attention seconds an ad earns from the platform it advertises on. To put it another way typically, the higher the average active attention the ad receives the longer the ad stays in memory (but there are diminishing returns). From these studies we have attention data, outcome data and decay coefficients. This is how we can determine the attention-memory threshold. This is nuanced by brand size and creative effects, but overall this pattern is generalizable.

Long term effects are important because not all people are ready to buy right then and there, when an ad hits them. So being remembered for longer means that the ad could still nudge a purchase long after someone has seen the ad.

5. Summary of Findings

Media that deliver higher levels of active attention enable good creative to be remembered for longer.

TAKE IT TO WORK

Just like attention decay, competing platforms have different rates of advertising impact decay after initial exposure. The attention data collected at the point of initial exposure helps to predict this (which helps with frequency planning).

Test #2 Mental Availability (long term measures, explicit memory)

1. Objective

Mental availability is a true north measure of brand strength, its relationship with market share makes it a leading indicator of market share change. An original study was initially conceptualized to understand whether attention could be directly linked to this measure. This study was the first in a series and was conducted in the USA with 12 test brands on three online video platforms, with 600 people who collectively viewed over 3300 ad views (both test and non test brands). The test was then repeated to test its generalizability in 4 additional countries, four additional platforms, 4 additional formats, with 55 test brands and 4,000 people who collectively viewed over 20,000 impressions (both test and non test brands).

2. How it Worked

We collected attention via gaze tracking on Mobile to determine whether respondents were looking directly at the ad or not while they were viewing media in real-time. After their viewing session they completed a mental availability survey which was indexed against a baseline to determine uplift.

Following their viewing sessions, our panelists participated in a mental availability survey. This survey was indexed against a baseline to assess mental availability difference between exposed and non exposed groups. We use Mental Availability under these circumstances because the panelist wanted to call on their explicit memory in an effort to associate all or any of the category entry points with the test brands (and competitors). We wanted to test explicit memory within the framework of semantic memory, and this is the best measure for this.

Semantic Memory is the type of explicit memory involving general knowledge, facts, and concepts not tied to a specific personal experience but is part of your overall understanding about the world. When you have information about brands stored in your semantic memory, it typically involves facts and concepts related to those brands, such as their logos, slogans, product categories, reputation, and other general information. For example, knowing that Apple is a technology company known for its sleek and innovative products like the iPhone and MacBook would be a part of your semantic memory. Similarly, understanding that Coca-Cola is a well-known beverage brand recognized for its iconic red label and classic taste would also fall under semantic memory. As such semantic memory plays a role in storing and accessing knowledge about brands and their attributes, contributing to your overall awareness and understanding of them.

3. Results

Our studies consistently indicate a strong positive relationship between Active Attention Seconds and Mental Availability Uplift (MA) ($r = 0.77$, $p < 0.05$). In simpler terms, when active attention is paid, there is a notable increase in mental availability uplift, whereas when no attention is paid, there is either no significant change or a negative impact.

The relationship between MA and attention is in line with platform performance i.e. poorer attention performing platforms and formats, deliver lower MA uplift (which makes sense given the relationship). Since MA is a competitive metric, where one brand gains, another loses within a finite market share, misattribution often leads to a decrease in MA for the tested brand. This effect can be substantial in some cases and less so in others, but it ultimately represents a shift in mental market share.

A second exposure seemingly serves to correct some of these 'errors', particularly for lower-performing attention platforms responsible for the initial misattribution. However, it's worth noting that the second exposure doesn't significantly increase MA. Instead, it corrects some of the brand misattribution issues from the first exposure. This means that after a second view, where creative has negatively impacted MA, there are slightly fewer misattributions to the competitor, but it also means frequency needs to be higher on lower attention platforms and formats which serves as a false economy.

If you recap on the consequences of attention switching in the previous section (Distracted Focus), this 'correcting errors' makes perfect sense. Higher attention platforms invariably have less switching so it is common sense that lower attention platforms have greater levels of misattribution, likely an effect of multitasking and little time.

4. Key Take Out

This shows that an increase in attention gives a brand some chance of market share growth, while decreases in attention will likely result in no growth, or at worst market share decline (refer Fig. 2.13 for context of an order of effects between attention and brand growth/decline). While this pattern holds true in a general sense, it is important to acknowledge that brand size and creative factors introduce nuances into the equation. Our studies have provided valuable attention and outcome data. By understanding the connection between attention and semantic memory, we can effectively validate the concept of the attention-memory threshold.

Considering the long-term effects of advertising is crucial because not all individuals are ready to make a purchase immediately when exposed to an ad. Building memory cues for future explicit retrieval plays a vital role in advertising. Without attention, the foundation for constructing memory structures is absent, and even worse, existing memory structures may deteriorate.

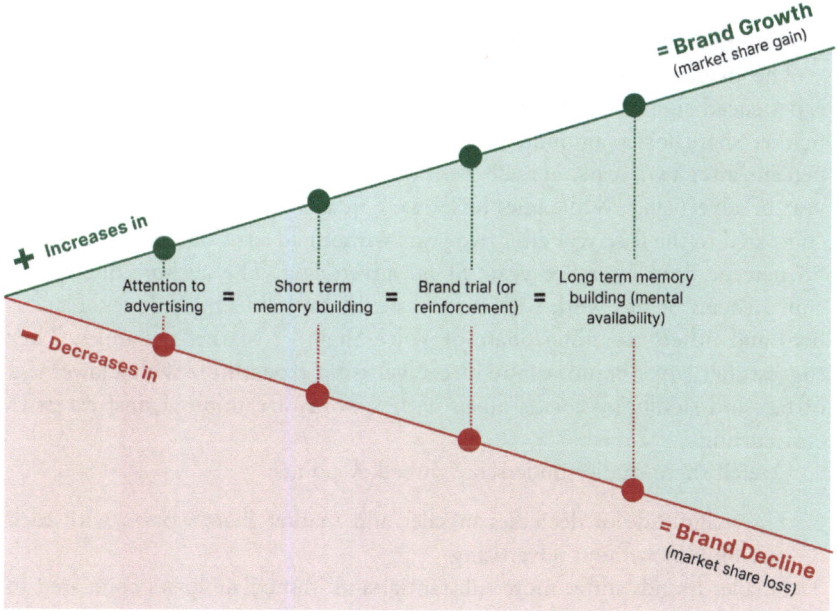

Fig. 2.13 The empirical path from attention to brand growth/decline

5. Summary of Findings

Media platforms that facilitate higher levels of active attention enable effective creative strategies to fulfill their role in building memory structures, contributing to long-term brand success.

MEANWHILE IN THE REAL WORLD As it turns out when brands go dark, not once but twice, chaos erupts.

It was appropriate in this section to call out this series of studies of advertising inattention and its impact on brand growth. While the authors don't use traditional methods of collecting attention data, nor do they talk specifically to the concept of attention, these studies consider the relationship of prolonged inattention to and the impact on sales and market share change. They focus on the effects of cessation of 'brand' or 'equity' advertising, versus 'activation' (see Long and Short of It by Les Binet and Peter Field).

The first study looked at two decades of advertising media spend and brand sales volume data from a global manufacturer of alcoholic beverages across ten different media platforms, including television, press, magazines, radio, online, cinema, out of home, and direct mail.

The second study, an extension of the first, considered similar spend data from 365 U.S. brands from 22 consumer goods categories. In both sets of data brands 'went dark' for at least one year (a complete cessation of advertising). One study assessed sales losses, while the other examined market share losses.

The overarching findings revealed that brands that stopped advertising experienced significant declines in both sales and market share. On average, market share losses amounted to a 10 percent decrease after one year, 20 percent after two years, and 28 percent after three years relative to the last year of advertising. While sales losses were quantified as a 25 percent decline compared to the base year after two years without advertising, and a staggering 58 percent drop after five years of no advertising. The authors discuss the consistencies of this work with prior research by John Phillip Jones, Danenberg and others regarding Share of Voice/Share of Market dynamics. They suggest that larger brands can reduce advertising expenditure with a lower risk of fast and significant losses, albeit with a word of caution against excessive cost-cutting.

Overall these studies underscore three key points:

1. The magnitude of decreases in sales and market share worsen with each passing year without advertising.
2. Smaller brands suffer more substantial and immediate losses compared to larger brands.

3. The decline in sales and market share is attributed to a shrinking customer base (penetration) rather than a loss of customer loyalty.

The moral of the story is that when brands stop advertising, they fail to capture attention to the core essence of what they offer. When this happens light buyers forget who you are and both sales and market share suffer.

A Sad Discussion About Broken Relationships

It's never fun when relationships end. But half of the battle for recovery and new relationships is to understand why the breakup happened, dust off, improve and move on to the next phase. This is what this section is about. Here we discuss three relationships that are impacted by 'dirty code' (Time-in-View).

Reach-Based Planning

Reach-based planning has been the basic premise of brand growth since the highly awarded statistician Andrew Ehrenberg (1926–2019) found some repeatable patterns within media spend and outcomes data (market share and sales). For over half a century, he contributed to marketing literature around systematic patterns in buyer behavior as they relate to how brands grow and decline. His main contribution was put forward as a collection of works with co-author, Gerald Goodhardt, in The Dirichlet: A comprehensive model of buying behavior (1984). His premise on reach-based planning was simple: focus your advertising dollars on reaching light buyers, rather than focusing on a futile attempt to get existing customers to become more loyal. His work was popularized in later works from the Ehrenberg-Bass institute, namely in How Brands Grow (2010) which simplified the concepts for advertisers to understand: advertisers should create strategies that prioritize maximizing campaign reach (ad exposure) to ensure that a brand message reaches as many individuals consistently in the target category as possible, within the budget constraints of the brand.

This all makes total sense, and sounds relatively easy. But it's not that simple anymore. The underlying measure (reach) that goes into this concept is not stable. This early work on reach based planning was written at a time when the pipes below advertising delivery were cleaner and you got what you paid for, unlike today. A time when measurement of actual human viewing was commonplace, unlike today. A time when an impression delivered the same volume of eye-balls regardless of which platform it was delivered, unlike today.

As such, audience measurement error under the surface of impression delivery significantly reduces the ability of reach based planning to even work, or for any form media planning for that matter. Today, you might buy a million impressions, your competitor might buy a million impressions but the volume of human attention achieved could be very different in each case. This has significant implications on the ability to deliver on objectives like mental availability at all.

If current reach-based planning worked, each impression would theoretically achieve 100% attention volume. This would mean that 100% of the impressions you buy are watched by 100% of the audience for 100% of the Time-in-View you pay for. But that is a fanciful ideal. The reality looks much different (Fig. 2.14). The diagram to the left of Fig. 2.14 demonstrates 100% attention volume where, for each second of Time-in-View, 100% of the audience looked at the ad. The one on the right one shows the reality of how humans interact with advertising, as discussed in the previous sections about attention switching (time and focus), attention decay and the dynamics of the user experience. In this example, due to diminishing attention over time, only 20% of the reach volume you think you are buying is achieved.

To make matters worse, in line with our earlier conversation about attention decay (in that underneath the hood there are literally tens of thousands of different distributions ranging from fast, faster, fastest, hybrid, slow, slower, slowest and everything in between) attention volume changes in line with attention decay. This is why the error under media planning is very complicated to equalize. If the underlying volume was the same across media types, it would be easy to fix with generic attention units, indexes or averages, but you can't because it's not.

This simple line must be repeated: attention decay distributions (which are a combination of how many people are viewing and how they are viewing) are literally the source of why not all reach is equal and they are the source for the solution too. Sticking to basics of reach based planning for the purpose of building mental availability, is only possible if we equalize reach and bring brand growth back to its glory days. More on how to do this in Chapter 5: A Guide to Now and Next.

TAKE IT TO WORK When you cannot quantify whether a human has viewed, brand growth becomes more a guess than science.

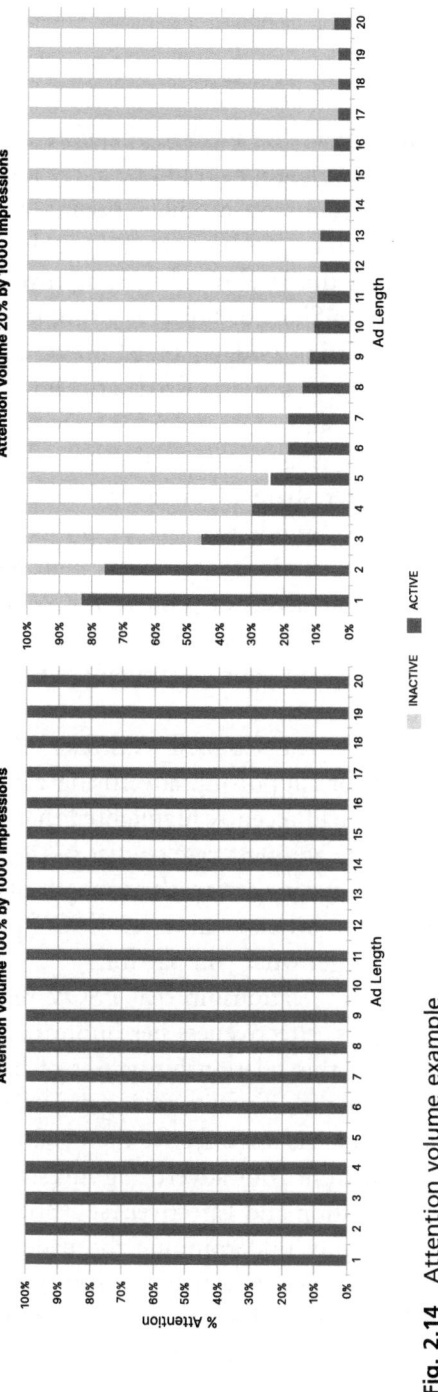

Fig. 2.14 Attention volume example

The ESOV Paradox

Section by Rob Brittain

Let's begin with the beauty in simple math.

A brand's sales are sourced from the market, therefore an understanding of advertising investment in the category should be a key input in determining the advertising budget. Decisions on product, pricing and distribution are all informed by an understanding of the category and competitors; therefore, it stands to reason that the level of advertising investment should also employ this too. ESOV (Extra Share of Voice) is a simple, empirically proven approach to planning advertising budgets based on an external view of the market, the external view here is key as a fixed ratio approach to advertising budget planning takes no account of competitive activity.

The calculation for ESOV is as simple as they come: Brand media share of voice minus Brand market share of category. Therefore, ESOV can be positive, neutral or negative. Brands that are supported by positive ESOV are competing for memory at an intensity that is high relative to their size and recent evidence shows the effects of positive ESOV go beyond growing market share. The beauty of this approach is it proves that if you're a smaller brand you don't need to outspend your larger competitors, what's important is how much you spend relative to your size.

Recent analysis from the Ad Council Australia (ACA) Effectiveness Database shows the power of supporting advertising campaigns with positive ESOV. However, Peter Field recently highlighted that the effectiveness of ESOV has declined over time amongst case studies in the IPA databank. So, what is going on here? Why are we seeing the strength of positive ESOV in some studies and its decline in others? This is the ESOV paradox (Fig. 2.15).

Now a reminder that you get what you pay for.

The answer lies in the core relationship that ESOV relies on…. that you get what you pay for. That is, effectiveness per impression is commensurate with cost per impression. If this relationship is out of balance, then you're not getting what you pay for and, if you're paying too much for less effective impressions, your share of voice is less effective than you think. This, in turn, is detrimental to the return from your advertising investment.

In our recent paper "Attention and Effectiveness" (Brittain & Field, 2023) we investigated this. The study underpinning the paper was a global first, combining high quality in-market effectiveness data with attention metrics for 39 campaigns in the ACA Effectiveness Database. In the study we clearly observed the power of higher attention media plans. The campaigns that

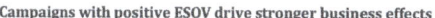

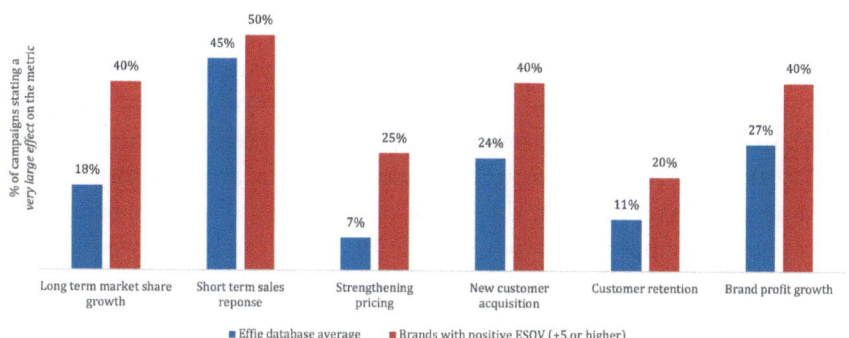

Fig. 2.15 "To ESOV and beyond", ACA effectiveness database, Brittain & Field, 2021

weighted their investment (50% or more) towards higher attention platforms delivered much stronger effects on their brand and businesses (Fig. 2.16).

It's clear that how the media budget is invested makes a huge difference. As a marketer you can make a great campaign and support it with a high attention media plan. However, you can also make a great campaign and support it with a low attention media plan. Needless to say, the former is much more effective than the latter. So we're getting much closer to the cause of the ESOV paradox, let's unpack it further.

The next step in the study was to look at the relationship between attention, ESOV and business impact so the sample was split further to look at both the weighting of investment towards higher attention (or lower attention) platforms and the ESOV supporting the campaigns. The results were

	N=	Avg Active attention seconds (campaign level)	% of campaigns stating a v. large impact on brand Mental Availability	Avg # of v. large business effects (INDEX vs total attention sample)
Lower attention media plan (<50% of media invested in high attention platforms)	21	4.6	35%	76
Higher attention media plan (>50% of media invested in high attention platforms)	18	8.1	52%	125
Difference (Higher vs lower attention media plan)		+3.5	+17pp	+49

Fig. 2.16 "Attention and effectiveness", ACA effectiveness database, Brittain & Field, 2023

very revealing. Amongst the campaigns with lower attention media plans, those that were supported by positive ESOV (as opposed to those supported by negative ESOV) were clearly more effective.

In terms of active attention, the difference between these two groups was minimal as they were investing across media platforms in a similar way. The major driver is the higher level of advertising intensity afforded by positive ESOV, these campaigns were competing harder for memory resulting in stronger effects. However, the magic really happens when high attention media plans are supported by positive ESOV. These campaigns were not only competing with a higher level of advertising intensity, but they were also doing so on media platforms where they received more attention, this had a big amplification effect. These campaigns (positive ESOV and high attention media plan) were, by far, the most effective group in the study (Fig. 2.17).

What is the biggest learning here?

When advertising budgets are constrained or reduced there can be a well-intentioned tendency to stretch the budget further by weighting investment into media platforms which have attractively lower CPM's. However, this is destructive to campaign effectiveness because your share of voice will be less effective than you think. Despite it being cheaper, you're not getting what you're paying for as the reduction in effectiveness per impression is greater than the reduction in the cost per impression.

What we now know is that attention mediates the relationship that under-pins the ESOV approach (that you get what you pay for) and this is the driver of the ESOV paradox. All media platforms can play a role; but it is the balance of investment across them that ultimately determines whether your campaign gets a lot, or very little, attention.

	N=	Avg Active attention seconds (campaign level)	% of campaigns stating a v. large impact on brand Mental Availability	Avg # of v. large business effects (INDEX vs total attention sample)
Negative ESOV and lower attention media plan	9	4.7	33%	55
Positive ESOV and lower attention media plan	12	4.5	42%	90
Difference (Higher vs lower attention media plan)		+3.5	+17pp	+49

Fig. 2.17 "Attention and Effectiveness", ACA effectiveness database, Brittain & Field, 2023

EXPERT INSIGHT: The ESOV Relationship Needs Resuscitating, Can Attention Economics Help? by Peter Field.

Since the early 1990s when Prof. John Philip Jones first formalized the SOV model, it has been widely accepted that if we want stable market share, we need to set our share of voice (share of category expenditure across media channels) level with our market share. And if we want growth, we will need extra share of voice—where our SOV is higher than our market share. This relationship has been a bedrock of media planning for many decades but has been jeopardized by the growth of digital media.

The reason for this is that to work, this purely financial model depends on reliable and equitable values being placed across diverse media exposures. That is to say that the commercial value of an exposure to an ad on platform A vs. on platform B is fully costed into the media prices of those two platforms. That is largely the case amongst 'legacy' media, but the arrival of the big digital media owners and their walled data gardens, broke the feedback loop between expenditure and growth: we have had to assume that exposures have equal value (and we no longer reliably know our share of voice). Attention research has revealed the assumption to be a major error—one we knew nothing of before. In fact, an exposure of the same ad served on different platforms can result in radically different impacts on mental availability, because the attention levels it will receive vary widely across platforms. So, the media money has not been reliably following the marketing value. This has had a major impact on the reliability of the SOV model.

Analysis of the UK IPA effectiveness data (around 650 digital era case studies) shows the progressive breakdown of the correlation between extra share of voice and mental availability since around 2007/8. This coincides with when performance marketing and the thinking that went with it, started to divert mass-market brands' communications budgets to digital media on a large scale. With no guidance on the long-term value of the digital media choices being made, this has inevitably led to the breakdown of the link between extra share of voice and market share growth—the John Philip Jones law that has guided media budgets for the last 30 years. At its peak around 2007/8 this relationship was exceptionally strong: easily significant at the 99% confidence level. It was a relationship that you could bank on, but since then it has lost most of that reliability (Fig 2.18).

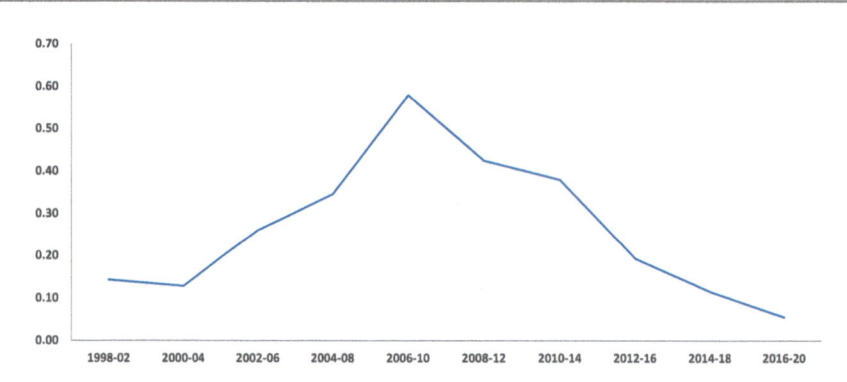

IPA   Base: IPA Databank, for-profit cases

Fig. 2.18 Correlation between ESOV & growth by period. IPA Databank, UK

There's no reason why this has to be the case. If the link between the cost of exposures on digital platforms and their commercial value can be restored, then the reliability of the SOV model will return. And the key to doing so is to apply Attention Economics to media planning.

RAPID RECAP

Let's take a longer look at a longer memory measure.

What is Mental Availability? Professor Jenni Romaniuk, the leading academic in this space, classifies Mental Availability as the strength (uniqueness) and prevalence (number of people) of the brand name and linked associations in a consumer's memory. Linked associations, if the advertiser has done their job correctly, act as cues that bring their brand to the surface of memory on different occasions, such as Coke and summer, De Beers diamonds and engagement, and here in Australia, Vegemite and breakfast. The more unique these associations are to your brand, the more likely the consumer will think of your brand over your competitor at the buying occasion.

Mental Availability has nothing to do with building brand love, intention to buy or any other proxy loyalty type measure. It is the simple notion of strengthening memory cues to increase the likelihood of your brand coming to mind when a purchase occasion or category cue arises, directly compared to your competitors. High mental availability is when that person has high awareness of the brand and knows what it does, and what it stands for.

Why does it matter? Being considered at the time of product purchase, versus not at all, has obvious implications on sales. A brand with strong Mental Availability is more likely to grow, at least not decline. In other words, mental availability and market share are significantly related. When MA goes up, so will market share. When MA goes down, brand decline will likely follow.

Of course, a caveat to the above is that the brand is physically available to buy. If a brand is out of stock or hard to access, a customer will choose your nearest competitor with little thought (because we are loyal to switching, not loyal to one). Just one reason that marketing and operations need to talk to each other. There's no joy in doing all of that advertising work only to have your nearest competitor scoop the sale.

In terms of measuring, Mental Availability is commonly both misunderstood and misrepresented. It is often passed off in brand research as brand awareness, consideration, brand personality or likelihood/intent of buying. But these are poor proxies and don't capture the underlying construct of Mental Availability nor do they account for market share baselines.

Mental Availability is considered a market-based asset. Maintaining and building it should be considered an absolute priority objective of advertising.

CPM (cost per meaningless thousand)

CPM (Cost Per Mille) is a metric based on two seemingly simple objective measures—the hard cost of the ad placement and the number of people reached. CPM is an industry standard way for an advertiser to quantify the value of different media. The idea of CPM is akin to grocery unit pricing. Grocery unit pricing is a labeling system introduced in the 70's to help consumers quickly compare the value of similar, but not identical, products. It's about standardizing cost against a common measure (such as liter) without the consumer having to do the complicated calculations at the point of purchase. Grocery unit pricing is about informed choice and displaying relative value. If the low sugar variant is more expensive per liter, but the customer is willing to pay for that feature, then so be it.

The trouble we face as an industry is that CPM is a metric that is impacted by a 'circular reference'. A circular reference in Excel (XLS), or a circular dependency in Google Sheets, happens when calculations create an endless loop, similar to a dog chasing its own tail. This occurs when a formula in a cell refers to itself directly or indirectly, causing confusion in the calculation process.

We've previously discussed the issues with measuring impressions, so one half of the two measures used in this standard and widespread metric is 'dirty code', but the 'cost' part of the CPM metric has its own performance challenges. This is where the circular reference problem kicks in.

Real-time bidding (RTB) was introduced in 2008 as a method for advertisers to purchase ad impressions on digital platforms through real-time auctions. The concept is straightforward: advertisers want to advertise, publishers want to sell their available ad spaces and an auction begins. The advertiser who wins the bid gains access to the impressions. While the highest bid often holds significance, the outcome of the auction can also be influenced by the rules and algorithms employed by the ad exchange or network, and this is typically non-transparent.

When contrasting this with the real estate market, a buyer seeks to acquire a property while a seller intends to sell one. However, in real estate auctions, the highest bid, typically exceeding the asking price, usually secures the property. These winning bids generally reflect the genuine overall value of the neighborhood. Even during rare economic events such as the COVID-19 pandemic, which temporarily inflate property prices, market conditions typically stabilize over time, returning to bids that accurately represent the neighborhood's relative value.

The key distinction lies in perceived value versus economic value. Perceived value is a subjective assessment shaped by individual opinions, brand perception, convenience, emotional appeal often varying among customers. In contrast, economic value is an objective evaluation grounded in a product's utility, functionality, and its relative market price. Economic value relies on quantitative factors and tends to provide a more consistent assessment of reality of value.

In RTB, the bidding system relies on perceived value, which can be problematic due to variations in impression quality, making them neither uniform nor relative. This flawed perceived value becomes the basis for bids, creating a feedback loop that reinforces the initial flaws. As a result, the 'reserve' price can create a false sense of quality, utility and functionality primarily driven by the bidding process itself.

And voilà, therein lies a circular reference.

So there you have it, CPM is a metric that is made up of two measures that are independently flawed (impression quality and cost relatively) coming together to form the foundation for how our industry values different media.

This is why this section is called cost per meaningless thousand.

TAKE IT TO WORK

Until we reach a point where we have reach/attention equivalence, cost per thousand will always mean cost per meaningless thousand.

Closing the Chicken or Egg Debate

Let's start with some song Lyrics (sung in Southern USA Country Style):

- *Which come first, the chicken or the egg?*
- *Which come first, the chicken or the egg?*
- *How could somethin' so fat and furry*
- *Come from somethin' so smooth and pearly?*
- *Which come first, the chicken or the egg?*

This charming children's Sesame Street song Written by Joe Raposo in 1972 was crafted to inspire young minds (Episode 0276). In reality, the answer to the biological question is that eggs existed long before chickens as a species evolved, but it serves as a metaphor for pondering the mysteries of nature and encourages children to think about more complex concepts.

This is relevant because a similar ongoing circular debate exists in the attention economy today.

Does the creative catch your eye and determine how many seconds of attention you pay? Or does the media platform define the seconds your creative content is afforded? A question typically followed by 'surely if we build better creative content, that will fix it?'.

The question 'which comes first' the media or the creative' underscores the ongoing discussion about what an advertiser is in control of in this highly distracted inattentive world.

Figure 2.19 illustrates one of many sets of data tested in this context. Brands A through M represent various creative executions, each deployed across different platforms in real-time scenarios, with consistent ad lengths. For instance, Creative A, lasting 15 seconds, was tested on platforms like TikTok, Facebook, and YouTube (note: these are not the actual platforms used here). By maintaining creative consistency across platforms, we can dissect the distinct impacts of media and creative on attention.

The data reveals differences in attention garnered from Brand A to Brand M. However, what becomes interesting is when we examine the data across rows. For example, when looking at Brand A on platform A, it achieved 7.2

	Platform A	Platform B	Platform C	Platform D	Avg. Attention Seconds	Loss Best to Worst
Brand A	7.2	4.5	3.4	2.3	4.4	-4.9
Brand B	7.0	5.5	3.3	2.9	4.7	-4.1
Brand C	6.9	3.7	3.3	3.2	4.3	-3.7
Brand D	6.5	5.1	2.9	2.8	4.3	-3.7
Brand E	6.4	4.1	3.2	2.7	4.1	-3.7
Brand F	5.9	4.3	2.7	2.5	3.9	-3.4
Brand G	5.8	3.8	3.1	2.7	3.9	-3.1
Brand H	5.5	4.8	3.4	2.4	4.0	-3.1
Brand I	6.0	3.9	2.8	2.4	3.8	-3.6
Brand J	6.1	3.8	2.5	2.2	3.7	-3.9
Brand K	5.5	2.8	2.5	2.3	3.3	-3.2
Brand L	5.4	3.9	2.3	2.5	3.5	-2.9
Brand M	4.6	4.3	2.5	2.4	3.4	-2.2

Platform attention performance: Best ⟶ to ⟶ Worst

© Amplified Intelligence 2024

Fig. 2.19   Example creative data by best/worst attention

seconds of attention, while the same creative on platform B obtained 4.5 seconds, followed by 3.4 seconds and 2.3 seconds. A similar pattern emerges with Brand M: on platform A, it secured 4.6 seconds of attention, while on platform B, it earned 4.3 seconds, followed by 2.5 seconds and 2.4 seconds. Look at any brand you will see the same pattern. While there is the occasional deviation in some sets of data, this is very rare.

This pattern indicates that every creative, whether strong (in its ability to capture attention) like Brand A or weaker like Brand L, experiences a consistent decline in attention across the same platforms, showcasing the impact of media placement over creative. If creative were the dominant factor in attracting attention, all creatives would perform equally across platforms and achieve the same duration of attention, which is not the case. The ability to capture attention for the creative, no matter how much effort was invested in it, is influenced by platform performance (and this performance is influenced by the user experience which was previously discussed). Importantly, this systematic pattern persists across all data collections, regardless of brand size, platform testing, format, or even programming, for example: the highest attention programming drives the most attention for ads, the lowest attention programming drives the least attention for ads.

Overall we typically see the average loss from best to worst between platforms (rows) is double the average loss between best to worst between creative (columns).

To make matters worse, the strongest creatives (i.e. Brands A, B, C) suffer the most—meaning the drop in attention when played on poorer quality platforms represents a greater number of seconds lost, than the seconds lost between best and worst platforms for average to weak creative (i.e. Brands K, L, M).

For example, examining Fig. 2.19, in the far right column you will see that Brand A loses 4.9 attention seconds when comparing best to worst platforms, while Brand M only loses 2.2 seconds. This is an interesting turn of events because normally the 'smallest' or 'weakest' elements are the most affected, in line with the Double Jeopardy effect, but in this case it's the 'strongest' (more on that in Chapter 4).

This work is yet another affirmation that impressions across platforms are not equal, primarily due to differences in the user experience of each platform. We can thank objective science and attention measurement for answering advertising's own chicken and egg puzzle. The winner is the egg (media).

TAKE IT TO WORK

The ability for creativity to shine is tempered by the performance of the media platform. Overall we typically see the average loss from best to worst between platforms is double the average loss between best to worst between creative.

As we conclude this section, let us express our gratitude to Nielsen for sparking the lively debate surrounding media versus creative. In a highly referenced article published by Nielsen in 2017, they contend that creative execution drives value more than media. Nielsen suggests that creative elements account for 47% of advertising effectiveness, surpassing media planning characteristics like targeting and reach, which contribute 36%. It's crucial to note how this report addresses media, stating:

It may seem obvious, but reaching a large number of consumers with advertising is critical to the success of a campaign: only consumers exposed to an ad can be influenced. This study examined 863 recent cross-media campaigns across all verticals and measured the volume of impressions for each of them, as well as the reach achieved with those impressions.

This paper often refers to creative versus media as a framework for analysis. The researchers combine reach, targeting and recency into a single 'media' group since these distinct factors all pertain to components of media planning and buying. With this grouping, we can more easily understand a campaigns, intrinsic creative qualities and its extrinsic media placement characteristics.

Fig. 2.20 Example of cross platform insertion code in creative benchmarking

A few key points to consider here:

1. Combining all three media factors into one, without accounting for the inequity in impressions, may introduce bias.
2. Measuring the 'volume' of impressions as a dependent variable without addressing the imbalance in impressions may lead to bias.
3. Not holding creative constant across conditions (including degree of switching), may lead to bias (Fig. 2.20 creative insertion code example that enables us to keep all creative constant to isolate effects).

We do agree on one critical point: creative is undeniably the linchpin for closing the sale. However, it is equally imperative to emphasize that the paramount element in garnering the attention necessary for the creative to even get the sale, in fact, the media.

2.3   The Great Unlearning

Think and Shift Differently

> The shortest and surest way of arriving at real knowledge is to unlearn the lessons we have been taught, to mount the first principles, and take nobody's word about them. Henry IV of England

"The problem with learning is unlearning", a headline perfectly crafted in a 2016 Harvard Review article by Mark Bonchek, founder of Shift Thinking and a specialist in transformative change. It emphasizes that the real challenge for companies lies in unlearning outdated mental models rather than just focusing on learning new ones. Bonchek talks about the importance of unlearning in the context of becoming a "learning organization" and the need to adapt to disruption and change, fast.

But he cautions it's not easy. In his experience even the best companies still struggle to practice what they preach. He thinks the problem is we focus too much on the popular (continuous learning) and less on the unpopular (continuous unlearning). But often the unpopular is challenging because reputation and career investment is at stake. Letting go might seem like shedding aspects of our identity, power, or established position, and that is risky and scary. Perhaps the irony is that often those with identity, power or established position are the ones in charge of change.

The concept of unlearning is not a new one, but one that we have all been unwittingly exposed to on a personal level in the recent few collective years of a pandemic and recession. We have all had to unlearn and relearn the rules around working arrangements, now we can't imagine being forced to work from a single location. We have all had to unlearn and relearn the rules around use of new technology, now we can't imagine life without telehealth. We have all had to unlearn and relearn the rules around socializing, now we all practice keeping distance.

Unlearning refers to the process of consciously letting go of or discarding previously held beliefs, assumptions, habits, or knowledge that may no longer be accurate, relevant, or useful. It involves challenging and dismantling preconceived notions or ingrained patterns of thinking and application to make room for new and updated information or perspectives. But it's not about forgetting either. It's about understanding what has changed, why it has changed and then how to apply this change for a better future. So less about holding on to the old ways, and completely rethinking what is possible in the future. Companies like Google, Uber, Airbnb, and Open AI are famous for removing limits to change the world. Unlearning is not always easy, as it often involves breaking away from the familiar, expending mental effort, self-reflection and ultimately moving out of your comfort zone.

Unlearning has three parts.

1. Recognition: Acknowledging that old mental models are no longer effective, relevant, or complete.

2. Ideation: Identifying or developing alternative mental models that better align with current reality, future goals and the changing environment.
3. Reinforcement: Rebuilding beliefs and ingraining new mental habits and reinforcing them through repetition and practice.

Unlearning is vital in all the 'sciences' social, applied, physical, and marketing is no exception. Perhaps the most impressive example of unlearning in recent history is collective unlearning that happened when the scientific community came together in COVID-19.

In the past it's taken four to 20 years to create conventional vaccines. For the new messenger RNA (mRNA) vaccines from Pfizer-BioNTech and Moderna, it was a record-setting 11 months. The process has changed forever the way drugs are developed.

John Cooke, M.D., medical director of the RNA Therapeutics Program at Houston Methodist Hospital's DeBakey Heart and Vascular Center, when asked in 2021 what he think the deepest lesions of 2020 brought us he said, "One of the biggest lessons we've learned from COVID is that the scientific community working together can do some pretty amazing things."

The pandemic triggered an unprecedented wave of global cooperation, uniting scientists, researchers, governments, and pharmaceutical companies in an effort to swiftly exchange crucial information and resources. This collaborative spirit allowed for rapid progress. Moreover, governments and international organizations played a crucial role by providing substantial financial support, enabling companies to invest significantly in vaccine research and development without bearing the usual financial risks.

Regulatory agencies, such as the U.S. Food and Drug Administration (FDA) and the European Medicines Agency (EMA), adopted expedited review processes that did not compromise safety standards. They implemented techniques like rolling reviews and offered guidance to vaccine developers, accelerating the approval process. The pandemic's worldwide scope facilitated large-scale clinical trials, ensuring a sufficient number of participants to swiftly assess the vaccines' safety and effectiveness.

Many countries issued emergency use authorizations (EUAs) for promising vaccines based on early data, enabling quicker distribution before full approval. To ensure ongoing safety, monitoring systems were swiftly implemented after the vaccines received emergency use authorization, allowing for real-time data collection and rapid responses to any emerging concerns.

In summary, the COVID-19 experience showcased the incredible potential of collective unlearning and collaboration. The unprecedented global cooperation, combined with substantial financial support, streamlined regulatory processes, large-scale clinical trials, and vigilant monitoring, resulted in the rapid development of vaccines that has transformed the future of drug development.

While not quite as miraculous and life altering as a vaccine, if this chapter has done nothing more than to begin the process of recognition and ideation for the purpose of preparing you to learn new things, it has done its job.

Unlearning Wanamaker

The whole point of this section is to establish the need to unlearn and to prepare you particularly for the big learnings you are going to read in this book. Unlearn everything you know, perhaps this one is one of the biggest:

"Half the money I spend on advertising is wasted; the trouble is I don't know which half." These are the famous words that John Wanamaker, the builder of the first mall in the US in 1876, said jokingly, but not jokingly. This quote reflects his understanding of the importance of advertising but also his frustration with its unpredictability.

Annoyingly, we have heard these words at every single advertising conference ever since.

But Wanamaker was an innovator, a driver of change, he also (less famously) said; "You can never ride on the wave that came in and went out yesterday." He would be horrified that 100 years after his death we are still riding on a wave that drastically underestimates his frustration.

In December 2023, the ANA (Association of National Advertisers) ANA Programmatic Media Supply Chain Transparency Study. When you unpack the ANA data and ad what we know from attention and digital, an eye watering number appears:

1. Global programmatic ad spend 2023 = US$558b
2. % of Programmatic advertising deemed 'loss of media productivity' (ANA 2023) = 35%
3. % of Programmatic advertising lost to 'transaction costs' (ANA 2023) = 29%
4. % of Programmatic advertising with attention = 20% (at best)
5. % Programmatic advertising that is passes ANA qualification AND gets attention = **10%**
6. $ Relative waste on programmatic advertising: US$506b

*Note: If A changes F will change, but E will remain the same. Based on the ANA report, wastage will always calculate to 10%.

So the replacement quote to the old Wanamaker quote should be this: **"90% of the money I spend on programmatic advertising is wasted; the trouble is I don't know which 90%".**

This is why there is a rally cry to 'think and shift' differently. Change is not popular, but once the CEO sees you wasting less than 90% of your digital budget, change will be popular again.

TAKE IT TO WORK

The new Wanamaker: 90% of the money I spend on programmatic advertising is wasted; fortunately now we do know which 90%

2.4   The Wrap Up: First Principles Thinking and Gary the Snail

First principles thinking is like taking apart a complex puzzle and rebuilding it from scratch, starting with unquestionable truths. It's like constructing a sturdy foundation before building a house. Just like an endlessly curious child, you keep asking 'Why?' and seek evidence at each step. This approach isn't just for rocket scientists; it works in any field where you predict or create something new.

Elon Musk, the master of first principles, swears by it for his success. Google "Elon and First Principles" for proof.

But the ultimate First Principle Thinking showcase was his 2017 interview with Chris Anderson (TED). He'd founded The Boring Company, aiming to dig tunnels faster than Sponge Bob's Gary the snail, who's 14 times quicker than regular tunnel machines. Musk's plan? Improve machines to outpace Gary by 4 or 5 times, to reduce costs and improve the economics behind tunnel construction. How? First principles thinking, of course.

In a Wall Street Journal article, Musk pointed out that relying on past experiences and analogies can stifle innovation. This is where Gary the Snail becomes an attention economy role model, free from past baggage, allowing us to dream big. 'Big Little Learnings' are key in this journey, providing answers to the 'why's' that drive us forward.

2.5   List of Contributors

Rob Brittain. Independent Marketing Consultant and Strategic Advisor

Rob Brittain is an independent marketing consultant and strategic advisor to CMOs, focused on enabling enterprise-wide marketing effectiveness capability. A published writer and speaker in his field, Rob is co-author of the "Advertising Effectiveness Rules" series of reports from the ACA Effectiveness Database with the globally renowned Peter Field. These include "Winning or Losing in a Recession", "To ESOV and Beyond" and "Attention and Effectiveness". Prior to becoming an independent marketing consultant Rob spent 20 years in client-side commercial roles including leading Marketing Effectiveness at ANZ Bank Banking Group and Marketing Analytics at Mondelez International across the Asia–Pacific region.

Peter Field. Marketing Consultant

Peter spent 15 years as a strategic planner in advertising and has been a marketing consultant for the last 25 years. Effectiveness case study analysis underpins much of his work, which includes a number of well-known texts in partnership with Les Binet: Marketing in the Era of Accountability, The Long & The Short of it, Media in Focus, Effectiveness in Context, and The 5 Principles of Growth in B2B Marketing. Other important authored and co-authored marketing and advertising texts include: Brand Immortality, Advertising in Recession—Long, Short or Dark?, The Link Between Creativity and Effectiveness, Selling Creativity Short, Why aren't we doing this?, The Crisis in Creative Effectiveness, The Alchemy of Effectiveness, To ESOV and Beyond and chapters in Eat Your Greens, The Effectiveness Code and the Sage Handbook of Advertising. Peter has a global reputation as an effectiveness expert and communicator and speaks and consults on this topic regularly around the world.

Moomal Shaikh. Principal Product Manager, Oracle

Moomal is a tech enthusiast with 10 + years of professional experience, specializing in the intersection of advertising, data, and tech. More recently, she has been exploring the effects of behavioral economics on the evolution of industry ecosystems, the adoption of new technologies, and the broader societal impact of media and advertising.

As a Principal Product Manager at Oracle, Moomal has owned the ideation-to-revenue process for a diverse portfolio of data analytics and ad-tech solutions, including spearheading measurement frameworks for audio, and developing streamlined tag solutions for publishers. She is thrilled to contribute her insights to The Attention Economy 2.0, hoping to provoke meaningful discussions on our evolving nexus with technology, advertising, and media.

References

Alter, A. (2017). *Irresistible: The Rise of Addictive Technology and the Business of Keeping Us Hooked*. Penguin Press.

ANA. (2023, December 5). *Programmatic Media Supply Chain Transparency Study: Complete Report*. https://www.ana.net/miccontent/show/id/rr-2023-12-ana-programmatic-media-supply-chain-transparency-study

Beal, V., Kennedy, R., Trinh, G., Hartnett, N., & Phua, P. (2021). When Brands Go Dark: A Replication and Extension. *Journal of Advertising Research,* May 2023, 2023–009. https://doi.org/10.2501/JAR-2023-009.

Binet, L., & Field, P. (2013). *The Long and the Short of It: Balancing Short and Long-Term Marketing Strategies*. Institute of Practitioners in Advertising.

Bonchek, M. (2016, November 3). Why the Problem with Learning is Unlearning. *Harvard Business Review*. https://hbr.org/2016/11/why-the-problem-with-learning-is-unlearning

Broadbent, S. (2000). What Do Advertisements Really Do for Brands? *Journal of Advertising, 19*(2), 147–165.

Danenberg, N., Kennedy, R., Beal, V., & Sharp, B. (2016). Advertising Budgeting: A Re-Investigation of the Evidence on Brand Size and Spend. *Journal of Advertising, 45*(1), 139–146.

Dawes, J. (2009). You Need More Customers: The Key Is How Many You Have, Not How Much They Buy. *Marketing Research Summer,* 30–31.

Ehrenberg, A. S. C. (1959). The Pattern of Consumer Purchases. *Applied Statistics, 8*(1), 26–41.

Ehrenberg, A. S. C. (2000). Repeat-Buying: Facts, Theory and Applications. *Journal of Empirical Generalisations in Marketing Science, 5*(2), 392–770.

Ehrenberg, A. S. C., Barnard, N., Kennedy, R., & Bloom, H. (2002). Brand Advertising as Creative Publicity. *Journal of Advertising Research, 42*(4), 7–18.

Ewens, K. J. (2022). *Divided Attention: The Value of Eye Tracked High and Low Attention in Consumer Behavior* (Doctoral dissertation). The University of Adelaide.

Field, P. (2008). Marketing in a Downturn: Lessons from the Past. *Market Leader, 42*, 1–7.

Field, P. (2017, April 18). *Peter Field: Short-termism is Killing Effectiveness.* Stuff (NZ). https://www.stuff.co.nz/business/91501478/peter-field-shorttermism-is-killing-effectiveness

Frascona 'Sochurkova, M. (2019). *Facebook Changes Post Size in Mobile News Feed.* Newsfeed.org. https://newsfeed.org/facebook-changes-post-size-in-mobile-news-feed/

González, V. M., & Mark, G. (2004, April). "Constant, constant, multi-tasking craziness" managing multiple working spheres. In *Proceedings of the SIGCHI conference on Human factors in computing systems* (pp. 113–120).

Hansen, F., & Christensen, L. B. (2005). Share of Voice/Share of Market and Long-Term Advertising Effects. *International Journal of Advertising, 24*(3), 297–320.

Hari, J. (2023). *Stolen Focus: Why You Can't Pay Attention—And How to Think Deeply Again.* Crown Publishing Group (NY). ISBN-13: 978-0593138519.

Jones, J. P. (1990). Ad Spending: Maintaining Market Share. *Harvard Business Review, 68*(1), 38–43.

Kirn, W. (2007). The Autumn of the Multitaskers. *The Atlantic, 1.*

Miller, E. K. (2017). *Multitasking: Why Your Brain Can't Do It and What You Should Do About It.* The Picower Institute for Learning and Memory and Department of Brain and Cognitive Sciences, Massachusetts Institute of Technology. ekmillerlab.mit.edu. Retrieved January 4, 2020.

Nelson-Field, K. (2022a). *Attention Applied: Time-in-view is the Downfall of Modern Measurement.* WARC.

Nelson-Field, K. (2022b). *Attention Elasticity: The Attention Economy's Chicken and Egg Question.* Opinion: Attention Revolution, The Media Leader.

Nelson-Field, K. (2023a). *Attention Applied: The Expectation-Reality Gap—An Important Consideration in the Year of Efficiency.* WARC.

Nelson-Field, K. (2023b). *Attention Applied: The Nuance of Size (and the Attention/Outcomes Relationship).* WARC.

Nelson-Field, K., & Ewens, K. (2019). *The High Value of Low Attention.* Admap.

Nelson-Field, K., & Jung, H. (2022). *The Shape of Attention: Mining Gold from Individual Level Attention Viewing Patterns.* WARC Exclusive.

Nielsen Catalina Solutions. (2017). *When it Comes to Advertising Effectiveness, What is Key?* https://www.nielsen.com/insights/2017/when-it-comes-to-advertising-effectiveness-what-is-key/

Rogers, R. D., & Monsell, S. (1995). Costs of a Predictable Switch Between Simple Cognitive Tasks. *Journal of experimental psychology: General, 124*(2), 207.

Seer Interactive. (2019, February 11). *YouTube Expands Advertiser Access to 15-Second Non-Skippable Ads.* https://www.seerinteractive.com/insights/youtube-15-second-ads

Tennø, H. (2022). Nobody Needs Metrics, What We Need Are Better Decisions. Medium. https://everythingnewisdangerous.medium.com/nobody-needs-metrics-what-we-need-are-better-decisions-9120f864d277

3

Attention Science Becomes a Science

One sometimes finds what one is not looking for.
Alexander Fleming (1928)

There is an iconic 90s Australian anthem, written and performed by legendary Australian songwriter and storyteller Paul Kelly called "From Little Things Big Things Grow'. The song is a protest song born from the country's history of social activism and indigenous rights and tells the story of the Gurindji people's struggle for land rights in Australia. It focuses on a specific and significant event in 1966 when Aboriginal stockmen and their families went on strike to demand better pay and land rights. This strike endured for several years and played a crucial role in advancing indigenous rights in Australia.

"From Little Things Big Things Grow" symbolizes the potential for growth, change, and progress that can emerge from even the humblest of beginnings. It serves as a poignant reminder that every significant achievement often commences with a small step or idea.

In this chapter, we continue along the same theme, directly following the concepts introduced in "Big Little Learnings." Little learnings initially arise from individual studies, but as they are repeatedly examined across hundreds of thousands, and sometimes even millions of data points, a remarkable phenomenon occurs—patterns begin to emerge and become generalizable and predictable.

This is the point where the study of attention transforms into a science, and marketers can bank on its reliability.

3.1   Good Science

Predictability in Attention Science

Andrew Ehrenberg (1926–2019) made a significant contribution by establishing reproducible quantitative patterns in the field of social science. In his 1993 article published in Nature, titled "Even The Social Sciences Have Laws," Ehrenberg showcased that even in areas like Marketing, often considered unpredictable due to the seemingly random nature of consumer behavior, there exist distinct regularities. He emphasized that uncovering human behavior patterns typically commences with existing knowledge and expectations, starting from small observations and building upon them.

Ehrenberg's fundamental belief revolved around the notion that scientific methods used in the physical sciences could be adapted and applied to the social sciences. In his 1969 work, "The Discovery and Use of Laws of Marketing," he presented five straightforward laws governing buyer behavior. He emphasized that the process of discovering such regularities parallels that of other scientific disciplines: collecting pertinent data and rigorously studying them, repeatedly. As Ehrenberg put it, "By examining consistent phenomena, one uncovers regularities. Science is as straightforward as that. The key is to select consistent phenomena as subjects of study."

He held the view that despite the inherent uncertainty in much of scientific knowledge, there exist fundamental lawlike relationships within observed phenomena. Systematically identifying and applying these relationships to practical problems drive progress in both scientific and practical domains.

This is where attention economics stands today. We are in the midst of a shift from Attention V1 to Attention V2. A shift from case studies to science where 'law like' patterns are guiding. This shift involves moving from relying on case studies to adopting a more scientific approach, where 'lawlike' patterns are replacing anecdotal evidence, ushering in a new era of understanding human attention.

Case studies have traditionally been the foundation of marketing strategies, often relying on specific instances to support their claims. For example, a company might say, "We did X with Brand Y, and it produced Z outcome."

However, this approach has a critical limitation—it's based on a single moment in time. If you change the conditions of the case study, the outcome is likely to be different. When differences can't be explained, the findings can't be confidently applied. It's like rolling a dice. Moreover, significantly different outcomes should raise concerns, as they are often inaccurate.

In contrast, science is built on the search for patterns and norms. When we conduct studies that reveal patterns, we establish a foundation that can withstand variations in conditions. Changing the test conditions of these studies is less likely to alter the results, and if differences do arise, they can usually be explained.

The litmus test for predictability and good science is replication. In empirical sciences, meaningful results come from building on existing findings rather than testing increasingly specific hypotheses. Replication studies aim to repeat earlier studies under similar circumstances to determine if the results can be reproduced. This is conducted using similar methods but with slightly varying boundary conditions, such as different countries, varying brand size or product categories. Doing this increases the likelihood that the results are valid, predictable and will hold over time and under fire. That is what makes them truly valuable. These are the types of results marketers can 'bet their house on'.

In our industry, where marketers are under increasing pressure to drive sales growth, there's a tendency to accept the results of studies that 'sound reasonable'. The result is a large amount of unsubstantiated advice, taken as fact.

Attention science represents a critical shift from relying on case evidence to establishing replicable norms using extensive data sets and advanced technology. Balancing the factors of predictability and unpredictability are ongoing challenges in scientific research, but this shift is essential for longevity, stability, and value in the attention economy.

Attention science matters because without applying scientific principles, simplistic approaches can do more harm than good. 'Good enough' is where we've come from, and we have spent the last couple of decades paying the price. Generalisable norms set the blueprint for successful attention prediction and without accounting for these patterns an attention model will be wrongly skewed by its own training parameters. Attention science not only offers a path to avoid marketing catastrophes but also provides an opportunity for positive, long-lasting change.

This chapter is dedicated to avoiding marketing catastrophes by providing reliable, generalizable norms for attention science. These norms are the bedrock upon which you can 'bet your house'.

MEANWHILE IN THE REAL WORLD

Data Snooping (also known as 'P-Hacking', 'data dredging' or 'p-value dancing') is a deceptive practice in data analysis. It involves the unethical manipulation of data to uncover patterns that can be presented as statistically significant, thereby inflating the likelihood of false positives. This dubious technique poses a significant threat to the integrity of scientific research.

In the first Attention Economy book, we presented an instance of 'research gone wild,' where an international team of 200 psychologists was commissioned to replicate some of the most famous psychology experiments in history. However, not only did half of the studies fail to replicate, but they also uncovered opposing findings compared to the original research. Reasons for replication failures can include anything from fluke to cherry picking, omission of outliers or not considering the whole picture (unknown variables that influence study outcomes).

A new case of data snooping has emerged which holds even greater irony to the concept of 'research gone wild'. In late 2023 the New Yorker wrote an article about Dan Ariely and Francesca Gino who were once famous for their research into why we bend the truth, and were found to (wait for it) bend the truth in their work. With academic credentials from esteemed institutions like Harvard and MIT, they had carved a niche for themselves in the exploration of human dishonesty. Ariely, in particular, had lent his insights to documentaries about prominent figures such as Elizabeth Holmes and had commented on the Enron scandal. Their notable paper titled "The Dark Side of Creativity," demonstrates that individuals with strong imaginative abilities tend to be more prone to deception. However, in 2023 their credibility took a hit when allegations of data manipulation surfaced. This brought to light the very behavior they had been studying—dishonesty—casting a shadow over their entire body of work.

This story serves as a valuable lesson, highlighting the negative impact of misguided incentives in the world of science, whether it's for academic recognition or gaining popularity among customers. It's a clear reminder of how crucial it is to maintain integrity in all aspects of scientific exploration and application. Moreover, it underscores the need for those who rely on scientific findings to appreciate and demand data that is generalizable and representative. In research, when things are vastly different than expected or vary significantly over different conditions and can't be explained, be cautious. It usually means it's not right.

Lewis-Kraus, G. (2023). They Studied Dishonesty. Was Their Work a Lie? The New Yorker. https://www.newyorker.com/magazine/2023/10/09/they-studied-dishonesty-was-their-work-a-lie

Researching the 'Non-researchable'

Researching the 'non-researchable' is a figurative phrase that describes the exploration of topics, questions, or areas of study that are exceptionally challenging, unconventional, or thought to be too complex or beyond the scope of traditional research. The concept often suggests pushing the boundaries of knowledge and pursuing unconventional or innovative approaches to better understand something previously deemed unattainable. It may involve using cutting-edge technology, developing new methodologies, or questioning existing assumptions and limitations.

Examples of topics that were once considered non-researchable but have been explored through creative and innovative approaches include the exploration of deep ocean ecosystems, the study of extremophiles in extreme environments, and the investigation of the human brain's intricacies.

In 2022, Nature Human Behaviour, a prestigious online scientific journal within the renowned Nature portfolio, celebrated its fifth anniversary as a respected publication. To commemorate this significant milestone, the journal released an article titled "The Future of Human Behaviour Research." In the article twenty-two leading scientists in some of the core disciplines within the journal's scope share their views on new directions in their disciplines. Their insights offer a valuable glimpse into the future of research on human behavior, with a particular focus on less-explored and innovative areas of inquiry.

The overarching message of the article is the necessity of expanding the scope of research disciplines to make them more diverse and pertinent. This expansion is seen as critical for addressing pressing societal challenges such as new technologies, artificial intelligence, political shifts, health crises, climate change, and others. In simpler terms, this article serves as a roadmap for 'researching the non-researchable'.

One noteworthy contribution in the context of the emerging field of attention science comes from Professor Claudia Wagner. She is a Professor of Applied Computational Social Sciences at RWTH Aachen University, Aachen, Germany, and serves as the Head of the Computational Social Science Department at the Leibniz Institute for the Social Sciences in Köln, Germany.

Professor Wagner describes computational social science as a multidisciplinary field that harnesses computational methods and cutting-edge technologies to collect, model, and analyze digital behavioral data, often in real-world settings or through large-scale designed experiments. These efforts are typically complemented by integrating other data sources to gain a holistic understanding of human behavior and social phenomena.

However, she highlights that while this field has made significant strides in shedding light on areas such as the spread of misinformation and the role of algorithms in curating information, it has somewhat overlooked critical questions related to data quality, accessibility, measurement validity, reliability, and their potential consequences. Professor Wagner suggests several key opportunities to address these challenges:

1. Privacy-Preserving Data Infrastructures: Establishing shared data infrastructures that respect privacy while collecting diverse data, including surveys and observational data, can enhance research and contribute to the reproducibility of findings. For example, longitudinal online panels in which participants allow researchers to track their web browsing behavior and link these traces to their survey answers will not only facilitate substantive research on societal questions but also enable methodological research (for example, on the quality of different data sources and measurement models), and contribute to the reproducibility of computational social science research.
2. Best Practices and Scientific Infrastructures: There is a need for best practices and support systems for developing, evaluating, and reusing measurements in computational social science. Learning from practices in survey methodology and other fields, such as medicine.
3. Understanding Feedback Loops: The fusion of algorithmic and human behavior invites us to rethink the various ways in which data, measurements and social theories can be connected. Research designs and product environments should be developed to systematically explore and enhance our understanding of these feedback loops.

Professor Wagner underscores the significance of addressing these issues to advance the field of computational social science, thereby enhancing the quality and impact of research. This expansion is not only essential for providing a roadmap to 'research the non-researchable' but also for elevating attention science to new heights. In essence, computational social science not only illuminates our comprehension of human behavior but also offers invaluable insights into propelling attention science into the future.

TAKE IT TO WORK

Human behavior is complex. The industry can't simply say 'we pick attention as the next viewability' but then fail to understand how attention works. Professor Wagners point on the need to rethink the fusion of algorithmic and human behavior and the various ways in which data, measurements and social theories can be connected, is onpoint. Vendors should understand nuance.

EXPERT INSIGHT: Key Principles from 'Non-Researchable' to 'Research-Ready' by Kellen Ewens.

1. The Importance of Scope Defining Using an Interdisciplinary Approach.

At its core, science strives to test the boundaries of our understanding about our world. Most commonly, science is iterative, building on our existing knowledge in a systematic way and laying the foundation for the next investigation. Other times, science emerges as the by-product of needing to address a particular problem, and the research solution is built backwards from execution to design. When joining an attention vendor in 2019 to help answer the yet unanswered question—can attention be used as a better and more reliable metric of media engagement?—it soon became clear that existing methods would not help to answer this question. Although aspects of attention, like selective or 'active' visual processing, had been extensively measured in past work, the nature of this research was highly experimental, typically positioning participants in extensively controlled and unnatural research settings. At best, participants would be required to wear somewhat uncomfortable headgear to monitor their focus, or at worst, be required to use head-stabilisation systems via a chinrest or bite-bar—neither of which effectively emulates the real-life environments in which most people encounter advertising.

Through collating thousands of papers on attention measurement approaches, we identified a recurring focus on active attention, a form of visual attention which is focused and explicit towards a particular stimulus. Study after study, from psychology to neuroscience, identified similar findings for advertising applications, namely that active attention commands the greatest value as a form of perception due to its links to enhanced brand and consumer outcomes. Given the popularity of these phenomena across literature fields, few of the findings surprised us, reinforcing the notion that active attention is a highly focused and valuable form of advertising perception. However, what was surprising was the rarity of research studies properly measuring the role of lower states of attention in advertising appraisal. Unlike active attention, a more 'passive' form of attention is less specific to a particular stimulus and is instead spread across several stimuli at one time. This apparent oversight in the literature left us with a myriad of questions spiraling into one another—how do passive states of attention function? How does the value of passive attention compare with that of active attention? And how could we measure the type of attention that exists when people aren't paying attention?

2. Moving From Lab Requires Computational Methods.

Clear on what we needed but unclear about how to get there, our design approach took us far and wide to related fields of study with a view to triangulate our ideal solution, using both an empirical and technical lens. From psychology, we sought theories on engagement and involvement to define our passive attention construct. From neuroscience, we studied two-stage models of visual processing to enhance our two-form solution. Looking to computer science, we leveraged the ideas of J.C.R. Licklider regarding the interaction of humans and computers in processing visual information, forming the conceptual basis of our neural network visual processing apparatus. And in the space created when overlaying all these concepts was our solution—a comprehensive, evidence-led, two-stage attention model based around a proprietary naturalistic (i.e., no need for wearable gear or laboratory tracking) remote eye tracking apparatus.

3. Persistence and Adaptability.

Then the hard work commenced. The need to put it all together to build research solutions that can collect the data required and prepare manuscripts to pass peer review. As I write here today, the non-researchable is now published and thus, researchable.

Seeing Through the Noise of Attention: A Diary of a Data Scientist

Section By Hayun Jung, Senior Data Scientist and AI Specialist.

As a data scientist, I've immersed myself in the rare and complex world of attention data to explore its potential in reshaping our understanding of attention in marketing use cases. This section sheds light on the evolution of attention data from isolated case studies to a robust scientific discipline. It offers insights into my personal experiences and the broader exploration of attention data, emphasizing its role in revolutionizing marketing strategies and enhancing consumer engagement. This not only showcases the evolution of attention science methodologies but also serves as a guide for harnessing its power in the dynamic landscape of marketing both for now and what's next.

The Rarity of Rich Data

In the field of marketing and consumer research, attention data often faces scrutiny due to its rarity and complexity. Critics argue that the high costs of collection, intricate preparation requirements, privacy concerns, and the inherent variability of human behavior might outweigh its benefits. However, a closer examination reveals that these very challenges make human attention data an indispensable asset in deeply understanding consumer behavior and enhancing marketing effectiveness.

It's vital to acknowledge that quality comes with a price. The meticulous environments and authentic scenarios required for collecting attention data ensure its relevance and applicability. These investments yield more accurate, reliable insights, ultimately saving resources that might be wasted on less effective marketing strategies derived from inferior data.

The true value of attention data lies in its ability to capture the multifaceted nature of human behavior, something that machine data simply cannot match. While machine data is often limited to metrics like clicks or scrolling or simple ad size, attention data goes beyond. It is important to recognize that attention data transcends the visual aspect and encompasses a range of responses, including audio engagement, emotional reactions, and physical actions.

This comprehensive approach combining visual, auditory, emotional, and behavioral data allows us to understand not only what captures attention but also what sustains it and importantly what truly influences consumer behavior. In truth, while privacy and ethical considerations present challenges in human data collection, they are not insurmountable and can be managed with GDPR equivalent policies to data collection, storage, transit and permissions. This is paramount in any study of human participants.

From Lab to Large

The depth and quality of insights provided by attention data are unparalleled, offering a profound understanding of consumer behavior that cannot be replicated by other data types. Advances in technology and methodologies are continually reducing barriers to representativeness and scale, making attention data more accessible and of better quality. This depth is invaluable in an era where consumers demand personalized, relevant, and empathetic marketing and marketers need truth sets that drive profound action (see more on Attention Profiles below).

My initial encounter with large-scale attention data was both challenging and exhilarating. It marked a venture into a world where every data point had the potential to unveil a new facet of human behavior. Coming from machine learning in a medical device context, access to human data of this scale, and beyond a lab, was exciting.

In this industry, a significant challenge arises due to the lack of standardization in measurement. Different businesses employ varying eye-tracking models and error maps with very different scale and representativeness, leading to discrepancies in the data. The absence of a standardized approach in measuring attention means that metrics like duration or binary probability can vary significantly in interpretation. This variation, combined with the absence of transparency in some attention indices, diminishes their effectiveness.

Moving Beyond Standard Metrics

The heart of attention data lies in its time-series nature. My role was to transform this raw data into reproducible and accurate metrics that can be practically applied. A role even more important as targeting cookies become redundant. However rapid adaptation and innovation were necessary to handle and analyze these massive time-scale datasets providing a more nuanced view of consumer attention.

Recognizing that duration alone was insufficient, I devised a method that didn't rely on arbitrary thresholds whereby I profiled ad views by grouping them based on various behavioral attributes, painting a more comprehensive picture of consumer engagement.

This approach recognizes the multidimensional nature of consumer engagement, offering richer insights beyond any surface-level metrics used in the industry today. By categorizing attention data, we capture the subtleties and nuances in how consumers interact with ads, acknowledging that human attention is inherently variable and influenced by many factors.

These included human attention factors such as distraction levels, peak and/or consecutive attention times, the frequency of attention shifts, and the average cycle of these shifts. Each attribute peeled back a layer of the complex human attention span, revealing that attention is not just a matter of 'if' but 'how' an ad is watched.

These profiles are generated by combining two types of data. First, there's machine based data, which includes implied attention metrics like ad visibility, scroll speed and pixel percentage, gathered automatically without human intervention. Second, we analyze human gaze distributions for the human factors mentioned previously. Combined, these attributes allow us to map attention behaviors more precisely, considering audience, device, and environmental factors.

A high correlation between ad formats and viewing patterns was observed, suggesting that the type of ad significantly influences how it is viewed. By integrating these data sources with post-viewing brand choice outcomes, we've managed to unveil the distinct value of each profile. Our ongoing research hypothesizes that factors like the content of the ad, its relevance to the brand, and the recency of consumer interaction might further explain variations in viewing patterns. These hypotheses are crucial in deepening our understanding of different elements that impact viewer engagement and offer valuable insights for future advertising strategies.

The practical implications of this work are immense. By understanding these Attention Profiles and Attributes, marketers can tailor their campaigns more effectively.

These types of viewing profiles allow us to move on from views alone, to how the audience engaged with the ad and what was the outcome it achieved. This approach aids in providing valuable insights to marketers, guiding them to optimize future campaigns and ensuring a meaningful exchange between the ad and its viewers.

It is clear that no single approach is a panacea; the field is complex and influenced by dynamic attributes and target differences. The strategy to categorize ad views by profiles aims to bring some uniformity and reliability to how we measure attention, accounting for the richness and variability of human engagement with advertising content. Additionally it gives us a way to build structured algorithms for predicting human behavior right down to the pre-bid level.

From Analytics to Science Including Diverse Data Types

The field of attention measurement is ever-evolving, with each dataset enriching our understanding and enabling us to refine our Attention Profiles and Attributes. This ongoing cycle of data collection, analysis, and application is not just about measuring attention; it's about understanding it in all its complexity, to make informed, effective marketing decisions in a landscape that's continually shifting.

Attention data, while insightful, gains significantly more depth when combined with other crucial data types:

1. Contextualizing Attention
The type of product being advertised is a crucial factor in interpreting attention data, as different products inherently require distinct forms of viewer engagement. For example, while a medical product advertisement might need an audience's extended focus for effective comprehension of details, a soft drink ad, like Coca-Cola, might achieve its impact with just a brief, intense exposure.

2. Brand and User Data Integration

The integration of brand-centric data and user demographics enriches the interpretation of attention patterns. This integration helps in customizing advertising strategies, tailoring them to specific audience segments based on their unique interactions and preferences.

3. Diversified Data Sources

Invest in and remain attentive to various data types, not just visual attention. Explore auditory, behavioral, and neurological data to gain a more comprehensive view of consumer engagement.

In conclusion, attention data, while a cornerstone of consumer research, is just one piece of a larger puzzle. By integrating it with brand, user, and other forms of data, we can achieve a more complete and accurate understanding of consumer behavior viewing profiles, leading to more effective and impactful advertising strategies.

Inspiring Action

Working with attention data has been a journey of ongoing learning and creativity. As a data scientist, I have embraced its complexities and potential to revolutionize our understanding of consumer behavior.

We stand at a pivotal juncture in the field of attention science, transitioning from a phase of conducting analytics with small, often old or aggregated data sets to embracing a more expansive, hypothesis-driven approach. Now, armed with a vast reservoir of attention data, we are empowered to formulate hypotheses and rigorously test them, opening new avenues of inquiry and discovery. But the future of attention science depends on our ability to adapt and uncover significant insights from this data. My advice to fellow professionals is to embrace these challenges and continually innovate, looking beyond surface metrics to grasp the true depth of consumer attention. This journey, though demanding, is incredibly fulfilling, providing unique opportunities to enhance how we understand and engage with consumers in a constantly changing market; it's a gateway to groundbreaking insights.

To those reading this book—whether you are a marketer, a researcher, or simply an enthusiast of consumer behavior—the call to action is clear. Embrace the complexities and opportunities of attention science. Contribute to this field, whether through research, application, or by challenging and refining existing methodologies. Your participation is crucial in shaping the future of attention science and, by extension, the landscape of marketing.

As we clear the noise, distilling vast amounts of data into actionable insights, we open up a world of possibilities. A world where understanding attention goes beyond mere observation to becoming a key driver of meaningful and effective marketing strategies. Let us continue to push the boundaries, to explore, and to innovate, as we forge ahead in this exciting field of attention science.

TAKE IT TO WORK

Science only works when good scientific principles are followed—good cross platform attention models should be collected and trained by the same mathematical values.

QUICK EXPLAINER

There are many factors that affect scientific predictability that customers of attention data need to consider.

These include well-established laws of nature, precise mathematical models, high-quality data and observations, and the ability to control variables in experiments, while challenges such as uncertainty in measurements and incomplete knowledge can introduce unpredictability. Here is a list of our top 5 to consider:

1. Data and Observations

The availability of high-quality data and observations is crucial for scientific predictability. Collecting precise and comprehensive data allows scientists to test hypotheses, refine models, and make accurate predictions about future events or outcomes.

2. Experimental Controls

In experimental sciences, the ability to control and manipulate variables within controlled settings enhances predictability. By conducting controlled experiments, scientists can isolate specific factors and study their effects, leading to more predictable results.

3. Mathematical Models

Mathematical models that describe the behavior of systems play a pivotal role in scientific predictability. These models use equations and algorithms to represent how variables interact and evolve over time. The accuracy and completeness of these models are essential for making reliable predictions.

4. Uncertainty and Measurement Error

Despite advances in measurement techniques, there is always a degree of uncertainty and measurement error in scientific observations. These uncertainties can introduce unpredictability into scientific predictions, particularly when dealing with small-scale phenomena or extreme conditions.

5. Incomplete Knowledge

In some areas of science, there may be gaps in our understanding or incomplete knowledge about the underlying mechanisms. This lack of comprehensive understanding can limit our ability to make precise predictions.

3.2 Laws of Attention

Andrew Ehrenberg's five "law-like" relationships in marketing have had a profound impact on the field of marketing. Derived from repeated observations and data-driven research, for five decades these principles have provided marketers with valuable insights into how marketing really works. They are all interrelated and all come to the same conclusion in terms of strategies for brand growth: That brand growth primarily stems from acquiring more customers, not from attempts to increase loyalty and moreover this focus should be on acquiring non/light brand buyers rather than attempting to increase the loyalty of existing heavy-buying customers.

Andrew Ehrenberg's most significant contribution to marketing was presented in collaboration with co-author Gerald Goodhardt in their seminal work, "The Dirichlet: A Comprehensive Model of Buying Behaviour" (1984). At its core, the NBD-Dirichlet model of consumer behavior is a powerful statistical tool that accurately describes consumer behavior and brand performance across a wide spectrum of conditions. His discovery reveals that a brand's customer base can be effectively described by a negative binomial distribution (NBD) of buying rates. Essentially, this distribution demonstrates a prevalence of light buyers (individuals with infrequent or near-zero purchase rates), a smaller number of moderate buyers, and very few heavy buyers across various conditions. Although the model is considered stationary, implying that brand growth is an uncommon and challenging feat, brands do indeed experience growth and decline over time. This insight provides valuable knowledge about the dynamics of market share shifts and equips marketers with strategies to nurture these infrequent occurrences.

The central tenet of Ehrenberg's work is that the path to growth is not primarily determined by marketers but is a statistical inevitability. This revelation demystifies marketing, revealing it to be more science than magic.

Two crucial generalizations, or 'laws' stemming from the model, fundamentally influence our approach to marketing and guide the methodology of media research, the Law of Double Jeopardy and the Duplication of Purchase Law:

The Double Jeopardy Law	The Duplication of Purchase Law
Law: Smaller brands have lower penetration and slightly less loyalty than bigger brands	**Law:** Brands share customers in line with their market share
The Double Jeopardy law reveals that purchase frequency and loyalty tend to remain relatively consistent across brands. This results in smaller brands not only having fewer buyers compared to larger brands in their category but also exhibit slightly lower customer loyalty. This phenomenon means that smaller brands face a "double jeopardy" of having fewer buyers and lower purchase frequency. For marketers, the key implication is that growing market share heavily relies on expanding the brand's customer base (increasing penetration), and that building loyalty requires first significantly increasing market penetration	The Duplication of Purchase law describes how competing brands share their customer base. It underscores that the extent to which a brand shares customers with its competitors depends on the size of those competitors. For instance, in the soft drink market, Coca-Cola, the largest brand, shares fewer customers with its competitors, while a significantly larger proportion of Dr. Pepper's customers (a smaller brand) also purchase Coca-Cola. This phenomenon demonstrates that customers consistently and predictably patronize a select group of brands, with one brand (typically the largest) being favored over others

Some other famous observations made by Andrew Ehrenberg and associates (that again are all interconnected with the main works above), include:

1. Consumer attitudes towards brands tend to shift primarily after trying a brand, rather than being significantly influenced by pre-trial advertising efforts.
2. Purchase intentions are heavily influenced by past buying experiences, which typically continue to shape future purchasing decisions.
3. In most product categories, competing brands tend to attract similar consumer profiles, resulting in limited brand differentiation within the category.
4. Brands with higher market share are typically thought of more at the purchase occasion, particularly among non-customers and infrequent buyers.

5. Brands typically have a larger base of light buyers compared to heavy buyers, and this group collectively contributes a significant portion of revenue.
6. It's easier to nudge many light buyers to buy once (or once more), than try to get heavy buyers to buy more heavily than they already do.

The work of Ehrenberg and associates has led to clear implications for marketers, and much of it sobering for those who think that with good advertising these norms can be overcome. This is not dissimilar to the work we have done in attention where in many aspects attracting attention for advertising is beyond advertisers' direct control and more in the hands of the placement on which it is delivered. So again, less magic, more science.

Our own 'big learnings' to follow, represent the culmination of all the 'little learnings' gathered over the past seven years presented in Chapter 2. These 'big learnings' are the overarching patterns that dictate how we engage with advertising, determining what captures our attention and what doesn't and why. Similar to established laws in marketing, each of these learnings has consistently proven true across extensive datasets, sometimes involving millions of human observations in a variety of conditions and over time. Also similar to the Dirichlet Model, the first body of work (The Hierarchy of Attention) underpins the others.

The significance of these laws cannot be overstated. These interconnected principles should serve as the bedrock for both helping advertisers tackle the challenges of media effectiveness and efficiency, and for the development of attention predicting products.

They are not merely case studies where a single brand has shown X or Y increase, but scientific and repeatable patterns using large-scale data applying computational scientific methods that represent the essential knowledge needed to understand how to navigate attention in media planning, buying and optimization. These are the 'Laws of Attention'.

The following section describes the law-like patterns found.

TAKE IT TO WORK

The 'Laws of Attention' are scientific and repeatable patterns using large-scale data applying computational scientific methods. These findings you can bet your house on.

The Hierarchy of Attention

Attention Law:	The structured arrangement of media and advertising elements determines the combined and weighted impact on the level of attention achievable.
Easier Summary:	Different media and advertising elements work together in a hierarchy to directly affect how much attention you can achieve. For example the same ad unit or format or genre will attract more or less attention depending on which platform or program it sits within. The same platform or program will attract more or less attention depending on which device it is played on. This is directly related to the user experience of each media element.
Deeper Dive:	How much attention your ad can achieve is directly impacted by the element above it. For example, your creative is impacted by the audience exposed to it. The audience exposed is impacted by the context (typically relevance) in which the creative is delivered. The ability for context to be noticed depends on the ad format. The ability for the ad format to be noticed depends on which platform it presents in. The ability for the platform to drive attention depends on the device it's viewed on. Putting it another way, you watch TV differently on a mobile device than a big screen, you view a 9:16 ad unit differently on a scrollable or non-scrollable platform, you watch for slightly longer if the ad is relevant etc. This is happening directly due to the switching behavior of the viewer which is directly due to the user experience of each of the media elements. And as such the marketing elements i.e. the audience and the creative, are directly impacted by this.
Implications:	For marketers this means that careful planning of the media elements (device, platform, format, context), to support the advertising elements (audience, creative) is essential for creating an advertising campaign that maximizes its ability to grab and hold the audience's attention (Fig. 3.1).

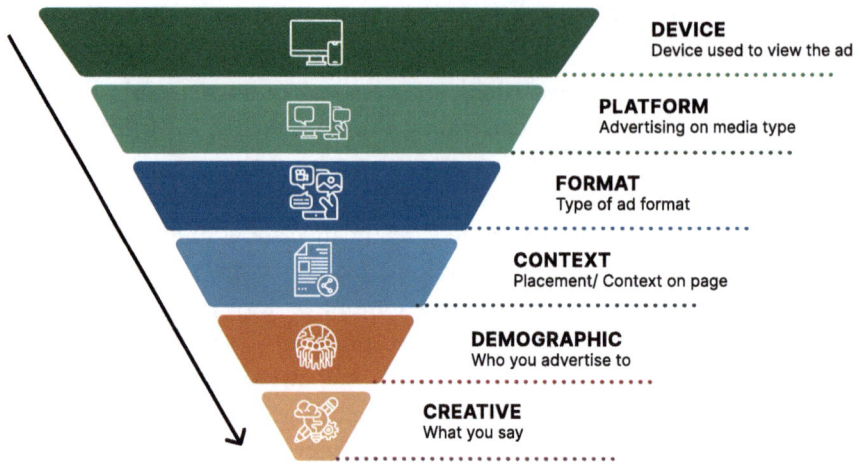

Fig. 3.1 The hierarchy of attention

Attention Elasticity

Attention Law: The range of attention seconds possible under the conditions of the media element.

Easier Summary: Attention elasticity is about the minimum and maximum potential attention time your ad will achieve on various media platforms or formats, which is also impacted by which device it is watched on.

Deeper Dive: Attention elasticity is a crucial concept that plays a pivotal role in defining the range of attainable attention seconds within the unique conditions of each platform or format. To grasp this notion more tangibly, think of it in terms of a box-and-whisker plot—a graphical representation that vividly portrays the distribution of attention seconds across various distinct quadrants, which helps advertisers to understand both the anticipated averages and the utmost extent of attention span that can be reasonably anticipated within a particular medium.

Another way to conceptually think about attention elasticity is like the physics of materials, where the elastic limit depends on structural properties of the substance in question. A steel bar, for instance, can only be stretched by approximately 1% of its original length, while rubber-like materials can exhibit an elastic extension of up to 1000%, due to their entirely different microscopic structures.

It is essential to grasp that each platform and format (which is impacted by the device it is delivered on) has its very own distinct elastic limit when it comes to attention. High-scrollability formats, for instance, tend to exhibit lower elasticity, offering a more restricted range of attention. Conversely, formats that are less inundated with distractions tend to showcase higher elasticity, providing a broader range of attention.

The implications of attention elasticity on creative strategy are profound and far-reaching. It highlights the fact that advertising creative executions operate within the confines established by the functional structure of the given platform. Merely enhancing the quality of creative content rarely breaks through established boundaries of attention norms. Even the most exceptional and captivating creative content can, at best, aspire to reach the uppermost level of the attention limit prescribed by the platform or format it occupies.

Implications: Attention elasticity literally shapes the opportunity for ad creative. It underscores that the capacity of creative content to capture attention operates within the inherent limitations set by platforms and formats. While there are strategies and triggers that can assist creative content in approaching these upper limits (more in Chapter 5), surpassing them is rare. To craft effective advertising strategies and maximize audience engagement, understanding and navigating these boundaries is imperative (Fig. 3.2).

Attention Viewing Profiles

Technical Summary: Consistent and structured behaviors that individuals exhibit when consuming information or content that provide an algorithmic description of how information is processed by individuals.

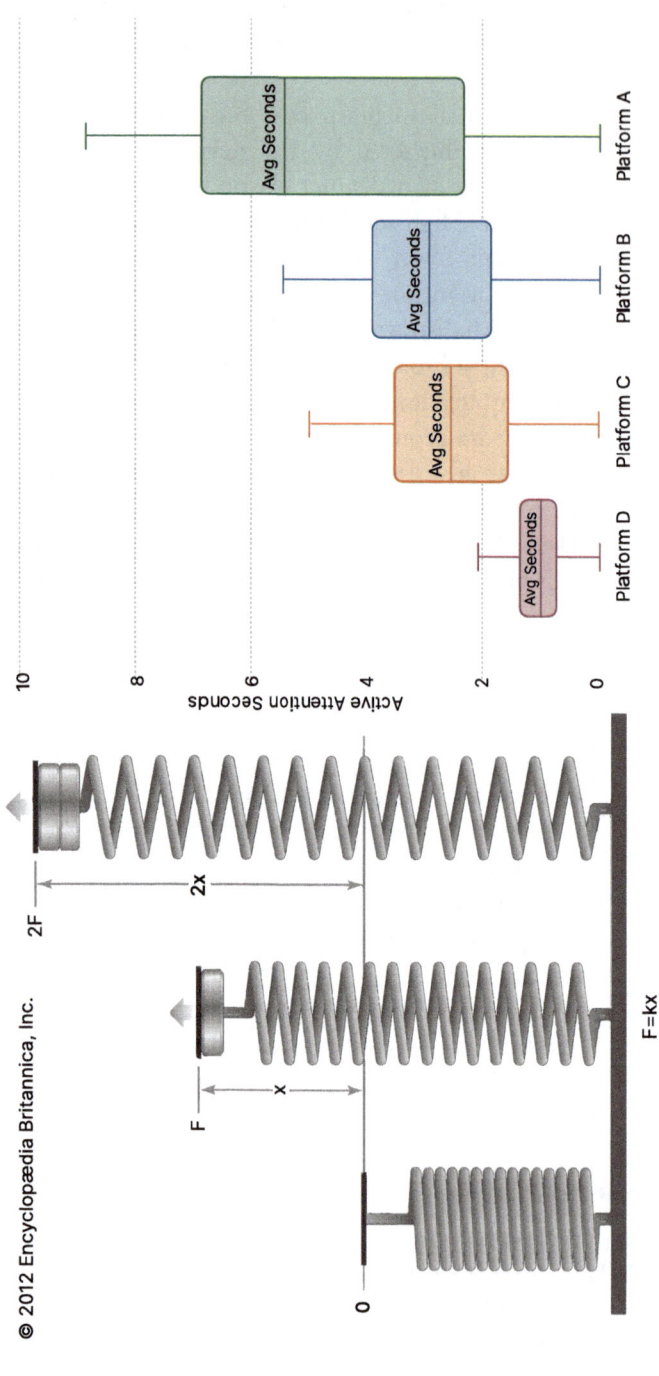

Fig. 3.2 The concept of attention elasticity

Easier Summary: People tend to display reliable and organized viewing habits when they are consuming content. These behaviors, called viewing profiles, can be systematically described using algorithms, which can be used in media planning and buying. Viewing profiles that tell us exactly how people pay attention and watch content in a structured way, by looking at where they focus their gaze, how often they stay focused, and when they switch between being attentive and less attentive.

Deeper Dive: We've long recognized that human attention goes beyond mere time spent, as human behavior is inherently complex. It's evident that spending 2 seconds on Platform A can yield different outcomes compared to Platform B. Utilizing unsupervised machine learning techniques to analyze gaze data reveals common viewing patterns, giving rise to distinct attention 'profiles.'

Attention profiles essentially represent the individual-level viewing behaviors of humans, quantified by parameters such as gaze fixation, gaze consistency, attention peaks, as well as the number and direction of transitions between passive and active attention states. These profiles serve as non-verbal indicators of attention, time, and focus, and they exhibit systematic patterns influenced by the constraints imposed by the user experience, which shapes how viewers interact with media (remember people watch the ads the way the platform trains them to).

What's particularly significant is that when we assess these attention profiles in relation to outcomes, even when the duration of attention is the same, different viewing profiles can have varying propensities to deliver upper or lower funnel results. Furthermore, although attention profiles have a high degree of generalizability, each platform and format possess a unique blend of attention profiles (as illustrated in Fig. 3.3). This explains why 3 seconds of attention on Platform A might hold more value than 3 seconds on Platform B, as Platform A may have a higher concentration of the specific viewing profiles that drive upper funnel outcomes.

As we progress in understanding human data, we have the potential to enhance these profiles by incorporating contextual factors, emotional responses, or other biometric methods. This integration of additional dimensions will further refine our ability to comprehend and harness the complexities of human attention in the ever-evolving landscape of media and advertising.

Implications: The discovery of hidden viewing patterns within individual-level attention data marks a significant leap forward in attention prediction. These profiles not only serve as invaluable tools for understanding what individuals are watching and how they are engaging with content, but also into how these profiles are linked on upper and lower funnel outcomes. These profiles exhibit a systematic and generalizable nature, far surpassing the predictive accuracy of any standard or aggregated probability measures. In essence, these attention profiles serve as the blueprint for precise attention prediction, paving the way for a new era in understanding and optimizing viewer engagement.

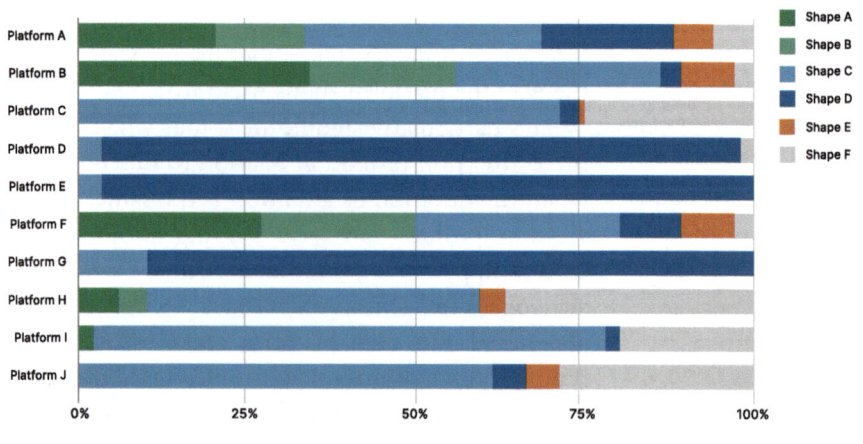

© Amplified Intelligence 2024

Fig. 3.3 Each platform has its own Attention Profile

Attention Jeopardies

As previously discussed, the conventional notion of 'Double Jeopardy' highlights the formidable challenges faced by smaller brands in the marketplace, often referred to as the 'double hit.' This concept finds its roots in the statistical patterns uncovered by Andrew Ehrenberg's groundbreaking research on purchase frequency. It underscores the dual disadvantage experienced by smaller brands, as they not only grapple with a smaller market share but also confront reduced purchase frequency among consumers. We observe a similar 'double hit' phenomenon when brands opt to advertise on platforms characterized by lower levels of consumer attention.

It's important to reiterate that this doesn't suggest that all advertising should exclusively target 'high' attention platforms, nor does it establish a universally defined 'sweet spot' that categorically distinguishes high from low attention. Instead, the main message is that marketing strategies must be adaptable to address the unique challenges presented by the dual disadvantage encountered on lower attention platforms.

In this final section, we unveil several attention-related 'double jeopardies' that have consistently emerged from our data so far.

1. **Mental Availability Imbalance**: Lower attention platforms drive less mental availability for you, and disproportionately more mental availability for your competitor.
2. **Frequency Requirements**: Lower attention platforms require more frequency to correct any wrongful misattribution to your competitor.
3. **Variable Engagement**: On lower attention platforms, more users switch more frequently between attention states.
4. **Creative Impact**: Lower attention platforms have more limited attention elasticity, making it harder for good creative to be better than average.
5. **Viewability Challenge**: Lower attention platforms exhibit a wider attention-viewability gap, resulting in a lower quantity of viewable inventory that achieves attention-viewability equivalence (seconds of time-in-view and 2 seconds of attention).
6. **Emotional Content Constraint**: The potential attention upside of positive emotional content is tempered on lower attention platforms.
7. **Impact on Creativity**: The best quality creative has more to lose on lower attention platforms than lower quality creative.
8. **TV Program Attention**: Lower attention TV programs also achieve lower attention levels for the advertisements aired during them.

3.3 The Wrap Up: Science Works Bitches

Question time at any 'in conversation' event can get interesting, but this one at the fourth annual Oxford universities Think Week event, takes the crown. It was filmed at the Sheldonian Theatre, Oxford, on Friday 15th February 2013 and is well worth a watch on YouTube.

Questioner: The question is about the nature of science evidence. You both said, and I think most people here would agree with you, that we're justified in holding a belief if there's evidence for it or if there are logical arguments we can find that support it. But it seems like this in itself is a belief which would require some form of evidence. If so, I'm wondering what you think would count as evidence in favor of that and if not how do we justify choosing that heuristic without appealing to the same standard that we're trying to justify.

Professor Dawkins: So…how do we justify, as it were, faith that science will give us the truth—is that the…?

Audience member (interrupting): How do we justify the scientific method?

Professor Dawkins: Yes, um…it works. It works. Planes fly, cars drive, computers compute. If you base medicine on science you cure people, if you base the design of planes on science they fly, if you base the design of rockets on science they reach the moon. It works…..(moderate pause)…bitches."

3.4 List of Contributors

Dr Kellen Ewens. Behavioral Scientist, Decision Design

Dr Kellen Ewens is a specialist behavior change researcher and practitioner operating at the intersection of attention, perceptions and actual behavior. With a strong background in applied psychology, graduating with a Bachelor of Psychological Science (Honors, First Class), and PhD-qualified in fields of consumer attention and digital advertising, Kellen leverages unique and innovative data-led research solutions to drive positive brand and commercial outcomes.

Hayun Jung. Senior Data Scientist and AI Specialist

Hayun Jung is a data scientist with a specialization in machine learning and AI, skilled in analyzing complex datasets to inform product development and business strategy. She holds a Master's degree in Information Technology and Business Intelligence from Carnegie Mellon University. Her experience includes roles at Amplified Intelligence and LBT Innovations, where she specialized in turning data insights into practical applications for ad tech and medical technology. Her work primarily involves bridging the gap between data analytics and real-world business solutions.

References

Bird, M., & Ehrenberg, A. S. C. (1966). Intentions-to-Buy and Claimed Brand Usage. *Operational Research Society, 17*(1), 27–46.

Bound, J. A. (2009). The Contribution of Andrew Ehrenberg to Social and Marketing Research. *Journal of Empirical Generalisations in Marketing Science, 12*(1), 1–12.

Box-Steffensmeier, J. M., Burgess, J., Corbetta, M., et al. (2022). The Future of Human Behavior Research. *Nature Human Behaviour, 6*, 15–24. https://doi.org/10.1038/s41562-021-01275-6

Ehrenberg, A. S. (1969). The Discovery and Use of Laws of Marketing. *Journal of Advertising Research, 9*(2), 11–17.

Ehrenberg, A. S., & Bound, J. A. (1993). Predictability and Prediction. *Journal of the Royal Statistical Society Series A: Statistics in Society, 156*(2), 167–194.

Ehrenberg, A. S., Uncles, M. D., & Goodhardt, G. J. (2004). Understanding Brand Performance Measures: Using Dirichlet Benchmarks. *Journal of Business research, 57*(12), 1307–1325.

Ehrenberg, A. S. C. (1968). The Elements of Lawlike Relationships. *Journal of the Royal Statistical Society Series A: Statistics in Society, 131*(3), 280–302.

Ehrenberg, A. S. C. (1990). A Hope for the Future of Statistics: MSOD. *The American Statistician, 44*(3), 195–196.

Ehrenberg, A. S. C. (1993). Even the Social Sciences Have Laws. *Nature, 365*(30), 385.

Ehrenberg, A. S. C. (2000). Repeat-Buying: Facts, Theory and Applications. *Journal of Empirical Generalisations in Marketing Science, 5*(2), 392–770.

Ehrenberg, A. S. C., & Bound, J. A. (2000). Turning Data into Knowledge. In C. Chakrapani (Ed.), *Marketing Research: State of the Art Perspectives (The Handbook of the American Marketing Association and the Professional Market Research Society)*. American Marketing Association.

Nelson-Field, K. (2022). *Attention Elasticity: The Attention Economy's Chicken and Egg Question*. Opinion: Attention Revolution, The Media Leader.

Nelson-Field, K., & Jung, H. (2022, May). *The Shape of Attention: Mining Gold from Individual Level Attention Viewing Patterns*. WARC Exclusive.

Royne, M. B. (2018). Why We Need More Replication Studies to Keep Empirical Knowledge in Check: How Reliable Is Truth in Advertising Research? *Journal of Advertising Research, 58*(1), 3–7.

4

The Reinvention of Invention

The most exciting companies create. They give us new ways of living, thinking or doing business, many times solving a problem we didn't know we had—or a problem we didn't pay attention to because we never thought there was another way. Before Uber, we hailed a cab by standing precariously close to traffic with an arm in the air. After Uber, that just seemed dumb.
Al Ramadam. Author Play Bigger (2016)

If you don't read another book, you must read this one. Play Bigger: How Rebels and Innovators Create New Categories and Dominate Markets. It is a book about ambitious thinkers tackling significant issues that often fly under the radar. Yet, when these issues or problems are uncovered, and inventive solutions are put into action, they lead to a surge in customer demand and the birth of entirely new categories. Playing Bigger is a book about inspiring and shaping markets, it is about setting the rules for the future. The authors originate from silicon valley, so this book naturally draws insights from iconic companies like Uber, Airbnb, Facebook, Snapchat and Tesla. But it also shines a light on lesser-known players, such as Birdseye in the early 1900s who invented the fast-freeze category.

© The Author(s), under exclusive license to Springer Nature
Singapore Pte Ltd. 2024
K. Nelson-Field, *The Attention Economy*, https://doi.org/10.1007/978-981-97-0084-4_4

With that said, in most cases, categories emerge as a progression from developments in existing ones. Take Airbnb, for example, they revolutionized short-term property rentals, even though hotels were already catering to travelers. Before Amazon transformed online book retailing, brick-and-mortar bookstores were the norm. Before Tesla introduced electric cars, gasoline-powered vehicles were the standard. And the list goes on. Most of the companies highlighted in this book aren't creating an invention that is entirely new, but they aren't simply selling us 'better' either. They are replacing something old with something different. So this is not a disruption for the sake of a disruption story, this is a creation story for the purpose of systemic improvement. They are reinventing an invention.

That's precisely why this chapter bears its title. We currently find ourselves at a similar crossroads, witnessing a transformation in the audience measurement landscape, transitioning from viewability to the emergence of a novel category that centers on human attention. In this context, we're not pioneering a new problem; instead, we're addressing a long-acknowledged measurement challenge. Brands have historically relied on their messages being seen to achieve desired outcomes, a requirement articulated as far back as 1898 by E. St. Elmo Lewis in the original guide for successful salesmanship. This chapter explores both the inception and evolution of the next generation of audience measurement: attention measurement and associated metrics.

4.1   How Categories Are Born

The Perfect Storm

When you look at the history of innovation it becomes evident that category generating businesses are born from predicting a perfect storm and executing a perfect response.

The term 'perfect storm' comes (loosely) from meteorology and became popularized through Wolfgang Petersen's 2000 film of the same name. The movie portrayed an extremely rare meteorological event in 1991 off the East Coast of the United States when Hurricane Grace merged with a significant North Atlantic low-pressure system and a cold front from Canada, creating an extraordinary super storm.

While the analogy of a perfect storm in innovation may not involve the same level of catastrophe, the fundamental concept remains the same: new categories emerge when visionary individuals anticipate a rare convergence of multiple interconnected events capable of rapidly driving significant industry transformation. This recognition, combined with the ability to execute a well-crafted business plan in the often time-limited window of opportunity, is essential just as the storm hits.

When examining the historical progression of categories, five common events have consistently driven the evolution of categories:

1. Scientific Discoveries
Throughout history, groundbreaking scientific discoveries have left an indelible mark. These include unraveling DNA's structure, harnessing electricity and magnetism, the serendipitous discovery of penicillin, and delving into the intricacies of quantum mechanics and greenhouse gasses. These revelations have driven progress in fields such as computing, genetic engineering, wireless communication, electrical engineering, antibiotics, sustainable practices, and more across all the branches of science.

2. Technological Breakthroughs
We've witnessed transformative changes driven by inventions like the internet, semiconductors, GPS, mobile tech, wearables, and AI. The internet revolutionized global communication and commerce, while miniaturized semiconductors powered electronic devices. GPS transformed navigation, and mobile tech made information access ubiquitous. Wearables, like smartwatches, are now part of daily life, and AI is reshaping industries. These innovations have not only altered our lives but also birthed new industries, shaping modern innovation.

3. Regulatory Change
Guided by shifts in government policies, regulations, and incentives, regulatory changes have wielded substantial influence over innovation dynamics. A favorable regulatory environment can encourage innovation and growth, be it through tax incentives or environmental regulations that significantly impact the trajectory and pace of change. Similarly, bans on food additives, substances, or carcinogens can spark the creation of entirely new categories. Recent measures related to data protection and content moderation regulations have also, and will continue to, leave their mark.

4. Global Events
Catastrophic events, including pandemics, recessions, financial crises, wars, natural disasters, and geopolitical shifts, have impelled innovation. The pressing need for solutions and adaptations to new challenges becomes evident during these times.

5. Cultural and Social Movements
Movements advocating for diversity and inclusion, mental health and well-being, equal rights, ethical consumption, and social responsibility

have exerted profound influence in industries over time. By shaping the values and priorities of society, these movements have inspired innovative approaches and ushered in new categories across various domains.

To bring this all back to reality, here are a few notable examples of category generating businesses. This is not an exhaustive list (obviously), just a few random category leaders to demonstrate the point. Each example is accompanied by a brief overview of the critical events that seemingly played a pivotal role in shaping their innovative journeys.

Fitbit   Cultural and Social Movements and Technological Breakthroughs: Fitbit's popularity can be attributed to technological advances, such as improved sensors and fitness tracking features, coinciding with a growing interest in health and fitness. This alignment of technological innovation and cultural interest has significantly increased consumer demand for convenient well-being monitoring.

Headspace Cultural and Social Movements and Global Events: Headspace's rise in popularity is closely tied to the increased awareness of mental health during the COVID-19 pandemic. Their meditation and wellness platform became essential for addressing stress and anxiety during this global event.

Netflix   Technological Breakthroughs: Netflix's dominance in the entertainment industry is a result of pioneering streaming technology, efficient video compression algorithms, and a commitment to producing high-quality original content.

Square   Technological Breakthroughs and Global Events: Square revolutionized payment processing with mobile solutions, and this transformation began during the 2009 financial crisis.

Teladoc   Regulatory Change and Global Events: Teladoc's success can be attributed to regulatory changes, particularly in telemedicine reimbursement policies, and the increased demand for remote healthcare services during the pandemic.

Tesla   Scientific Discoveries, Technological Breakthroughs and Regulation Change: Tesla's remarkable success is rooted in groundbreaking advances in battery technology, electric vehicle (EV) innovations, and favorable pro-electric vehicle policies. These factors converged to reshape the entire automotive industry, responding to both scientific discoveries related to greenhouse gasses and changing environmental regulations.

Uber   Technological Breakthroughs and Regulatory Changes: Uber transformed the transportation industry with smartphone technology, supported by regulatory changes in taxi licensing that they actively lobbied for.

MEANWHILE IN THE REAL WORLD

This is a reminder to Airbnb just how easily regulation change can shape, then shake, a category.

In September 2023 New York City was the latest city to enforce stringent regulations on short-term rentals through platforms like Airbnb, including the prohibition of entire-home rentals, a two-guest limit, and the requirement for hosts to be present during renters' stays. These measures have undeniably made a profound impact on New York City's short-term rental market, leading to a staggering 77% decrease in the number of Airbnb listings which represents the disappearance of thousands of Airbnbs and other short-term rentals. The city has issued a warning to travelers, cautioning them to expect elevated expenses during the holiday season, as hotel room prices in New York City have surged by 1.92% in just a span of two months.

Over the last 2 years, similar regulations have been enforced in dozens of cities around the world said to address housing shortage concerns, tax loop-holes and maintain control over the short-term rental market. These regulatory changes represent a significant transformation in the short-term rental sector and could re-shape the category as a whole.

In Australia as at October 2023, "gig" workers on digital platforms in various sectors including food delivery, ride sharing and on-demand care, are commonly classified as contractors rather than employees, which means they aren't entitled to benefits like minimum hourly wages or sick leave. However, the Australian government is considering legislation that will enable the Fair Work Commission to establish minimum standards and conditions for workers on these platforms.

Uber has warned that if these reforms are enacted, consumers could face significant price increases, with daytime Uber rides potentially rising by 55% and public holiday costs by 85%. For UberEats, weekend orders may surge by up to 125%, and on public holidays, the increase could be as high as 160%.

Consequently, consumers are expected to reduce their Uber trips by up to 65 million annually and order 75 million fewer meals from UberEats due to the anticipated higher prices. A massive shake up to a category down under.

So why is this even relevant here?

It's relevant because there's a rare perfect storm on the horizon, the biggest our industry has witnessed in 30 years. This perfect storm serves as a catalyst for change, and we are currently witnessing the emergence of a new measurement category, with attention measurement at its core.

Let's quickly consider the relevant critical events and how it relates to our industry:

1. Regulatory Change: Death of the 3P cookie estimated late 2024.

For the past three decades, cookies have served as the bedrock of the digital ecosystem, facilitating critical functions that advertisers rely on, such as cross-site personal identification to drive audience targeting, retargeting, frequency capping, and measurement. But cookies have not been without controversy, primarily due to their intrusive tracking capabilities and the concerns surrounding user privacy. However, in response to mounting distrust regarding the collection and sharing of personal data by Big Tech companies, governments and regulatory bodies have stepped in to implement stricter data protection laws. Notably, Europe's GDPR and the United States' CCPA have ushered in a phase-out of cookies due for completion at the end of 2024.

This represents a landmark regulatory shift in the history of the internet, and its ramifications are substantial to brands who spend advertising dollars online (2024 forecasted global digital spend $645b). Marketers who rely on tracking humans via cookies to improve personalized marketing, audience segmentation and multi-touch attribution models will need an alternative solution, while publishers are facing increased difficulties in monetizing their websites. Without adequate alternatives the loss of 3P cookies will lead to less informed decision-making and marketing inefficiencies (plus advertisers may become more dependent on the data and targeting capabilities offered by walled garden platforms, which have transparency and data quality issues unto themselves).

2. Cultural and Social Movements: Brands are calling for improvements in measurement data quality.

Advertisers are rising up and demanding higher standards of measurement in digital advertising. This revolt has been brewing overtime and has had a few nuanced themes. In chronological order these themes include:

(a) **Call for transparency in media**: Between 2015 and 2019 several prominent Chief Marketing Officers (CMOs) from major companies like

Unilever, P&G, and Mars have expressed serious concerns about the lack of transparency and measurement issues in digital advertising. Keith Weed of Unilever highlighted the problem of digital ads not being seen, with statistics from Nielsen and Google suggesting a significant portion of ads go unnoticed. He stressed the need for industry standards to eliminate fraud in digital advertising and emphasized the importance of ensuring that advertisers are paying for the eyes of real humans, not bots. Marc Pritchard of P&G called the digital media supply chain murky and fraudulent, emphasizing the lack of compliance with standards, unreliable measurement, hidden rebates, and the prevalence of fraud. He also cited the sluggish growth in advertising despite massive spending, which raises questions about the return on investment for advertisers and the quality of the audience reached. Mars CMO, Andrew Clarke, echoed the concerns about transparency and measurement, emphasizing the need for better visibility of key metrics and partnerships with platforms to achieve transparency. These CMOs collectively highlight the urgent need for the industry to address these issues and improve accountability in digital advertising while ensuring that advertising investments are reaching real human audiences effectively.

(b) **Call for better metrics that deliver media value**: The call for change persisted after 2019, albeit with a nuanced shift. In the wake of the pandemic's financial blow to most advertisers, the conversations moved from a 'demand for transparency' to a 'call for effectiveness'. The key to achieving this effectiveness lay in better measurement. By this point the inadequacies of impression measurement and the realization that 'not all reach is equal', had become widespread. Fast forward to 2022, and the term "alternate currencies" began to gain traction, with attention being one of them. In this context, the term "alternate" served as a direct sucker punch to Nielsen, which had once been a trusted source of reach data but was now cast under a cloud of doubt regarding its ability to accurately measure cross-media impact and provide value to advertisers. Nielsen was not alone in facing this mounting pressure for meaningful metrics. Viewability measurement, viewed as a broader concept rather than a singular blow to any specific vendor, also came under scrutiny for its underperformance. Advertisers started to understand the difference between 'served' and 'seen'. As of 2023, the drive for more relevant metrics continues to significantly reshape the industry.

A few verbatims from heavy hitters to show the rally is real:

(i) **Keith Weed, CMO Unilever. (2015)**: "I have real concerns about measurement. It's like having billboard ads underwater, it's a complete and utter waste of our money. I believe we should get what we pay for. There are more bots on the internet than humans, so are you paying for the eyes of a bot or human eyes? Clearly we all want to pay for the eyes of a human, and we need real action as an industry to make sure we get standards that we all agree are right, to ensure that fraud is taken out of the way we buy digital advertising."

(ii) **Andrew Clarke, CMO Mars. (2017)**: "Concerns about media transparency and digital measurement are obviously top of mind right now. We invest billions of dollars each year to drive growth, and frankly we still don't have the visibility we need to make sure we're getting the best possible return. We simply need better visibility of the key metrics, and we don't have them. We are partnering with the likes of Google and Facebook, etc., to get the transparency we're looking for, so we can better invest to drive our intelligent reach. But we haven't got the transparency of audience numbers, we haven't got the transparency of viewability across channels, and that's important for us in terms of how we make our creative. This is a tough space and we, as a big advertiser, need to get involved to help drive the industry."

(iii) **Marc Pritchard, CMO P&G. (2017–2019)**: "The digital media supply chain is murky at best, and fraudulent at worst." "We serve ads to consumers through a non-transparent media supply chain with spotty compliance to common standards, unreliable measurement, hidden rebates and new inventions like bot and methbot fraud." "The bigger issue driving this push for transparency is the lackluster growth among brands spending big on advertising. We're not growing enough, despite spending an astounding $200 billion in advertising in the US, the growth rate of our collective industries is pretty anemic."

(iv) **Walter Flaat, CDO Dentsu Canada. (2019)**: "In five years' time, we need to look at why we are using reach currencies. In essence, they are a compromise. Reach planning won't exist, either, because effect planning is already rising sharply, or it will be used less and less. Planning can certainly be done on effect currencies."

(v) **Danny Clayman, VP Northern Europe Xandr. (2020)** "In 2020, we expect to see technology companies work even more closely with advertisers and publishers to develop new tools to capture the attention of consumers across screens, devices and formats around the world."

(vi) **Dan Meier, Reporter Videoweek. (2023)**: "Now some 29 percent of upfront buys are expected to be transacted on alternate currencies, according to Advertiser Perceptions, as agencies seek viewership guarantees across different screens and devices."

(vii) **Chrissie Hanson, CEO OMD USA. (2023)**: "Let's start with looking at the ad - have you seen it or not? That seems like a reasonable starting point. When we think about attention, it comes from our original desire to show an improvement in the way we harness our clients' dollars to do better outcomes. OMD started with gaze analysis that determines where a viewer is looking based on their eye movements and facial features."

(viii) **David Cohen, CEO IAB USA. (2023)**: "Change will accelerate fast, and by 2030 our industry will look markedly different. My advice: Don't wait for change to come to you; be part of driving it."

(ix) **Linda Yaccarino, CEO X. (2023)**: "Good measurement fuels that great content experience. But insufficient measurement completely undermines the process. Without better measurement, the industry can't give anyone — audiences or advertisers — the premium content experience they deserve. And it doesn't just affect the people watching or the publishers. Inaccurate measurement drives media inflation, and affects everything from production decisions, to brand partnerships, to agency structures, and so much more."

(x) **Kristiaan Kroon, Chief Investment Officer OMG. (2023)**: "There is a clear need for these products as the Australian CTV market is becoming far more complex for advertisers… Alternative audience measurement is inevitable."

c. **Call for a reduction in carbon across the ad-tech supply chain**: In recent times, there has been a growing movement within the advertising industry to address a newer aspect of environmental responsibility. While brands have traditionally been held accountable for their green marketing practices, advertisers are now facing pressure to take measures to reduce the carbon emissions associated with their media buying activities, particularly across the ad-tech supply chain. This carbon footprint in the ad-tech supply chain is largely attributed to the bid request process and ad campaign delivery, which involve the transmission of massive data volumes between publishers, SSPs, DSPs, and various other vendor servers. This shift in perspective represents a direct response to the prevalent issue of 'greenwashing', where many brands appear to meet the minimum sustainability requirements primarily for competitive advantage, often without a comprehensive consideration of the climate crisis across all aspects of their business. Hence the pressure on advertisers to take this to the next level of scope 3 emissions, and address the media supply chain.

MEANWHILE IN THE REAL WORLD

Over the past decade, another significant cultural and social movement has been brewing within the advertising industry: the push for enhanced brand safety standards. Brand safety encompasses a range of strategies designed to safeguard a brand's reputation and prevent potential revenue loss when advertising online. This critical aspect revolves around the careful avoidance of ad placement alongside inappropriate or unethical content that could inadvertently tarnish the brand's image. While brand safety may not have a direct impact on the perfect storm driving the attention metrics category, it indirectly reinforces the prevailing concerns about the reliability of digital advertising and the opacity of the programmatic ecosystem. This further bolsters the call for improved data quality and transparency in the industry.

IAB's inappropriate content list includes:

1. Adult & Explicit Sexual Content
2. Arms & Ammunition
3. Crime & Harmful Acts to Individuals and Society and Human Right Violations
4. Death Injury, or Military Conflict
5. Online Piracy
6. Hate Speech & Acts of Aggression
7. Obscenity and Profanity
8. Illegal Drugs/Tobacco/E-Cigarettes/Vaping/Alcohol
9. Spam or Harmful Content
10. Terrorism
11. Sensitive Social Issues

https://iabtechlab.com/press-releases/tech-lab-releases-for-comment-content-taxonomy-to-improve-brand-safety-support-brand-suitability/

3. Technological Breakthroughs: Computer Vision AI and Behavioral AI.

In 2017, IPSOS Audience Measurement published a report heralding the dawn of what they dubbed the 'fifth age of audience measurement', where they suggest that "by 2025 new methodologies will be re-calibrated in response to a fast-changing media environment and where the quest for total understanding of audiences will be higher than it has ever been." In this report several pillars underpinned this forecast:

Platform Neutral	Audiences will be measured from wherever they consume media content, whenever they are exposed to it.
Passively Collected	Data will be collected passively by installing technology on respondents' devices with minimal demands on their part. Rather than prompting individuals to recall their media habits, permission will be requested to install an app on their phones for automated behavior tracking.
Big Data	In television, access to second-by-second details of the content households view is possible through more advanced set-top boxes. Internet usage, including accessing streamed video or audio and making online requests for text or imagery, will be monitored using router meters and other methods.
Hybrid	Measurement will progressively blend data from external sources, including a significant portion of big data, with sample-based data that transforms device data into insights about individuals utilizing those devices.
Data Science	Data Scientists will leverage modern techniques and robust computing power to integrate and enrich datasets while maintaining balance and fairness.
Respondent Friendly	Audience measurement solutions will be designed with the human panel member at the core, accommodating their lives rather than imposing on them.

Their forecasting has indeed proven accurate. It's evident that as we fast forward to 2025, we now have access to highly advanced human measurement methods. These methods include privacy-conscious computer vision techniques seamlessly integrated into smartphone apps, quietly gathering extensive data through JavaScript Tags (covering channel choices, content dimensions, and context), facial landmarks (for tracking attention and emotions), and data on outbound network traffic to identify what people are viewing on streaming services, linear channels, or social media. The data collected through these innovative methods can be skillfully modeled to predict human behavior, encompassing aspects such as attention, emotions,

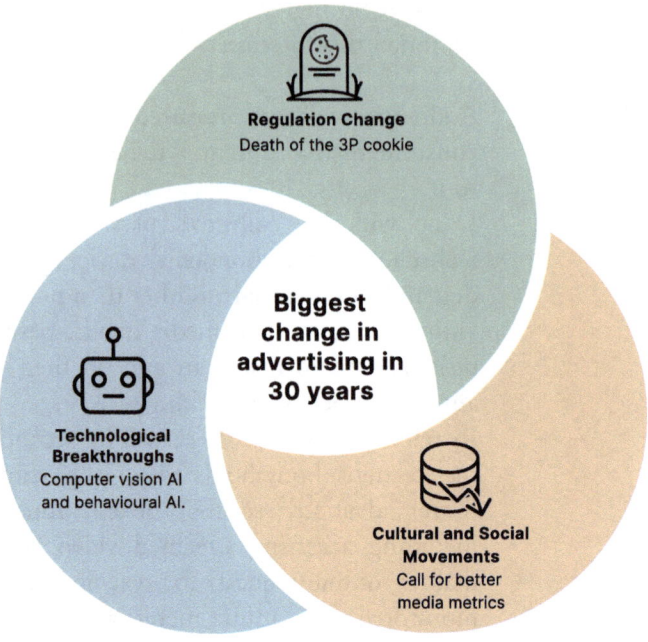

Fig. 4.1 The media perfect storm

contextual relevance, and outcomes. As Language Models like GPT-3 continue to advance at a rapid pace, the potential for extracting value from human data is poised to grow exponentially over time.

In just six years, significant technological advancements have shifted our focus from whether an ad has been served to how an ad has been viewed and the responses it has generated. Welcome to the fifth age of audience measurement (Fig. 4.1).

The Perfect Response

What did Fitbit, Tesla, Uber, and Netflix do when they sensed a significant challenge on the horizon? They responded with innovative strategies, creating entirely new categories that revolutionized their respective industries. This transformative process is currently unfolding in the media and advertising space, driven by enabling technologies and a coalition of change-oriented investors, including agencies, brands, publishers, and industry bodies. This collective effort is injecting fresh perspectives into an era where traditional measures of human viewing, such as traditional reach data, faces heightened scrutiny. The evolution of attention measurement represents a profound advancement touching upon technology, ethics, and effectiveness within an industry eager for change.

Why is this evolution so crucial? Because attention data simplifies decision-making, providing transparency in performance throughout the media lifecycle. This not only helps brands, agencies, and platforms financially by reducing unnecessary spending across the advertising ecosystem, but it also contributes to a greener advertising environment by cutting down on carbon emissions linked to excessive ad impressions as resources are redirected from non-value-adding advertising. All of this means that viewers' experiences with media improve as the quality of content and advertising increases while extraneous 'noise' is removed. This enhancement in the exchange of value between viewers and media content is a significant contribution to the betterment of our world alone.

In light of this, attention is rapidly emerging as one of the most fitting responses to the challenges faced by the industry. It offers a promising path forward that aligns with the evolving advertising landscape, positioning stakeholders for a more prosperous and sustainable future.

TAKE IT TO WORK

Categories are born from the perfect mix of a perfect storm and perfect response. This is the position attention measurement is right now. On the edge of the perfect storm, waiting for widespread validation to deliver the perfect response.

QUICK EXPLAINER

Let's consider 'Attribution Cookies' versus 'Attention Tags'.

In the ever-changing world of online tracking, the upcoming end of third-party cookies has led the ad-tech industry to explore new ways to maintain an efficient bidding system, assess the success of ad campaigns, manage revenue per thousand impressions (RPMs), and adjust targeting strategies to suit the evolving business landscape. Among these alternatives, attention tags emerge as a noteworthy contender. Here is a super fast overview to explain the distinctions between attribution cookies and attention tags and highlights their potential benefits for advertisers.

Attribution cookies and attention tags are both measures used to gauge the effectiveness of online advertising, but they do so in different ways:

Attribution cookies serve as a means of measuring attribution in online advertising. They provide advertisers with insights into what viewers were exposed to and their subsequent online activities. For example when you visit a website, a cookie is transmitted to your browser, which stores various personal details like your preferences, login information, browsing history specific to that website, and more. Essentially, they help pinpoint and credit the touchpoints within a user's journey that ultimately lead to a conversion. This process involves collecting a substantial amount of personal data.

On the other hand, attention tags take a different approach by concentrating on measuring the engagement of a single ad placement or impression in isolation. They are less invasive in nature. For instance, attention tags collect data related to media consumption and media placement, such as the URL, scroll speed, and content placement dimensions. However, they do not track the viewer's preferences or subsequent online activities. Their primary purpose is to provide advertisers with insights into the level of attention each impression receives, but this data cannot be traced back to an individual or their behavior such as clicks.

In summary, Attribution cookies track the user, and they gather a significant amount of personal information. while Attention tags track the ad placement, collecting very limited personal information.

In essence, attribution cookies focus on the user and gather extensive personal data, while attention tags are primarily concerned with tracking ad placements and collect minimal personal information, making them a less intrusive alternative in the evolving landscape of online tracking.

Trade Bodies Unite

Once a storm has hit, and the general industry starts to rally around a perfect response, the final part of category generation (in measurement specifically) is trade body involvement.

A trade body, or council, association, group, foundation, is a group of experts gathered to promote common interests and play a vital role in supporting and advancing the interests of businesses within a specific industry. They typically provide a range of services and activities aimed at promoting industry growth, advocating for favorable policies and enhancing the overall success of their members. Business groups, industries, or even governments usually fund and support them.

In our industry, there are two distinct types of trade bodies, each with its own strategic focus and contributions. Some trade bodies take the lead in activities such as establishing industry standards, shaping regulations, fostering a common language, promoting best practices and documenting ethical standards. On the other hand, there are trade bodies that prioritize professional development programs, build educational initiatives, run marketing conferences and facilitate networking opportunities for their members.

The trade bodies focused on the former set of activities play a crucial role in the early stages. They lay the foundation by advocating for the category, creating a regulatory framework and setting the industry's ethical and operational standards. Conversely, the trade bodies focusing on education, conferences and networking are instrumental in the later stages of category development. They help bridge the 'innovation diffusion' gap by equipping industry professionals with the knowledge and skills needed to navigate the emerging category successfully which ultimately contributes to the growth and maturation of the category.

Without discounting the incredible value to the media ecosystem of trade bodies such as World Federation of Advertisers (WFA), The Incorporated Society of British Advertisers (ISBA) and The Coalition for Innovative Media Measurement (CIMM), The Association of National Advertisers (ANA) and others, the three trade bodies that have been most influential in the early advancement of attention measurement and metrics specifically are The American Research Foundation (ARF), The Interactive Advertising Bureau (IAB) and The Media Ratings Council (MRC). Their contributions are all different, yet all valuable in shaping this category.

Here is an overview of their separate initiatives and progress.

1. The American Research Foundation (ARF)

Their charter: To further, through research, the scientific practice of advertising and marketing.

Technology has been both a boon and a bane to marketers: more ways to connect with customers, but far more complexity. There has never been a more critical need for solid information, standards, and transparency. Businesses can only grow when operating on correct information and real insights—drawn from empirical research, objective experiments and valid market tests. Since 1936, the Advertising Research Foundation has been the standard-bearer for unbiased quality in research on advertising, media and marketing. Its powerful knowledge, unifying standards and best practices. Headquartered in New York City.

The attention event: The Attention Measurement Validation Initiative.

The ARF Attention Validation Initiative is a three-phase, empirically-based evaluation of the rapidly evolving field of attention measurement and prediction in marketing. The objective of the initiative is to promote a deeper understanding of attention measurement, ensure the reliability of measurement approaches, foster transparency and common standards, and provide valuable guidance to stakeholders in their pursuit of effective attention measurement strategies.

In the first phase, the initiative involves mapping the landscape of attention measurement providers to create an Attention Atlas, aiming to enhance transparency specifically in how vendors position themselves and their methods. This was a highly rigorous phase including both quantitative and qualitative analysis. Phases two and three will focus on Creative Attention and Publisher Attention solutions into 2024.

The initiative is a collaborative approach so research suppliers, media companies, and agencies with unique approaches to attention measurement in any media, were invited to participate. Additionally the initiative receives support from both an Academic Advisory Committee and a Brand Steering Committee, which includes senior researchers and practitioners from companies such as Coca-Cola, LinkedIn/Microsoft, MARS, McDonald's, and The Attention Council, among others. The committees devised the RFI questionnaire used to collect information on all the methodologies, approaches, and business practices from the attention measurement ecosphere.

Scott McDonald, CEO and President at ARF (ARF PR 2023), "*Attention is one of, if not the most, critical component of the ARF Model of Advertising Effectiveness but it is also one which has not been empirically studied. As new attention measurement services come to market, the industry has been asking us to help them gain transparency into the validity, reliability and predictive power of these measures. This Atlas will be the first step in helping marketers make more informed decisions around choosing a method and supplier– clearly outlining the solutions' rightful application to advertising and media evaluation.*"

Greg Pharo, Global Senior Director at Coca-Cola (ARF PR 2023), "*This is an initiative that we are passionate about given the growing interest in attention metrics and the promise of new more accurate metrics. With attention shifting from tactic to strategy across global marketing practices, it is vital to understand exactly how these solutions work and their impacts on the industry, to help advertisers secure better outcomes including avoiding ad waste.*"

The progress: Both a comprehensive literature review and the Vendor Validation/Attention Atlas is complete. Across the two stages complete, 26 vendors participated as did 180 advertising professionals from both the buy and sell side. The literature review is a 29 page document outlining attention literature from the definition of attention, to measuring it, to the attention economy more broadly. The Atlas describes the attention measurement space in detail, illuminating this nascent sector. The report includes two sections. The first section describes what methods are being used, what these companies report and how and what they measure, be it ad creative or the media environment. The second section includes in-depth overviews of the 26 participating attention measurement companies.

The summary: The vendor validation component gives the reader a clear understanding of how each vendor operates, where their strengths and weaknesses are in both industry understanding and methodological rigor. The methods employed to extract these reports were both rigorous and fair. This Atlas is a must read for those looking for a single reference point as to the players and the data available in the ecosystem. Readers should also be highly confident that the research means employed to collect this data are perhaps the most rigorous and independent in the industry.

2. The Interactive Advertising Bureau (IAB)

Their charter: The Interactive Advertising Bureau (IAB) empowers the media and marketing industries to thrive in the digital economy.

Since 1996, The IAB has done critical research on interactive advertising, while also educating brands, agencies, and the wider business community on the importance of digital marketing. In affiliation with the IAB Tech Lab, IAB develops technical standards and solutions and is committed to professional development and elevating the knowledge, skills, expertise, and diversity of the workforce across the industry. Through the work of its public policy office in Washington D.C, The IAB advocates for its members and promotes the value of the interactive advertising industry to legislators and policymakers. Headquartered in New York City.

The IAB has a long history of successful lobbying and initiatives for positive change. In June 2011, the IAB, in collaboration with the ANA (Association of National Advertisers) and the 4A's (American Association of Advertising Agencies), introduced the Guiding Principles of Digital Measurement. These five principles laid the groundwork for the "Making Measurement Make Sense" initiative and provided a solid foundation for the advancement of the viewability metric. The underlying rationale for this metric was common-sense: if an audience wasn't exposed to an ad, it couldn't possibly have any meaningful impact. Before this initiative measurement error, non-human traffic, below-the-fold delivery and slow loading were rife. They were modestly reported as impacting up to 50% of served online impressions.

The collaboration between ANA, 4A's, and IAB also gave rise to the creation of the Trustworthy Accountability Group (TAG). TAG stands as the leading global initiative dedicated to combating criminal activity and bolstering trust within the digital advertising industry. TAG carries out its mission by actively working to eliminate fraudulent traffic, facilitating the exchange of threat intelligence, and advocating for brand safety. This is achieved through the concerted efforts of industry leaders who come together to analyze threats and disseminate best practices on a global scale. Notably, TAG holds the distinction of being the first and sole Information Sharing and Analysis Organization (ISAO) for the digital advertising sector. This official designation by the U.S. Department of Homeland Security underscores TAG's pivotal role as the primary platform for sharing critical threat intelligence within our industry.

In 2014, the IAB Technology Laboratory (Tech Lab) was established as a non-profit consortium with a global member community dedicated to developing foundational technology and standards to foster growth and trust in the digital media ecosystem. Comprising digital publishers, ad technology firms, agencies, marketers, and other industry participants, the IAB Tech Lab concentrates its efforts on addressing critical areas such as brand safety and ad fraud, identity, data, and consumer privacy, ad experiences and measurement, and programmatic effectiveness. Some notable contributions include the development of the OpenRTB real-time bidding protocol, the ads.txt anti-fraud specification, the Open Measurement SDK for viewability and verification, the VAST video specification, and the Project Rearc initiative aimed at privacy-centric addressability.

The attention event: The Attention Task Force.

In 2023, the Interactive Advertising Bureau (IAB) launched the Attention Task Force, an initiative focused on understanding the attention economy and in particular attention metrics. Its primary objective is to develop a common language for data signals and measurement techniques, thereby ensuring consistency in how attention metrics are understood and utilized as well as consistent measurement practices.

The IAB has placed significant emphasis on the establishment of a strong groundwork for attention measurement within the digital advertising landscape. To this end, they have devised a three phase strategy for the Attention Task Force. Phase one is about stakeholder engagement; gathering input from various stakeholders to gain insights into their specific needs and capabilities. Phase two is about the development of educational resources to create informative guides and practical examples that promote a shared understanding of different attention measurement methods. Phase three revolves around collaborative discussions among agencies, brands, publishers, and technology providers to establish clear criteria for measuring attention to ensure industry-wide alignment.

Angelina Eng, Vice President Measurement & Attribution at IAB (Adweek 2023), "*In the rapidly evolving landscape of digital advertising, brands are in a race to capture consumer attention across various channels including banners, videos and social media content. As a result, the concept of attention has become a crucial metric for understanding the impact of advertisements. However, as we delve into the realm of attention metrics, a collaborative and coordinated approach is essential to ensure proper measurement and establish a solid foundation. With a solid foundation and unified efforts, attention metrics can indeed become a valuable asset, enhancing ad effectiveness and driving meaningful consumer engagement in the evolving digital landscape.*"

The progress: Phase one is complete, Phase two is in progress at the time of this writing.

In 2024, the IAB plans to work alongside the Media Rating Council to set attention metrics standards, but they are taking a cautious approach to ensure they carefully consider the complexities involved, spanning logistical, operational, and financial dimensions, before fully embracing attention as a currency in the digital advertising landscape.

The summary: The IAB Attention Task Force initiative is unique to the IAB Tech Lab in the USA. In contrast to some IAB reports from other countries, which seem hastily compiled, this initiative adopts a more deliberate and collaborative approach to ensure comprehensiveness, consideration and accuracy is presented to the industry. While the level of methodological detail is not as extensive to that of the ARF reports, the IAB serves a different purpose. Its succinct educational resources, and its ability to enlist the MRC, play an invaluable role in the development of this category.

QUICK EXPLAINER

The following initiatives in this list, driven by trade bodies, are also changing the media and measurement landscape. While not explicitly related to attention measurement, they deserve an honorable mention here.

1. The Incorporated Society of British Advertisers (ISBA) Project Origin

ISBA is the UK's exclusive representative body for brand owners in advertising. They aim to unite marketers, provide industry insight, and advocate for positive changes. Their core purpose is to establish a transparent and responsible advertising environment that earns public, advertiser, and legislative trust. They work to empower transparent and sustainable advertising relationships, promote inclusivity and sustainability, and collaborate with members and partners to offer leadership and guidance. Origin is ISBA's advertiser-backed program designed to create a blueprint for cross-media measurement as part of a global initiative recognizing the value of advertising in a changing consumer landscape. It addresses the need to measure campaign reach across digital and broadcast platforms while highlighting the absence of standardized measurement methods. ISBA's "Project Origin," aligned with WFA principles, fosters collaboration among advertisers, platforms, broadcasters, and media agencies to advance cross-media measurement.

2. The Coalition for Innovative Media Measurement (CIMM) Multi-Currency Transition Initiative and Lexicon

The Coalition for Innovative Media Measurement (CIMM) is an organization in the United States that focuses on advancing media measurement practices and methodologies especially in the context of television and cross-platform advertising. CIMM is a division of the ARF (Advertising Research Foundation). Two significant initiatives undertaken by CIMM include a 2022 Deloitte-commissioned study on the transition to a multi-currency TV advertising market. This study examined the challenges and benefits for various industry participants, aiming to establish priorities for industry collaboration in preparation for a multi currency market. Another key initiative, Lexicon 4.0, originated in 2010 and updated in 2021, providing over 2500 definitions to clarify Advanced TV Advertising and Return Path Data for the media industry, facilitating understanding amid technological advancements and supporting innovation in TV measurement and advanced advertising.

3. The Association of National Advertisers (ANA) Programmatic Media Supply Chain Transparency Study

The WFA is the only global network for marketers and represents 90% of global marketing communications expenditure—roughly US $900 billion per year. Our goal is to make marketing better by championing more effective and sustainable marketing communications. GARM is an initiative established under the auspices of the WFA in response to growing concerns surrounding brand safety and the overall quality of online advertising environments. Its core mission is to enhance the digital advertising ecosystem by tackling critical issues such as hate speech, harmful content, and misinformation. GARM actively engages in partnerships with industry to establish robust standards and industry best practices that foster responsible advertising and ensure secure online environments for brands.

3. The Media Ratings Council (MRC).

Their charter: Media Rating Council seeks to improve the quality of measurement services and data source products to provide a better understanding of the applications (and limitations) of the information and services delivered. The Bylaws of the MRC document the organization's mission as:

1. To secure for the industry and related users measurement services that are valid, reliable and effective.
2. To evolve and determine minimum disclosure and ethical criteria for measurement services.
3. To provide and administer an audit system designed to inform users as to whether such measurements are conducted in conformance with the criteria and procedures developed.

The MRC is a not-for-profit organization, established in 1963 at the request of US Congress, to perform accreditation for rating and ad measurement service companies like Nielsen, comScore, Linkedin, Amazon DSP and iSpot.tv. Companies paying to be accredited by the MRC, align themselves to the MRC Minimum Standards and open themselves up for auditing (undertaken by Ernst and Young). Each time a measurement firm changes its methodology or releases a new product it requires an audit.

The initial set of standards was introduced in 1964, encompassing key areas such as (a) ethical practices and operational standards, (b) disclosure requirements, and (c) guidelines for electronic advertising delivery. Since that time, a multitude of guidelines and standards have been established, spanning a wide range of topics, from click measurement protocols to guidelines for measuring in-game advertising among others.

One of the most notable and perhaps contentious standards emerged in 2014 when the MRC unveiled the 'Viewable Ad Impression Measurement Guidelines,' which gained widespread recognition under the term 'viewability'. This groundbreaking standard fundamentally changed the way ad impressions were counted, stipulating that a substantial portion of the ad content must be displayed on the user's screen for a significant duration to qualify as a valid impression. Shortly after, in 2015, the Wall Street Journal noted the MRC to be "The most powerful player in media you've never heard of." However, a decade later, with its transformative impact on the measurement of ad impressions, one would expect that this no longer holds true.

The attention event: Outcomes and Data Quality Standards.

At the time of this writing, the attention event for the ARF differs significantly from the initiatives of the ARF and IAB mentioned earlier. Instead of focusing on initiatives aimed at working through what attention is, their approach is to work through what it is not.

In late 2022, the MRC introduced a standard pertaining to 'Outcomes and Data Quality.' These standards offer guidance on efficient data collection, cleaning, and integration and identify user actions that contribute to desired outcomes, including ad exposure, interaction/engagement, and conversion. The MRC underscores the significance of this step, as outcome measurement without accurate delivery and exposure measurement would be non-actionable and could lead to a misallocation of media spending. They also state that this step is vital as to not confuse outcome measurement with audience measurement.

The MRC's stance on attention and outcomes is clear: that outcomes measurement providers should consider advertising exposure or contact by the consumer as well as their attention or impact for any audience if causality is to be assessed. And they suggest doing this by referring back to the ARF's New Media Model as a reference for measuring Attention, a model explored in greater detail in Chapter 1.

Given the complexity and importance of this standard, this next section transcribes in verbatim, with no paraphrasing, the section in the Outcomes standards that specifically relates to attention, section 'A Sad Discussion About Broken Relationships'.

There is a solid summary thereafter for those more time poor (Fig. 4.2).

MRC Outcomes and Data Quality Standards, Section 'A Sad Discussion About Broken Relationships': Beyond measuring media and ad exposure (rendered and viewable), establishing presence of an audience via "eyes/ears on" or attention and engagement are critical factors in determining

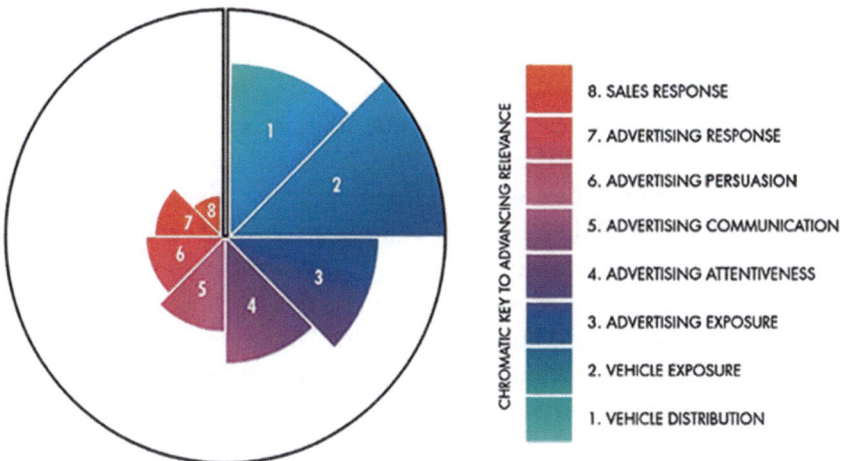

Fig. 4.2 The ARF New Media Helix (*Source* ARF Making Better Media Decisions 2022)

meaningful exposure of an advertising message by the consumer. These criteria have an unequivocal bearing on the advertising's actual contact with, or impact on, consumers, the consumer's consequent actions and ultimate brand Outcomes. As such, Outcomes measurement providers should consider Advertising Exposure or contact by the consumer as well as their Attention or impact for any audience if causality is to be assessed. Direct measurement of Attention is not required for Outcomes measurement in all cases due to feasibility and privacy considerations, however its direct significance to causality should be recognized.

The Advertising Research Foundation's (ARF's) Media Model may be used as a reference for measuring Attention. The first 3 levels of the ARF Media Model (Vehicle Distribution, Vehicle Exposure and Advertising Exposure) are covered by certain aspects of this Standard and more broadly as part of various MRC and/or IAB Standards and Guidelines (the 4th level, Advertising Attentiveness, is the subject of this section). Further, the last 2 levels of the model (Advertising Response and Sales Response; levels 7 and 8, respectively) are the very subject of this Standard, and Outcomes providers are encouraged to consider the additional details espoused in the ARF's Media Model in these areas. Finally, levels 5 and 6 of the model (Advertising Communication and Persuasion) are related to Sentiment, Lift and other cognitive, behavioral and perception KPIs discussed above and planned for further standardization as a subsequent planned phase of this Standard.

While some aspects of Advertising Attentiveness are touched on with regard to discussion of Engagement above, Outcomes services that include direct measurement of advertising exposure or contact (Level 3) and/or impact on the consumer should consider this aspect (the 4th level) of the ARF Media Model to the extent feasible. Specifically, the ARF defines Advertising Attentiveness as "the degree to which those exposed to the advertising are focused on it – ranging from a very brief exposure (or 'scan') that is likely to leave very little memory trace, to intense focus with cognitive and emotional engagement that can lead to enduring recall and impact attitudes and behavior – both positively and negatively."

The ARF includes guidelines on the predictive and performance measurement of Advertising Attentiveness, but the salient point is that beyond confirming presence of an ad, presence of a user and the opportunity to see the ad, whether or not the ad was actually seen (contact), engaged with (contact with notice), paid attention to (impact) and ultimately retained in memory, is of fundamental importance in measuring the ad-lifecycle and a consumer's actions (at each Level of the Ad's life-cycle) all of which are required to generate a response as part of Outcomes measurement. This consideration may include the degree of attentiveness that may be impacted by simultaneous consumption of other media depending on qualitative media factors like, location, environment and other stimuli.

Consumer attention measures that are not direct measures of physical or confirmed cognitive attention that are instead indirect measures for Attention (such sustained tuning or duration with an ad or commercial, presence of users and other interaction attributes), must be clearly distinguished from direct measures of Attention. Such indirect measures are still considered Audience measures that require viewability and SIVT as discussed above. Any such indirect measures must be appropriately described in disclosures including the nature of measurement.

Finally, as discussed as part of the scoping section above, there are certain cognitive and behavioral aspects of methodology that may be involved in Attention that go beyond passive measurement and involve measurement techniques beyond simple studies/survey and panels—for example, neuro studies, eye-tracking, cross-site behavioral and benchmarking analyses, etc. Likewise, more complex aspects of these products such as models that seek to disentangle the generally established relative effects of media contact and creative impact on Outcomes represent difficult areas to standardize. While consumer Attention measures are included in this phase of these Standards, to the extent they are derived from either first- or third-party measurement of consumer's media and ad exposure (with contact, i.e., "Eyes-On" or "Ears- On" as a minimum)/activity, more advanced methodologies and models employed within them are intended to be addressed as part of a later phase of these Standards.

The summary: The MRC is different from the other trade bodies due to the regulatory nature of their charter. So their job is to put official 'lines in the sand' specifically related to measurement services in the media and advertising industry, rather than educate stakeholders. The four key points to consider from an attention perspective are these:

Advertising Attentiveness: This concept, defined by the ARF, is a pivotal element and should be used as a baseline for both outcomes and how they link to attention and is defined as the degree to which people exposed to an ad are focused on it, ranging from brief exposure to intense engagement.

Distinguishing Direct and Indirect Attention Measures: Attention measures that are not direct measures of physical or confirmed cognitive attention (such as advanced methodologies like eye-tracking, neuro studies, and explicit consumer reporting) that are instead indirect measures for Attention (such sustained tuning or duration with an ad or commercial, presence of users and other interaction attributes), must be clearly distinguished from direct measures of Attention.

Outcomes and Causality: Outcomes measures should not be confused with or misrepresented as audience measures. Outcomes measurement providers should consider Advertising Exposure or contact by the consumer as well as their Attention or impact for any audience if causality is to be assessed.

Future Standardization: This standard is the first of what seems to be a few initiatives on the drawing board to manage attention measurement and associated metrics.

MEANWHILE IN THE REAL WORLD

Is this a case of 'Attention by Association' or could it be a rerun of the 'Like' button debacle?

In 2009, Justin Rosenstein delivered a marketing masterstroke for Facebook by co-inventing the Like button which single-handedly changed the nature of how we consider advertising success. While other metrics (such as, views, shares, comments, ratings) had been introduced on YouTube a few years earlier, the Facebook Like button was the first time perceived customer approval was directly linked to a brand (as opposed to content) at such scale. The use of the word 'Like' conveyed not only human interaction but also an endorsement of the brand. But as it turned out, this was wrong.

A comprehensive analysis of the top 200 brands, ranked by the number of "Likes" they garnered in 2012, revealed a surprising revelation: the word 'Like' may not carry the connotations that advertisers initially presumed. The study unveiled a stark reality; in any given week following the initial 'Like' button engagement, a mere fraction—specifically, less than 1% (0.45%)—of these enthusiastic brand 'likers' demonstrated the inclination to revisit the brands they professed affection for.

Well it seems, some 15 years on, such marketing genius is happening again but this time in the attention category.

At CES in 2022, DoubleVerify made a big announcement. They announced they had successfully achieved MRC accreditation for their newly registered DV Authentic Attention® product. An aggregated proxy measure made up of multiple data points collected directly from the publisher and/or captured on a device. Including 'ad presentation' factors such as share of screen, time on screen, ad size, audibility and 'engagement' factors such screen touches, screen orientation changes, skipping, scrolling video playback, and audio control interactions and more.

However soon after the announcement, Andy Brown, CEO of The Attention Council, was quick to voice his concern, not over the accreditation in itself, but the need for clarification of the connectivity to attention. Andy said: *"The journey towards the creation of an agreed metric for attention took a couple of interesting turns this week. At CES Double Verify issued a release to inform the market that their proxy metric approach to measuring attention had been accredited by the Media Rating Council (MRC). What exactly does this mean and what are the implications? Firstly we should start with applauding DoubleVerify for achieving the accreditation. If significant media dollars are to be spent against attention metrics (of any kind), then transparency is critical. That said, it is important that we understand what the MRC is doing here. They are NOT setting the definition for the measurement of attention (based on an evaluation of the relative effectiveness of the method). They ARE verifying that DV are 'doing what they say they do' in respect of their measurement solution. In other words this is not like the digital viewability standard."*

Andy's sentiment makes sense given what is known about human attention data. Even though the 'engagement' measures might be 'physical interactions' as defined in various MRC standards, these factors can translate to BOTH attention and inattention. Moreover each of these factors require different relative importance weightings that only human data can reveal (see more of this in Chapter in A Human Informed Hybrid Model).

So how did DoubleVerify get MRC Accreditation? Simple, as Andy said they were accredited for the metrics they do collect, the physical interaction factors collected by tag and device, but not on the construct of attention itself. Until the MRC gets involved in 2024, no standards for direct human attentiveness have been set.

Could this be another Justin Rosenstein moment?

Attention Data Demystified

The Definition of Definitions

> Failures of attention management are undoubtedly responsible for many business catastrophes, but because attention is one of those pesky intangible assets, it's difficult to document its presence (though its absence is surely felt). (Thomas H. Davenport and John C. Beck)

It's time to shift our focus from how the category was born to where it stands today. A crucial starting point is to clear up any confusion about the words we're using. While organizations like the IAB Tech Lab and the MRC seem to have moved on from the debate over how exactly attention is defined, many are still stuck in the semantics and are hesitant to move ahead without consensus.

But what is happening right now is a mix up in the definition of definitions.

To be clear, the conceptual definition of attention has been set by seminal academics and practitioners in psychology and other sciences for more than a century. And if you flick back to Chapter 1 to re-read the 7 definitions representing this century-long understanding of the intricacies of attention, you will see these definitions are all quite similar—including the ARF's which the ARF refer to as the baseline. To prove the similarity point, when we plug in all 7 published 'best in class' definitions from Chapter 1 in to ChatGBT and ask it to summarize, this is the definition returned which is highly similar to the ARF version (which makes sense because the ARF version is based on a meta analysis not their own independent research):

> Attention is the mental process that involves focusing cognitive resources on specific stimuli or aspects of the environment, leading to a state of heightened mental activity and concentration. It can vary in intensity, from brief and fleeting exposures to intense cognitive and emotional engagement, and it plays a crucial role in memory, attitude formation, and behavioral responses. (ChatGPT 2023)

The point here is that the definition of attention is highly researched, it is consistent and it is universally agreed in the science world so the advertising industry should accept this.

However, what the industry should be asking for is alignment on is the operationalization of attention—this is different.

Definition and operationalization are two distinct concepts often used in research and scientific inquiry, particularly in fields like psychology, sociology, and other social sciences. One is a noun, one is a verb.

A theoretical definition tells you what a concept means and sets the foundation for research to clarify 'what' is being studied. While an operational definition tells you 'how' to measure or observe it in order to quantify the concept in a concrete and objective manner.

For example, a theoretical definition for the concept "customer satisfaction" is often defined as the degree to which a customer's experience with a product or service conforms to expectations and the ideal experience. While the operational definition might be; customer surveys to rate their experiences with this brand and competitive brands on a five-point scale: Very Satisfied, Satisfied, Neutral, Dissatisfied, and Very Dissatisfied.

So with the definition of attention set, it's time to move on to the unpacking of the 'operationalization of attention'.

The Attention Economy Taxonomy

Now that we've established the 'what' we are trying to measure, let's dive into the 'how' we measure it. The Attention Economy Taxonomy, is hard to say but important to understand.

This section showcases the main methods used to collect and model attention data. It does not call out vendors, you can look at the good work of the ARF Attention Atlas to look at comparisons, but what it does do is it attempts to simplify the complex by categorizing data into methodological themes.

To make it more accessible, we'll employ a hierarchical approach, breaking things down into different levels. We'll start with broad categories and gradually drill down to more specific details. Think of it as peeling layers of an onion. We've organized these into five tiers for each of the four primary methods of collecting attention data: biometric methods, non-biometric methods, and data signals. This approach aims to simplify the complexity while maintaining comprehensiveness.

Additionally, this section includes call-out explanations to clarify some research terms used here. For instance, we'll distinguish between probabilistic and deterministic data, define the differences between metrics and measurements, and granular data versus aggregated data. These explanations should provide context to the concepts discussed. To get started, familiarize yourself with the 'Attention Methodological Taxonomy Snapshot' table and then proceed from there (Table 4.1).

Table 4.1 The attention methodological taxonomy

	Biometric methods		Non biometric methods	Non-human
Tier 1: Data Source Categorization	Human			Non-human
Tier 2: Primary Collection Methods	Biometric methods		Non biometric methods	Data signals
Tier 3: Sub-Methods	Visual	Neuro	Psychological	Ad exposure & user interaction factors
Tier 4: Measures	Visual time & visual focus	Emotional arousal, valence outlook, response latency	Quantitative scales, qualitative response	Binary probability
Tier 5: Metrics	Attention decay, Attention:AdLength Equivalence, Attention:Viewability Equivalence, Attention:Impression Equivalence	High/Low Counts, Attention Scores, Measure Duration & Variation	Outcomes/Insights	Media Quality Scores, Attention/Engagement Indexes

*This is not an exhaustive list of measures and metrics, it simply represents what is typical in the market at the time of writing

Human, Biometric and Visual

Tier 1: Human

Human attention measurement, in its essence, involves the <u>direct</u> quantification of human behavior. It encompasses the assessment of physical or confirmed cognitive attention, where the engagement of ears, eyes, or the brain with advertising content is explicitly verified through biometric means. These methods offer objectivity and quantifiability, shedding light on how people react to different stimuli and tasks.

Tier 2: Human, Biometric

Biometric methods are relevant in psychology, neuroscience, human–computer interaction, and marketing research. These methods involve the examination of physiological, neurological, and neuropsychological signals to understand human behavioral characteristics. They provide insight into an individual's attention or engagement, deepening our understanding of how people respond physiologically to external stimuli.

Tier 3: Human, Biometric, Visual

Visual methods involve the use of cameras to capture information, typically in the form of video footage, from the surrounding environment. Subsequently, machine learning models are deployed to process the collected footage and extract relevant information. These techniques have broad applications across various fields, including computer vision, healthcare, security, and social sciences like ethnography. They serve as valuable tools for data gathering, enabling analysis, recognition, and understanding of human emotions, attention, and other non-verbal cues that may be challenging to obtain through alternative methods.

The following methods are the most widely used in attention measurement and involve tracking and recording visual engagement to ads and content:

(a) **Eye Tracking**: One of the most well-known methods is eye tracking, which tracks and records a person's eye movements, including where they look, how their gaze moves, and how long they focus on specific points or objects. This method can investigate visual perception, attention, and decision-making processes in various fields, including advertising, usability testing, and human–computer interaction research. It can be applied both passively, using devices like smartphones with built-in cameras, or in controlled laboratory settings (often if used in neuromarketing cases).

(b) **Facial Detection**: This technology and process entail identifying and pinpointing human faces in images or video frames captured by cameras. It determines the movement of a person's head concerning a particular point or object, offering insights into their attention and focus on that point. Furthermore, facial detection and analysis are crucial for recognizing and classifying emotions based on facial expressions. Facial detection is especially valuable when the distance between the camera and the individual is too large for effective eye gaze detection and contributes to creating models for age verification, often necessary for privacy considerations.

(c) **Pose Estimation**: Pose estimation is a computer vision technique that focuses on estimating the positions and orientations of a person's body parts, including the head, torso, arms, and legs, within an image or video. While it may not be as widely recognized as some other visual methods in attention-based data collection, it holds significant value for attention models in scenarios where there is a need to track objects or individuals (including multiple people) from a distance in real-world environments, such as cinema or outdoor settings. Pose estimation also helps differentiate human presence from other objects or animals and can contribute to the development of models for age verification.

Tier 4: Human, Biometric, Visual, Measures

(a) **Attention Time**: The amount of time (in seconds, or sub seconds) a human spends focusing their attention on a specific task, areas of interest, content, or object.

(b) **Attention Focus**: The degree of fixation, direction of fixation, or viewing consistency, across time on a specific task, areas of interest, content, or object. Attention focus provides a deeper understanding of conscious awareness and mental processing than attention time alone.

Tier 5: Human, Biometric, Visual, Metrics

(a) **Attention Decay**: Decay curves are distributions of attention time and focus.

(b) **Attention: AdLength Equivalence**: Proportion of attention time relative to ad length.

(c) **Attention: Viewability Equivalence**: Proportion of viewable inventory (by relative MRC standards) that achieves the equivalent attention seconds and proportion of ad pixels on screen.

(d) **Attention: Impression Equivalence**: Proportion of attention volume relative to impressions bought.

QUICK EXPLAINER

This is a quick quantification of measurement versus metrics.

'Measurement' and 'Metrics' are closely interconnected concepts, and they are often used interchangeably but they hold distinct meanings and serve different roles in the data and analysis journey.

Measurement refers to the process of quantifying or evaluating something using standardized units or criteria. This process includes assigning numerical values to specific attributes or characteristics of an object, process, or phenomenon. Measurement provides the foundational raw data or observations required to comprehend and evaluate various aspects of a system, process, or performance. For instance, measuring an object's length in inches, the temperature in degrees Celsius, or the time in seconds are all examples of measurements.

Metrics are specific quantitative measures derived from measurements, providing context and meaning by expressing relationships between measures. They serve to assess, compare, or monitor performance, enabling insights, goal evaluation, and informed decision-making. Examples of metrics include ratio of lengths, relative temperature and time intervals or distributions.

So one is the process of acquiring data, while the other are quantitative measures derived from that data. A measure is a number, while a metric measures a relationship between numbers. Metrics add context to measures for understanding and application and measures precede metrics.

However a warning: when metrics lack a solid foundation of accurate and reliable measurements underneath, several problems can arise, including:

1. Inaccuracy

Inaccurate measurements can lead to metrics that do not reflect the true state of the system or process being assessed. This can result in misleading conclusions and decisions based on flawed data.

2. Poor Decision-Making

Metrics are often used to guide decision-making. If the measurements upon which these metrics are based are flawed, decisions made using these metrics may be suboptimal or even detrimental to the organization's goals.

3. Misallocation of Resources

Incorrect metrics can lead to resources being allocated inefficiently. For example, if a metric used to assess the performance of a marketing campaign is flawed, the organization may end up investing in the wrong marketing strategies.

4. Difficulty in Improvement

Metrics are also used to identify areas for improvement. If the measurements are unreliable, it becomes challenging to pinpoint specific weaknesses and take corrective actions effectively.

This goes back to the old adage of 'garbage in, garbage out' or 'good data in, good data out'. This simple saying highlights that if you start with accurate and reliable information, you'll get good and dependable results. It's a fundamental principle in fields like data analysis and decision-making, emphasizing the importance of trustworthy data for achieving valuable outcomes.

Human, Biometric and Neuro

Tier 1: Human

Human attention measurement, in its essence, involves the direct quantification of human behavior. It encompasses the assessment of physical or confirmed cognitive attention, where the engagement of ears, eyes, or the brain with advertising content is explicitly verified through biometric means. These methods offer objectivity and quantifiability, shedding light on how people react to different stimuli and tasks.

Tier 2: Human, Biometric

Biometric methods are relevant in psychology, neuroscience, human–computer interaction, and marketing research. These methods involve the examination of physiological, neurological, and neuropsychological signals to understand human behavioral characteristics. They provide insight into an individual's attention or engagement, deepening our understanding of how people respond physiologically to external stimuli.

Tier 3: Human, Biometric, Neuro

Neuro-based assessments originally emerged from the medical field, where they were used for diagnosing and treating nervous system and brain function disorders. However, they have gained significant relevance in social sciences, especially for evaluating two crucial aspects of audience response: attention and emotion. These aspects are closely associated with indicators of emotional and subconscious reactions to advertisements. There are three primary types of neuro measures, and within each of these, we explore the most commonly employed methods for assessing attention:

1. Neurological Assessments (direct brain)
2. Physiological Assessments (heart, pulse, blood, pupil, skin, sweat)
3. Psychological Assessments (indirect brain via response)

1. **Neurological Assessments (direct brain)**: these methods involve the use of medical-grade devices to directly measure real-time changes in brain activity. These assessments are conducted to gain a deeper understanding of how attention-related processes affect the brain. These types of assessments can only be conducted in the lab.

   (a) **Electromyography (EMG)**: This diagnostic and research technique is employed to measure the electrical activity of muscles. EMG captures the electrical signals generated during muscle contractions, offering valuable insights into muscle function and the neural pathways governing muscle movements.

   (b) **Functional Magnetic Resonance Imaging (FMRI)**: FMRI is a neuroimaging technique used to measure and visualize brain activity in real-time. It does so by detecting changes in blood flow and oxygenation levels in the brain that are associated with neural activity.

2. **Physiological Assessments (heart, pulse, blood, pupil, skin, sweat)**: these methods encompass the analysis of various physiological responses that offer insights beyond brain activity, shedding light on an individual's cognitive processes, including attention. These assessments help researchers understand how the body reacts during various cognitive tasks, attentional states, or in response to specific stimuli. In many of the cases in-lab data collection is necessary, although there are some portable and wearable technologies surfacing, particularly related to EEG.

   (a) **Facial Electromyography (EMG)**: Small, adhesive electrodes are attached to specific facial muscles of interest. These electrodes are designed to pick up the electrical signals generated by the contraction and relaxation of these muscles. This is used to understand changes in emotional arousal related to specific stimuli.

   (b) **Facial Detection**: This technology and process involve identifying and localizing human faces within images or video frames captured by cameras. In the context of neuro studies, facial detection and analysis play a vital role in recognizing and categorizing emotions based on facial expressions.

(c) **Galvanic Skin Response (GSR)**: GSR is a measure of changes in skin conductance that can provide valuable insights into emotional arousal and attentional responses. It is commonly utilized in research focused on emotional attention, including studies that examine physiological reactions such as skin conductance and sweating in response to advertising stimuli.

(d) **Electroencephalography (EEG)**: In this procedure, flat metal electrodes are placed on the scalp using conductive gel. These electrodes capture electrical signals produced by neurons in the cerebral cortex, forming the EEG signal. Neurons communicate via electrical impulses, and EEG records their activity.

(e) **Heart Rate Variability (HRV)**: A method used to evaluate the fluctuations in time intervals between consecutive heartbeats. This approach offers valuable insights into the activity of the autonomic nervous system and can be applied to the study of attention and stress responses. Research often focuses on monitoring changes in heart rate and pulse measurements as indicators of emotional and attentional reactions to advertisements.

(f) **Pupillometry**: Pupillometry involves measuring changes in pupil size, which can be indicative of cognitive load and attentional processes. Pupil dilation can reflect changes in cognitive effort and arousal levels.

3. **Psychological Assessments (indirect brain via response)**: These techniques primarily gauge response times during problem-solving and recognition tasks. They indirectly reveal unconscious implicit associations, attention, and attitudes.

(a) **Continuous Performance Test (CTP)**: CPTs are computerized assessments designed to measure sustained attention and response inhibition. Participants are presented with a series of stimuli, typically letters or numbers, and are tasked with responding to specific target stimuli while disregarding non-targets. This test serves to evaluate attention, impulsivity, and response time.

(b) **Stroop Test**: The Stroop test assesses cognitive flexibility and the ability to restrict automatic responses. Participants are asked to name the ink color of words that are color names themselves (e.g., the word "blue" printed in red ink). Performance on this test provides insights into selective attention and cognitive control.

Tier 4: Human, Biometric, Neuro, Measures

(a) **Arousal:** The strength or and variability of a physiological or neurological response. The physiological response varies depending on the method i.e. heart rate, pulse rate, blood flow, pupil fixations, skin response, sweat levels.
(b) **Valence:** The degree to which each of the body's two motivational systems is more strongly activated, the positive (appetitive) system or the negative (aversive) system.
(c) **Response Latency:** Verbatim and open-ended, free-text responses, which offer qualitative insights providing rich context, nuanced information, and deeper insights into respondents' perspectives.

Tier 5: Human, Biometric, Neuro, Metrics

(a) **High/Low Counts:** Percentage/count of respondents high/low arousal/ valence.
(b) **Attention Scores:** Emotions/Arousal(seconds) by aggregated score.
(c) **Emotion/Arousal/Blink Rate Duration:** Measure duration (seconds) by ad on screen.

Human, Non-Biometric and Psychological

Tier 1: Human

Human attention measurement, in its essence, involves the direct quantification of human behavior. It encompasses the assessment of physical or confirmed cognitive attention, where the engagement of ears, eyes, or the brain with advertising content is explicitly verified through biometric means. These methods offer objectivity and quantifiability, shedding light on how people react to different stimuli and tasks.

Tier 2: Human, Non-Biometric

Non-biometric methods encompass approaches to measure or analyze human behavior or characteristics without relying on the capture of unique physiological or behavioral traits of individuals. Unlike biometric methods, non-biometric data is generally less sensitive and carries lower privacy risks. However, it can be susceptible to biases or errors stemming from self-reported behavior, perception, awareness, emotion, and sentiment. Researchers often employ a combination of methods to gain a holistic understanding of how individuals perceive, engage with, and respond to advertising content.

Tier 3: Human, Non-Biometric, Psychological

Methods such as surveys and interviews are most commonly used in fields like psychology, marketing, and social sciences to understand human behavior and preferences. These non-biometric methods provide a range of tools for researchers and psychologists to gain insights into human psychological processes and behaviors.

(a) **Surveys:** These methods are employed to gather feedback from viewers concerning their attitudes, preferences, and responses to specific products or advertisements. Participants can provide insights into which elements caught their attention and whether the content influenced their perceptions, sentiment, memorability, recall, consideration or purchase intentions.

(b) **Interview & Focus Groups:** In-depth interviews and focus group discussions go beyond the surface-level insights obtained through surveys. They offer a deeper exploration of participants' emotional responses and thoughts concerning content and advertisements. Through open-ended conversations and group interactions, these qualitative methods enable a more comprehensive understanding of why certain content or ads evoke specific reactions and how these responses influence individuals' perceptions and decision-making processes

(c) **Ethnography:** Ethnographic research involves direct observation of individuals interacting with advertisements in real-world settings, such as their homes or during shopping trips. This approach offers valuable insights into the authentic viewing environment and the various factors that shape attention. It's worth noting that ethnography was the original choice for robust attention research, preceding the development of eye gaze and facial detection technologies. It continues to be a foundational method for studying attention due to its capacity to offer direct yet passive, largely non-self-reporting insights into human interactions. Ethnographic research can include self-reported diaries and logs.

Tier 4: Human, Non-Biometric, Psychological, Measures

(a) Quantitative Response: Individual responses obtained from structured and predefined answer choices, enabling numerical measurement and facilitating straightforward statistical analysis.

(b) Qualitative Response: Verbatim and open-ended, free-text responses, which offer qualitative insights providing rich context, nuanced information, and deeper insights into respondents' perspectives.

Tier 5: Human, Non-Biometric, Psychological, Metrics

(a) **Outcomes/Insights:** An outcome based metric is understanding whether the measure lines up with the goal. i.e. did the attention measure relate to brand lift, memorability, consideration, favorable sentiment, intention to buy, willingness to pay or any other performance based goals.

Non-Human, Data Signals and Ad Exposure/User Interaction

Tier 1: Non-Human

Gathering non-human attention serves as a strategy for ad tech vendors to participate in the attention measurement industry, especially when direct assessments of physical or confirmed cognitive human attention aren't feasible. Proxy measures through data signals act as indirect indicators of attention towards a stimulus or content. However, the accuracy of these measures on their own, especially when compared to direct and biometric measures, is often subject to scrutiny. Nevertheless, these measures do provide significant scalability in the digital landscape, where direct attention measurements face limitations due to human panel sizes and privacy concerns.

Tier 2: Non-Human, Data Signals

Measuring attention through devices involves indirectly quantifying human behavior by harnessing data signal proxies collected through JavaScript Tags from devices and publishers. These tags possess the capability to gather a wide array of data, including factors related to media consumption and implied on-screen engagement, as well as important backend contextual data such as ad placement and user device information. These measures are then modeled to infer human behavioral traits.

Tier 3: Non-Human, Data Signals, Ad Exposure & User Interaction

Data signal proxies rely on the collection of two primary sets of data to infer consumer attention. The first set involves data that verifies whether an ad has been served (ad exposure signals), and the second set consists of what the

ARF call, 'physical interaction factors' that serve as proxies for engagement (user interaction signals, a proxy for whether an ad has been seen).

(a) **Ad Exposure Signals**: These are the 'ad served' factors. These are often referred to as hygiene factors and encompass specific data signals that quantify whether the ad was rendered and viewable. This usually includes viewability verification, ad time-in-view and ad aspect ratio.

(b) **User Interaction Signals**: These are considered the 'ad seen' factors. These are often referred to as proxies for human engagement. This usually includes ad cursor movement, screen orientation, mute/unmute actions, volume adjustments, ad clicks, device key presses, and many more. Without these indicators, the level of human engagement could not be inferred in any way beyond basic viewability verification services.

Tier 4: Non-Human, Data Signals, Ad Exposure & User Interaction, Measures

(a) **Binary Probability**: Attention collected from devices is generally categorized into binary states and measured within a range of probabilities. This approach does not consider moments of complete inattention or occasional instances of 100% full attention. Instead, it most commonly captures attention levels that fall somewhere in between these two extremes, but the amount of attention in terms of duration, or the degree of focus cannot be predicted.

Tier 5: Non-Human, Data Signals, Ad Exposure & User Interaction, Metrics

(a) **Media Quality Scores**: Categorical media quality scores for grouping inventory along a continuum including high, med, low attention/ exposure probability.

(b) **Attention/Engagement Indexes**: Media quality broken down by measure to Low/High Engagement and Low/HIgh Attention.

QUICK EXPLAINER
What is the difference between 'Deterministic' versus 'Probabilistic' data?.

Deterministic and probabilistic data represent two distinct approaches to describing and analyzing information in various fields. The main distinction between deterministic and probabilistic data lies in their treatment of uncertainty and predictability.

1. Deterministic Data

Deterministic data is all about certainty and predictability. Each data point or piece of information has a clear and unambiguous value that can be precisely determined. There's no inherent randomness or uncertainty in deterministic data. The data is fixed and doesn't change on its own. Deterministic models use specific rules or equations and provide exact results. They don't allow for variations because they solely depend on input data and preset rules. For example, in the context of human data, measurements like a person's height are deterministic. When you measure an individual's height, you typically get an exact, fixed value that doesn't change unless there's a significant physical change (e.g., growth due to age). A deterministic model for predicting a person's height based on age might follow a simple rule like "height increases by an average of 5 centimeters per year during the growth phase." In this case, you can precisely predict a person's height by using their age as input, assuming that they follow this deterministic growth pattern.

2. Probabilistic Data

Probabilistic data aims to embrace uncertainty and randomness. Instead of giving exact values, it presents a range of possible values, each with a probability or chance of happening. Probabilistic data adds randomness or variability into the mix. The exact value isn't predetermined but is described using probabilities. Probabilistic models work with uncertain data, such as ranges of possible values and their probabilities. They're usually based on statistical methods and probabilistic principles, which help quantify uncertainty and randomness by providing a distribution of possible outcomes, each with a likelihood. This distribution considers the variability and uncertainty in the data. An example related to human data can be found in medical diagnoses. Consider a medical test for a disease. The test may provide a range of possible outcomes, such as 'positive' or 'negative', and each outcome is associated with a probability. For instance, a test result might indicate a 80% probability of being negative and a 20% probability of being positive. These models take into account various factors, including test results, symptoms, and medical history, to calculate the probability of a person having a disease. Instead of providing a definitive diagnosis, Bayesian networks offer a range of probabilities for different disease outcomes, reflecting the inherent uncertainty in medical diagnostics.

A Human Informed Hybrid

In short, attention data can be categorized into two main groups: human-centric and non-human-centric. We have briefly identified that no data is perfect and that each data set has its own limitations, but let's go deeper on these. The most pressing pros and cons for these data types revolve largely around accuracy and scale, let's start with a quick fire summary:

Human Data Pros:	**Accuracy.** Human biometric data is the source of truth. It is observed and deterministic. It is a direct quantification of human behavior at very granular levels of humans consuming media naturally.
Human Data Cons:	**Scale.** Collecting biometric data can be costly, and it may pose privacy risks in regions where it's classified as sensitive under data privacy laws. Privacy concerns are controllable when samples are smaller.
Non-Human Data Pros:	**Scale.** Data signal proxies are the source of scale. It can reach gargantuan numbers of impressions in a day, with little to no privacy concerns.
Non-Human Data Cons:	**Accuracy.** Data signal proxies are not directly linked to human behavior. It is inferred and probabilistic. Tag based solutions need to use aggregation, probabilities and ranges to manage the complex task of predicting human behavior.

The scale conversation is obvious, but let's do some fun simplistic math to show the point.

In 2022, Nielsen reported their human panel assets in the USA to be around 500,000 individuals across multiple digital platforms. If we use the 'very' loose adage of each person being exposed to 5000 ads per day, removing non-digital (25% non-digital), we get human attention data on close to 2 billion impressions per day. Tag based Data Signals: In 2022, there are reportedly 307 million internet users in the United States being exposed to loosely 5000 ads per day. Using the same math tag based methods will get us attention indicators on 11 trillion impressions per day. This is a data pool more than 5000 times greater.

This is an unrealistic expectation (notwithstanding the privacy and cost implications to collect human attention data from a Nielsen size panel), but you get the point about scale.

The accuracy conversation is more complex, so we need to dig deeper.

To illustrate the complexity of predicting human attention, think of it akin to solving a 4D puzzle rather than a 2D one (see Fig. 4.3). The complexity arises from how humans genuinely engage with media. Beneath every device, platform, format, and ad-unit lies complicated and highly variable viewing behavior, encompassing intricate profiles of attention duration and focus. While viewability and engagement data are useful, predicting attention on 2D signals is susceptible to a substantial margin of error without a thorough comprehension of these intricate human viewing patterns (refer to Viewing Clusters in Chapter 3).

The 2 dimensions used in market for human attention prediction are 'served' and 'seen' (hygiene and engagement signals) but the missing dimensions include:

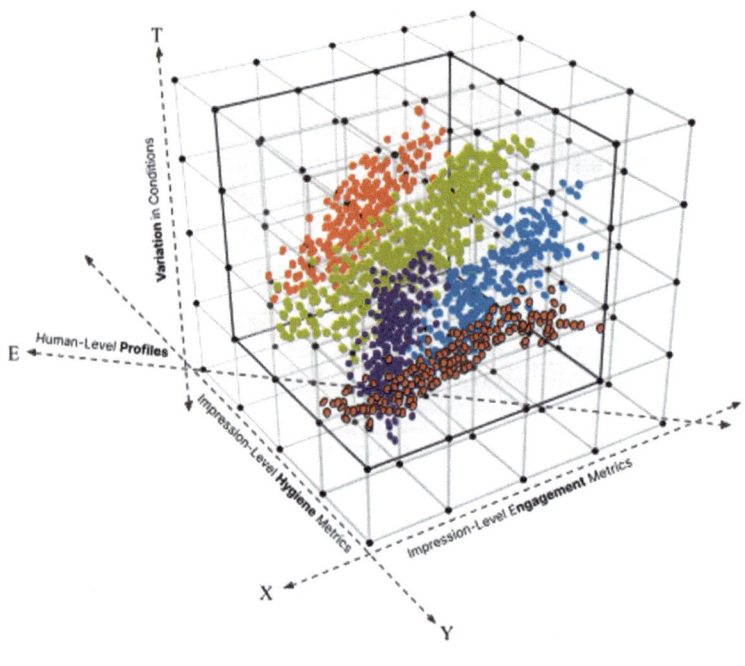

© Amplified Intelligence

Fig. 4.3 The multidimensional human Rubik's Cube

1. **Human Viewing Profiles and Factor Weightings**: Impression-level engagement factors inherently hold indicators of attention, but can also be contributors to <u>BOTH</u> attention and inattention to the ad. <u>AND</u> the impact of these factors on attention varies depending on the context in which the ad unit is exposed, necessitating adjustments in factor weighting for different formats and under diverse conditions. This context is not related to the same context in the 'ad relevance' sense, although that does play a mediating role too, this type of context for example is where a 9:16 will render a very different amount of attention depending on where it is placed, meaning ad coverage plays a role but its impact is mediated by many other factors. This goes the same for Time-in-View, volume etc. etc.... The humble Rubik's Cube boasts an astonishing number of possible combinations—43,252,003,274,489,856,000—take this to 4D and the puzzle gets a whole lot harder.

2. **Variation in Conditions**: When media owners make adjustments to their platform's user experience, such as altering ad unit aspects, sound settings or ad load rules, it can disrupt the functionality of predictive models. These disruptions can effectively 'break the prediction puzzle.' Small user experience changes occur monthly (we see that in our collection code), while larger ones take place every 6 to 12 months. Therefore, it's crucial to continuously collect data from real human interactions to keep these models up-to-date and enhance their accuracy.

To address the accuracy versus scale debate the answer is simple, the future of attention economics needs an amalgamation of both. A hybrid approach blends deterministic and probabilistic data elements, resulting in a more holistic and accurate representation of complex systems and a scalable solution.

TAKE IT TO WORK

Human attention is complex. A hybrid approach blends deterministic and probabilistic data elements, resulting in a more holistic and accurate representation of complex systems and a scalable solution.

MEANWHILE IN THE REAL WORLD

Did you know that OpenAI uses hybrid methods to gain human-level outputs?

In 2019, before OpenAI was one of the most famous brands on the planet, they conducted a noteworthy experiment that gained considerable attention. In a modest building in San Francisco, the then 'promising' researchers from OpenAI tested Dactyl, a robotic single hand designed to solve a Rubik's Cube. They of course received huge praise for their success, but it was the training method that stood them apart. An article about the experiment in the New York Times highlighted that, for quite some time, while other researchers had been programming robots to solve Rubik's Cubes as quickly as possible, OpenAI had focused on self-learning to achieve "human-level dexterity." To do this they utilized reinforcement learning techniques to train the robotic hand to handle objects with a remarkable level of skill and adaptability, just like a human. The learning process involved both physical and virtual simulations, with the robotic hand learning through trial and error. It basically learned to be human-like from watching real humans solve the puzzle. The article also emphasizes that prioritizing self-learning over speed to a result ultimately gains greater breakthroughs. There is a lesson here for our industry.

Even their newest breakthrough, ChatGPT uses a vast amount of human training data to learn and generate its responses. Its training data was a large collection of publicly available sources such as books, articles, websites, and other human written material pre 2022. After the pre-training phase the model is refined by human input on the fly. While it fine-tunes itself in flight, it continues to get direct input from human reviewers so that it addresses responsiveness, biases and handles new scenarios. This iterative feedback loop, where human data plays a crucial role, exemplifies the synergy between humans and machines in a hybrid model.

This type of training data is commonly referred to as 'Ground Truth' and its importance is well established in artificial intelligence systems.

As Karthik Narasimhan, a computer scientist at Princeton University, aptly puts it, "Humans learn through a combination of both doing and reading. We want machines to do the same." Pre-training machines with human data empowers machines with essential concepts and information, much like reading a manual before using new software. It not only accelerates their learning process but also guides them toward mastering skills they might otherwise struggle to acquire.

The Critical Importance of Ground Truthing

In the field of supervised learning, "ground truth data" denotes data that serves as a "provable" or "true" answer to a specific question. This type of data is collected through direct observation of actual real features and real context—in this case, real humans doing real things. The quality and accuracy of this ground truth data has a significant and direct impact on how well predictive algorithms work. And the more complex the prediction task, the deeper and more accurate the ground truth data needs to be. In simpler terms, to train a complex machine learning model effectively, the more comprehensive and true-to-life the observed data is, the better it represents the thing we're trying to predict. This is important because solid ground truth data is foundational to any Hybrid Model for our industry.

Determining how much ground truth data is enough for complex prediction tasks like understanding human behavior depends on several factors specific to the task and the level of accuracy required. Here are some considerations to consider in attention economics:

1. **Task Complexity**: If the task involves simple, binary predictions, you may require less ground truth data. However, for intricate, multifaceted predictions, such as predicting human behavior in diverse scenarios, you'll likely need a more substantial amount of ground truth data.
2. **Variability of Behavior**: Consider the diversity and variability within the human behavior you're trying to predict. If human behavior in your domain is relatively consistent and predictable, you may need less ground truth data. Conversely, if behavior varies widely depending on context, individuals, or other factors, you'll need a larger and more diverse dataset to capture this complexity.
3. **Data Quality**: Ensure that your ground truth data is of high quality. Inaccurate, aggregated or noisy ground truth labels can hinder the performance of predictive models. Quality assurance and validation processes are crucial to minimize errors in the ground truth data.
4. **Sample Representativeness**: The ground truth data should be representative of the population or behavior you aim to predict. If your dataset only covers a narrow segment of the population or specific situations, it may not generalize well to broader scenarios. In such cases, you'll need more diverse and representative data.
5. **Temporal Dynamics**: Human behavior can change over time due to various factors. If your prediction task involves understanding temporal changes or trends in behavior, you may need time-series data and a longer historical dataset to capture evolving patterns accurately.
6. **Validation and Testing**: Implement rigorous validation and testing procedures to evaluate your model's performance. Cross-validation and testing on held-out datasets can help you gauge how well your model generalizes to new, unseen data.

In summary, the amount of ground truth data required for complex prediction tasks varies depending on the specific circumstances and objectives.

Starting with a reasonable dataset and progressively increasing it while monitoring model performance is a practical approach. Ultimately, the adequacy of ground truth data should align with the complexity of the task, the variation in behavior across conditions and the level of accuracy needed for meaningful predictions. Without solid ground truth, hybrid models will fail.

TAKE IT TO WORK

Ensure that your ground truth data is of high quality. Inaccurate, aggregated or noisy ground truth labels can hinder the performance of predictive models.

Data DNA for Successful Attention Models

The diagram to follow (Fig. 4.4) describes how the data sets should connect for the future success of hybrid models in attention economics. At its core it's about a clear, but profound, data interface that connects the ground truth and data signal proxies to provide a clear map of attention measurement for a functional and enduring ecosystem.

1. **Ground Truth Database**: This dataset includes non-aggregated human biometric attention data combined with non-aggregated data signals collected from the <u>same</u> individuals during ad viewing. Collecting both biometrics and data signals from the same individual provides the linking data to connect the human and the non-human data.

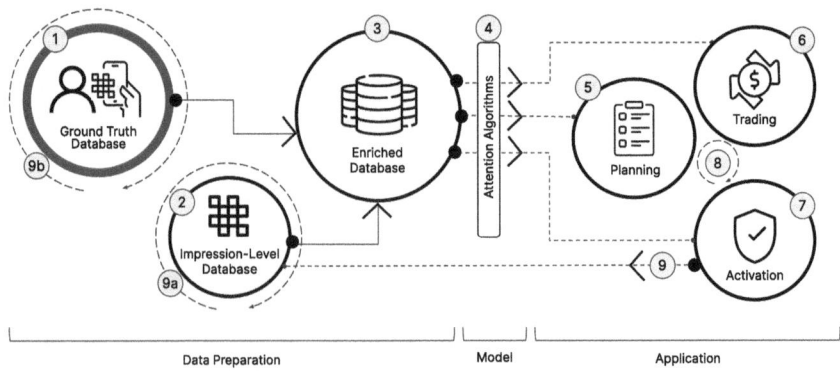

DNA of The Attention Economy. © Amplified Intelligence 2024

Fig. 4.4 Data flow for sustainable attention measurement

2. **Data Signal Database:** This dataset is non-human and includes data signals collected via JavaScript Tags from devices and publishers in the general course of impression delivery. This includes factors related to media consumption and implied on-screen engagement as well as ad placement and user device information. The Data Signal Database serves as a valuable source of information about the digital environment and the circumstances surrounding ad impressions.

3. **Enriched Database:** The Enriched Database is created by merging data from both the Ground Truth Database and the Data Signal Database. It combines the human-centric biometric data with the digital environment-related data signals. The inclusion of both biometric data and data signals from the same individuals is vital because it provides a contextual link between the human reactions (biometric data) and the environmental or situational factors (data signals) at the time of ad exposure.

4. **Attention Algorithms:** Distinct attention models are then built from the Enriched Database addressing attention time and attention focus to support metrics such as Attention Decay, Attention:Viewability Equivalence, Attention:Impression Equivalence and more. These models and metrics are then used in the main use cases of product delivery.

5. **Attention Models for Media Planning:** These models, designed for media planning tools, apply weightings to existing media plans to optimize for attention and enhance spending efficiency based on campaign objectives.

6. **Attention Models for Media Trading:** Custom probabilistic models developed for media trading enable advertisers to bid and purchase media using attention signals, factoring in the right combination and weighting of attention indicators at the point of transaction.

7. **Attention Models for Media Verification:** These models facilitate in-flight campaign optimization by measuring attention and assessing campaign performance for impressions after they are delivered.

8. **Feedback Loop between Applications:** While not part of the machine learning data flow as such, it's essential to note how each application informs the others. As advertisers and agencies progress through the ecosystem, each phase improves the performance of the next. For example, optimized planning enhances decision-making in trading, and optimized trading improves verification outcomes, leading to more effective media mix scenario planning.

9. **Ongoing Collection and Tracking:** Regular updates to all data are necessary to continually improve machine learning models to manage any changes in conditions. All new verification data feeds back into the

impression-level database, which, in turn, contributes to the enriched database.

Why is all this important?

Why does this matter? Because without applying rigor and striving for a clear, integrated roadmap, simplistic approaches to attention measurement can potentially do more harm than good. Our industry and the advertisers funding it have evolved from a point where "good enough" sufficed, and we are still paying the price through wasted media dollars spent on digital ads that were often not seen.

It is also important because human informed measurement is finally returning to the media landscape after it went missing for 30 years. Upon its return, we must request transparent validation from vendors claiming any presence of human data in their models. The MRC will inevitably consider a standard around 'how much ground truth is enough', until then this chapter should at minimum form part of any vendor RFI.

> **TAKE IT TO WORK**
>
> Beware the attention proxy that has little to no human ground truth. These are band aid fixes applied to a fracture in our industry that needs a full plaster cast.

4.2   The Future State of Currency

The Formation of a 'Non-currency' Currency

Currency has always been a representation of value, enabling civilizations to engage in the trade of goods and services. As time has passed, its form has evolved from primitive bartering to paper money, and most recently, digital currency. However, one aspect has remained constant: a currency's universal acceptance and stability within its regional ecosystem as the medium of exchange.

The term 'currency' gained prominence in advertising during the mid-twentieth century, coinciding with the rise of television advertising. This era necessitated standardized measurement and valuation systems. By the 1980s and 1990s, 'currency' solidified itself as the industry standard for measuring audience reach and related metrics, including ratings points and cost per thousand impressions.

It was never designed to maintain universal stability over time. Its creators failed to anticipate technological shifts and the evolving landscape of future ad delivery systems. This early currency was specifically tailored for measuring linear television audiences, disregarding the diverse measurement methods used across various media, such as radio, outdoor, and others. Even in the 1980s, not all reach was equal, highlighting the persistent issue with media currency.

While measurement has always presented challenges, recent research has brought to light the disparities between legacy and digital media. This has catalyzed a movement to enhance data quality and explore alternative currencies. NBCU's deconstruction of the US TV landscape serves as a notable example of this shift.

Outside of the advertising world, currencies designed for specific conditions or purposes are often termed 'complementary currencies'. These currencies address particular economic or social challenges, such as unemployment crises or liquidity shortages, when the national currency falls short. Complementary currencies typically have limited acceptance beyond their specific context or community and are not intended to replace the primary national currency.

Some examples include the Chiemgauer in Bavaria, the Sardex in Sardinia, and perhaps the most famous, The Continental. During the American Revolutionary War (1775), the American Congress issued paper money to its colonies as a new independent currency called The Continental. Within five years, the currency's value had plummeted to about 1% of its face value, causing chaos for the newly independent American people. By 1785, Congress introduced a new currency, the US dollar. However, the collapse of The Continental had left Americans wary, leading individual states to issue their own bills of credit, ignoring the federal government. In late 1792, the Coinage Act was enacted to regulate the United States' currency, with the silver dollar becoming the only lawful tender. A decimal system was introduced shortly after.

In the advertising industry today, a similar phenomenon is unfolding: a fragmentation of media measurement and a shift toward alternative currencies in response to the depreciation of our master currency. The industry is exploring new methods to measure value in the absence of stability, considering metrics related to attention, emotion, and context to bridge the gap.

In early 2023, Deloitte, CIMM, The 4A's, and the ANA collaborated to provide insights and perspectives on the transition to a "multi-currency" TV market. Some key points from the report include:

1. The current state of the multi-currency transition is characterized by a "test and learn" phase involving early trials, experimentation, and initial systems integrations.
2. There is consensus that multi-currency systems represent the future of the TV/video marketplace, with expectations of two to three coexisting vendors, but no more than five.
3. While big data plays a role it alone will not serve as the future of measurement and panels will continue to be vital in currency creation, serving purposes like calibration, personification, or validation.
4. Reconciling different metrics for the same "currency" event is a challenge in the alternative currency landscape, prompting questions about the effort required to arrive at the same number.
5. Plausible future scenarios include one dominant currency alongside independent measures, multiple currencies anchored to a common foundation, and wholly independent currencies.
6. The multi-currency transition is a collective effort, not driven by a single organization or initiative.

The evolution of measurement and currency in advertising signifies a significant transformation in the industry's landscape. We find ourselves in the midst of this transitional phase, with many unanswered questions. However, one thing is clear: the future of multi-currencies (or measurement to complement the chosen currency) is inevitable, and how we adapt to this change will shape the next three decades of our industry.

MEANWHILE IN THE REAL WORLD

It appears that a public breakup with Nielsen has taken place in the Land Down Under.

An overdue move by a bold CEO in Australia broke up with traditional measurement during their upfronts in late 2023. Mark Frain, CEO of Australia's biggest streaming service has said that measurement is too reliant on claimed behavior and wants to make their customers feel more secure about their ad dollars on their platforms. "We are taking measurement into a new age. A future where your investment is accurately measured." This will literally shake the foundation of TV measurement and start the ball rolling for change.

Foxtel decided to break away from the OzTAM ratings system, marking a significant shift in Australia's television measurement landscape. Foxtel Media

CEO Mark Frain announced that Foxtel would support a new viewing measurement system initially based on data from its million set-top boxes, with Kantar providing the analysis. However, the more groundbreaking development is the collaboration with US-based measurement provider VideoAmp, potentially reshaping TV measurement in Australia for the first time since 1999, forming the Video Futures Collective. This move reflects a shift in the industry's dynamics, similar to the changes in 1999 when OzTAM replaced Nielsen as the ratings provider.

Australia appears to be heading down a path similar to the frustrated US media sector, with the emergence of alternative currencies. While this transition may bring complexity, it is considered inevitable, and advertisers need to prepare for a multi-audience currency universe. The outcome may ultimately lead to a reunion between broadcaster assets and digital streaming services, but the path forward remains uncertain as the market evolves, creating room for alternative currencies.

A Marketplace of Measurement—The $600B Problem That No One Has Solved

Section by Jonah Goodhart

Digital advertising turned 30 in 2024. In those three decades, we have gone from $0 to $600 billion in annual global digital advertising spend. More than two-thirds of all money spent on advertising now goes to digital formats and channels. That is pretty incredible. What is also pretty incredible is that with that much spend, there is no measurement standard for digital advertising. How is it possible that we could be spending so much as an industry and not have consistent and trusted standards for measurement? Let's start with a little context.

Why does digital advertising measurement matter? In short, because it is supposed to tell marketers what works and what doesn't. Digital advertising, it has been said, is the fuel of the internet. It is what funds the vast majority of services and activity. For most digital content and service providers, advertising is their largest income source. In 2023 Google generated over $297 billion in annual revenue, with around 80% of that coming from digital advertising. Those ad dollars fund the ubiquitous search engine that most of us use, the #1 video service in YouTube, the #1 email service in Gmail, the #1 maps service in Google Maps, and so on. Google is the #1 recipient of advertising revenue on the internet. The #2 recipient, Meta, generated more than $126 billion in revenue in the same time period, around 97% of which was from digital advertising. And of course those ad dollars fund the services that billions of people around the world use such as Facebook, Instagram, WhatsApp, and more. And while there are examples of digital content and service companies that generate more of their revenue from non-advertising sources, like Netflix and of course Amazon, these companies are increasingly focused on digital advertising as key parts of their strategy. Netflix began selling digital ads in 2022 after famously saying they never would and Amazon, with $40 billion in digital advertising revenue in 2023, is the leading platform in the fastest-growing part of the digital advertising sector, called Retail Media. Any way you slice it, digital advertising and its success or failure is closely linked with the scaled services many of us think of as the internet itself.

Also, to date and in aggregate, digital advertising has seemed to work. Examples from large public companies demonstrate the direct impact to revenue from advertising spend, the majority of which is digital. Industry analyst Brian Wieser highlighted sales growth in earnings reports tied to increased advertising for some of the top CPG brands, including the world's largest advertiser, Procter & Gamble. P&G posted sales growth with "significant increases in marketing," L'Oreal reported sales growth "supported by heavy levels of advertising," and Colgate reported sales growth with "advertising spending increases of 20%." And it's not just CPG brands—companies like T-Mobile and Verizon both increased ad spend as of the time of this writing. So we can conclude that something must be working here. The challenge, though, is that there is little consistency in digital advertising, especially compared to legacy forms of marketing.

1. All Impressions Are Not Equal.

For the last 60 years, there have been five major mediums for advertising—television, radio, newspapers, magazines, and out-of-home. Formats in these mediums were more or less consistent. An ad on TV looked the same whether it was running on NBC or ABC or CBS or cable for that matter. It was always 15 or 30 seconds in length, always had audio on, and always covered 100% of the screen. Radio ads were traditionally 30 seconds long and in some cases 60 seconds. The difference from one platform to another was not usually noticeable to the consumer. Newspaper and magazine ads were standard sizes and formats too. Full page ads, half page ads, quarter page ads, back page ads, etc. The physical size of a newspaper (height and width) as well as a magazine, was also standardized. There was some variety but they were mostly consistent and predictable. Out-of-home had some variety but again, there was consistency (14 feet in height and 48 feet wide as an example).

With digital, we find ads that use some of the "old" standards but with an almost unlimited number of variations. Video ads can be bought as 15- or

30-second slots, but they can also be 6 seconds or 10 seconds or 3 seconds. They might take up 100% of the screen or 40% of it, depending on the format and environment. They can be skippable, auto-muted, or not. Newspaper and magazine ads might mostly be understood now as "digital display" and while there are some standards in that world, they are numerous and complex ("standard" display formats today include 728 × 90 pixels, 300 × 250, 300 × 600, 160 × 600, 970 × 250, 970 × 90, 300 × 1050, 120 × 60, 120 × 20, 640 × 1136, and more). Even in out-of-home, where there are standard billboards, the digital versions have reinvented sizes and now support standards like a height of 6 feet or 10 feet and widths of 12 feet or 30 feet. What all of this adds up to is a massive amount of complexity and, said simply, inconsistent ad experiences.

When digital wasn't as prominent, we could turn a blind eye to some of its challenges and complexities. Today, though, we live in a digital-first world. In the U.S., consumers spend more time streaming TV content than watching broadcast or cable, more time with digital audio than traditional radio, more time with digital news than with physical newspapers, and more time with digital magazines than physical ones. So the world has gone digital—no news there. But in the process, we have lost any consistency of formats and created a host of new problems (like bot impressions, made-for-advertising sites, brand safety challenges, lack of cross-platform identity solutions, gamification of many of the metrics we do have, and much more).

These collective problems have created a challenge when it comes to measurement. We can no longer simply ask how many impressions did you buy or in how many households did your ads run? Those concepts have become somewhat meaningless. The idea of "reach" needs to be qualified or caveated if we are talking about digital. If I bought 100 million impressions that were never on a viewable part of the consumer's screen, should I count those as "exposures"? Most brands would say no. If my ads were technically viewable (on the consumer's screen for some minimum standard of time like one or two seconds), but the placement garners minimal actual attention, does the viewability really matter if I am trying to judge impact? Perhaps not. If I got a viewable ad in a placement that someone did more likely pay attention to, but that someone was not at all in my target market (like an ad for AARP benefits shown to a 15 year old) or I reached the right group but in the complete wrong context (like reading about heart attack symptoms on WebMD and seeing an ad for buying web domains), it also misses the mark. And if I did get all of these things right—I served a viewable ad, in a context that made sense, to someone who likely could have paid attention to it and was in the right target market, but the ad itself didn't resonate—there was no emotional connection, no memorable effect—did the rest of it make a difference?

2. We Need to Stop the Siloes.

To be successful in digital advertising, brands must ensure their ads are valid and viewable, in attentive environments, shown to an appropriate audience, in an appropriate context, with a creative that resonates. And ultimately they need to measure outcomes (actual sales as well as concepts like brand awareness and brand favorability), and they need to connect those outcomes back to the ads they bought. In other words, they need to leverage smart unified measurement that focuses on the impact of their advertising. As an industry, by and large we are failing to do this today. We make decisions in siloes without seeing the "whole board". We choose media without knowing what creative will be running. We pick audiences without understanding context. And we choose optimization metrics like viewability or attention without also ensuring we have done our jobs in the other areas, oftentimes leading us to prioritize metrics that are in conflict with each other (like reach and viewability) and to deprioritize outcomes.

So how do we get smarter about digital measurement and as a result, digital advertising? With over 200 companies in the ad measurement space, there is clearly no one silver bullet solution—rather, there is an opportunity to leverage what many of these great companies are doing in a more intelligent way. We can bring metrics together. We can unify and harmonize measurement signals so they work with each other and not against. We can see the "whole board" (or most of it anyway) in one single place and we can decide on a centralized and smart repository.

These 200 measurement companies, though, can't solve the problem themselves. Many of them are competitive with each other and would be diametrically opposed to sharing their data with each other. Also, they will each naturally be incentivized for their proprietary metrics to be the most important, to be the so-called "metrics that matter", discouraging innovation in the name of competition. To move the industry forward, we need an independent platform that can unify the right signals on behalf of brands and publishers. We need a solution that is agnostic to the underlying metrics. We need a solution that encourages innovation and competition.

3. Bringing All the Measurement Solutions Together Might Bring Us Closer to the Holy Grail.

An independent measurement cloud with an embedded measurement marketplace may be one such solution. The concept of a measurement cloud is straightforward—unify and harmonize metrics and data in a centralized cloud-based platform that makes real-time modeling and decisioning seamless. The idea of an embedded marketplace is also critical to drive competition and as a result innovation. Most marketers or brands have some of the necessary solutions: they have a reach provider and a verification and brand safety solution, and perhaps have some of the other areas like audience or contextual intelligence or creative intelligence. But they rarely have all these things in one unified and actionable place, and they definitely don't have a seamless marketplace that augments their measurement stack with whatever they need in the moment they need it, on demand. The marriage of a marketplace inside of a measurement cloud stack is core: it is the seamless interaction of these two worlds that will help future-proof the digital advertising market.

For the 25 years that I have been in digital advertising, people have been asking "what metrics matter?" The answer, I believe, is not uniform. It depends on the category being advertised, the specific product or service being messaged, whether the brand itself is new to market or has been around for a long time, whether the brand story is simple to get or whether it needs some explanation—and much more. The metrics that matter are custom to the goals of the marketer. That is not going to change. What is now possible, though, is that we can create a set of tools that will help answer these questions in a clear and thoughtful way customized to the specific challenge the brand or publisher is exploring.

With an independent and agnostic approach, we can ask and answer questions that can bring us closer to the Holy Grail—getting the right ad in front of the right person, in the right environment, at the right time, and continually optimizing towards a desired outcome. The better we get at this framework, the better digital advertising measurement will do and the more digital itself can flourish on behalf of all of those who depend on it.

4.3   The Wrap Up: A Year in Ad Tech Will Make Anyone Grumpy

What a difference a year makes. We can all get cynical and grumpy in the ad tech business, it appears that these sentiments have found a home in ChatGPT itself.

In a blog post written by Dr. Augustine Fou in late 2022, a renowned figure never known to shy away from humorously highlighting the mess that characterizes the programmatic ecosystem, ChatGPT was approached to provide synonyms for certain ad tech terms that Dr. Fou deems as "questionable."

ChatGPT was still in its early stages at that time. Fast forward a year, and we revisited the same query, seeking a fresh response from ChatGPT. The results were even more cynical than before. Given the ChatGPT algorithm is continuously trained by user feedback, looks like lots of humans are thinking programmatic is BS, just as Dr Fou does (Table 4.2).

https://www.linkedin.com/pulse/adtech-acronyms-synonyms-bs-august ine-fou/

Table 4.2 A fresh response from Chat GPT

	Chat GPT response	
	2022	2023
Programmatic buying	Letting the computers do the shopping for your ads in real-time	Ads on autopilot—because human creativity is apparently extinct
Real-time bidding	The digital equivalent of a fast-paced auction for ad space	It's like a cutthroat auction for ads, where your budget gets devoured faster than you can say "rip-off."
Audience targeting	Zeroing in on the people most likely to buy your stuff and bombarding them with ads	Inviting people to your party, just so you can manipulate them later
Cross-device targeting	Stalking your customers across all their devices, like a digital private investigator	Stalking your customers relentlessly across their gadgets, because privacy is a joke to us
Brand safety	Making sure your ads don't end up on any sketchy websites or next to any NSFW content	Shielding your brand from the treacherous depths of the internet's cesspool
Viewability	Ensuring that your ads actually have a chance of being seen, unlike that billboard your company wasted money on	Ensuring your ads are in-your-face annoying, because subtlety is overrated
Programmatic direct	Cutting out the middleman and letting the robots buy your ad space directly from the source	Bypassing the middleman but still getting ripped off for ads

4.4   List of Contributors

Jonah Goodhart. Co-founder of Mobian and Montauk Labs

Jonah Goodhart is the Co-Founder of Mobian and Montauk Labs. Previously, Jonah was the Co-Founder and CEO of Moat (acquired by Oracle) and founding investor in Right Media (acquired by Yahoo). Jonah was also a Co-Founder of WGI Group, an investor in more than 100 companies.

References

Ad Age. (n.d.). P&G Slashes. https://adage.com/article/cmo-strategy/p-g-slashe/309936

Ad Age. (n.d.). *IAB's 2024 Predictions: Why Creator Economy, AI, and Privacy Regulations Will Have a Big Year.* https://adage.com/article/opinion/iabs-2024-predictions-why-creator-economy-ai-and-privacy-regulations-will-have-big-year/2526566?utm_campaign=Oktopost-2023-11+Native+Posts&utm_content=Oktopost-Facebook&utm_medium=social&utm_source=Facebook

ARF. (2023). *The ARF Sets Out to Map Attention Measurement Landscape as Phase One of Attention Validation Initiative* [Press release]. https://thearf.org/wp-content/uploads/2023/04/ARF-Attention-Validation-Initiative-Phase-1-Launch_FINAL-Release.pdf

Baker, R. (2015). Unilever CMO Calls for 100% Viewability and 'Real Action' on ad Fraud. *AdNews.* https://www.adnews.com.au/news/unilever-cmo-calls-for-100-viewability-and-real-action-on-ad-fraud

Barwise, P., Bellman, S., Lang, A., Varan, D., & Weber, R. (2015). How Reliable Are Neuromarketers' Measures of Advertising Effectiveness? *Journal of Advertising Research, 55*(2), 176–191. https://doi.org/10.2501/JAR-55-2-176-191

Burrowes, T. (2017). 'Murky' Digital ad Chain Holding Industry Back, Warns Unilever CMO Keith Weed. *Mumbrella.* https://mumbrella.com.au/murky-digital-ad-chain-holding-industry-back-warns-unilever-cmo-keith-weed-474029

Campaign Asia. (n.d.). *Exclusive Q&A: Mars CMO Andrew Clarke on Transparency and Fighting for Your Agencies.* https://www.campaignasia.com/article/exclusive-qa-mars-cmo-andrew-clarke-on-transparency-fighting-for-your-agencies/433521

Clarke, A. (2023). *Exclusive Q&A: Mars CMO Andrew Clarke on Transparency and Fighting for Your Agencies. Campaign Asia.* https://www.campaignasia.com/article/exclusive-qa-mars-cmo-andrew-clarke-on-transparency-fighting-for-your-agencies/433521

Eng, A. (2023). The Rush to Measure Attention Calls for a Collaborative and Coordinated Approach. *Adweek*. https://www.adweek.com/media/universal-def inition-attention-measurement-coordination/

Gozman, V. (2022). The Slow Death of Third-Party Cookies. *Forbes*. https://www. forbes.com/sites/theyec/2022/09/12/the-slow-death-of-third-party-cookies/?sh= 5cbf38ff4026

IAB's 2024 Predictions: Why Creator Economy, AI, and Privacy Regulations Will Have a Big Year. *Ad Age*. https://adage.com/article/opinion/iabs-2024-predictions-why-creator-economy-ai-and-privacy-regulations-will-have-big-year/ 2526566?utm_campaign=Oktopost-2023-11+Native+Posts&utm_content=Okt opost-Facebook&utm_medium=social&utm_source=Facebook

Ipsos. (2017). *Passive Simplicity*. https://www.ipsos.com/sites/default/files/ct/public ation/documents/2017-08/Passive_Simplicity.pdf

Ipsos. (n.d.). *Audience Measurement 50: Pushing Boundaries*. https://www.ipsos.com/ en/audience-measurement-50-pushing-boundaries

Krstić, J., Kostić-Stanković, M., & Cvijović, J. (2021). Green Advertising and Its Impact on Environmentally Friendly Consumption Choices: A Review. *Industrija (Ekonomski Institut, Beograd), 49*(1), 93–110. https://doi.org/10.5937/industrij a49-31692

Levy, M. G. (2023). Machines Learn Better if We Teach Them the Basics. *Quanta Magazine*. https://www.quantamagazine.org/machines-learn-better-if-we-teach-them-the-basics-20230201

Marketing Week. (n.d.). *Mark Ritson on Viewability and Fraud*. https://www.market ingweek.com/mark-ritson-marc-pritchard-viewability-fraud-speech/

Meier, D. (2023). Now Some 29 Percent of Upfront Buys are Expected to Be Transacted on Alternate Currencies, According to Advertiser Perceptions, as Agencies seek Viewership Guarantees Across Different Screens and Devices. *Videoweek*. https://videoweek.com/2023/05/10/alternate-currencies-to-be-given-airtime-at-upfronts/

Metz, C. (2019). If a Robotic Hand Solves a Rubik's Cube, Does It Prove Something? *The New York Times*. https://www.nytimes.com/2019/10/15/technology/ robot-hand-rubiks-cube.html

Moore, G. A. (1991). *Crossing the Chasm: Marketing and Selling High-Tech Goods to Mainstream Customers*. Harper Business.

MRC Outcomes and Data Quality Standards September 2022 Final. https://med iaratingcouncil.org/sites/default/files/Standards/MRC%20Minimum%20Stan dards%20-%20December%202011.pdf

Nelson-Field, K., & Taylor, J. (2012). *Facebook Fans: A Fan for Life?* Admap, WARC.

Nelson-Field, K. (2022). *Attention Applied: The DNA of the Attention Economy*. WARC.

Nelson-Field, K., & Jung, H. (2022). *The Shape of Attention: Mining Gold from Individual Level Attention Viewing Patterns*. WARC Exclusive.

News.com.au. (n.d.). *Uber Warns of Price Hikes up to 85% Due to Workplace Law Shakeup*. https://www.news.com.au/finance/work/at-work/uber-warns-of-price-hikes-up-to-85pc-due-to-workplace-law-shakeup/news-story/4b6398f39c27608 3dee5ebda53d190f6

Noble, T. (2013). Neuroscience in Practice: The Definitive Guide for Marketers. *Admap, 48*(3), 30–45.

Online Advertising Spending Worldwide. *Statista*. https://www.statista.com/statis tics/237974/online-advertising-spending-worldwide/

P&G slashes. *Ad Age*. https://adage.com/article/cmo-strategy/p-g-slashe/309936

Ramadam, A., Peterson, D., Lockhead, C., & Maney, K. (2016). *Play Bigger: How Rebels and Innovators Create New Categories and Dominate Markets*. Piatkus.

Ritson, M. Mark Ritson on Viewability and Fraud. *Marketing Week*. https://www.marketingweek.com/mark-ritson-marc-pritchard-viewability-fraud-speech/

Rogers, E. (2003). *Diffusion of Innovations* (5th ed.). Simon and Schuster. ISBN 978-0-7432-5823-4

Shields, M. (2015). The Most Powerful Player in Media You've Never Heard Of. *The Wall Street Journal*. https://www.wsj.com/articles/BL-269B-2957

Statista. (n.d.). *Online Advertising Spending Worldwide*. https://www.statista.com/sta tistics/237974/online-advertising-spending-worldwide/

Unilever CMO calls for 100% Viewability and Real Action on ad Fraud. *AdNews*. https://www.adnews.com.au/news/unilever-cmo-calls-for-100-viewability-and-real-action-on-ad-fraud

Universal Definition of Attention Measurement Coordination. *Adweek*. https://www.adweek.com/media/universal-definition-attention-measurement-coordinat ion/

Williams, T. (2023). New York Is Cracking Down on Airbnbs to Ease Housing Pressures. Here's How The Big Apple and Other Cities are Regulating Short-Term Rentals. *ABC News Australia*. https://www.abc.net.au/news/2023-09-07/new-york-airbnb-crackdown-major-cities-short-term-rentals/102825318

Yaccarino, L. (2023). Premium Predicament: What's Being Measured? [LinkedIn post]. https://www.linkedin.com/posts/lindayaccarino_premium-predicament-whats-being-measured-activity-7018552255326904321-R15n/

5

A Guide to Now and Next

"Media and creative need to work together, the silos create ineffectiveness and
inefficiencies now more than ever."
Brian Jacobs 2023.

In 2022, AI and Society Strategist Sofia Pires in her award winning body
of work on System 3 thinking, reminded us of a quote from roboticist Hans
Moravec back in 1990 where he claimed that we were approaching a "water-
shed in the history of life - a time when the boundaries between biological
and post-biological intelligence will begin to dissolve." According to Pires,
this long-anticipated juncture has now arrived, with artificial and human
intelligence seamlessly intertwining in ways that often escape our notice. Pires
introduced the groundbreaking theoretical concept of System 3 thinking,
building upon the foundation laid by Nobel laureate Daniel Kahneman
in 2012 regarding the intricacies of human cognition and decision-making
across various contexts.

System 1 thinking is fast, automatic, and intuitive and largely involves
unconscious thought processes. This mode of thinking demands minimal
effort and attention and relies on heuristics and shortcuts to help us make

rapid decisions and judgments, though it can be prone to biases and potential for error. System 2 thinking is slow, deliberate, and analytical and largely involves conscious effort and mental energy. This mode of thinking requires more effort and attention and is often used for complex tasks that require problem-solving and decision-making. It is less prone to biases and errors but can be time-consuming and mentally taxing.

While System 3 thinking is not an established concept in cognitive psychology, Pires suggests that it represents a more nuanced level of cognitive processing or an additional layer of decision-making beyond Systems 1 and 2. It is intricately tied to the integration of artificial intelligence (AI), poised to become an integral facet of human cognition. In essence, System 3 entails humans thinking swiftly and automatically, with the full support of AI-driven deliberate and analytical thinking.

In this new era for brands, we face unique challenges. Consumer attention towards advertising is currently at an all-time low due to measurement system complexities and the unalterable user experience of media platforms. Consequently, the influence of creativity on decision-making is evolving significantly. The question arises: how can brands make a lasting impact in this environment? How can we bridge the gap between creative and media silos to work effectively, especially given the substantial challenges, and opportunities, brought about by technology? As we move into a phase where AI is poised to exert even greater sway over our thoughts and interactions with media and brands, this chapter addresses some core fundamentals of how brands can proactively position themselves to achieve visibility 'now' and to build long term strategies and memorability for the 'next'.

5.1   The Paradox of AI Generated Attention

Section by Sofia Pires
In the 1970s, a time when the world wasn't yet at our fingertips, and we didn't casually carry trillions of bytes of content in our pockets, Nobel laureate economist and cognitive psychologist, Herbert A. Simon, delivered a prophetic message: as information becomes abundant, attention becomes the scarce resource.

Today, we can all relate to this feeling of being personally overwhelmed and struggling to wade through the vast sea of content.

However, there's a twist when we consider the role of generative AI in producing content to maximize human attention.

Contrary to Simon's famous quote, "A wealth of information creates a poverty of attention," when it comes to generative AI it's the opposite that is true: **more information can lead to greater attention.**

To clarify this argument, I'll start by explaining how generative AI works today (at the time of publishing this text) and how the concept of attention underpins its recent success. Then, I'll delve into how this connects with human attention, and I'll finalize by suggesting strategies that we can use to maximize it.

Note that my focus in this analysis is on **how to use Generative AI to drive human attention**, the latter defined as the ability to actively process specific information in the environment while tuning out other details. I am intentionally leaving out other opportunities to use generative AI in marketing that are not directly related to this task.

I'm also stripping a lot of the complexity of the topic with the purpose of leading you through the core thinking and getting to a framework for action.

1. In both humans and AI, attention is dependent on context

As marketing professionals, artists, politicians, teachers, or even parents, communication is our main tool to create attention.

With the advent of Generative AI, we can now explore novel ways to maximize our efforts. To do so, we must start by understanding the new capabilities of machines and the traditional processes of human beings.

I'll start by giving a brief overview of how generative AI works through its own mechanisms of attention, which will then guide us in this exploration of how we maximize human attention using AI.

a. In AI, "Attention" is how large language models understand context

Natural Language Processing (NLP) is what enables Generative AI to understand human direction without the need for code, complex rule-based computer instructions.

NLP is the branch of computer science focusing on teaching machines how to make sense of human-generated data, and how to learn from this data. As new, better NLP systems emerge, anyone can now communicate with computers in our natural language and get the machine to generate text, images, video and audio.

The tipping point of this process has been the recently developed transformer model, based on deep artificial neural networks which are not only able to efficiently recognise individual words, but also to understand them in their context.

That has been a game changer for Generative AI, and what in computer science is called the attention mechanism: when the model considers all words in the text and assesses their relevance in each context. For instance, if we write, "a man on a bank fishing," the AI understands that "bank" refers to a riverbank rather than a financial institution because the words "bank" and "fish" are given the highest weights in the neural network.

When we strip away the layers of complexity in how generative artificial neural networks function, we see that their "understanding" of natural language is often driven by the context.

This ability to effectively process context inputs is evolving rapidly, such as in the recently released Language Learning Model (LLM) called LongLLaMa, based on Meta's LLaMA, which is pioneering focused transformer training for context scaling. This means that the number of prompts or data input into the system can be much higher without losing accuracy.

As we increase input data, we improve context. The more we improve context, the better the systems become at aiding human users in creating content that maximizes consumer attention.

b. In humans, attention is determined by contextual determinants

Psychology has identified determinants that affect attention in human beings. These are external factors such as intensity, size, motion, contrast, repetition or novelty of the stimuli, and internal factors like personal interest, emotions, moods, goals, and past experiences, amongst others.

Although this is not news to communication professionals, up until now it has been impossible to factor in all those contextual determinants into the content we create.

But thanks to the new transformer models, all those determinants can be factored into how we use generative AI, which I'll explain further.

The basic principle is that as we increase the input data into generative AI, we also increase accuracy in the understanding of the context that the audience is in.

2. The more the data, the richer the context, the higher the attention AI can generate

We have been reliant on the belief that comms professionals must possess a deep understanding of human attention, gained through years of empirical observation, experience, and researched consumer insights. Usually, this understanding is distilled into a culturally relevant truth that drives creative ideas and is a standard requirement for any creative briefing.

With generative AI, we no longer need to be filtering down knowledge into one killer insight. In fact, we shouldn't. The more data parameters we input, the better the AI will comprehend what is interesting and how to generate the most relevant response to each and all individuals, thus capturing their highest attention.

In summary, the more the information, the richer the context, the more relevant and interesting the content, the higher the attention.

This approach to using the generative AI models to maximize attention through painting the richest picture of context is what I'm calling **AI-Generated Attention.**

But this is not a single-point solution, as we'll see below, where I suggest different ways to explore it.

3. A framework for brands to generate attention with Generative AI

The ability to drive attention will depend on the brand's approach to it, which I'm simplifying visually into two axes: customisation level and engineering complexity (with a direct correlation to costs and implementation timelines) (Fig. 5.1).

The choice of what to do depends on needs and resources available. To better assess it, I'll expand on each of these approaches separately.

a. Prompting and iteration
In this, the process of AI-Generated Attention is empirical and experimental. The LLM will follow instructions based on small amounts of data that it is able to take in. In this, because we're just using an external LLM

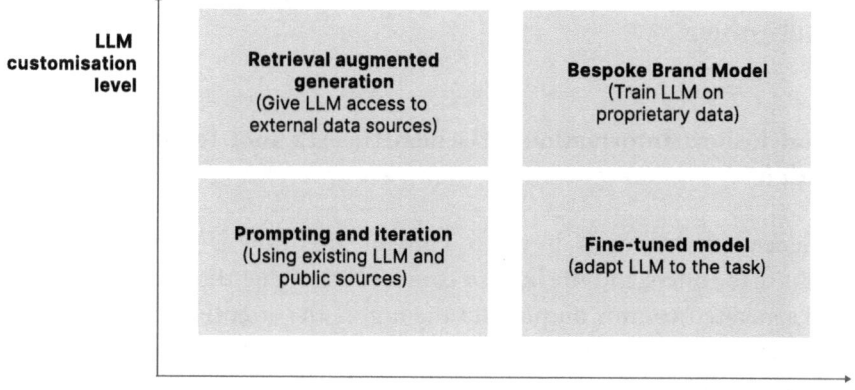

Fig. 5.1 Pires Attention/GenAI Framework 2023

such as ChatGPT, we must always assess if and how we want to input confidential information.

b. Retrieval augmented generation (RAG)

This is about plugging-in external or proprietary audience research data. The advantage is to link relevant data that improves the understanding of our audiences' context, besides the base knowledge of the LLM.

Note: *Prompting and iteration and Retrieval augmented generation* can only take in data such as text, images, audio and video. Tables with numerical data will have to be transformed into conclusions through a supervised learning model, which would take more than 6 months to train and deploy.

c. Fine-tuned model

This approach is to adapt existing open-source models to the comms task we have. This is obviously limited by open-source models' availability to what we require, but one can only anticipate that as time goes by, the number of those pre-trained models will increase dramatically.

d. Bespoke brand model

This is where attention becomes truly personal. This is the model that dominates context because it has been trained on proprietary data. To maximize consumer attention, this Generative AI model will be able to factor in external comms characteristics intensity, size, motion, contrast, repetition or novelty of the stimuli, and internal determinants like personal interest, emotions, moods, goals, past experiences, amongst others. It will continuously learn from consumer interactions and become increasingly better at providing the right answer, to the right person, at the right time. It's worth clarifying that all these approaches must respect legal and ethical principles. Even where regulation is still playing catch-up, I recommend looking into the industry advisory bodies, such as the IPA and ISBA's guiding principles for agencies and advertisers on the use of generative AI in advertising.

4. Conclusion: Information is Generative AI's tool for driving human attention

AI Generated Attention is when Human attention is maximized by AI systems that understand the human context. The richer the context, the better is the generated comms output and the higher the attention level it achieves.

To maximize AI-generated attention in our brand comms, we must provide the best possible picture of the context we are in. This approach no longer relies on finding the insight that will lead to the magic solution, but it focuses on using a large spectrum of personal and context-rich attention data. The right approach ranges from applying the basic prompting to proprietary data-driven models, as illustrated in the matrix above.

The paradox of AI generated attention lies in the amount of data required to maximize human attention. In a world with an increasing wealth of information, AI-generated attention can be harnessed as a valuable resource to stand out and enrich brand-consumer interactions.

It's the start of a new era where a wealth of information creates a wealth of attention.

TAKE IT TO WORK

Contrary to Simon's famous quote, "a wealth of information creates a poverty of attention," when it comes to generative AI it's the opposite that is true: *more information can lead to greater attention.*

5.2   Modern Distinctiveness

In his January 2022 No Mercy No Malice blog post, Scott Galloway drew our attention to the enduring legacy of Steve Jobs with the memorable phrase, "When I Say Steve, You Say Jobs." Although Galloway's blog primarily focused on the distinction between vision and fraud in Silicon Valley, it serves as a timeless reminder of our brain's innate ability to establish connections and associations when the appropriate mental training data is present. Then in late 2023, the notable Bill Harvey drew our attention to a concept similar to this, but by this time the emergence of GenAI was in full swing. He emphasized that 'we each have a ChatGPT within us,' suggesting that humans possess a comparable predictive function within our own brains, which had largely gone unnoticed for an extended period. Harvey pointed out that, much like ChatGPT, our internal mechanism forecasts our upcoming thoughts based on our past thoughts (akin to training data) and our most recent thoughts (similar to the autocomplete prompt). This internal biological AI, playfully referred to as the 'robot' by Harvey, enhances our thoughts by employing familiar language patterns we've used previously. In both instances, whether it's the inner 'robot' or ChatGPT, their predictive ability owes its success to the substantial training data they've absorbed.

As we think about the direction of generative AI, and consider Sofia's insights regarding the contextual information needed for AI-Generated Attention and System 3 thinking, it becomes clear that there are a couple of other points to make about how creativity will fit into the next era of memorability.

Training Data for Your Future Brand

Firstly, using context cues to grow a brand isn't new at all. Professor Jenni Romaniuk has been advising brands for quite some time on the idea of 'training' consumers' own neural networks to recognize distinctive brand assets, preparing them for the crucial moment of purchase. Distinctive assets are things that strongly tie the brand in the memory of most consumers. These can encompass various creative aspects like logos (think of the Nike Swoosh), colors (such as Cadbury Purple), fonts (like the Coca-Cola type-face), shapes (like the iconic VW Beetle), slogans (who doesn't recognize Just Do It), characters (like Rich Uncle Pennybags from Monopoly), ad styles (think Red Bulls high-energy vibe), or auditory elements, like a catchy jingle (remember the Stuck on Band-Aid tune).

The moment you utter something like 'Finger lickin' good,' it immediately triggers recognition in most of us, and your brain likely conjures up the image of the brand's equally famous character with the white beard and mustache. However, a word of caution—simply using these elements in the background or as an afterthought in advertising won't transform them into genuine assets. To be truly considered a Distinctive Asset, an element should evoke the brand (and only that brand) without any prompting, and it should do so for nearly 100% of consumers, almost 100% of the time. Achieving this is no mean feat; it demands time, unwavering commitment, and financial investment. But here's the catch, for distinctive assets to remain in memory, they need to be visible. However, as discussed in previous chapters, this is not as straightforward as it may seem due to three key problems:

1. Many online ads are viewed for very brief periods, often falling below the attention-memory threshold. This makes it difficult to refresh memory cues and nearly impossible to create new assets (see Fig. 5.2).
2. Even when we are paying attention, our focus frequently shifts between attentive and inattentive states. As a result, brands can easily go unnoticed during moments of inattention, especially because branding is not always continuously present.
3. Brands often adapt their content to fit the specific youthful or authentic 'theme' of the platform they're on. While this can be effective for grabbing attention, more and more we notice that recognizable assets are not prominently featured.

All of this leads to a situation where new consumers of a product category, including the younger generation, and occasional buyers of a brand, do not receive sufficient exposure to these assets. They are not adequately trained to associate, for example, 'The Golden Arches' with 'Burgers,' resulting in insufficient familiarity and frequent misattribution to competitors. This pattern is evident in the attention and outcomes data collected over the past several years, explaining the low attention/high misattribution double jeopardy pattern mentioned in Chapter 3.

Figure 5.2 serves as a reference for brands, aiding them in contemplating the utility of various attention levels, as previously examined in Chapter 2. Media platforms that support heightened levels of active attention contribute more to the establishment of distinctive assets. Conversely, at lower levels of attention, their role is to refresh.

TAKE IT TO WORK

Context cues (distinctive assets) are the glue between your brand and your customer's memory. This is more important than ever in this highly distracted world, coupled with a time where the lines between AI and reality are blurred. Build and protect them at all costs.

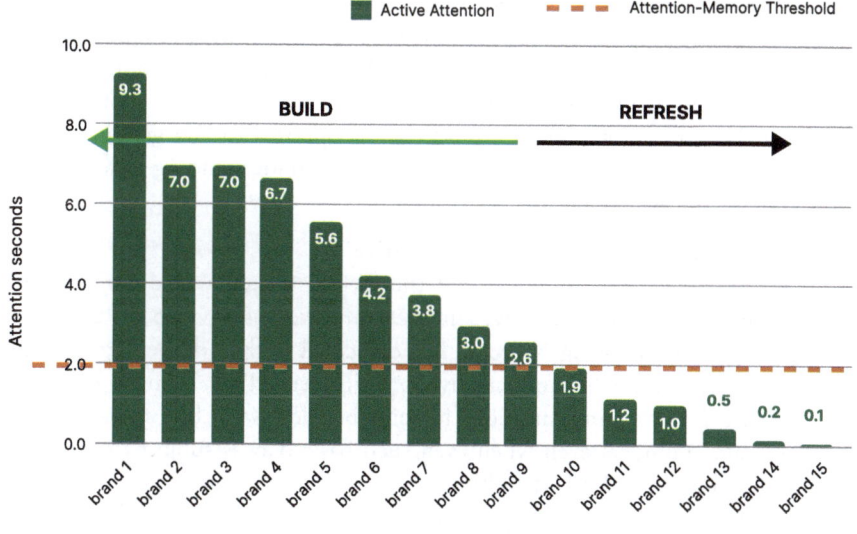

© Amplified Intelligence 2024

Fig. 5.2 The attention-memory, build-refresh guide

EXPERT INSIGHT: Moving From the 'Pathetick' to the Sublime by Brian Jacobs

"Whatever is common is despised. Advertisements are now so numerous that they are very negligently perused, and it is therefore become necessary to gain attention by magnificence of promises, and by eloquence sometimes sublime and sometimes pathetick." (Samuel Johnson, 'The Idler' No.40, 20th January 1759).

We have always known that some ads work better than others, and that for ads to work at all there has to be not only an opportunity for them to be seen, but for them actually to be noticed.

Even I do not personally remember Dr Johnson, but I do remember a study done by the agency I was working at in the 1980's, Leo Burnett, whose legendary Media and Research Director, Dr Simon Broadbent took himself off to individuals' homes and spent a few evenings sitting in their living rooms watching family members watching television.

Even back then, in a simpler time, before the invention and emergence of online media forms, it was obvious that different TV shows attracted different levels of attention and so did different editorial contexts in print media. But the obsession with opportunities to see, the biggest possible gross numbers and the lowest cost-per-thousands, meant that Simon felt it necessary to put a more considered, nuanced view to our clients.

No creative sets out to bore the audience into ignoring his or her work, whilst in media the best of us have tried to plan with attention levels in mind ever since we first learned what an audience was.

Media vendors conducted studies on the fluctuation of TV attention levels between programs and within ad breaks during programs. Additionally, they investigated the effectiveness of ads placed on inside covers compared to those appearing on pages within the magazine. But these were about justifying higher prices for premium positions, as opposed to any genuine wish to understand consumer behavior, and to use that understanding to feed into the content the agency created.

1. The division between media and creative

Unfortunately, the complexities of the media market, where a video on one channel is simply not viewed in the same way as a video on another (despite them both being 'videos'), has coincided with a deepening of the division between media and creative practitioners. This in turn has led to a desire for over-simplification, for an obsession with lowest common-denominator numbers even when even such basic data is subject to misuse, misunderstanding and mis-definition.

We need to take a breath and remind ourselves what exactly it is we're trying to do. We are trying to place a piece of commercial communication in front of the right people in such a manner as to increase the chances of it being noticed. Every commercial communication is different, every channel is different, every audience is different. An individual watching TikTok watches content on it differently from the way he or she watches YouTube, Netflix or broadcast TV. And that individual's behavior is different from his neighbor's. We're playing three-dimensional chess, with audience, channel and creative variables and with each and every combination producing different outcomes.

2. Some advice for your three-dimensional chess game

Fortunately, these days we don't have to rely on an ad legend sitting in peoples' homes to understand how people are noticing ads (or not). We have access to massive amounts of data and decades of expertise. Simon would have loved it. Unfortunately, there are no easy answers though. There are patterns and similarities but there are also exceptions, which is where competitive advantage lies. Headline averages can only take you so far; they're a guide, a benchmark to aim to beat. So it's better to treat every campaign plan as unique, to consider all channels as different, and plan how and where you first create and then deploy your communication assets accordingly. And moreover, media and creative need to work together, the silos create ineffectiveness and inefficiencies now more than ever.

Do these simple things and your advertising will improve, and it will be noticed. Perhaps more importantly, it will trend towards 'the sublime' and away from 'the pathetick'.

Context Cues and GenAI

Another thing to consider is this—the content you create today will play a significant role in shaping the training data for future generative AI systems. To illustrate this point consider the following straightforward, non scientific, example: we provided two widely used image-generating AI with four very similar requests, differing only in the product category:

1. Design an ad for **cola** in USA
2. Design an ad for **running shoes** in USA
3. Design an ad for **fried chicken** in USA
4. Design an ad for **coffee** in USA
5. Design an ad for **burgers** in USA

When examining the top 4 AI-generated ads from both tools (Fig. 5.1), it became evident that these ads prominently featured branded elements from

Coca Cola in nearly all cases (88%, including the polar bear), even though there was no specific request for this. As you move down the list, the utilization of the Nike Swoosh decreased to 50%, and for KFC, it was even lower at 38%. Notably, none of the recognizable assets associated with Starbucks and McDonald's were explicitly utilized in any of these ads. Overall, the average proportion of AI-generated ads with distinctive assets included unprompted was 44%. However, if we specifically instruct the AI to design 'an ad for Nike,' 'an ad for Starbucks,' and so on, that average nearly doubles. The key point here is that while the training data contains information about these brands, the AI doesn't always recognize the associations between the brand categories and the specific brands when generating content unprompted.

It's essential to understand that generative AI operates based on neural networks that have undergone extensive training using vast datasets comprising text, images, audio, and video. These networks generate new content by recognizing patterns they have learned from the existing data. Consequently, the presence or absence of specific brand assets in the ads, and its connection to a specific category, sheds light on the characteristics of the historical training data.

None of us truly knows where generative AI will lead us in the future, but there has never been a more crucial time for brands to establish a foundation of 'mental training data.' This includes recognizable brand cues that are directly linked to the category, in anticipation of what lies ahead. Your contributions to content creation today will likely have a significant impact on shaping the capabilities and inclinations of generative AI systems and our own "inner robots" in terms of recognizing and representing your brand in the future (Fig. 5.3).

TAKE IT TO WORK
Branding itself may not directly capture additional attention, but it plays a crucial role in influencing outcomes such as driving sales.

MEANWHILE IN THE REAL WORLD
Are you ready for a 70's rewind?
    In 1972, David Ogilvy, celebrated for his influential book "Ogilvy on Advertising," which has educated countless generations of marketers and introduced the concept of 'The Burr of Singularity.'

Fig. 5.3 Brand unprompted GenAI ads

He said, "The average consumer now sees 20,000 commercials a year; poor dear. Most of them slide off her memory like water off a duck's back. Give your commercials a flourish of singularity, a burr that will stick in the consumer's mind. One such burr is the mnemonic device or relevant symbol—like the crowns in our commercials for Imperial Magazine."

He recognized back then that standing out from the crowd was crucial and being distinctive was key. This point is even more significant today given his reference to 20,000 commercials exposed to in a year, is likely per day now. A decade prior to his foundational book, Time magazine anointed him with the title of "the most sought after wizard in the business."

As it also happens, he required a lesson in addressing a woman as a 'poor dear'—a reflection of the 1970s, with all its good and bad in the advertising world.

EXPERT INSIGHT: The Predictability of Attention by Dr. Jared Cooney Horvath

It would not be wrong to say that there are no two identical carpenters in the world. Each artisan possesses his or her own unique vision, temperament, and kinaesthesia. This means it would be practically impossible to develop meaningful universal principles with regards to the larger craft of woodcraft.

Luckily, all carpenters are forced to use the same basic tools. Each artisan must employ nearly identical hammers, chisels, and sandpaper. This means it is entirely possible to develop meaningful universal principles with regards to the tools used to undertake woodcraft.

Who cares?

It would not be wrong to say that there are no two identical consumers in the world. Each customer possesses his or her own unique aims, history, and understanding. This means it would be practically impossible to develop meaningful universal principles with regards to the larger field of human awareness.

Luckily, all consumers are forced to use the same basic tools. Each customer must employ nearly identical neurons, neurotransmitters, and neurological networks. This means it is entirely possible to develop meaningful universal principles with regards to the biological substrates used to drive human attention.

Although dozens of these universal principles exist, two are of primary importance and worth exploring here.

The first concerns **'dorsal filtering'**.

Simply put, when attending to common stimuli, every human being employs the dorsal attention network: this network acts as a sensory filter which effectively separates relevant from irrelevant stimuli. It is your dorsal filter allowing you to focus on these words while ignoring the sensation of your clothing against your body, the smells wafting through the air around you, and the sounds ticking your ears right now.

Here's the important bit: the dorsal filter is not passive—it does not cleanly process incoming stimuli in order to show you the world how it truly is. Rather, the dorsal filter is active—it explicitly tweaks incoming stimuli in order to show you the world as you think it should be.

> The fcst taht you can raed tihs pagararph wtih mnimimal eforft is tetsaemnt to the inrecdblie pwoer of yuor dosral flietr to cahgne inocmnig ifonramtoin to fit yuor ideas for the wrlod. Unofrutntaley, tihs laeds to a vrey ssrcy cnocluison…

When employing the dorsal filter, human beings are not truly living in the world around them; rather, they are living in their own minds. We all use our previous experiences of the world to build predictions about incoming stimuli, meaning most of us are literally living in the past, not the present moment.

This leads to the second universal principle of attention: **'ventral shifting'**.

When human beings are confronted with stimuli that do not match their current predictions—when incoming information is unlike anything experienced before—then the dorsal filter is unable to function and will shut down. When this occurs, the brain shifts into the ventral attention network and, physiologically, everything changes.

As an example of this shift, what is this image below?

If you're like most people, you have no clear prediction for what this image should be, so something in your biology has changed. You may notice that your heart rate and breathing have slowed; that your pupils have dilated; that your skin is generating a small tingle. Most people refer to these physical sensations as 'confusion' or 'curiosity'.

If you felt anything, that is the sensation of your ventral network kicking on; that is the sensation of leaving your predictions behind and landing in the true and real present moment. Right now, your brain is furiously trying to build a new schema, mental model, or prediction that you can employ if you ever come across a black and white image like this again in the future.

It is an inescapable fact that human beings will never learn better, faster, or easier than after making the ventral shift because their entire biology has entered into a mode that facilitates mental updating.

What does any of this mean for the fields of marketing, advertising, and branding?

I will leave that to you to determine. I promise, filtering this information through your specific expertise will lead to far more meaningful and useful revelations than anything I could come up with sitting here at my computer.

I will, however, say this: once people make the ventral shift, they are biologically primed to learn—unfortunately, this does not guarantee effective learning. There remain universal principles of memory, feedback, and motivation that must be considered if we hope to guide individual change in specific directions.

And lest I leave you hanging…

Now that you have a prediction, your brain can comfortably move back into dorsal mode and you'll wonder how you ever struggled to make sense of that original image.

The Age of Average

The call to rediscover the value of context cues may not, ironically, receive the attention it deserves. In the backdrop of the 'Age of Average,' as coined by Alex Murrell (Fig. 5.4) during a keynote address at the West Of England Design Forum in late 2022, a troubling trend spanning the past two decades emerges. A substantial portion of content, ranging from user-generated content to branded advertisements, taglines, and logos, has shown minimal stylistic evolution. This pattern is primarily driven by a tendency to conform to prevailing norms, particularly in response to the era of social media, where straying too far from the norm can be deemed risky. Consequently, many brands opt for alignment with their peers in an attempt to reach broader audiences, resulting in the emergence of 'blanding.'

'Blanding' is characterized by brands adopting a minimalist and homogenized aesthetic, marked by elements like sans-serif fonts, clean lines, restricted color palettes, and an overall simplification of their visual brand identity. The core objective of blanding is to project timelessness, crafting a brand that appears contemporary and appealing to a broad audience. Murrell's observations extend beyond consumer brands, affecting various domains, including television shows, app icons, city skylines, motor vehicle designs, and more.

Fig. 5.4   Alex Murrells, The age of average

However, the implications of this trend are profound. Over the past two decades, we have effectively conditioned future generative AI tools (as well as future consumers) with a backdrop of uniformity. Reversing this homogenization necessitates a concerted effort to reintroduce contextual distinctiveness into our digital landscape. This underscores the critical importance of nurturing unique and easily recognizable brand assets in an era where differentiation and individuality are becoming increasingly crucial, particularly in our continued reliance on AI and advanced technologies.

In 2023, a notable instance of this trend was highlighted by Ethan Decker, the founder of Applied Brand Science. When news emerged that a long-standing healthcare giant intended to replace its iconic, time-honored script logo of 130 years with a more contemporary design, purportedly signaling a renewed emphasis on pharmaceuticals and medical devices, Decker shared his thoughts on LinkedIn. In his LinkedIn post, he remarked, "J&J blandifies their 136-yr-old logo. It's like putting carpet over beautiful old pine floors." (Fig. 5.5).

In summary, most brands, even well-established ones, are unintendedly engaged in the process of 'untraining' the younger generation while assisting the older generation in forgetting about them. This comes largely from the choices made in the media planning stage, but also from choices about fitting in. However, the ability to achieve quick recognition with minimal prompting will become increasingly crucial in the evolving landscape of AI and System 3 thinking. Brands should regard their distinctive assets as valuable training data for both the now (inner thought processes of consumers)

1886

Johnson&Johnson

2023

Johnson&Johnson

Fig. 5.5 Ethan Decker's Blandifying

and the next (emerging AI technologies), and find better ways to maximize their opportunity for attention. These assets will serve as a lifeline in the future.

EXPERT INSIGHT: The Importance of Distinctive Assets (A Small Brand Story) by Dan White

Being distinctive means having characteristics that make something quick to recognise and easy to distinguish from alternatives. Brands should strive to be as distinctive as possible because of the commercial benefits distinctiveness can bring.

Our brains are engineered to spend as little energy as possible as we navigate our daily lives. This means we only pay attention to things that might be relevant to us, and we take decision-making shortcuts whenever possible. Distinctiveness in marketing is effective because of our need to preserve precious mental energy. It plays three important roles:

1. Getting noticed

Our minds only pay attention to things around us that are potential threats to our physical or emotional wellbeing or opportunities to improve them. This is why we notice things, including marketing activities, that stand out from the environment and are either new and unexpected, or highly familiar and known to be relevant. This explains why highly distinctive advertising is so effective.

2. Building brand memories

One of the big challenges with advertising is making sure the ideas and feelings it creates become connected with the brand in people's memories. If a brand has spent time and money to establish a set of distinctive assets in people's minds, these can be featured in advertising to ensure new, long-lasting brand associations are forged. Leveraging distinctive brand assets means that every dollar spent on advertising will have greater impact and a longer-lasting effect.

3. Triggering brand memories

If we need to buy something, any brand that comes to mind is more likely to be chosen. Our minds assume that a salient brand is the good option—after all, that's how we make most of our decisions in day-to-day life. We tend to rely on our gut instinct. If a brand has built up a set of distinctive assets—a logo, mascot, jingle, or even a unique visual style—these can be used along the path to purchase to trigger brand recognition and relevant associations, making the brand feel like an obvious choice.

When I left the corporate world and needed to create my own, personal brand, I was keen to leverage what I'd learnt about the importance of distinctiveness. From day one, all of my illustrations have used the same three colors, the same font (which is based on my handwriting), and the same graphical style (which has been easy, since it is the only way I know how to draw!). Based on the feedback I have received, the distinctive style of my illustrations has enabled me to build a brand that has become well-known within the world of marketing. For a small brand (a freelance illustrator and accidental entrepreneur), this is the ultimate opportunity to compete with bigger brands. Turns out creativity does have the power to punch through the sea of ordinary.

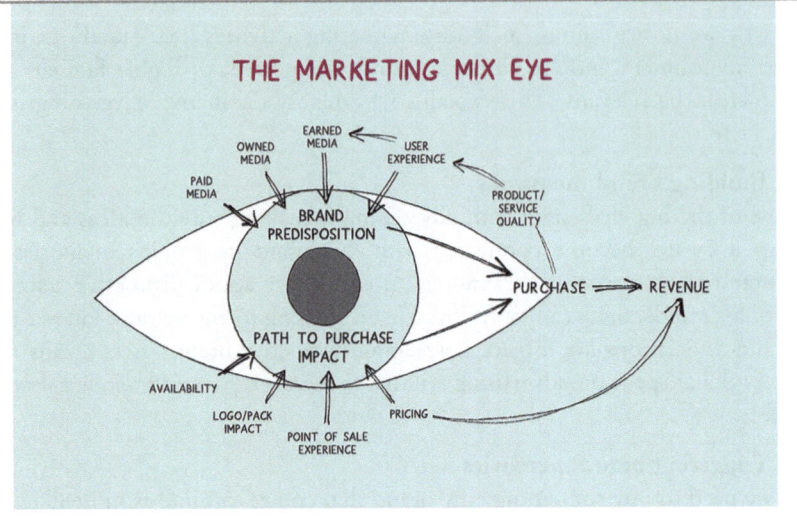

THE MARKETING MIX EYE

https://migroup.com/blog/dan-white-powerful-marketing-visuals/

MEANWHILE IN THE REAL WORLD: A Masterclass in Advertising in a Low Interest Category

Just before Christmas 2023, Andrew Tindall, Global Partnerships Director as System1, posted an endearing shout out to a company that doesn't perhaps have the most interesting or the most inspiring product, but a product nonetheless everyone needs particularly at Christmas. This company sells batteries, everyone needs them, but no-one really thinks about them, certainly not in any salient way. Except the Duracell Bunny. We all know him. The Duracell Bunny made its debut in 1973, establishing itself as an enduring symbol of long-lasting power using Television as its stage. In Duracell's original ads, battery-powered toy rabbits gradually slowed down, leaving only the Duracell-powered one active. The concept of these ads lasted decades.

Mind you it wasn't always smooth sailing for this little pink dynamo.

In 1988, Duracell let its trademark lapse and was no longer running the campaign. That's when rival Energizer swooped in and created a near identical asset to its competitor and a near identical ad style to boot. Energizer then filed for its own trademark, which was followed by Duracell filing for a new trademark, referencing the original campaign. But it was too late, and Duracell ended up agreeing to an out-of-court settlement that gave Energizer rights to use the bunny in the United States and Canada, and Duracell the rights in the rest of the world.

Duracell hadn't advertised in 5 years but in 2023 resurrected the long established Bunny with a sweet Christmas Ad by Wunderman Thompson. The ad was about Santa and Rudolph who crash landed in the snow because Rudolph's nose ran out of batteries and they couldn't see to fly. Luckily the Duracell

Bunny was near who raced to the rescue replacing the lower quality zinc batteries with long lasting Duracell for the safe return to the Christmas eve skies.

In November 2023 System1 did a review of the ad, and offered clever advice regarding the value of distinctive assets in a low interest category in a low attention world. Andrew Tindall said:

"No child wakes up on Christmas day excited about the little pack of batteries taped to their new toy. In fact, no one cares about batteries ever. It's energy. As close to a commodity a thing can get.

That's what makes the consistent commitment to the Duracell Bunny by Wunderman Thompson so genius. Orlando Wood has shown the repeated use of these brand characters over multiple campaigns leads to great immediate and future business effects with the IPA (Institute of Practitioners in Advertising).

Firstly, they are great as they ensure the brand is omnipresent throughout the advertising. Our own research has shown that, no matter the channel, our focused attention comes in bursts/pulses. There's no guarantee which part of the creative will hold the most focus. If you have a branded character on the screen all the time, the creative is actively branded throughout.

And no, a logo at the bottom of the creative doesn't do the same job. No one is drawn to this or wants to look at it. A character earns your attention. People often get this wrong with brand assets in advertising. Just because they are on the screen doesn't mean the job is done.

Secondly, the Duracell Bunny carries the story and with it emotion. Here, it's dropped into a culturally relevant situation. It gives the brand a reason to show up. They could have shown us the now iconic black and gold batteries with messaging that they last longer. Or they can land this in an emotional way to earn our attention and build stronger memory structures."

Credits given to: Luis Estrada López, Neil Godber, Ants Bell, Jason Berry, Alex Horlock, Jonny Park, Lizzie Alleyne, Victoria Riggo, Rudi Macloskey, Marco Montanaro, Laura Spendolini and Katie Oldfield.

Original Post: https://www.linkedin.com/feed/update/urn:li:activity:713124 9619635695616/Ad: This Christmas choose Duracell. By Wunderman Thompson. www.duracell.info

There are lessons in here for us all:

1. Emotions nudge attention: Emotions are one of the few triggers that help to nudge up attention on any platform.
2. Protect your distinctive assets: The greatest asset, and the most important intellectual property you will ever have, are your distinctive assets. Grow them, protect them, keep them relevant and present.
3. Distinctive assets are even more important in a low attention world: When you have only 1 second before the creative you have put blood, sweat and tears into is rudely skipped over, the one thing that might mean that 1 second is not a complete waste of investment is if your distinctive assets present early. This might not mean a character like the Duracell Bunny, this could be color, ad style or sonic assets.
4. Teach the newcomers: If you want these to be relevant in decades to come you have to assume that newcomers and/or youth will not have such

fluency with the brand. Only high attention media can do that (where ads are watched beyond the attention-memory threshold).

5. Be patient and track results: Even after years off air this distinctive asset still indicated strength of brand recognition. When your CMO is sick of the asset, often consumers aren't.

5.3   Attention Triggers

We are in a constant state of divided attention, we don't stop and engage with advertising in any sustained or focused manner. Instead, we switch frequently between attention and in-attention across the entire course of the ad being on screen. This distracted focus poses a formidable obstacle for brands aiming to convey their message effectively. In this environment, the concept of attention 'triggers' becomes crucial. Remember as discussed in Chapter 2 and 3, this distraction is normal, it cannot be altered in any significant way as it is a direct consequence of the nature of the user experience itself, however triggers can act as catalysts to re-engage and refocus the distracted mind, similar to how you might snap your fingers in front of someone's face to get a moment of attention, but are not typically the cause of longer viewing (which is ultimately constrained by the user experience as discussed).

This attention-switching phenomenon isn't exclusive to advertising; it extends to our daily lives. For example, when we're walking down the street, we often operate in a subconscious state until something triggers our attention. This trigger can be a railway crossing signal up ahead (a bottom-up trigger) or a friend honking their horn and calling out our name as they pass by (a top-down trigger). Once the train passes or our friend drives away, the importance of our attention diminishes, and we return to our subconscious thoughts, like remembering to buy dinner ingredients.

In the extensive literature on attention theory, there is a consensus among scholars in the fields of attention and dual processing regarding what happens to our attention during subconscious and conscious states. When exposed to certain stimuli, such as advertising content, our state of consciousness and subsequent level of attention can change based on the guidance triggers within.

There are two main types of guidance triggers mentioned in the literature: top-down and bottom-up triggers.

Top-down attention is driven by personal goals and intentions, often referred to as endogenous attention. For example, when we consciously search for something online or come across a personally relevant advertisement, we direct our attention with purpose and control, even if briefly. In such instances, our primary focus shifts to the intended task, and we engage in conscious thinking. However, when we realize that the information we actively sought is irrelevant, we revert to either lower levels of attention or a more pre-attentive state.

Conversely, external triggers driven by the stimulus itself, often referred to as exogenous triggers, fall into the category of bottom-up triggers. For instance, when an advertisement incorporates elements such as strong emotions, animated visuals, or loud sounds, it automatically captures our attention at a lower, more instinctive level. In this situation, the advertisement becomes a peripheral rather than a central focus, requiring less demanding, semi-conscious processing. Bottom-up attention triggered by stimuli tends to fluctuate rapidly, and this has implications for advertisers when designing content aiming to create surprise or novelty. This also underscores why emotional content can be effective but typically does not fully break through the threshold of sustained attention. It's worth noting that many advertisements are viewed in a passive, low-attention state rather than an active one, making bottom-up triggers a central aspect of creative strategy.

Bottom-up attention triggers can take various forms:

1. **Unexpected Elements:** Surprise twists, surprises, or sudden changes in the narrative, imagery, visual or auditory presentation can jolt viewers out of their distracted state and refocus their attention on the ad.
2. **Emotional Hooks:** Content that evokes strong emotions, whether it's humor, empathy, excitement, or nostalgia to either the story or a character tends to capture and retain viewer attention more effectively.
3. **Interactive Features:** Interactive elements that encourage viewer participation, such as clickable links or immersive experiences, provide a sense of participation and engagement, increasing the chances of sustained attention.

In summary, in an era synonymous with distracted focus and frequent attention shifts, attention triggers play a vital role in capturing at least some level of viewer attention. When viewers momentarily divert their attention from an advertisement, strategically placed attention triggers can reignite their interest and redirect their focus back to the content. In this way, attention triggers serve as valuable tools for advertisers to ensure not all of their message is lost in the sea of distractions. Let's dive into a couple.

Unexpectedness

A recent book by Dr. Jared Cooney Horvath, titled 'Stop Talking, Start Influencing,' along with his award-winning education program called 'The Learning Blueprint,' sheds light on the concept of unexpectedness and its implications for advertisers struggling to capture attention. In his work, he discusses an experiment by Ben Jones, a former creative director at Google, who set out to explore human attention by attempting to create what he called the 'Most Skippable Ad' ever. His primary goal was to understand what exactly leads people to disengage from digital advertisements.

Initially, Jones believed that nothing would captivate viewers less than a 30-second advertisement on YouTube featuring only a black screen—devoid of visuals, audio, or any content whatsoever. He thought this minimalistic approach would undoubtedly lead everyone to skip the ad, providing a clear baseline to study the elements necessary to capture attention effectively. To test his theory, Jones aired the 30-second black screen advertisement. To his surprise, almost no one chose to skip it. Remarkably, a significantly larger number of people were willing to endure 30 seconds of a blank screen compared to the more flashy and attention-grabbing ads available. This served as evidence of one of the fundamental principles of attention, which is 'unexpectedness,' and how to harness it. When people browse YouTube, they typically expect digital ads with flashing images, thumping music, and a loud sales pitch. So, when they encounter an ad with absolutely nothing—simply a black screen—their expectations are disrupted, triggering their attention.

Dr. Cooney Horvath explains that this happens because the brain is constantly trying to predict what will happen next, positioning itself ahead of the unfolding world. The key takeaway from this section is that to truly capture an individual's attention, one must disrupt their predictions—and the best way to do this is by NOT delivering what they anticipate. He states that when a prediction fails, the brain shifts its focus to the present moment, intensifying attention and activating memory networks to work at full capacity. In other words, when a prediction is thwarted, the brain becomes ready to absorb and retain new information to make sense of what it encounters. However, the book emphasizes a crucial point: a prediction can only be broken once. Once a new prediction forms, the same material cannot disrupt it again. Knowing that an ad has a black screen makes it unlikely for viewers to engage with it again for an extended period. It's a bit like a punch line that is not funny once you've heard it. This insight underscores the importance of innovation and novelty in capturing attention.

His work also discusses other relatable examples, such as stumbling on miscounted stairs in the night, spilling coffee by reaching for a mug that was not in the spot you thought it was, or encountering an unexpected obstacle while driving which shocks your system. These instances evoke a heightened sense of attention because inaccurate predictions lead to consequences, sometimes good sometimes bad. Consequently, when a prediction fails, the brain enters a state that allows for quick and effective 'updating' of information in order to avoid this failure in the future.

Dr. Cooney Horvath suggests, "keep them uncertain, keep them guessing, and you will keep them paying attention." However, he also emphasizes that attention is just one part of the story; once you have the audience's attention, you must still educate them in a way that leads to deep, lasting, and accurate memories. This is where the concept of context cues becomes significant.

TAKE IT TO WORK

Viewers switch focus easily. Advertisers need to understand the triggers that snap viewers out of their normative zombie state.

MEANWHILE IN THE REAL WORLD

It would seem Blankety Blanks was a 1970's Version of ChatGPT (another 70's rewind).

Blankety Blanks was an Australian game show in the 1970s based on the American game show Match Game. There was also a UK version called Lily Savage's Blankety Blank which ran for 11 years on BBC1. The Australian Blankety Blanks was hosted by Graham Kennedy on Network Ten from 1977–1978. It only ran for two seasons, but its legacy lives on in Australia today. Apart from its classic 1970s colorful, yet cringe-worthy displays of sexual innuendo, blue eye-shadow and smoking on stage, Blankety Blanks was essentially a comedy program with a game format built around it.

The host read a short scenario (often laced with double entendre) which, at some point, contained the word BLANK. The contestants and celebrity panelists then had to fill the BLANK with a word of their own. The BLANKS written by the celebrity panelists often lead to scenes of hysteria, particularly because in the 70 s highly suggestive BLANKS were the essence of the comedy. With characters like Ugly Dave Gray, Dawn Ding a Ling, Noel the Null Fairy and Peter the Phantom Puller you can likely understand why it could never be repeated on television today.

This is a comedic example of what Professor Horvath says in his book about filling in the blanks. Both Blankety Blanks Australia (1970s) and Horvath's first book (2019) were published at a time before generative AI was a household staple. Perhaps the creators of Blankety Blanks should connect with Bill Harvey and Dr Horvarth, as they have all dabbled in the mysteries of the 'inner robot'.

Emotions

It's a well-established fact, supported by extensive research, that our emotions play a crucial role in grabbing our attention and influencing our behavior. Emotions can be thought of as powerful signals that not only capture our focus but also guide our actions. When we experience intense emotions, our bodies react instinctively without requiring conscious thought.

In the study of emotions, researchers often employ two fundamental (orthogonal) dimensions: 'valence,' which represents whether an emotion is positive or negative, and 'arousal,' which quantifies the intensity of our emotional responses.

Arousal measures the strength of our emotions, encompassing feelings like excitement, sadness, surprise, or even discomfort. Valence, on the other hand, categorizes emotions as either pleasant or unpleasant. While some experts argue that only positive emotions are effective in advertising, psychologists contend that both positive and negative emotions can be impactful in engaging people.

While the literature on this subject is extensive, there is a consensus across disciplines regarding the relationship between emotions, advertising, and attention. These collective findings universally agree that emotions function as attention-grabbing mechanisms and play a significant role in enhancing memory, accelerating comprehension, reducing errors, prolonging focus, and elevating recall and preference for products and brands. In a nutshell emotions have long been considered a conductor for further cognitive and behavioral outcomes.

None of this is new news. What is new though, is how emotions aid attention under the constraints of the user experience.

Let's briefly revisit the discussion in Chapter 2 regarding the chicken and egg debate, as well as the Attention Elasticity concept discussed in Chapter 3. It's important to recall that our research indicated that both strong and weak creative content (determined by the total number of active attention seconds) experience a consistent decline in attention across different platforms. Our findings show that the platform's functionality plays a major role in capturing attention while the strength of the ad execution, from a creativity perspective, has less impact. This finding has important implications for advertisers, as it implies that enhancing the quality of creative content rarely results in breaking through established attention limits.

However, there remains a notable distinction between the best and worst creative content in terms of the amount of attention it garnered, as illustrated in Fig. 5.6 (avg. 40% difference). The question arises: What accounts for this difference? In other words, why is the creative content of Brand M perceived as less effective than that of Brand A?

Building upon the foundation laid by Rob Brittain in Chapter 2, in collaboration with Peter Field and the Ad Council of Australia, a third phase of research was conducted and presented by WARC at Cannes Lions 2023 titled 'The Triple Opportunity of Attention.' Using data from the Effies database, one of the objectives of this work was to uncover the creative elements that consistently make one ad execution more successful in capturing active attention than another. The key to this distinction, as revealed by the research, lies in the emotional strength of the creative content. However, this work went further into understanding how such creative elements work under the constraints of the media.

All of the Effies ads were examined through the lens of our own attention collection system in parallel with System1's emotive Star Rating system. Our findings align with existing literature, confirming that high arousal emotions indeed have a notable impact on the amount of attention earned. In this study, we observed an overall increase of 12% in active attention

	Platform A	Platform B	Platform C	Platform D	Loss Best to Worst %
Brand A	7.2	4.5	3.4	2.3	-68
Brand B	7.0	5.5	3.3	2.9	-59
Brand C	6.9	3.7	3.3	3.2	-54
Brand D	6.5	5.1	2.9	2.8	-57
Brand E	6.4	4.1	3.2	2.7	-58
Brand F	5.9	4.3	2.7	2.5	-58
Average — Brand G	5.8	3.8	3.1	2.7	-53
Brand H	5.5	4.8	3.4	2.4	-56
Brand I	6.0	3.9	2.8	2.4	-60
Brand J	6.1	3.8	2.5	2.2	-64
Brand K	5.5	2.8	2.5	2.3	-58
Brand L	5.4	3.9	2.3	2.5	-54
Brand M	4.6	4.3	2.5	2.4	-48
Loss Best to Worst %	**-36**	**-49**	**-32**	**-31**	

Stronger Creative ↑ / Weaker Creative ↓

Platform Attention performance: Best ⟶ to ⟶ Worst

© Amplified Intelligence 2024

Fig. 5.6 Example creative data by best/worst attention, split by weaker/stronger creative

seconds when comparing high-emotion ads to their low-emotion counter-parts. However, the upside of high emotional content is highly dependent on the platform on which the ad plays. For example, there is a greater uplift in active attention seconds between high and low attention on the high attention media than there is on the low attention media.

To illustrate this point, let's refer to Fig. 5.7. We noted a mere 3% difference in active attention seconds between high and low emotive content on a low-attention platform, whereas this difference soared to 18% on a high-attention platform (with a mid-level increase of 14%). It is essential to reinforce that these results pertain to identical creative executions, indicating that the same creative whether it is high or low intensity emotion performs better or worse, in line with the overall performance of the platform (as we have said earlier).

In essence, emotions undeniably play a significant role, but the choice of media platform still remains the dominant factor. In other words, while high arousal emotions can boost attention seconds, their ability to amplify attention is constrained by the inherent limits of the chosen platform, akin to the

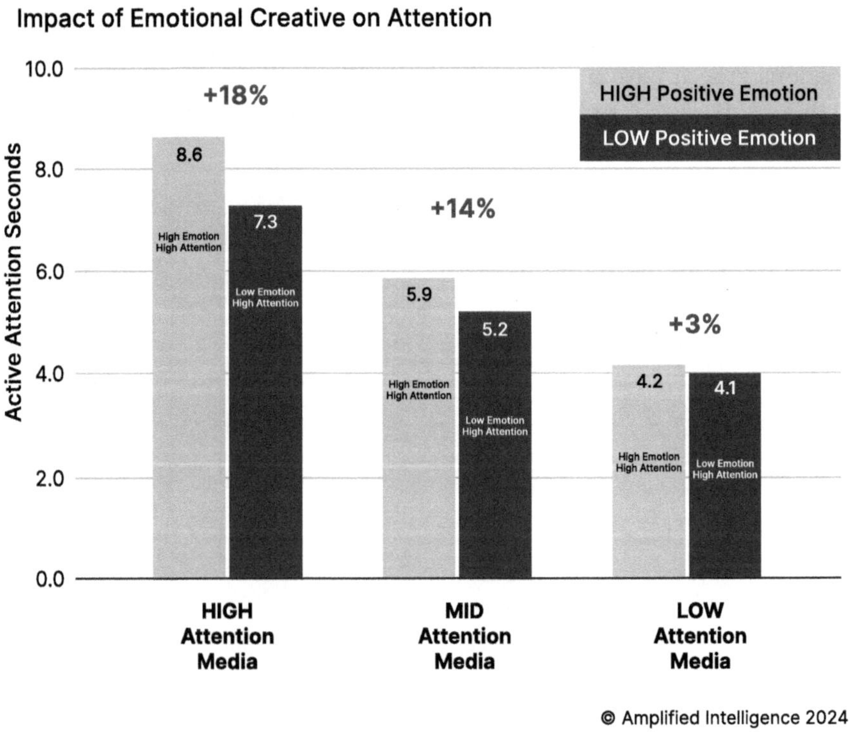

Impact of Emotional Creative on Attention

© Amplified Intelligence 2024

Fig. 5.7 High/low emotional creative on high/low attention media

concept of an elastic limit. Meaning highly emotive creative will only extend attention therefore up to the natural 'attention ceiling' of the platform. It also tells us that testing creative in an artificial way tells you at best whether Creative A and B are different, at worst it will tell you nothing as to what to expect in the real world.

TAKE IT TO WORK

Emotions help, but BLANKS without BLANK simply cannot work. Advertisers should work to BLANK all creative.

EXPERT INSIGHT: The Art and Science of Emotive Advertising by Orlando Wood.

If media science can tell us something of the canvas for our work, I'd like to describe what we might put on that canvas for broad and popular appeal. I'm going to describe how we might create advertising that moves, and I'm going to turn not just to psychology to help us, but also to art history, because as Bill Bernbach once put it, "Only art can make you feel, and only feeling can make you act."

Advertising is rather like putting on a show, so I'm going to tackle this in three acts.

Act 1: A Masterclass from Popular Culture

Let's begin with a masterclass from popular culture—a scene from a very famous film, *Star Wars VI: Return of the Jedi*—"He is my brother" (TM & © Lucasfilm Ltd. (LFL) 1997). I'd invite you to watch the scene, listen to the dialogue and above all look at the faces of the characters during this pivotal moment in the film. If you can't find it or are rushed for time, I have sought to convey it below.

Scene start>>

The Death Star detonates in a spectacular explosion. Ewoks, droids and rebels excitedly dance and hoot.

Threepio *(excitedly)* "They did it!".

We cut to Han and Leia. Han has been attending to Leia's wound. Han is kneeling on the right; Leia is sitting to our left. Both are looking up at the sky, with the Ewoks still whooping behind.
Han Solo turns his head to look at Leia, his face etched with concern.

Han: "I'm sure Luke wasn't on that thing when it blew."

Leia: *(Looking away into the middle-distance, contemplative, as if straining to hear a voice)* "He wasn't. *(And then with a slight flick of the eyebrows)* I can feel it."

Han: *(Swallows, pulls back a little, his face tightening and turning away slightly, then softly)* "You love him… *(he forces a reconciled smile)*, don't you?".

Leia: *(Re-engages, returns Han's look, smiles, shrugs slightly, hiding nothing, appearing puzzled)* "Yes."

Han: *(Face hardening, as if realizing his luck is changing, seeking to conceal his indignation)* "All right. I understand. Fine. *(He pauses.)* When he comes back – I won't get in the way."

Leia: *(Closes her eyes, lets out a breath, smiles, shakes and lowers her head, and then looks up at Han, looking him in the eye)* "No, it's not like that at all… *(She pauses, leans in, places her right hand on Han's shoulder)* he's my brother."

Han's eyes widen and he glances to his left, his head follows, his mouth is open, he turns his head again, this time fully away to his left. Leia places her open hand gently on his left cheek, turns his head back to face her, and she draws his head towards her radiant face. She kisses him.

Marking the turning point, the score moves here from John William's 'Luke and Leia' theme, to 'Han and Leia' theme.

The camera pans out to show Han's face mid-kiss, he is still thinking, his eyebrows move, he pulls back from the kiss, open-mouthed, his eyes and his whole face lifts, with joy, relief and elation. And a close-up of Leia reveals delight and warmth in her face and eyes too.

An Ewok appears, waving his arms.

Han now fully understanding the situation, draws Leia close with his open right hand, mirroring Leia; they kiss. He pulls away in a sharp movement, but continues to engage her with a loving look. They both turn to draw the adjacent Ewok into their embrace.

Scene end>>

Anyone who has ever seen the film will no doubt remember the scene. The betrayal of emotion on the human face at a moment of revelation—an emotional turning point in the narrative. Italian artists in the 17th-century had a term for precisely this; they called it *moto e azione. Moto,* from the verb *movere,* 'to move', meaning the stirring of the passions betrayed visibly to the outside world; and *azione*—bodily actions, poses, and expressions that mark crucial moments of the story. For this was the 'age of affect'—a popular kind of art—when artists would conceive their paintings and sculptures around emotional turning points such as this one, like stills from a film. They knew that to create affect, you have to show affect; that to move, you have to show movement. And if an insight of some kind could be revealed at this emotional turning point, this would only serve to amplify its emotional force. If you look at Caravaggio's *Boy Bitten by a Lizard* or Bernini's *David*, you will see exactly this creative principle at work.

Act 2: *Moto e Azione* in Advertising

If *moto e azione* was important in 17th Century art, then it is critical in advertising today. There was one agency who, I believe, implicitly understood this. Alongside DDB, they were at the forefront of the creative revolution in the 1960s and 1970s in the UK. They were called Collett Dickenson Pearce. Look at any of their work—perhaps start with the Hamlet cigar or the Cinzano commercials—and you will see how central it was to their success. This was an agency that intuitively understood how to convey emotion—and elicit it in the viewer –through the bodies and faces of their characters, and often with an emotional turning point. They also understood that if the brand was central to the moment of revelation, they could amplify further the ad's emotional force. *Moto e azione.*

To understand the relationship between attention, emotion and creativity, I look to the work of neuropsychologist and philosopher Dr Iain McGilchrist. McGilchrist is perhaps the world's expert on brain lateralization. Since the 1960s there has been a mistaken belief that the left and right hemispheres might do different things. It is not that they do different things, but that they do things *differently*, have different modes of attention, as McGilchrist might put it. McGilchrist explains that the right hemisphere presents the world to us with a 'broad-beam' attention, has greater emotional depth and plays a pivotal role in understanding context, metaphor, music, and humor. It is also better associated with memory—in particular memory of people, places and events (episodic memory)—and the communication and understanding of emotion through the body. The left hemisphere by contrast, brings a 'narrow-beam' or focused attention to bear; it breaks down what is presented to it into smaller parts, seeks to control and manipulate what it sees. It is rather direct, linear, with little sense of lived time or narrative; it is not so understanding of people, depth, music or humor either.

In a collaboration with Ad Council Australia ("Triple Opportunity"), Karen Nelson-Field, Rob Brittain and I embarked on an analysis of creative that involved studying campaigns to identify the features that might be associated with the modes of attention associated with the left and right hemisphere's modes of attention—broad or narrow. We then overlaid these on business effect data for each campaign captured by the ACA. The results unequivocally highlighted the superiority of right-brained advertising—what we might describe as advertising with *moto e azione*. With their greater emotional depth and narrative appeal, the 'right-brain' campaigns outperformed the left-brained on both long-term objectives and overall effectiveness. This is because right-brained advertising is better able to lodge the brand in memory. Furthermore, we uncovered evidence that right-brained advertising, advertising with *moto e azione,* also works on those in the market now, to create short-term impact. It therefore helps both present and future earnings.

Final Act: The Triple Opportunity: Crafting Advertising Success

For any company wanting to squeeze greater value from their advertising—seeking to create both present and future earnings—*moto e azione* is a highly valuable artistic principle. As I show in Look out, advertising with human vitality, implicit communication and spontaneous changes in facial expression is more likely to capture attention, elicit an emotional response, create fame and result in lasting business effects. In our collaboration, Karen, Rob and I provided evidence for three growth opportunities for advertisers today—media selection, creative strength and investment above your size. High-attention media, emotive advertising, and positive extra share of voice (ESOV) are key to unlocking lasting advertising success. Creative strength is an important part of this winning recipe.

Key Points to take to work:

1. Emotive advertising does more than simply extend the attention paid to your advertising; it helps to Create mental availability by lodging your brand in memory and bringing your brand to mind before any other in the buying moment. It can therefore establish business effects now and into the future.
2. Creative can develop an emotional response in the viewer by drawing on the artistic principle of *'moto e azione'*; the outward expression of internal feeling via the face and body, the moment of revelation, an emotional turning point.
3. For the strongest business outcomes, it is high-attention media, with emotive advertising (for broad-Beam attention) supported by high investment (positive ESOV) that is needed.

Why Viral Cats Have No More Lives

Circa 2012 was a time when most thought putting a cat on a skateboard would guarantee a viral hit, much research was being done on how to crack the viral code. Some work of our own published in 2013 put a quick end to the romance that free reach was easy to gain if you simply built 'better' creative executions (The Science of Sharing, Oxford University Press). It was a wake-up call for those who believed that going viral was as simple as crafting the perfect meme.

This work was built on the foundational work of Berger and Milkman in 2010, which explored the connection between emotional responses and the sharing of articles from the New York Times to consider the relationship between emotional engagement and distribution efforts, often referred to as 'seeding' at the time.

Berger and Milkman proposed a physiological perspective, suggesting that the level of "arousal," a well-established emotional construct, plays a crucial role in driving viral diffusion.

Questions we sought to answer included:

1. Do videos that evoke high-arousal emotions tend to be shared more frequently than those eliciting low-arousal emotions?
2. How does the concept of Valence, the emotional tone (positive or negative) of content, factor into the sharing equation?
3. What carries more weight in driving sharing: the inherent qualities of the creative content itself or the distribution efforts?

To conduct our research, the team (from Ehrenberg Bass Institute) utilized two substantial datasets: one containing non-commercial content and the other featuring branded content, both totaling 400 videos. The focus of this work was on real sharing data (many tens of thousands of shares per day), steering clear of predictions, views, or other proxies for online audience behavior. We used emotional arousal pairs, as a more objective measure than traditionally used subjective scales. In addition, we scrutinized videos with both high and low sharing levels, not just those that achieved viral success (see Fig. 5.8).

The core findings were ahead of their time:

Positive		Negative	
High Arousal	Low Arousal	High Arousal	Low Arousal
Hilarity	Amusement	Disgust	Discomfort
Inspiration	Calmness	Sadness	Boredom
Astonishment	Surprise	Shock	Irritation
Exhilaration	Happiness	Anger	Frustration

Fig. 5.8 Arousal/Valence Grid. Nelson-Field, 2013

1. While creative quality certainly enhanced the likelihood of sharing, it was the distribution efforts, or 'seeding,' that remained the driving force behind video sharing.
2. Creative quality was dubbed the 'icing on the cake,' indicating that content with high-arousal emotions was more likely to be shared above the expected average.
3. The intensity of emotions, whether they were high or low arousal, emerged as a more significant factor than valence (positive or negative) in predicting sharing behavior.
4. Videos that evoked high-arousal emotions managed to break through the clutter of online content and were the most memorable among viewers.

This research didn't just dispel myths about virality; it provided invaluable insights for marketers. At the time, many were surprised by these findings, given how deeply ingrained the (wrong) concept of virality had become in marketing strategy. It also offered a clearer perspective on what marketers could achieve with their creative content within the constraints of digital media.

A decade later, revisiting this research serves as a reminder that even during the early stages of digital media, the user experience of the platform was already challenging our preconceived notions about how advertising operated. At the time though, we didn't really understand it that deeply and the flow-on effects this would deliver. This underscores the enduring importance of distribution efforts (the egg) as the primary driver of the success of the creative content (the chicken).

TAKE IT TO WORK

Just when you thought all viral cats were expired, they pop back up with life number 9 to remind us that distribution efforts are the primary driver of the success of creative content. In other words, media distribution plays a bigger role than most people think—the perfect scenario is amazing content and a good distribution strategy.

MEANWHILE IN THE REAL WORLD

Here is an example of when a brand gets it right using the perfect trio of triggers.

"Compare the Meerkat" is a highly successful and long running advertising campaign that aired on British and Australian commercial television for comparethemarket.com, a price comparison website under the BGL Group. For close to 15 years, this brand has consistently used emotion, unexpectedness and contextual cues (visual and auditory) linked to the brand.

Launched in January 2009, created by advertising agency VCCP, the campaign features Aleksandr Orlov, a CGI anthropomorphic Russian meerkat, and his family and friends. Orlov, depicted as an aristocrat and the founder of comparethemeerkat.com, humorously expresses frustration over the confusion between his website and comparethemarket.com, cleverly playing on the similarity between the words "market" and "meerkat." His catchphrase, "Simples," became iconic. The campaign achieved substantial popularity, propelling comparethemarket.com to become the fourth most visited insurance website in the UK, up from its previous ranking at 16th in January 2008. Entrepreneur David Soskin also noted that the wordplay between "meerkat" and "market" in the campaign was effective in overcoming the high cost of the latter keyword in sponsored search engine listings.

The campaign has been running ever since, with many new meerkat characters, including baby Oleg, to keep unexpectedness going. Today the website offers downloads like wallpapers, ringtones, and an iPhone application. There is nothing that resembles the 'age of average' here.

https://www.comparethemarket.com.au/meerkat/download/

The Science of Magic: A Lesson From a Professional Thief

Before we move onto the media side of the 'now' and the 'next', what could be more fun than a confession from a professional thief. In 2008, a fascinating paper titled "Attention and Awareness in Stage Magic: Turning Tricks into Research" was published in the prestigious Nature Journal.

The authors of this paper come from diverse backgrounds, including neuroscientists, magicians and a professional pickpocket named Apollo Robbins (who has since become a trusted advisor for law enforcement officials, specializing in fraud, theft, and scam trends).

The paper was presented at a 'Magic of Consciousness' Symposium in Las Vegas, known as the city of illusions. It coincided with the annual meeting of the Association for the Scientific Study of Consciousness attended by an academic audience including neuroscientists, psychologists, and philosophers who were all keen to explore the psychologically puzzling aspects of magic.

The New York Times reported, "After two days of presentations by scientists and philosophers speculating on how the mind construes, and misconstrues, reality, we were hearing from the pros: James (The Amazing) Randi, Johnny Thompson (The Great Tomsoni), Mac King, and Teller—magicians who had intuitively mastered some of the lessons being learned in the laboratory about the limits of cognition and attention."

Their paper explores the world of magic, an art form rich in its history of captivating and redirecting attention while skillfully exploiting the inherent constraints of human perception and awareness. It discusses how the fundamental principles of stage magic have been carefully refined over centuries and highlights the increasing interest in applying these principles within the broader field of cognitive sciences.

Upon reading this paper, it becomes evident that the principles behind successful magic are remarkably similar to those behind successful marketing.

Both magicians and marketers share a common challenge: understanding how to manage inattentional blindness. In simple terms, inattentional blindness means not noticing something surprising or obvious because your attention is elsewhere or you're not paying enough attention to consciously see it. This concept illustrates the limits of how selective our perception can be, as discussed in more detail in Chapter 1.

One classic example of inattentional blindness is the 'gorilla experiment,' conducted by psychologists Christopher Chabris and Daniel Simons. Participants were asked to count basketball passes in a video, and many failed to notice a person in a gorilla costume walking through the scene, because they were so focused on counting passes. This is an example of inattentional blindness where individuals can miss things, even if they are in eye-shot.

Another example, more relevant to advertising, is the 'Triple Dipped Chicken Experiment.' A social experiment by Bite Back 2030 demonstrated how advertising priming can influence food choices without people realizing it. Teens in the experiment ordered 'triple dipped chicken' from a menu because they had been exposed to influencer ads and posters all morning on their way to the restaurant. The majority of teens chose the triple dipped chicken option over 49 other food choices. Comments from the surprised teens included statements like "I didn't even notice that," "I scrolled straight past," "That's scary", "I don't remember that." It's important to note that this video carries a serious message. Bite Back 2030 is a youth activist movement in the UK advocating for higher standards in 'Big Food' to combat the obesity crisis. Their message to food giants is "fuel us, don't fool us."

Both of these experiments underscore the importance of considering gaze time and gaze focus at two different attentional levels (active and passive). One is deliberate and focused mental processing (eyes on ad) while the other involves peripheral and unintentional focus (eyes nearby the ad). Both are valuable but yield different outcomes for brands, just as it did in these experiments.

Interestingly, there are striking parallels between magic principles and advertising triggers. Both involve the redirection of attention and awareness to achieve goals like building trust, increasing awareness, enhancing memory, shaping perception, and captivating audiences. The key distinction, though, lies in their direction: magic aims to divert attention away from the 'gold,' while advertising strives to direct attention towards it. Advertising seeks to eliminate inattentional blindness, whereas magic aims to create it. It's as straightforward as that. Below, in Table 5.1, you can find an overview of the shared applications of triggers in these two very different, yet seemingly similar, social sciences.

It turns out there is a lot to learn from the science of magic. Magic and advertising triggers share a common emphasis on capturing attention and fostering awareness through elements like unexpectedness, novelty, and emotion. The good news is, you don't have to be a wizard to incorporate magical techniques into your advertising strategies.

MEANWHILE IN THE REAL WORLD

Here is a cheer to the magic of humanity.

It turns out Magicians and Humane Technologists have a lot in common too. For instance, take Tristan Harris, a Co-Founder of the Center for Humane Technology; he actually started his career as an actual magician. He then studied persuasive technology at Stanford University, ultimately applying his knowledge, such as understanding triggers to guide and redirect attention, to his own startup and later at Google. During his tenure at Google, he started to raise awareness about the perils of technology that manipulates attention for profit, a topic we'll jump into further in Chapter 8 on Ethics.

The Center for Humane Technology stands as a highly respected non-profit organization with a mission to champion the responsible and ethical design of technology, ensuring it serves humanity rather than causing harm. They are dedicated to addressing the ethical and societal dilemmas posed by technology and digital platforms, including giants like Google and Facebook and others who demand our attention. While Harris trained as a Magician, his co-founders started with less impressive jobs like mathematician, dark matter physicist and mindfulness teacher. Together, they are reshaping the course of history for the better.

So it is official, between David Ogilvy and Tristan Harris, one does need to be a wizard to be a marketer.

Table 5.1 Magical marketing triggers

	Magic	Marketing
Context Cues	Magicians employ context cues by integrating props, settings, or narratives that make their illusions appear more plausible and relevant. These cues establish a context where the magic seems logical and natural	Marketers use distinctive brand assets or elements to trigger recognition and association with a brand in the minds of consumers. These cues can include things like logos, colors, fonts, shapes, slogans, characters, ad styles, and auditory elements
Repetition	Magicians use repetition by performing the same illusion multiple times, often with variations, to create familiarity with the audience. This can lead the audience to believe they understand the trick, only to be surprised by a twist	For brands, repetition plays a crucial role in enhancing brand recognition when using context cues. By consistently and repeatedly exposing consumers to distinctive brand assets it reinforces their memory and association with the brand. This reinforcement makes it more likely for consumers to recall the brand when making purchasing decisions
Emotion (Humor)	Magicians often incorporate humor into their performances to emotionally engage the audience. Humor creates a relaxed atmosphere, making the audience more receptive to the magic	In marketing, humor is used to capture the audience's attention, evoke positive emotions, and enhance brand or product memorability. Humorous ads can stand out and leave a lasting impression on consumers

(continued)

Table 5.1 (continued)

	Magic	Marketing
Emotion (Awe)	Magicians aim to leave the audience in awe and wonder, creating a lasting impression of their performance. Magic afterall is a form of entertainment	Awe is a high arousal positive emotion that elicits 'wow' reactions and a sense of connection to something greater. It's most effective when products emphasize their desirability and seem distant in time, leading consumers to perceive them as valuable, even if they don't fulfill an immediate need
Motion	Magicians use seemingly innocent and commonplace actions to conceal their secret maneuvers. These actions are seamlessly integrated into their performance, creating the impression that every movement serves a specific purpose. This misdirection deceives the audience, as they are less likely to focus on actions that appear ordinary and logical	Italian artists from the seventeenth century coined the term "moto e azione," emphasizing the importance of showing movement and emotion to create effect. This principle remains highly relevant in advertising, where the inclusion of dynamic actions, poses, and expressions at key junctures in the narrative elevates emotional resonance and captivates the audience

EXPERT INSIGHT: Why Attention Seekers Need to Get With the Program by Peter Hammer

According to the Cambridge Dictionary, the idiom "get with the program" means to "accept new ideas and give more attention to what is happening now." This sentiment is relevant for advertisers who "get with the program" by way of TV program sponsorships, who have also accepted new ideas of advanced TV measurement such as attention.

To understand the impact of sponsorships on attention, our team at the Marketing Scientist Group created a large-scale viewing experiment for Paramount ANZ, exposing 2,200 Australian TV viewers to different advertisements and sponsored programs including MasterChef Australia and Australian Survivor.

The research participants were shown different combinations of brand/ad placements, from a standard TVC through to a fully-integrated sponsorship for eight different brands. The experiment was conducted in homes using computers, smartphones/tablets, and TVs, employing eye-tracking technology (with permission) so we could understand what viewers were looking at when watching the content and advertising.

This research forms part of a larger body of work investigating the impact of integrated content and TV sponsorships, and is the first study where we have made attention the primary focus. As such, we were able to identify four new insights on how TV program sponsorships deliver attention and impact for brands, especially when compared to standard TVCs.

1. Deeper TV sponsorships create more "opportunities to see", which results in more attention

Deeper TV sponsorships have more assets, which creates more "opportunities to see" a brand across content and advertising. The study found that there was 3.4 × more brand time for those shown fully-integrated sponsorships compared to a standard TVC alone. Eye-tracking data confirmed that these fully-integrated sponsorships also generated more attention seconds (3.5x) for a brand, as it was shown in more places across TVCs, billboards and integrated content.

2. Integrated content is typically more impactful due to increased attention

TV sponsorships with integrated content generated more uplifts in key metrics than other elements (TVCs and billboards) because viewers paid more attention to brands during content than in ads. For example, we found viewers were more likely to have their eyes-on-screen during a brand mention within content (+17%) on average, as compared to when a brand was mentioned within the ad break.

3. When people pay attention to visual brand assets it increases memory metrics

Eye-tracking data showed that when viewers gazed at a variety of different brand assets (e.g. logos, products, etc.) within content and ads, they gave higher responses for a brand across a range of metrics. The biggest uplifts were in memory metrics, including top-of-mind awareness (+37%), the average number of associations linked to a brand (+16%), as well as lifts in brand-asset fame (+18%).

4. Attention to brand assets in content primes viewers to pay attention to subsequent advertising

Eye-tracking data showed that viewers were more likely to pay attention and recognise an advertisement, regardless of the spot, if they had gazed at the product placed within content prior to the ad break. Interestingly, when the TVC featured the same product asset as the content, it had even higher results for attention and recognition. This aligns with other research that high-lights the priming / halo effects that comes from sponsorships and integrated content with product placement.

The findings of this study are a call to action for advertisers, to look beyond standard TVCs and consider the opportunities presented by TV program sponsorships. In particular, we have proven sponsorships can create more "opportunities to see" a brand, which results in more attention and impact on memory, especially when they are integrated within the content, as it primes viewers for subsequent advertising. In other words, for those advertisers seeking attention, it's time to get with the program!

5.4 Making Reach Great Again

We'd like to extend our apologies in advance to anyone who might have mixed feelings about the title of this section heading. Its intention wasn't to evoke thoughts of someone else's campaign catchphrase; rather, it was chosen because it seemed to be the most fitting choice for this concluding section of the chapter.

In the preceding chapters, we've gone deep into the root causes of the measurement challenges in our industry (along with the resulting ripple effects), explored the true nature of attention, conducted a thorough examination of the methods for collecting attention data, and scrutinized the credibility of the metrics it provides. We've dissected it, placed it under the microscope, asked 'why' repeatedly, and now, it's time to reassemble the pieces.

This last section begins with a concise summary of the current practical applications in the market—in essence the 'now' for attention and media. From there, we dive precisely into what the title suggests: exploring ways to make reach meaningful once more—the 'next' for attention and media.

The Now: The Fab Four

Currently, there are four (fabulous) primary uses of attention data in the market, benefiting agencies, brands, and publishers. In summary these applications include (see Fig. 5.9):

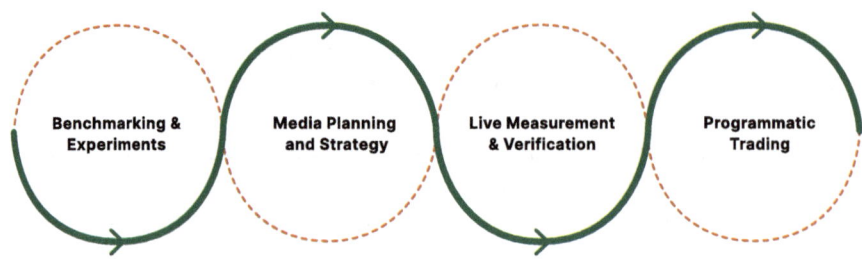

Fig. 5.9 The fab four

1. **Benchmarking and Client Experiments:** This involves comparing performance and conducting experiments to enhance advertising strategies.
2. **Media Planning and Strategy:** Utilizing attention data to optimize media spending, improve campaign planning, and achieve better audience engagement.
3. **Live Measurement and Verification:** Real-time assessment of ad performance, ensuring that campaigns effectively capture and retain audience attention.
4. **Programmatic Trading:** Leveraging attention metrics for informed bidding and optimizing ad inventory selection to maximize ROI.

Note that specific details may vary by vendor, so consult resources like the ARF Attention Atlas for vendor-specific offerings. But below is slightly more detail on some of the use cases surfacing. Note: The perfect scenario in a future attention ecosystem is for each attention application to improve the performance of the next. For example, optimized planning should enhance the application and decision-making in trading, and optimized trading should enhance the verification application. Hence feedback loops have the potential to drive continuous improvement and as the industry matures, we can expect them to play an increasingly crucial role in enhancing overall performance.

1. Benchmarking and Experiments

Benchmarking and experiments hold a crucial place within advertising and marketing, serving several vital purposes:

a. **Hypothesis Testing Ground:** Attention experiments offer the perfect laboratory where hypotheses related to factors like attention and brand presence, as well as attention and ad frequency, can be put to the test.

b. **Enhancing Advertising Strategies:** Brands and agencies use these experiments to kickstart the improvement of their advertising strategies. Through these experiments, they gain valuable insights into the intricacies of attention in various scenarios and under diverse conditions.

c. **Establishing Performance Baselines:** Media benchmarking creates a starting point for understanding the attention capabilities of different platforms and formats. The attention data collected from these experiments becomes the foundation for essential performance metrics that guide future creative and campaign planning.

d. **Comparing Creative Performance:** Creative benchmarking systematically evaluates how distinct advertising campaigns perform in capturing attention across a wide array of media platforms and formats.

2. Media Planning and Strategy

Media planning workflow tools, including APIs and web platforms, have emerged to optimize advertising efforts with a focus on attention and efficiency:

a. **Reach Optimization:** These tools select media channels, formats and ad lengths to maximize the reach and impact of advertising campaigns to achieve both short and long-term brand goals. It can also be used to negotiate favorable rates to maintain control over advertising costs (also see Equivalizing below).

b. **Demographic Insights:** Allows deeper insight into how attention performance influences campaign outcomes across different demographics.

c. **Carbon Reduction:** The measurement and use of attention data in planning workflows also allows advertisers to minimize excessive ad impressions (thereby reducing carbon emissions) and derive more value from quality impressions.

3. Live Activation and Measurement

Live activation and measurement involves using a JavaScript tag to assess campaign performance based on the parameters of attention. This concept offers several benefits for advertisers and publishers:

a. **Realtime Campaign Optimization:** Attention measurement and verification contribute to enhanced campaign optimization by supplying essential metrics for assessing audience engagement from the perspective of attention.

b. **Propensity Marketing and Enhanced Targeting:** Attention metrics enable propensity marketing, allowing advertisers to identify and target consumers more likely to take action based on their attention levels, offering improved predictive capabilities for outcomes and conversion propensity.

c. **Optimizing User Experience:** Publishers and platforms can enhance inventory pricing and optimize the user experience by considering the attention performance of their users.

d. **Predictive Insights:** These metrics offer predictive insights into ad effectiveness, helping marketers understand the correlation between ad attention and outcomes in real-time.

4. Programmatic Trading

Attention based programmatic trading is a method of buying ad inventory that places a strong emphasis on the level of audience attention it is likely to achieve:

a. **Prioritizing High-Performing Inventory:** Advertisers can prioritize ad inventory that excels in capturing audience attention. This can translate into improved campaign performance and a higher return on investment (ROI).

b. **Attention-Driven Optimization:** Advertisers can dynamically fine-tune their bids based in real-time. This ensures that their ads not only capture but also maintain the audience's attention, leading to more successful campaigns.

c. **Custom Bidding Algorithms and Pre-Bid Segments:** Using attention API data, and combining it with other data sources, advertisers can build custom bidding algorithms that prioritize attention for improved conversion rates inside DSPs.

TAKE IT TO WORK

The value of feedback loops in attention measurement and metrics are underestimated. Continuous improvement plays a crucial role in enhancing overall model performance.

EXPERT INSIGHT: Is Measurement in Trading akin to the Survival of the Fastest? by Adam Heimlich.

In the media process of yesteryear, measurement came last in a long series of tasks. It was the caboose of the train. Only after a media campaign has been strategized and activated, went the thinking, could its effects be measured. A modern model would position measurement on the circumference of a circular media process—after you purchase a placement, yes, but also before you purchase again. In this configuration, the manual process of applying what you learned to the next campaign is automated. The campaign morphs from what was expected to what is actually needed to achieve its desired outcome. Measurement is the locomotive, driving purchase decisions toward the optimum.

The key question for advertisers is who owns that train? Or, less poetically, who decides what training data your machine learning is trained on?

Increasingly, advertisers are wielding this power. More competition in AI tools for advertisers is bringing more choice and sovereignty for those willing to adopt them. Be assured: When the brands whose budgets fuel the industry apply their learning to machine learning, different values bind its decisions. After all, what are algorithms, if not rules for decisions? For many years, the best advertisers approached automated buying with caution. It was necessary for brands to let their analytics team catch up to digital media and supervise what its robots had opted to bid for and buy. When AI is trained by sellers to decide for buyers, the relationship is naturally tense, if not adversarial.

Attention is a prime example: though every advertiser agrees it matters, no publisher's ad algorithm is trained on attention signals.

It comes down to measurement. Even a high-quality publisher with an affluent audience lives and dies by daily clicks and attributed conversions. These metrics improve with the volume of ad placements, not quality. Advertisers periodically raise alarms about fraudulent websites, clickbait websites, websites made only for advertising. These are all names for the same thing: sellers exploiting poor predictions of value by machines advertisers use but can't control. Steering against the autopilot is a tedious way to travel. But to input your exact destination into the learning machine, your own guardrails and standards, your own custom metrics, and your own choice of analytics partners—so you can take your hands off the manual controls and let your decisions be made automatically, a million times per second? That's scary. What will you learn? Having stepped up and taken accountability for all of that, there's no longer any room for a marketing team to hide.

A Rapid Fire Case Study about Complex Interactions

In complex systems like human behavior, interactions between variables can lead to unexpected outcomes (emergent properties). This is why it's crucial to understand the relationship between attention and outcomes because it is more complex than it may initially seem. This rapid fire research is interrupting the flow of the chapter because of its importance to attention application and product. Ultimately this study shows the need for a nuanced understanding of attention, and how these subtleties can greatly impact outcomes, general business results and campaign success.

In partnership with a leading soft drinks company this work aimed to look beyond simply assessing 'which media works best' to dig deeper into interactions that might have implications for its whole advertising approach. Specifically, we wanted to understand whether bigger brands in their portfolio respond to attention differently than smaller brands in their portfolio, and moreover what this meant for the attention/outcomes relationship?

The study conducted a comprehensive analysis by first gathering gaze data from over 1,000 individuals and analyzing more than 2,300 ads. Its primary objective was to give us a baseline of attention both focus and time, including active, passive, and non-attention across various media platforms in real-time. Then we built a robust logistic regression model to validate the smaller sample comprising an additional 41,801 human observations spanning 41 product categories and 2,155 unique brands of observations collected previously. This allowed us to thoroughly analyze interaction effects on various outcomes, including brand presence, brand size (market share), switching behaviors (attention focus), and audience demographics.

Takeaway #1: Passive And Active Attention Work Differently For Different Sized Brands

Active attention plays a more substantial role in brand choice overall than passive attention, but the brand's size moderates the significance of each type.

Both small and large brands see improvements in brand choice for every second of active and passive attention, which also underscores the importance of attention duration. However, the research uncovers that smaller brands can achieve four times the brand uplift per second of active attention compared to their larger counterparts. In contrast, larger brands benefit more from each second of passive attention, while smaller brands derive greater value from each second of active attention they garner. This distinction likely arises from the established mental presence of larger brands and the effectiveness of their distinctive creative assets.

Takeaway #2: Eyes-on-Brand Attention is Vital to Outcomes

The research also revealed that the likelihood of consumers selecting a brand was notably influenced by the level of human attention directed towards the specific branded elements, such as the logo or other branded assets. The concept of "eyes-on-brand" attention emerged as a pivotal metric for driving favorable outcomes, signifying the exact moment when the brand is visible and a viewer is actively engaged.

Despite the soft drink brand's relatively strong performance in terms of branding quality, with branding frequency and timing surpassing typical creative standards in all ads examined, only 42% of these branded moments garnered active viewership. The situation worsened on platforms character-ized by rapid attention decay, where most viewers quickly lose interest and tend to avoid, scroll past, or skip ads. On such platforms, a mere 35% of participants actively viewed the initial 42% of branded moments. This dual impact affects both the frequency of brand exposure and the size of the audience reached, both of which significantly influence outcomes.

Our findings highlight that while the likelihood of brand selection is influ-enced by multiple factors, the "eyes-on-ad" attention remains one of the most substantial contributors. These results underscore that it's not only the duration of attention that matters but also how individuals engage with the content and the factors we refer to as attention time, attention decay, and attention focus.

Takeaway #3: Outcomes are Heavily Mediated by Brand Size and Eyes on Brand

Given takeaways 1 and 2, it's not surprising that this study highlights the critical role of ensuring that the branded moment is visible and emphasizes the impact of brand size on achieving immediate outcomes. This research also reveals that these factors can introduce bias and mislead a model attempting to predict attention because the relationship direction is incorrect. Attention can forecast outcomes, but outcomes cannot reliably predict attention. If a large brand can generate the same amount or probability of attention but yield fewer results than a smaller brand, how can outcomes be used to forecast attention? Similarly, if a poorly branded ad can attract the same amount or probability of attention but generate fewer results than a well-branded ad, how can outcomes predict attention accurately? These nuances highlight the significance of interaction effects (Fig. 5.10).

TAKE IT TO WORK

Big brands behaving differently is not surprising. Therein lies the importance of considering nuance in attention products.

EXPERT INSIGHT: Big Brands and Absolute Attention by David Porter.
It turns out surrogate measures fail big brands.

Jumping from agencies to brands was something of a culture shock for me, despite many years working agency-side on CPG brands. I was pulled up short by new colleagues' obsession with "competitiveness", expressed through share of voice and message frequency. We all want brands to compete, but media experts were coming to the view that these old metrics were not fit for the digital age. But how, then, to stay competitive? Marketing thinking has evolved since, with a growing consensus that reaching one new viewer is preferable to reaching the old ones repeatedly. And that, although a fully

Fig. 5.10   The nuance of size

funded media plan can help, it's even better to have awesome creative assets. This is generally best understood by those whose audiences lean towards digital media, where share of voice is impossible to measure as you cannot track competitor spends and impressions. And frequency becomes academic in the absence of a standard unit of measurement such as the 30″ commercial.

Many big brands have tried to unpick this, seeking out surrogate measures: "if we can't measure competitors' spends, what can we measure? If each digital format is unique, what's the numerical expression of how different they each are from a TVC ('equivalence')?" These complex, long-term projects could prove to be either wild-goose chases or superseded by advanced versions of Attention Measurement. Brands sought new measures because the old ones stopped working. But those old metrics were themselves a compromise, being proxies for what was—at the time—unmeasurable. That's no longer the case.

What marketers really want to know is: "Who's watching my messages? Really watching? Which parts do they watch most and least? On which platforms and formats does each asset get watched the most?".

– Not the "hidden pixel no human will ever see" kind of watching.
– Not the "turned away until the ads are over" kind of watching.
– Not the "you'll just have to trust me about viewability" kind of watching.
– Not the"we did an attention study once and applied the findings to all our campaigns" kind of watching.

Without this knowledge, much of what brands "know" about themselves and their competitive set is decidedly sketchy. What's the point in comparing brands' media impressions if we don't realize that Brand A gets five times Brand B's attention for the same money? How can we set the most budget-efficient reach targets, or targets sufficient to deliver the attention-memory threshold required to build adstock models? It's time to admit that we went with the old proxies because they were all we had. But now we have marketers wringing their hands over a decline in marketing effectiveness while staring much of the solution in the face.

Media planning based on real human attention is now a reality. Brands can know which assets will attract the most human attention and be guided towards making them even stronger. They can match their hardest-working assets to the hardest-working platforms and formats specific to their campaign, updating plans in real-time to make the most of this knowledge. And they can understand how competitive their creative: media blend is within their competitor set.

Here is my advice to Dreamers and Early Adopters.

Artificial Intelligence will add great qualitative richness to the "yes, they are watching" feedback—within months, not years. Chapter 7 hears from

Attention Early Adopters and Dreamers. The most successful marketers will need a foot in both camps.

To the Early Adopters: Brands can use Attention to become more competitive today, to sharpen assets to perfectly fit the chosen platforms and formats, while placing a value on their media based on how many humans are actively watching (spoiler alert: media owners are all over this space already!).

To the Dreamers: There's plenty more to push for. As AI gives us richer, real-time Attention knowledge, we will start to fix three things that keep marketers awake at night:

- Absolute Viewability: brands can know from an independent source, how many eyeballs landed on their.
- message and for how long. Verification and viewability measurement will be transformed.
- Absolute Safety: we must recognise that a totally clean and safe internet is just a dream. But AI–fueled Attention metrics will steer brands—and hopefully the public—away from the darker corners of digital, most of the time.
- Absolute Truth: all the science we grew up with such as reach building, multi-media planning, adstocks, competitive metrics and so on, will spring back to new life. But this time around they will be absolutely fact-based.

5.5   The Next: Equivalence

"Today, we buy reach, tomorrow we might buy attentive reach. The shift will be abrupt." Sorin Patinilet MARS (WARC Guide to Attention, 2020)

The industry has been dealing with data quality issues for a long time, this is not news to anyone. At the core of this predicament lies a fundamental discrepancy in reach volume to attention volume. For example, when an audience reach vendor or publisher reports that 1,000 people were exposed to an ad (traditional reach), it might transpire that only 300 individuals actually viewed the content. This 70 percentage point difference in volume is a significant (unintended) miscalculation in our industry. It is the same old, 'served does not equate to being seen' conversation, but most media planners don't think the discrepancy in a volume way. This is why we are in the 'not all reach is equal' predicament and is also why traditional reach metrics have a weaker connection with business outcomes than they used to (as described in much of Rob Brittain's and Peter Field's work).

Reach has been the cornerstone of media planning and buying for nearly 75 years, deeply ingrained in the infrastructure and workflows of professionals worldwide. Understanding the number of people reached remains essential for achieving brand growth, focusing on reaching a broader audience to enhance penetration over loyalty, for example. Does reach require a significant overhaul? Yes. Should it be completely replaced? No.

Over the past 15 years, there has been a surge in the 'outcomes economy,' driven by a commercial opportunity that arose while traditional reach was not delivering the desired results. But it's akin to a dog chasing its tail—we're not addressing the core issue, just pursuing a different solution (that in most cases only gives you a tenth of the story if you are lucky).

Does this mean that outcomes are unimportant for brands? No. What it signifies is that by addressing the fundamental challenges our industry faces, we can dispense with superficial vendor metrics and instead brands can leverage their own longitudinal business metrics directly linked to campaign reach. These are metrics already integrated into workflows and board reports, such as sales, market share changes, and cost of goods sold. Equivalizing reach simply means these reports will look healthier from an efficiency perspective.

Human Attention data was built to equivalize

Human attention data is the one type of supplementary data that can truly fix the discrepancies in reach. Reach is human, attention is human. Reach is a count of people exposed, attention is a count of people viewing. Reach is both volume and time based, attention is both volume and time based (i.e. count of people and count of seconds). These similarities make it easy for the two sets of data to work together. It was built to do this job.

Essentially, equivalizing reach, which we refer to as 'attention adjustment,' involves incorporating traditional reach curve data and integrating attention data from an enriched database. This process results in an attention-adjusted reach curve that correctly accounts for the varying impact of media mix components such as platform, format, and demographic. It serves to highlight the disparity between the expected traditional reach and the attention-adjusted reach, all along the same continuum as traditional reach curves.

To simplify, think of it as adding a third dimension to reach planning. Budget and reach are the foundational elements of reach planning, while attention introduces the third dimension, allowing us to equalize the overall real reach volume (Fig. 5.11).

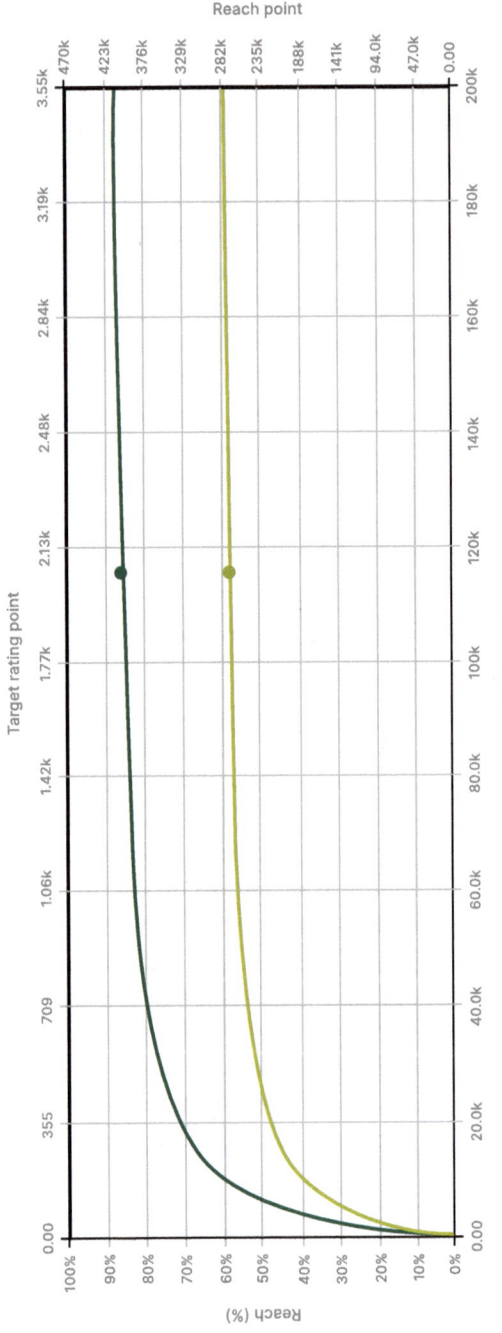

Fig. 5.11 Example attention adjusted reach curve

In 2023, Richard Kirk, while associated with Zenith, introduced a concept called 'Right Reach.' This approach calculates reach by taking into account not only the volume of attention but also factors like persistence and relevance, using coefficients as a foundation. Kirk's research has consistently shown that this adjusted reach metric is a more accurate predictor of campaign success compared to traditional reach measures. In an article for MediaLeader, Kirk discussed two potential solutions to the issue of reach measurement. He proposed either rebuilding how we calculate reach (mentioning C-Flight and Project Origin as examples) or quantifying attention and using it to modify reach, resulting in what he called 'attentive reach,' which serves as a reliable proxy for effective reach.

In his words, 'Right Reach' is a bit of both and Zenith built a series of tests off by factoring a channel's ability to reach the target audience using a series of coefficients, based on cross-channel data, including:

1. Attention: how much attention can this channel generate? More attention equals greater business results.
2. Persistence: how likely is it that the viewer is enjoying the content the ad sits next to? Highly engaged viewers are more likely to correctly recall and attribute ads to brands.
3. Relevance: how easy is it to put the ad next to content that is thematically similar? And how easy is it to buy that context at scale?

He reported that their testing revealed that their 'Right Reach' method provided a clearer understanding of both restored and effective reach. Figure 5.12, shown below, presents the results of their analysis spanning several campaigns conducted over a two-year period, with calculations based on weekly reach data. This figure illustrates the difference in the correlation between traditional reach and outcomes (specifically, traditional sales) before and after implementing the 'Right Reach' approach. Essentially, it highlights the contrast between the relationship of traditional reach and sales and the relationship between 'Right Reach' and sales. According to their findings, they discovered that the connection between traditional reach and sales was severely weakened, while 'Right Reach' exhibited a strong correlation with sales, indicated by an r-squared value of 0.6.

Kirk said "I'm convinced we can improve on this effort to calculate effective reach. Hopefully planners reading this will join that discussion. It feels vital they do: if we can increase the confidence advertisers have in the link between spend and outcomes, brands will lean into fragmentation. And when empirical planning methods deliver that link, it means brands can evolve their

Brand (all large, national advertisers, in top 5 of their categories)	Period	Success Metrics	r2 – Reach vs success metric	R2 – Right Reach vs success metric	Improvement
Price comparison website	2021-22	Yougov Attention	0.37	0.46	+24%
Price comparison website	2021-22	Yougov Ad Aware	0.4	0.45	+12.5%
Premium confectioner	2019-21	Yougov Ad Aware	0.25	0.47	+88%
Grocery retailer	2019-22	Yougov "Quality" perception	0.22	0.48	+118%
Grocery retailer	2019-22	Yougov Purchase Intent	0.29	0.5	+72%
Bank	2020-21	Ipsos Spontaneous Brand Awareness	0.25	0.36	+44%
Bank	2020-21	Ipsos Spontaneous Brand Awareness	0.16	0.4	+150%
Bank	2018-19	Yougov Spontaneous Brand Awareness	0.25	0.39	+56%
Pet food	2021-22	Incremental sales value from media, derived by client's MMM	0.09	0.59	+555%
Grocery retailer	2019-22	Yougov Ad Aware	0.27	0.40	+48%

Fig. 5.12 Zenith right reach test

media mix faster, whilst saving money through a better-informed negotiation position. There has never been a better time to be a media planner. Just five years ago, this was not expected. Media markets were largely predictable, and the consensus was that media planning would be largely automated and in-housed. Even MediaCom's head of planning, Steve Gladdis, was asked if he feared his job was going to be taken by a robot. Instead, rapid media fragmentation has created an environment in which strong planning craft has never been more valuable to advertisers."

AI will facilitate a smoother equivalization process, and the next generation of systems must be equipped to handle this data efficiently, possibly through the implementation of data cleaning rooms. In a 2023 Medium article, Jim Warner from Snowflake addresses this issue by emphasizing the need for planning and buying optimization systems to incorporate multiple datasets. These datasets should include traditional audience reach metrics alongside components for assessing attention across various sources.

Warner asserts that despite the increasing accessibility of outcome measurement, reach and frequency metrics remain valuable tools for marketers to measure and manage their campaigns effectively.

When reach is attention adjusted it solves many other effectiveness problems 'down the line'

When equivalence is established, it brings back the normalcy to all the previously disrupted relationships we discussed in Chapter 2. Reach-based planning becomes comprehensive, ESOV (Excess Share of Voice) functions effectively, and the metric known as "Cost per Meaningless Thousand" can revert to being the straightforward "Cost per Thousand." This allows reach to once again serve as a valuable currency alongside other metrics such as emotion and context.

However, it's important to note that equivalence doesn't solve the issue of human attention decay, which is a permanent fixture. This means that attention elasticity will continue to be a recurring pattern, which in turn places limitations on creative strategies within these constraints.

Nevertheless, what equivalence achieves is providing a clear picture of the situation you are dealing with. You can then plan and purchase media based on this reality, much like the golden age of media planning. This is the future of equivalence: considering attention-adjusted reach alongside factors like Placement, Audience, Content, Context, and the cost-to-Return on Advertising Spend (ROAS) ratio.

EXPERT INSIGHT: Causing Change in Marketing, Advertising and Media by Bill Harvey.
The key to change is design thinking and proving business results.

There has been remarkably little change in the Big Picture of how things work in the marketing field in the past half Century. Mostly the changes which have occurred relate to new media providing more choice for consumers and advertisers. The optimization practices continue to be focused mostly on oversimplified sex/age targets, with lowest CPM and highest reach being the main considerations. Contextual impact weights continue to exist on the fringes and improve every year, but do not affect most buys. I learned a few tricks as to how to introduce changes and my work that has been widely adopted included ADI/DMA (a way of lining up sales with ad impressions geographically), passive peoplemeters like the PPM, addressable ads, measurement of advertising sales effects using big data singlesource, use of big data for audience measurement.

The trick is to get prospective clients to help you invent the product, building trust by showing real business results repeatedly, avoiding adding to workflows. The value of rigorous methodology seems diminished in the absence of hard sales and brand equity measures, because if the advertiser feels iffy about modeling as a way of measuring business success, methods which improve ROI will not be taken seriously enough. Random Control Trials are slowly becoming recognized as a way of giving advertisers enough confidence in the outcome measures to scale up use of methods that amplify advertising effectiveness, including our own research that is forging alignment between ad and context, and between ad and recipient, in both cases in terms of motivation. I'm looking forward to putting these amplification methods together into a "cocktail" which maximizes ROI and brand equity. We already have numerous trusted third party validations on these amplifiers separately, and the measures of the combined cocktail will be coming soon.

As it turns out, science flourishes when hip-shooting stops.

The main drag on making marketing a true science is the general attitude of hip-shooting on creative based on research designed to prove preconceived ideas, and treating media as having very little to contribute other than as many impressions as can be bought as cheaply as possible. This is not the ideal culture in which science can flourish. The more bulletproof the sales effect measures, the sooner marketers in droves will realize that a little more scientific care and feeding of creative and media decisions can double, triple, and quadruple success rates in actual company profits.

We proved that with TRA and today thousands of companies are using big data sales measurement of advertising, albeit many of them have yet to validate their specific methodologies, and in a recent study I conducted for the Coalition for Innovation in Media Measurement (CIMM), we found that marketers and their agencies had become turned off by verbal-response brand lift studies which always showed positive results, causing a return to marketing mix modeling as a more trustable way of estimating the real business effects of marketing and advertising.

The next decade in these fields pivots entirely on how trustable are the chosen methods for measuring return on ad spend (ROAS). With modeling being the least distrusted method today, amplifier methods will gain adoption more slowly, until definitively trustable sales effect measurement is a proven reality.

TAKE IT TO WORK

Sweeping statements from academics about buying big media for reach based planning are out of touch in this landscape. When a platform is twice as big, but a reach point delivers half the human attention, any value in being big is canceled out.

MEANWHILE IN THE REAL WORLD

As always the indelible Tom Roach was on point when he wrote a piece in marketing week mid 2023 about attention and creativity. He said that "Solving the attention issue in digital advertising is key to improving creative effectiveness. It will take a combination of good old-fashioned creativity and a good new-fashioned understanding of what works on each platform. Simple, but hard."

The core recommendations presented in his opinion piece are summarized as follows:

1. Attention is the Challenge

Solving the problem of grabbing and retaining people's attention in digital advertising is crucial for improving creative effectiveness. This requires a combination of creativity and an understanding of what works on each platform.

2. Shift in Advertising Landscape

The advertising landscape is evolving with a focus on brand-building creativity. Video content and creator-driven entertainment platforms are playing a significant role in this shift.

3. Overcoming Short-Termism

Digital advertising has suffered from short-termism due to its historical focus on targeting in-market prospects. To achieve sustainable growth, brands need to reach new audiences and move beyond ads that only appeal to immediate buyers.

4. The Attention Problem

Attention research highlights that a substantial portion of digital ads does not receive enough active attention to impact brand memories positively. The key difference between brand-building and direct-response ads is the duration of active attention, which affects their long-term impact.

5. Media Dynamics

Each platform has a unique set of dynamics, and understanding these dynamics is crucial. It's essential to tailor ads to specific platforms, optimizing for the platform's rules and algorithms.

6. Creative Approach

Creativity plays a significant role in maximizing attention on a platform. Adherence to platform best practices, such as using emerging story arcs and evoking high-emotion, is essential to drive brand awareness and lift.

7. Influence of Creators

Creators who understand their platforms well can create attention-grabbing content. Collaborating with creators can lead to more effective advertising, particularly on platforms like TikTok.

8 Budget and Consistency

Brands should focus on fewer platforms and select them deliberately to maintain consistency in their brand strategy. Closer alignment between media and creative planning is essential.

9 Continuous Adaptation

The advertising landscape continues to evolve, and brands need to adapt to new platforms and strategies as they emerge.

His article emphasizes the importance of creativity, understanding platform dynamics—and the synergies between them—it is a good summary of how to stop silos and adapt to new trends to effectively capture and retain the attention of digital advertising audiences.

https://www.marketingweek.com/attentions-the-problem-creativitys-the-answer-as-ever/

5.6   The Wrap Up: How Brands Blow

How Brands Blow, a collaboration between Ryan Wallman and Giles Edwards, is a fun book published by self proclaimed silly sods (by …Gasp!, the Proper Marketing agency that's been Creatively Memorable & Boringly Effective™ since 2009). It's a mix of both funnies and facts about ad effectiveness and amazing copy (but not as you know it). It's much less boring and a lot more fun than other books of its kind (which is the point, make copy interesting and people will possibly like it). It teaches us about 'happy-vomits,' 'Radvertising,' 'branding as a vegetable,' and a lot of duck hunting. All things marketers should know about!

Our Top 3 Funny Blows:

1. BRAND LOVE   **(and a bit of surveillance capitalism)**

Brand: What an amazing customer journey it's been. From the first time you looked at me across that crowded supermarket aisle, I knew you were the persona for me. When you took me home, well, let's just say nobody has ever interacted with my touchpoints like that. And then the engagement! I just want you to know that it will always be my mission to surprise and delight you. Love, your one true brand.

Consumer: I used you once because I was desperate. Leave me alone, you loser.

2. GREAT ADS OF 2023

Headline: This is an ad.

Body Copy: But it's not really an ad. It certainly doesn't have a logo, so you'll never know who it's for.

Fineprint: But it just solved climate change and created world peace. Because Gen Z or something.

Extreme Fineprint: We think capitalism is evil too. Now give us money.

3. TEMPLATE FOR EVERY MANS WATCH AD

Illustration: Picture of a watch.

Headline: An appeal to the male ego (that makes no sense or is out of context).

Body Copy: Some crap about astronauts or pilots.

Fineprint: Logo

So if advertising isn't about interacting with one's touchpoints, creating world peace or pilots, how then 'do brands blow'? In closing this chapter the answer is simple, 'this isn't Ryan' and 'this isn't Giles' tell us:

1. **IT GETS ATTENTION** (it might need to be semi-sweary).
2. **IT INCORPORATES THE BRAND NAME AS AN INTEGRAL ELEMENT** (like Zig or Zag).
3. **IT COMMUNICATES WHAT THE COMPANY OFFERS** (and no hackneyed buzzwords).
4. **IT USES DISTINCTIVE BRAND ASSETS** (so BCF-ing gets stuck in your head).
5. **IT HAS REACH AND FREQUENCY ACROSS MULTIPLE CHANNELS** (this isn't exactly particle physics we're dealing with).
6. **IT STAYS THE COURSE** (Short-termism bedevils modern marketing).
7. **IT'S FUN** (although one person's 'fun' is another's 'I'd rather be disembowelled with a Rogue Double Grip 170 fishing gaff').

Fig. 5.13   This is not Ryan

Fig. 5.14   This is not Giles

8. **DOES IT DO THE EFF-ING JOB?** (stick to the basics, no need to push the boat out) (Figs. 5.13 and 5.14).

5.7   List of Contributors

Giles Edwards. Founder …Gasp!

Giles is the Founder of …Gasp!, the Proper Marketing agency that's been Creatively Memorable & Boringly Effective™ since 2009.

He believes in "Proper (timeless) Marketing"; tactics change, people don't. And its vital role in the Boardroom. He talks about this and more at industry events and alongside esteemed guests on the hugely popular UK Top 2 marketing podcast, Call to Action®. Launched in Feb' 2019, he's subsequently hosted and interviewed some of the industry's greatest minds collecting > 350,000 unique listeners from across the globe.

In 2019, Giles and Ryan Wallman collaborated, to write, design and publish the bestselling book, 'Delusions of Brandeur'; a no-holds-barred commentary on modern marketing and business. Industry legend Dave Trott remarked, "I love this book. Anything I spend my time on, I either have to learn something or be entertained, with this book I get both—along with great art direction.

More recently, in April 2020, Giles launched the charitable initiative ISOLATED Talks®. It's a rallying call across the lockdown divide for the advertising industry to unite and share ideas that help others whilst part-nering with organizations and charities such as Samaritans; to Creatively Support Mental Health. "It's one of those ideas I wish I'd had myself"—Dave Birss.

Peter Hammer. Managing Director, Marketing Scientist Group

Peter Hammer is the Managing Director of the Marketing Scientist Group, a research and data company using science and technology to help media businesses and marketers grow their brands. He was previously the Head of Insights and Analytics across Asia–Pacific for Warner Bros Discovery, and has held senior research, data and strategy roles at Yahoo7 and Turner Broadcasting, and is an alumnus of the Ehrenberg-Bass Institute.

Peter specializes in audience measurement, content/advertising effective-ness and brand research. His work is regularly featured in trade media and global conferences, and he is published in the Journal of Advertising Research.

Bill Harvey. Co-founder of Research Measurement Technologies (RMT), co-founder of TRA Inc. (acquired by TiVo)

For over 35 years Bill Harvey has been leading the way in media research with special emphasis on the New Media. He is often asked to provide his vision of the future of some specific part of the media world. Bill is known to many as a media futurist.

Bill Harvey after a history of innovation co-founded TRA, the first company to show that naturally occurring purchase and media data can be used to create the first actionable process for true ROI measurement and optimization. In 2012 TiVo acquired TRA, now called TiVo Research.

Today, beyond consulting for many companies, Bill has co-founded Research Measurement Technologies (RMT), which is developing a programmatic ROI optimizer that will benefit advertisers and content creators. RMT has breakthrough IP in two areas:

1. Discovery of the 265 drivers of viewing, accounts for 76% of the information in Nielsen ratings.
2. Ability to grow the sales of stalled brands.

a. Media Optimization

Bill has spent over 35 years leading the way in media research with special emphasis on the New Media. As the 24 year-old strategy head of the American Research Bureau (now Arbitron), he invented the Area of Dominant Influence or ADI, an audience-based definition of television markets that Nielsen emulated as the DMA, and which was called by Sales & Marketing Magazine "the most widely used marketing tool in the world today". The ADI has profoundly influenced the advertising and television industries.

Harvey benefited from entering the advertising business exactly as the first mainframe computers were being turned to the task of media optimization. This led him to become one of the early pioneers of optimizers—and a media researcher who had to also learn about media effectiveness in order to program the optimizers. Media effectiveness as a subject falls between media research and advertising research and so Harvey was one of the few media researchers who crossed the line to combine both disciplines. He was most fortunate to have been tutored and mentored by some of the giants in the advertising and research industries including Mike Drexler, Erwin Ephron, Helen Johnston, Timothy Joyce, Burt Manning, Len Matthews, Hal Miller, Ed Papazian, Sandy Reisenbach, Jim Rosenfield, Arnie Semsky, Lester Wunderman, and too many others to mention here.

Before joining Arbitron, Harvey was a media research executive at Grey Advertising, Kenyon & Eckhardt, and Interpublic, specializing in the development of media optimizers.

b. Author and Speaker

Bill authored Mind Magic, a book on self-transformation, which has been used as a course text at thirty-four universities including NYU and UCLA. A popular speaker at media and futurist conferences around the world, he has written and been the subject of numerous articles in a wide range of consumer and media trade publications. From 1979 to 1999 his monthly newsletter, The Marketing Pulse, helped decision-makers at leading advertisers, agencies and media companies understand important trends in media technology. That newsletter in 1979 accurately predicted the 3-network share of audience as it would be in 1990, and made many other projections that turned out to be prophetic, including predicting permission marketing, and coining terms that became generic such as clickstream and click throughs. In January 1999 that newsletter merged into The Myers Report.

c. New Electronic Media

In 1972, Harvey founded New Electronic Media Science (NEMS), a marketing media research consultancy that has served nearly 70 top advertisers and agencies, all major MSOs, virtually all major networks and all major Hollywood studios in the area of New Media. NEMS consulted for QUBE and numerous other early trials, for AT&T in the development of the 900 Number, had its first online service in 1972 and put the first online questionnaire on CompuServe for World Book in 1982. NEMS created International Research Services (IRS), which worked with research companies in 34 countries and compiled and harmonized ratings data from these countries into comprehensive reports for a number of Hollywood studios and networks. NEMS had clients in the U.S., Canada, U.K., France, Germany, Italy, Spain, the Netherlands, Japan, Australia, and a number of other countries.

d. Next Century Media (NCM)

In conjunction with IBM and Leonard Matthews, former CEO of Y&R and of Leo Burnett, Harvey founded Next Century Media (NCM). Next Century Media began as the leading interactive media advisor to advertisers, advertising agencies, entertainment and media companies worldwide, and evolved into an enabler and service provider for addressable TV commercials and TV clickstream measurement. NCM led the development of addressable television advertising and interactive media measurement standards, working with the ANA, 4A's, ARF, IAB, FAST, Audit Bureau, NACHO, CableLabs, and CASIE. Harvey was the originator and drafter of the CASIE Principles which set the privacy standards for the industry. In 1995, in cooperation with Arbitron, NCM published The CyberMeasurement Index, the first compilation of Internet clickstreams to a common standard, in which AOL was a leading participant; 34 agencies subscribed to the report. This was the first experiment in the amalgamation of clickstream data from multiple sources.

e. Media Effectiveness

NEMS and NCM were leaders in the field of Media Effectiveness Measurement, the quantification of the higher order business effects of one medium versus another. Harvey believes that this is the Holy Grail within the marketing business: the ability to place an ROI value and not just an eyeballs value on a specific advertising investment. In the 70s, NEMS was highly active in this field, and among the notable studies conducted in that era was the measurement of a CBS Special sponsored by Ralston Purina, whose attitude shift and commercial recall scores tripled their scatter plan norms, and the measurement of the same ads in Black Enterprise Magazine versus Newsweek, showing again three times the effectiveness for an average ad among upscale Blacks if the ad were seen in the context of their own specialized magazine.

Adam Heimlich. Founder and CEO, Chalice Custom Algorithms

Adam Heimlich is Founder/CEO of Chalice Custom Algorithms, a NY-based software company building tools for advertisers who want to control the AI that spends their money.

Dr. Jared Cooney Horvath. Director, LME Global

Jared Cooney Horvath (PhD, MEd) is a neuroscientist, educator, and author of the best-selling book Stop Talking, Start Influencing: 12 Insights from Brain Science to Make Your Message Stick. He has conducted research and lectured at Harvard University, Harvard Medical School, the University of Melbourne, and over 750 schools internationally. Jared has published 6 books, over 50 research articles, and his work has been featured in numerous popular publications, including The New Yorker, The Atlantic, The Economist, and PBS's NOVA. He currently serves as Director of LME Global: a team dedicated to bringing the latest brain and behavioral research to teachers, students, and parents alike.

Brian Jacobs. Co-Founder Crater Lake and Co. (ex Leo Burnett, Carat, UM, Millward Brown)

Brian Jacobs has spent over 50 years in the advertising business including spells at Leo Burnett (UK, EMEA, International Media Director), Carat International (Managing Director), Universal McCann (EMEA Director) and Millward Brown (EVP, Global Media). He has worked in the UK, EMEA and globally based in the USA. He has lived through shifts from full-service ad agencies to media agencies; from traditional single-commercial-channel TV to multi-faceted digital channels; and from media planning to multi-disciplinary communication planning.

Over his time in agencies Brian was responsible for media activities on several major accounts across multiple geographies—including P&G, The Coca-Cola Company, and adidas. He also represented the agency sector on numerous UK and European media industry committees, including the BARB Management Committee.

In 2006 Brian started Brian Jacobs and Associates (www.bjanda.com), a consultancy business that numbers advertisers, start-ups, media agencies, research agencies and trade bodies amongst its clients.

Brian has co-authored two books on the media industry. 'Spending Advertising Money' with the late Dr Simon Broadbent was published in 1984; 'Social Media Marketing' with Jouko Ahvenainen, Alan Moore and Ajit Jaokar appeared in 2009.

His free blog (The Cog Blog) has clocked up over 450 editions since 2013 and is widely read throughout the industry. It is republished in the US by MediaVillage.

Brian is a regular speaker and chair at media and audience measurement events.

BJ&A along with the real-time experience business MESH Experience, the advanced analytics firm Navigation, and the creative strategists Totman Stride recently established Crater Lake and Company (www.craterlakeandcompany.com), a collective focussed on making sense of data and research by breaking down silos and working collaboratively across disciplines.

Brian serves as a Non-Executive Director at MESH Experience.

Sofia Pires. AI & Society Strategist, Winner of the President's Prize for Outstanding Body of Work in the 2022 IPA Excellence Diploma in Brands

Sofia Pires is a unique thinker with a strong comms background having led strategy for HSBC, HP, Unilever and Diageo at WPP and Omnicom media agencies. Beyond corporate, she has spoken at forums such as Ignite London and lectured at the University of Greenwich.

Over the past 5 years, she delved into Artificial Intelligence at the University of Cambridge, the LSE and the Singularity Group, exploring its intersection with society and its impact on work across industries.

Sofia won the President's Prize for Outstanding Work in the 2022 IPA Excellence Diploma, for her novel approach to what she coined System 3, when AI and human cognition converge.

David Porter. David Porter Advisory (ex-Unilever, WFA, MMA & WPP)

David is an independent strategic advisor specializing in media and marketing-related issues with a particular focus on Asia Pacific. His career spans 27 years in London-based agencies, followed by 18 years in Asia and the Middle East.

He retired from full-time media work in March 2022, leaving his role as Vice President, Global Media for Unilever. He led the CPG giant's award-winning Media team across a geography bounded by Morocco, Russia, New Zealand and South Africa: "Most of World" as opposed to "Rest of World".

During 12 years with Unilever, the company was frequently the most awarded organization in Asia in terms of marketing effectiveness, topping local and regional rankings at the Effies Effectiveness Index and the MMA Smarties awards. In recent years, David helped to transform Unilever into one of the region's most effective data-driven marketers.

While in Asia, he was Chair of the APAC Mobile Marketing Association and has been an advisor to the World Federation of Advertisers, where he was previously its Vice President for APAC. David has a long association with the Effies marketing effectiveness awards, chairing the APAC competition in 2020 and twice leading APAC juries, as well as being a judge on many occasions. During this time David featured regularly in Campaign magazine's APAC's Power List.

Now based with his family in BC, Canada, David's advisory roles include work with Australian attention measurement company Amplified Intelligence, founded by this book's author.

www.linkedin.com/in/davidporter裴德为

Ryan Wallman. Executive Creative Director and Head of Copy, Wellmark

Ryan is Executive Creative Director and Head of Copy at Wellmark, a Melbourne-based creative agency that specializes in healthcare. In his former life, he was a doctor and worked for several years in psychiatry.

An internationally acclaimed copywriter and marketing commentator, he has written for numerous industry publications, including Marketing Week, the Australian Financial Review and The Economic Times. He is also author of the bestselling book 'Delusions of Brandeur' and co-author of 'Eat Your Greens: Fact-Based Thinking to Improve Your Brand's Health'.

Something of a contrarian, Ryan is known for his no-nonsense approach to marketing, and has twice been listed in Business Insider's 'Best 30 People in Advertising to Follow on Twitter'.

Along with his medical degree, Ryan has a Master of Marketing from Melbourne Business School and a Graduate Certificate in Professional Writing. He has vowed to never study again.

Dan White. Freelance Brand Consultant, Illustrator & Trainer

Dan White is a business innovator. His ideas, frameworks and visualizations have influenced generations of marketing and insights professionals and are built into many of the world's leading brand measurement, media evaluation and copy-testing systems.

Dan's career includes a decade as a marketing analyst, another as a brand and communications consultant and a third as a Chief Marketing Officer. Dan splits his time between client consultancy, training, platform speaking, illustration and writing. He is the author of 'The Smart Marketing Book', 'The Soft Skills Book', 'The Smart Branding Book' and 'The Smart Advertising Book'.

Orlando Wood. Chief Innovation Officer, System 1

Orlando Wood is Chief Innovation Officer of the System1 Group, Honorary Fellow of the Institute of Practitioners in Advertising, and author of highly respected publications Lemon (IPA, 2019) and Look out (IPA, 2021).

Orlando is widely regarded as an advertising thought leader and his work on creative style influences both thinking and practice. Through a unique combination of neuroscience, cultural history and advertising research, he describes a shift in advertising style that has occurred in today's technologically disrupted world and explains how this has undermined advertising's effectiveness. Importantly, Orlando's work also provides evidence and guidance to show how we might reverse it.

Orlando has led the IPA's Creativity and Effectiveness research for many years, looking at the greater effectiveness associated with fluent devices (a term he coined) and the features of advertising that sustain attention, elicit emotion and achieve lasting business effects.

Orlando regularly collaborates with others in the industry to understand how advertising works. In 2022, he collaborated with Peter Field and Karen Nelson-Field to present 'Triple Jeopardy' at The Cannes Lions Festival, describing the three threats to advertising effectiveness. In 2023, he returned to Cannes with Karen-Nelson Field, Rob Brittain and Peter Field to present 'Triple Opportunity', a study that confirmed the benefits of positive ESOV invested in emotive creative on high attention media.

Orlando frequently runs creative effectiveness masterclasses for advertisers, including sessions for marketers at The Cannes Lions International Festival of Creativity and The Marketing Academy. His work has won recognition from the ARF, the AMA, Jay Chiat, ISBA, the MRS, ESOMAR and the IPA.

References

Astudillo, C., Muñoz, K., & Maldonado, P. E. (2018). Emotional content modulates attentional visual orientation during free viewing of natural images. *Frontiers in Human Neuroscience, 12,* 459.

Bergmann, H. C., Rijpkema, M., Fernández, G., & Kessels, R. P. C. (2012). The effects of valence and arousal on associative working memory and long-term memory. *PLOS One, 7*(12). https://doi.org/10.1371/journal.pone.0052616

Brave, S., & Nass, C. (2009). Emotion in human-computer interaction. In A. Sears & J. A. Jacko (Eds.), *Human-computer interaction fundamentals.* CRC Press.

Brittain, R., & Field, P. (2023). EsoV and beyond—Part 2. https://advertisingcoun cil.org.au/industry-reports/esov-and-beyond-part-2/

Brown, S. P., Homer, P. M., & Inman, J. (1998). A meta-analysis of relationships between ad-evoked feelings and advertising responses. *Journal of Marketing Research, 35*(1), 114–126.

Chabris, C., & Simons, D. (2010). The invisible gorilla: And other ways our intuitions deceive us.

Derbaix, C. M. (1995). The impact of affective reactions on attitudes toward the advertisement and brand: A step toward ecological validity. *Journal of Marketing Research, 32*(4), 470–479.

Dodgson, L. (2019, October 18). A social experiment eerily predicted teenagers would all order 'triple dipped chicken' at a restaurant after they were unconsciously targeted by influencer ads and posters. https://www.insider.com/social-experiment-predicts-what-food-teenagers-will-order-video-2019-10

Dolcos, F., Katsumi, Y., Moore, M., Berggren, N., de Gelder, B., Derakshan, N., Hamm, A. O., Koster, E. H. W., Ladouceur, C. D., Okon-Singer, H., Pegna, A. J., Richter, T., Schweizer, S., Van den Stock, J., Ventura-Bort, C., Weymar, M., & Dolcos, S. (2020). Neural correlates of emotion-attention interactions: From perception, learning, and memory to social cognition, individual differences, and training interventions. *Neuroscience & Biobehavioral Reviews, 108*, 559–601.

Ehrenberg, A., Barnard, N., Kennedy, R., & Bloom, H. (2002). Brand advertising as creative publicity. *Journal of Advertising Research, 42*(4).

Ehrenberg, A. S. C. (1988). *Repeat-buying: Facts, theory and applications* (2nd ed.). Oxford University Press.

Fernandes, M. A., Koji, S., Dixon, M. J., & Aquino, J. M. (2011). Changing the focus of attention: The interacting effect of valence and arousal. *Visual Cognition, 19*(9), 1191–1211.

Florack, A., Egger, M., & Hübner, R. (2020). When products compete for consumers' attention: How selective attention affects preferences. *Journal of Business Research, 111*, 117–127.

Frederickson, B. L., & Banigan, C. (2011). Positive emotions broaden the scope of attention and thought-action repertoires. *Cognition and Emotion, 19*(3), 313–332.

Friestad, M., & Thorson, E. (1986). Emotion-eliciting advertising: Effects on long-term memory and judgment. *Advances in Consumer Research, 13*(1), 111–116.

Harvey, B. (2023). Powerful mind part 39. Human Effectiveness Institute. https://www.humaneffectivenessinstitute.org/we-each-have-a-gpt4-within-us/

Hourihan, K. L., Fraundorf, S. H., & Benjamin, A. S. (2017). The influences of valence and arousal on judgments of learning and on recall. *Memory & Cognition, 45*, 121–136.

Jager, D. T., & Russeler, J. (2016). Low arousing positive affect broadens visual attention and alters the thought-action repertoire while broadened visual attention does not. *Frontiers in Psychology, 7*, 1652. https://doi.org/10.3389/fpsyg.2016/01652

Janiszewski, C., Kuo, A., & Tavassoli, N. T. (2013). The influence of selective attention and inattention to products on subsequent choice. *The Journal of Consumer Research, 39*(6), 1258–1274.

Jefferies, L. N., Smilek, D., Eich, E., & Enns, J. T. (2008). Emotional valence and arousal interact in attentional control. *Psychological Science, 19*(3), 290–295.

Jeong, E. J., & Biocca, F. A. (2012). Are there optimal levels of arousal to memory? Effects of arousal, centrality, and familiarity on brand memory in video games. *Computers in Human Behavior, 28*(2).

Johnson, G. (2007, August 21). Sleights of mind. *The New York Times*. https://www.nytimes.com/2007/08/21/science/21magic.html

Katsuki, F., & Constantinidis, C. (2014). Bottom-up and top-down attention: Different processes and overlapping neural systems. *Frontiers in Systems Neuroscience, 8*, 138.

Kirk, R. (2022). We can better manage media fragmentation by measuring 'Right Reach'. The Media Leader. https://the-media-leader.com/we-need-to-lean-into-fragmentation-by-measuring-right-reach/

Macknik, S. L., King, M., Randi, J., Robbins, A., Teller, T., & J., & Martinez-Conde, S. (2008). Attention and awareness in stage magic: Turning tricks into research. *Nature Reviews Neuroscience, 9*(11), 871–879.

McConnell, M. M., & Shore, D. I. (2011). Upbeat and happy: Arousal as an important factor in studying attention. *Cognition and Emotion, 25*(7), 1184–1195.

Memmert, D. (2006). The effects of eye movements, age, and expertise on inattentional blindness. *Consciousness and Cognition, 15*, 620–627.

Mitchell, T. A., & Nelson, M. R. (2018). Brand placement in emotional scenes: Excitation transfer or direct affect transfer? *Journal of Current Issues and Research in Advertising, 39*(2), 206–219.

Murrell, A. (2022). The age of average. https://www.alexmurrell.co.uk/articles/the-age-of-average

Nelson-Field, K. (2013). *Viral marketing: The science of sharing*. Oxford University Press.

Nelson-Field, K., Riebe, E., & Newstead, K. (2013). The emotions that drive viral video. *Australasian Marketing Journal, 21*(4), 205–211.

Poels, K., & Dewitte, S. (2018). The role of emotions in advertising: A call to action. *Journal of Advertising, 48*(1), 81–90.

Roach, T. (2023). Attention's the problem, creativity's the answer—As ever. Marketing Week. https://www.marketingweek.com/attentions-the-problem-creativitys-the-answer-as-ever/

Romaniuk, J. (2018). *Building distinctive brand assets*. Oxford University Press.

Saxton, B. T., Myhre, S. K., Siyaguna, T., & Rokke, P. D. (2020). Do arousal and valence have separable influences on attention across time? *Psychological Research Psychologische Forschung, 84*(2), 259–275.

Shapiro, S., & MacInnis, D. J. (2002). Understanding program induced mood effects: Decoupling arousal from valence. *Journal of Advertising, 31*(4), 15–26. https://doi.org/10.1080/00913367.2002.10673682

Simons, D. J., & Chabris, C. F. (1999). Gorillas in our midst: Sustained inattentional blindness for dynamic events. *Perception, 28*, 1059–1074.

Sutherland, M. R., & Mather, M. (2017). Arousal (but not valence) amplifies the impact of salience. *Cognition and Emotion, 32*(3), 616–622.

Teixeira, T. S., Wedel, M., & Pieters, R. (2012). Emotion-induced engagement in Internet video advertisements. *Journal of Marketing Research, 49*(2). https://doi.org/10.1509/jmr.10.0207

Teszka, R. (2011). The crossroads of magic and science: Sleights of mind: What the neuroscience of magic reveals about our everyday deceptions. *Cerebrum (New York, NY), 2011*, 2–2.

Treisman, A. (1998). Feature binding, attention and object perception. *Brain Mechanisms of Selective Perception and Action, 353*(1373), 1295–1306.

Warner, J. (2023). Reach & frequency in the age of outcomes. Medium. https://medium.com/snowflake/reach-frequency-in-the-age-of-outcomes-927bb3157973

Wallman, R., & Edwards, G. (2023). *How brands blow*. Gasp Books.

6

From Realization to Application; the Diary of a CPO

An expert is someone who has succeeded in making decisions and judgements
simpler through knowing what to pay attention to and what to ignore.
Edward de Bono

When you're in the market for a new house, you turn to an architect. When
plumbing issues rear their head, a skilled plumber becomes the expert you rely
on. Each of these experts plays a pivotal role when their specialized skills are
needed, and their expertise proves invaluable when your own abilities reach
their limits.

In this chapter, we introduce you to a seasoned expert: Alex Pacey, a
distinguished Chief Product Officer (CPO) for Omnicom Media Group who
has built attention-focused products from the ground up. His expertise is
evident in his ability to simplify the complexities of attention and identify the essential components that hold the greatest significance for both his
agency and clients. Alex has been a student of attention economics since day
one, and since graduation he now assumes the role of an architect, metic-
ulously designing blueprints for product solutions, managing home owner
expectations and leading the construction team to bring them to life.

In this chapter Alex brings you 'take it straight to your boss' advice on
the successful integration of attention metrics and how all the pieces of the
'people, product, process' come together.

K. Nelson-Field, *The Attention Economy*, https://doi.org/10.1007/978-981-97-0084-4_6

He is both humble and humorous in his advice. Enjoy the read.

6.1   My Diary Prelude

By Alex Pacey (OMG)

Being asked to write this chapter was undoubtedly a nice little boost to the ego at least initially until the realization that a completion date nears and confidence in my ability is put under self-induced scrutiny. I should point out at the outset that I am not a writer, and this is the largest body of text I will have produced since my University dissertation in 1995 which was titled "Human Resources Management in Further Education." I have no idea what it was about and I'm not sure I did then either. This chapter will at the very least be more useful than that particular endeavor was – that's a promise I feel confident putting in writing.

The aim of this chapter is to give you, the reader, some insight into the experience of setting the wheels in motion to bring attention measurement into your business. In it I will endeavor to talk through the decision-making process and what I (and the broader team involved) have learned through the process. Much of the content will be, I hope, just as applicable to any new product or process as it is to the specifics of Attention Measurement, But before we do that let's set a bit of context about my role in our company and how attention landed on my lap!

Since starting this role, it's become clear to me that there are multiple interpretations of what a Chief Product Officer does. Certainly, the avalanche of unsolicited emails and LinkedIn messages I receive leads me to believe that most out there think that I'm responsible for the purchase of almost anything available on the open market. So, let's clarify. I'm involved with two of the key functions within Omnicom media agencies—Strategy and Planning.

These functions in a media agency involve the development and implementation of overarching plans and approaches that guide the agency's activities, decision-making processes, and resource allocation to achieve ours and our client's business objectives. They are responsible for aligning the agency's offerings with market demands, identifying opportunities for growth, and ensuring that the agency remains competitive in the ever-changing media landscape. The strategy function encompasses a wide range of activities, including market research, competitor analysis, client insights, trend forecasting, and the formulation of long-term goals and tactics. It provides a framework for the agency to navigate challenges, make informed choices, and optimize its resources to deliver effective and innovative solutions to clients.

Overall, they act as a compass, guiding the agency's direction and helping it stay ahead in a dynamic and competitive industry.

In short, it's my role to provide the best possible environment for these elements to flourish. It has been my experience that the key to succeeding in doing this lies in the push to make headway in two key areas—Product (and within it, process), and People. As we move further into the chapter, I will present the challenges faced and tactics used through the lens of these two pillars but first let's look at what I mean when I say Product and People.

6.2   Factors of Influence or Change

Product Development

Overseeing the development and enhancement of the agency's products and services. This is asking questions like; are we staying ahead or at the least keeping pace with the needs of the market? This includes understanding market trends, conducting market research, and identifying client needs. By collaborating with cross-functional teams, such as client teams, technology, and data analytics, we ensure that the agency's products align with client objectives and meet market development and ensure continuous improvement to stay competitive in the evolving media landscape.

Product Process

The process component focuses on establishing efficient and effective workflows and procedures for product development, delivery, and optimisation. This involves working closely with teams to define and streamline processes, ensuring clear communication and collaboration across departments. We look to facilitate the implementation of agile methodologies, enabling faster iteration and responsiveness to market changes. By continuously evaluating and refining processes, we improve operational efficiency, minimize bottlenecks, and enhance the overall productivity of the agency.

Product Branding

It may seem somewhat superficial to say how we 'talk' about what we do is as valuable as what we 'are doing' or 'how we do it', but all I'm really talking about here is branding. It's so important to provide language that enables your team to shorthand to clients and other interested parties what it is we can do for them. This isn't just about the new function or product like attention measurement. Taking a commonly performed task or process and turning it into a standardized and scalable product is incredibly valuable. This productising or branding of a repeated function allows the agency to leverage its expertise and best practices, ensuring consistent and high-quality outputs while saving time and effort.

Product Simplification

I'm not entirely sure why, but it has been my experience over 24 years that a lot of people work very hard to make what they do seem very complex, providing an avalanche of acronyms and obfuscatory language and words. For example I remain unconvinced that ideation is a real word or that information needs to be "cascaded". Success for me has always come in the form of doing the opposite of this, of attempting to get to the core of any challenge in the most matter of fact way possible. Without doubt this is at its most powerful when mobilized properly to get a group of people to rally around something. People want to know what they're going to be doing and why it's important—what's at the heart of the matter. They are less than interested in hearing you try to sound smart.

People Buy-In

It seems embarrassingly self-evident as I type this, but I've seen it done poorly enough times, often by myself I'll admit, that it clearly bears repeating—nothing will be achieved without the buy-in of your people. Anything that is developed from a product perspective must be done with those who will use it firmly in front of mind. Nothing you build or synthesize is done in isolation, it will have a knock on effect, at least if it's successful, for your people and the existing processes and structures within which they work. I would argue that we need to be giving equal weight to the consideration of how any product will land with your people as you do to the development of the product itself you are asking for problems. But really, how often do we truly do that?

Product and People Synthesis

Put simply, how does everything work together? How does any new thing affect what we're already doing? It's fundamental in my role to try to have the broadest possible view of all the processes and structures that we have in place. Without this knowledge it's incredibly hard to evaluate whether any proposed change will be beneficial or not. If I can't do this for myself then it makes it next to impossible to get a larger cohort of people to embrace a new or indeed existing process.

The interplay between product and people and all the intricacies within and around them, cannot be understated when considering something new. Especially a new category like attention measurement. This holistic approach is the foundation for better product innovation and meaningful change in an organization.

TAKE IT TO WORK

Simplicity is key for effective change. Great ideas, clear communication, and straightforward problem-solving can unite people and drive success.

6.3 The Polarising Issue of Media Measurement

So let's turn our attention (ahem) to the matter at hand, the central point of this chapter and the book itself, the application of attention measurement into a business. To my mind, to understand the importance of attention measurement it's important to share something of the context into which attention measurement lands.

Since the advent of digital media, agencies have lived with something of a polarization of approaches to targeting our brands' consumers. Accepting that there is a good deal of nuance to any approach, if we simplify it, you can either:

1. Target all potential category buyers—an approach championed by the good folks at the Ehrenberg-Bass Institute for Marketing Science or;
2. Look to use the tech and targeting options available to me to isolate and engage more specific behavioral audience targets.

The Ehrenberg-Bass Model challenges the notion that marketers should exclusively focus on a specific target audience. Instead, it emphasizes the importance of reaching and appealing to all potential buyers within a product category. Some implications of this perspective include:

1. Broad Reach: Marketers should invest in strategies that allow them to reach a wide audience, ensuring that the brand is visible and accessible to as many potential customers as possible.
2. Mass Communication: Mass marketing efforts, such as advertising and promotional activities, can be effective in increasing brand awareness and attracting a larger customer base.
3. Continuous Presence: Maintaining a continuous presence in the market helps to reinforce the brand's visibility and attract both new and repeat buyers.

However, in parallel, the media industry in Australia is experiencing a proliferation of new measurement techniques as viewing habits undergo significant changes. With the rise of digital platforms, streaming services, and mobile devices, traditional methods of measuring audience viewership are being seen as less effective in capturing the full spectrum of consumer behavior. As a result, media companies, advertisers, and researchers are actively exploring and adopting innovative measurement techniques to gain a comprehensive understanding of audience engagement.

Overall, both approaches to targeting have challenges. Targeting all category buyers puts the emphasis firmly on broad audience reach delivery which raises the question—what is reach? Up to this point, traditionally when we talk about reach, what we're actually talking about is an 'opportunity' for our ad to be seen. On the flip side of the coin when we think of taking a much more targeted approach, the challenge here is that whilst there are many brilliant companies offering measurement solutions, they often lack breadth and mean you are measuring a portion of your media spend (albeit very well).

This is the environment into which attention measurement lands and in turn why its potential is so great. Attention measurement offers for the first time an applicable, cost effective deeper measure of consumer engagement with your advertising message—not just who has the 'opportunity to see' but rather who is actually 'seeing'.

More specifically, for those of us over here in media agency land, the attention conversation evolves the reach vs cost equation by providing us a truer measure of 'effective reach' or 'quality reach' if you prefer. From a media vendor perspective this has the potential to change the selling equation. Consider these two examples from different points on a 'quality' versus 'effective' reach spectrum:

1. A mass reaching social media platform that delivers reach on a vast scale, but one must pause to consider the effect on attention given the user's ability to speed scroll through content;

or;

2. The more limited reach of the movie theater that can now lean on a new industry wide metric to confirm its long-held belief that its audiences are indeed fully engaged on the big screen experience.

It is by no means a one or the other scenario as amongst other things the above examples don't take into account relative cost, but it's easy to see the impact attention has on the choice architecture.

While it may seem obvious, the importance of attention in advertising cannot be overstated. Attention is the gateway to perception, memory, and persuasion. If your ad doesn't receive attention, it doesn't have a chance to make an impact.
David Ogilvy (1963)

TAKE IT TO WORK
The attention conversation changes the reach vs cost equation by providing us a truer measure of 'effective reach' or 'quality reach'. This changes the game for media vendors.

6.4   Factors of Influence for Successful Attention Integration

Now let's look at what I've learned specifically about the implementation of attention and a new measurement product in our processes. Let's consider this learning through the lens of the two pillars we discussed earlier, People and Product.

People Identification (Your Internal Target Audience)

I did weigh up whether this should sit under People or Product as it will clearly affect both but ultimately, I landed here. A question we asked ourselves straight away with attention was are we trying to 'raise the floor' or 'raise the ceiling'? Is attention measurement going to be the domain of a few of the brightest and best in our building or is this something that a much broader team is going to need to understand and leverage? Understanding this was absolutely central to our decision processes from day one, and informed everything that happened from there on out.

We also had to consider the amount of time and resources that we were willing to commit to the change to attention. The degree to which we were willing to change up our existing products or processes. The level at which we looked to pitch any training documents and sessions, or indeed whether we needed them at all.

Having said all that, ultimately, we cheated. We decided it had to be both, or rather it would naturally become both. This was driven by two beliefs:

1. Ultimately over the medium to long term we felt that attention measurement and the ability to plan using attention metrics would become 'hygiene'. That is to say that it would become something expected as it's so fundamental to understanding effective reach. That being the case, it needed to be something that everyone who worked on a client response understood. So—raising the floor.
2. Knowing our teams there would naturally be individuals who would 'lean in' and look to gain much more than a basic understanding of attention. So—they would help us to raise the ceiling.

QUICK EXPLAINER
Raise the ceiling or raise the floor?

The concepts of 'raising the floor' and 'raising the ceiling' are often used in the context of setting or redefining standards or expectations, whether in personal development, business, or various other fields. They represent different approaches to improvement and progress.

Raising the Ceiling aims to reach higher levels of performance, quality, and achievement by setting ambitious goals. It encourages creativity and innovation, and drives competitive advantage, but it can be costlier and riskier. Raising the Floor involves increasing the minimum standard to an acceptable level. It prioritizes efficiency and risk reduction, providing consistency rather than disruption.

One is about higher results with higher risk, one is about reliable results with lower risk. Often the answer is both, reward is a trade off.

People Preparedness (Before Engaging Your People)

If you're reading this book, then it's a fair assumption that you already have a view on how attention could slot into your current offering. For us, our goal was to have a broad perspective on the value of attention within our process *before* we engaged the broader contingent of people who would ultimately be tasked with using this new attention measure. Because of the nature and complexity of our industry it's rare that a large number of people will have a high level view on all the possible implications of inserting a new metric into your process. They will however have a deeper view on the effect on their specific area of expertise, often in ways that you hadn't considered. For this reason, it's hugely beneficial for you to be able to provide that 'top down' view to your leadership team before you engage your people. With that said it's just as important that your initial view is flexible enough to be able to clearly take on the feedback and input from your broader team, particularly those identified as lean-in individuals. Lean-in individuals are your stars, and their input should be valued and seen by others as such. By providing that top down view to the leadership before you engage your team, not only will this motivate others to engage and step forward, but it will stop any potential disillusionment from lean-in individuals who can quickly become detractors.

> **TAKE IT TO WORK**
>
> Lean in individuals are your stars, and their input should be valued and seen by others as such. Those that lean in are often those who are capable of raising the ceiling.

People Preparedness (During Early Stages of Engagement)

Our approach to the dispersal of knowledge on attention was first 'inspire', then 'educate'. To do this you need to get the experts in front of your people.

For us this meant getting our chosen attention partner in front of as many of our people as possible, talking them through the research that had been done to validate what we were doing, and to provide early and clear use cases. This was an intentional approach knowing the best and newest approaches to media and marketing are the most interesting to our people. The benefit of this approach provides an environment for people who have a predilection to lean-in, to actually do so. It's been our experience that there's a much higher likelihood of success when smart people come forward themselves rather than it being us that 'identify champions' to the cause. Your best people are always disproportionately busy because everyone wants a piece of them so if they buy in of their own volition then it's the best possible outcome.

People Buy-In (Create an Environment for Champions to Succeed and Flourish)

Having a core group of lean-in individuals was incredibly satisfying, but the onus was on us to provide an environment for them to flourish and feel like their input was valuable and worthwhile. Lean-in types will not invest unless they know that our approach is likely to lead to change. We had to be prepared to accept that multiple people could offer more valuable perspectives than the initial leadership team, which was not only acceptable but desirable. In this context, effective leadership involves identifying where the skills of highly motivated individuals can be optimally utilized and setting the right framework for them to operate within, while allowing them the autonomy to take the lead. With that said, I have continued to learn that a key part of this job is actually getting these guys to do less. Sounds odd, but put another way, getting them to understand that most people won't go to the lengths they do when considering the effect of attention on their day-to-day roles. So creating an environment for champions to flourish is sometimes reminding them it is a long distance race, not a sprint.

> Whatever you do in life, surround yourself with smart people who will argue with you.
> John Wooden (Hall of Fame US Basketball Coach)

People Training Methods (Focus on the Fundamentals)

I've spoken at some length above about 'lean-in' individuals. The fact is that there is a much larger contingent of your people that won't do this (there must be a 'double jeopardy' pattern in there somewhere). That's not to say non 'lean-outers' aren't interested or aren't smart and talented people. Their focus may be elsewhere, they may be too slammed capacity wise to lean in on this particular subject. Sometimes they may be leading the charge within their own specific team which you may be unaware of. But for simplicity's sake let's refer to those who lean-in, as 'your people'. Training is for your people.

So, let's talk about the focus of your training. And focus is the key word here. If you are interested enough to be reading a book on the subject of attention, then it's likely you might fall into a trap that I certainly have over the years, trying to impress with your newly found knowledge vs actually training them.

Your initial training on Attention should focus entirely and exclusively on usable information. In a fast-developing area like this one the temptation is to constantly worry about keeping pace and whilst that is important it's not as important as the fundamental building blocks of attention. For example, your people knowing your perspective on how attention alters a client brief is considerably more valuable than them remembering that TikTok added a new format that is higher in attention than the others.

TAKE IT TO WORK

Attention should focus entirely and exclusively on usable information. Don't worry about introducing 'new' into the training programmes, make sure 'your people' are savvy on the fundamentals.

So what were our fundamentals? Our initial training program focused on answering 3 core questions:

1. What is attention?
2. How is it measured?
3. How are we approaching it for our business and our clients?

Nothing more complicated than that. We made a real effort to remove anything superfluous so that the sessions were about fundamentals, and our team were told that. They were told there would be follow up sessions when necessary and that we could customize materials for specific client needs (more on that later).

By the way, always offer to train your clients and external partners. It serves two purposes wonderfully. Firstly, you demonstrate to your partners that your business values are keeping pace, and in front of, new market opportunities. Secondly, and speaking candidly, once your internal team knows that their clients know about this they'll recognise the necessity to pick it up and run with it themselves.

> **TAKE IT TO WORK**
> Always offer to train your clients and external partners, it serves multiple purposes.

People Training Methods (Repeat, Repeat, Repeat)

It's been my experience that when landing and embedding anything new in an existing process you are constantly pushing against what I've (perhaps charitably) termed "knowledge elasticity." That is to say that whenever you push a group to learn new ways of doing things it's prudent to work under the assumption that a high percentage will revert to the way they had previously been doing things. If attention is to become part of your ongoing process, then it cannot be a 'one and done' approach to any training that you roll out. Be prepared to repeat training regularly, to provide updates and where possible turn successful work into case studies to be shared with the group. Case studies in particular are a wonderful way to both reassure people that this can be done and to motivate people to keep up with the new capabilities.

Another tip, consider adding attention measurement to the relevant staff induction documents, it's a relatively uncomplicated way to begin the training process and let new recruits know it's something you value.

> **TAKE IT TO WORK**
> If attention is to become part of your ongoing process, then training cannot be a 'one and done' approach. And consider adding attention measurement to staff induction documents, this sets the tone from day one (plus they will be well prepared for continuous training).

People Training Methods (Arm Yourself to Overcome the Attention Skeptics)

Earlier in the chapter I raised the question; "what is reach", well for most who work within the media industry it's one of, if not the, pre-eminent measurement metric and has been since the year dot i.e. how many people is your campaign going to reach? and, how many reach points will it take to achieve your objectives? With the advent of universally applicable attention measurement, we are now able to look at what percentage of that reach is actually being seen. As this book suggests, that is a big change. And when trying to make that change you are going to be met with some resistance. It's inevitable. In my mind I consider there to be a 'Skepticism Spectrum' it's loosely a formed concept, but it runs the course from the "I don't know, I kinda like things the way they are" end, all the way through to the "well this won't work and I'm going to tell everyone why" wavelength. Ok, so I'm being a bit flippant with the naming conventions, but I suspect you know what I'm driving at. Resistance to change is hard wired into us. To our brains change equals danger.

Through this process of bringing in attention metrics into our processes we've come up with a few tactics to counter the skeptics:

1. Be clear on the clear FAQs and have answers for them—on your journey to understanding attention there are going to be questions that you and your team encounter as you build up to training the larger cohort. These will no doubt rear their heads again once you begin the process of training. Make sure you have answers in place for when the training rolls out. Remember though, be confident in the fact that it is ok to not have all the answers with a measurement this new. It's actually an opportunity to demonstrate to your team that you're pushing boundaries, and in turn fairly revealing about certain individuals if they expect all the answers to be in place.
2. Lean on the experts—Good attention vendors will understand that most people they deal with are on a steep learning curve and are motivated to spread the word and help. Lean on them! The closer you can get your people to the source of truth the more impactful the message.
3. Mobilize your lean-in individuals. People trust others that "look like me", you only need to look at the explosion of "influencers" as proof of this (I didn't say that was a good thing!). Your lean-in individuals are your internal influencers. We have found them to be a wonderful way to engage skeptical individuals on their terms in a safe environment and get into the specifics on an issue that maybe couldn't be handled in a group training environment.

TAKE IT TO WORK

Skepticism to change is absolutely normal. Lean in on the lean-in team members, they are like your very own influencers.

People Management (Make Sure the View from the Top Matches the Day-to-Day Reality)

Clearly, this is not a point unique to the context of Attention measurement, but having worked for the best part of 25 years in media I think I'm on safe ground to say that it's an industry that isn't shy about weaponizing hyperbole. To me it's one of the least appealing facets of this industry's personality that 'talkers' too often triumph over 'walkers', that the dream is often seen as more important than the reality. This can and does work for business that I and you, reader, both know, however it only ever actually works from an external facing perspective i.e., what the business appears to be able to do.

When it comes to implementing a new measurement approach it's absolutely vital that the vision you put forward to your people is anchored in what is possible. That's not to say that you shouldn't be excited about what is potentially possible or give a sneak peak into upcoming developments you're considering. But ultimately it's vital that the narrative you put forward is one driven by what's possible now with the tools, people and processes you currently have in place. I cannot overstate the value of everyone in your business being reassured that you as the leadership team understand the pressure your broader team face day to day when working to make new things a reality and fitting them into existing or even new frameworks. Additionally, there are some hugely advantageous side effects:

1. Confidence greases the wheels of forward motion. If your team is confident that what you have put together clearly reflects their day-to-day reality, and that it works 'on the ground', they are exponentially more likely to put it in front of a client and present it with confidence.
2. Functionality = fixture. Nothing will make attention measurement in your business wither on the vine quicker than it not being able to function within the parameters of your existing workflow and processes (more on that later). It won't matter how many training sessions you do and how often you and your leadership team sit around scratching your heads. If a planning manager working on Client X can't get it to work, it's over.
3. Top to bottom alignment builds culture, this is a wonderful side effect. Nothing builds on culture like alignment, like everyone in your business looking up at the top and thinking; "they get me and they understand what I'm going through." If you are rolling out something as fundamental as attention, and you are saying "this is a huge change in the way we see measurement, it's a huge change in the way we expect you to do your job and speak to your clients, oh and by the way we've built approach aligns

with what you currently do", then that sends such a powerful message to your people. They will know you value the experience they have at work and that you understand them. Don't undervalue that opportunity.

TAKE IT TO WORK

Top and bottom alignment builds culture, so be a 'walker' not a 'talker'. Make sure the vision you put forward to your team is anchored in what is possible, but free enough to allow them to set sail. That sends a powerful message to the team about how management values them.

While there is a long list here about arming people for success and change, let's move on to the other 'P' in the family—product.

Product Perspective (Build a Distinct Perspective on Attention)

One of the paradoxes with attention measurement is that it's so fundamental that it can seem overly simple. The flip side of this conundrum is that you will rarely have the time it takes to download all the knowledge that exists within a book (such as this one) in a way that is usable in the day-to-day cadence of your business relationships.

The most effective way we have found to have clear cadence, is have a distinct point of view for your business on attention, these are two of ours:

1. Spend time understanding the implications of attention on your marketing plans and make a conscious decision on how fundamental this will be as part of your approach/dogma. There is no 'one size fits all' approach and what works for you might not work for others.
2. If we remove any other noise, attention measurement is about getting more humans to spend time processing your messaging to influence a purchase, action or belief.

What if you try to do the same with your business? Can you articulate in simple terms what your business is trying to do and what would you say is its core vision or mission and do you know the process by which you're looking to achieve this? If you're clear on that then you will make understanding where attention fits in a lot simpler and give yourself a better platform for understanding if you can build a distinctive position.

Product Processes (Embed Attention in Your Existing Process and Product Suite)

There is the convergence of a couple of things I've talked about earlier that come to bear here. Firstly, the growing complexity of the media marketplace and proliferation of measurement techniques. Secondly, the need for your people to understand how attention is going to affect their day to day lives, the work they do and the products and processes they use to complete it. The danger here is an irony, bringing in attention to your business adds complexity when its entire purpose is to provide clarity. Put more succinctly, most of your people are not looking for another thing they need to worry about!

For that reason where at all possible you should focus on ingesting attention metrics into existing platforms rather than building something new or, maybe worse, bolting on—the problem with bolt on(s) is they tend to drop off!

Just like we advise clients to test new creatives, websites or media approaches, Invest the time to consider how attention can improve what you already do in a way that is easy for the majority of your team to understand. It's much easier to get a team's head round a product update vs a brand new product entirely.

> **TAKE IT TO WORK**
>
> Spend the time and resources to integrate (good) attention data or models into your systems. The trouble with bolt-ons is that they fall off.

Product Validation (Demonstrate Cause and Effect)

One of the most enduring practises in advertising is the classic before and after shot:

1. A tired house with a fresh lick of new paint
2. 15 minutes a day to go from flab to abs
3. Adding stock to your Bolognese

It's used ubiquitously because it works, it's a shortcut to what we all want to understand—cause and effect. If I do X, Y *will* happen.

So, with that said any integration of attention metrics into a product that looks at optimizing or planning to reach needs to be able to demonstrate the 'before and after' impact to understand the delta between traditional OTS reach and attention adjusted reach. Only by understanding this can you start to use attention data to help shape your recommendations for the better. The biggest factor to wrap your team's head around when moving from OTS to attention adjusted reach is the certainty that your estimated attentive reach and frequency will be lower than your traditional reach & frequency, often significantly when it comes to frequency. This is no reason to sound the alarms and rethink your entire existence as a marketer. In most cases, media plans for most clients are only incrementally different to the previous years plan and just because you now have a quality metric to better forecast effective reach does not mean your previous campaigns are any more or less effective, you just have a greater understanding of how effective they were and could be in the future.

This is an opportunity for agencies, marketers, and brands to drop the YOY vanity metrics and reporting bravado to seek greater clarity on how they should be allocating budget across channels and platforms. Practically, unless you have all your budget invested into a single poorly performing channel attention wise, the introduction of attention metrics into your planning will not drastically change the channels that appear on the media plan, nor the formats to a degree.

The most misunderstood element of attention planning is that all the media budget will be funneled into the channel with the highest attention scores and that simply is not true. As much as I love cinema, great media planning when considering attention data is understanding the seismic difference that you can have by allocating effectively between both high and low attention platforms (they play a key role also).

Without getting into the role of diverse types of attention and the nuances of how much attention you need for the common objective you are trying to achieve, good attention planning is about understanding how attention metrics, reach potential and cost of media intersect across all channels within the intended mix.

For example, a 10% shift from channel A to channel B across your plans does not sound like something you should put in bright red font in a client presentation, even if it could yield a modest 5% incremental effective reach points for the same budget. However, such a shift across multiple plans across multiple years, will compound into a much larger impact. Cause and effect, "1% daily improvements compound to 37 times better annually" James Clear (2022).

TAKE IT TO WORK

The most misunderstood element of attention planning is that all the media budget will be funneled into the channel with the highest attention scores and that simply is not true. Good attention planning is about understanding how attention metrics, reach potential and cost of media intersect across all channels within the intended mix.

Product Global/Localisation (Lean on Global but Then Make It Local and Client Specific)

Being part of the Omnicom global network has provided considerable advantages in our journey to deeply integrate attention strategy and data here in Australia. One major advantage is our access to a diverse group of highly intelligent individuals worldwide who face similar challenges. We often learn from them as they are in many cases more advanced in addressing challenges, have learned valuable insights that we haven't, or have encountered issues that we may have overlooked. This has undeniably given us the chance to partner with high quality attention vendors much earlier than we otherwise would have, had we not had the global scale as an agency. Our business's size and extensive reach have definitely opened doors to collaboration opportunities that would typically have arisen at a later stage.

With that said its vital to strike a balance here:

If you lean too much on global output, there can be a suspicion both internally and externally that you lack local expertise or nuance. If you ignore global learning or knowledge, then the risk is that your findings can appear to lack replicability or lack heft. There's no perfect mix here and ultimately comes through experience and knowing what works best for your business and its clients. However, we have found that a mix of three components works well:

1. Universally applicable global knowledge: this communicates scale and the widespread acceptance of attention. This ultimately breeds confidence in sharing findings up the chain to clients and more senior staff members.
2. Local nuance: in Australia, we've observed the unique aspects of our market. Specifically, attention measurement might mean something different for the evolving BOVD and streaming landscape, and its viewers, in these shores. Experience shows us that often a global insight or global research finding can be interpreted as having a lack of relevance to

a local market. Whilst there are certainly globally applicable findings and commonalties. For example, in the way that we humans interpret and process information, rightly or wrongly these can be trumped by a perceived cultural difference or local nuance.

3. Instance specific examples: a bit of a mouthful but what I mean here is what do we know that is specific to the people or client that we are talking to. For example, if your client is historically heavy TV advertisers what does attention measurement mean for them and crucially what does it change in how you're going to approach their business. Let's face it we don't want to expend all this energy and time to tell a client everything will remain the same.

Product WIP (Work in Progress Is Good Enough)

There was a period not too long ago when all the talk was about 'having a start-up mentality', and this was regardless of the size of the business you worked in. During this period there was a lot of inevitable bandwagon jumping and talk of 'always being in beta', the idea that concepts and products are always developing and never truly finished. This always struck as something difficult to implement in a business the size of Omnicom, but now more than ever this rings truer to me. The fact is that attention measurement is not just new to your business, its new full-stop, relative to more established forms of measurement.

This forces us to work with something that will be by its very nature changing and evolving. You can choose to see this one of two ways. Firstly it's a risk, we don't know everything, and things are changing so how do we talk to staff and clients? Or conversely (and this is the way I've approached this for the business that I work within), see this as a moment of liberation. After a career of trying to always have the answer it's been refreshing to know that nobody has all the answers on something this new. What this has meant in terms of a product approach is that we don't wait for things to be 'finished' before sharing with the team.

There is a power and value in staying ahead of the curve, and experience, introducing innovative ideas to a client's business, even when you anticipate changes, is essential. Clients constantly express the desire to be challenged and our experimentation with proof of concepts in attention measurement has allowed us to do just that. I would encourage you to do the same.

TAKE IT TO WORK

There is power and value in experimenting with attention measurement. It keeps you in front of the curve and your clients happy.

Product Rollout (Build a Roll Out Plan but Make It Flexible)

One of the clearest learnings we have taken from this ongoing experience is the need for flexibility. Part of a partnership, such as the one we have with our valued attention partner, is that we learn new results and implications constantly. As exciting as this is, it can play havoc with your best laid plans. How you approach this is going to come down to you, your team and what you know of how your business works best. For us the floor vs ceiling thought came back in here—specifically in understanding the fundamentals that are unlikely to change and making sure that everyone is comfortable with that, all the while keeping a core group of lean-in individuals up to date with all relevant developments as they occurred. Proved invaluable in assisting us to understand the implications of the changes. They also played a crucial role in bridging the communication gap back to their respective teams, guiding us in determining the most effective ways to convey or withhold information about these changes. They have been, and continue to be, our internal influencers.

6.5   The Wrap Up: A Category Changing Summary

I hope you read this whole chapter and I hope that I have delivered on my promise of making it useful. We are all so busy, our attention spans are diminishing, which means summaries are good. So here you go! Here is my summary on how to engage your people to help you change a category:

1. Identify your internal target audience.
2. Form a broad point of view before engaging your people.
3. Get the experts in front of your people.
4. Create an environment for attention champions to succeed and flourish.
5. Focus training on the fundamentals.
6. Repeat, Repeat, Repeat.

7. Arm yourself to overcome the attention skeptics.
8. Make sure the view from the top matches the day-to-day reality.
9. And when building out your product.
10. Build a distinct perspective on attention.
11. Embed Attention in your existing processes and product suites.
12. Demonstrate cause and effect.
13. Lean on global, but then make it local and make it client specific.
14. Work in progress is good enough.
15. Build a roll out plan but make it flexible.

Lastly, a note for you and your team building the attention approach in your business. Stay the course! Hold fast! Whilst there is undoubtedly a correlation between the quality of a new idea or approach and its likelihood to succeed, it's not the whole story. People revert to old ways, lean-in individuals leave for new pastures, global people make changes, your focus gets pulled elsewhere (which is ironic since we are talking about attention). It's a familiar story. Ultimately if you want attention in your business if you see it as fundamental then it's there for the long haul and ultimately most permanent change happens incrementally. People see others succeed and want a piece of it. New business gets won because of it and new people get inducted into your business where attention is BAU.

Be consistent, it will happen.

Alex Pacey.

6.6 List of Contributors

Alex Pacey. Chief Product Officer, Omnicom Media Group

Alex Pacey is an industry leader with over 23 years' experience focused on communications strategy and planning. As a multi award winning planner Alex has helped guide some of the globe's biggest brands across myriad categories. Moving into leadership roles Alex helped lead multiple agencies to Agency of the Year honors across multiple years. In his latest role as Omnicom's Chief Product officer Alex is responsible for the product that supports both Strategy and Planning functions across Australia's largest media group.

7

The Investors

Here's to the crazy ones. The misfits. The rebels. The troublemakers. The round pegs in the square holes. The ones who see things differently. They're not fond of rules. And they have no respect for the status quo. You can quote them, disagree with them, glorify or vilify them. About the only thing you can't do is ignore them. Because they change things. They push the human race forward. And while some may see them as the crazy ones, we see genius. Because the people who are crazy enough to think they can change the world, are the ones who do.
Think Different Campaign. Apple Inc. (1997)

The extreme change in the media measurement landscape recently is a credit to the dreamers who saw the value of change in the first place, and to the tireless early adopters who dared to follow. In this chapter we shine a spotlight on these visionary individuals.

Dreamers are individuals who possess an uncanny ability to foresee the impending need for transformation long before it becomes evident to the majority, and act on it. These people had the foresight and the unique set of skills to champion ground-breaking attention measurement agendas through the intricate channels of their respective organizations, while galvanizing others to their cause. Being a dreamer is not an easy job; it's a path fraught with challenges that only the most resilient souls dare to tread. The

K. Nelson-Field, *The Attention Economy*, https://doi.org/10.1007/978-981-97-0084-4_7

path to change is often paved with skepticism, doubt, judgment and frustration. When a dreamer succeeds, they become a hero in their organization, but a misstep can result in gardening leave. Early adopters are individuals who seize the opportunities to experiment, acquire knowledge and advance an innovation, when many are still pondering their next move. These people lean in to progress, underscoring the significance of proactive and forward-thinking approaches in a world that often hesitates in the face of change. Being an early adopter comes with its fair share of risks too, but their role is crucial in providing ideas the initial momentum they need.

The relationship between dreamers and early adopters is symbiotic. Dreamers rely on early adopters to champion and support their ideas from concept to reality. Early adopters, in turn, gain an edge by embracing these fresh concepts and enjoying the benefits of groundbreaking solutions, products, or services before they become mainstream. This collaboration is pivotal in propelling innovation and progress, bridging the gap between imaginative thinking and practical application.

This chapter is a collection of simple stories about the adventures of extraordinary people. These are stories from round pegs in square holes that helped to shape a category.

7.1   The Dreamers

> **The Dreamer Brief:**
> The **'why'** they bothered getting involved with attention economics movement
> The **'plan'** they took
> The **'how'** they brought others along for the journey
> The **'wins'**, the learnings

Kristian Claxton, GroupM

Icebreaker Question: What's the most embarrassing thing you've ever done in public and lived to tell the tale?

Icebreaker Answer: Back in 1999, when I was a cringe-worthy 16-year-old, I had the pleasure of visiting San Antonio, Ibiza, with my dear mother—yes, embarrassing, I know! One evening, we found ourselves at a bar sipping on cocktails when a bunch of rowdy 18–21-year-olds, clearly riding the highs of life, decided to do some karaoke. And, of course, they couldn't resist shoving the microphone right in front of me. Picture this: my voice cracking like a pubescent teenager while attempting Celine Dion's "My Heart Will Go On." Let's just say, it was a Titanic disaster of epic proportions!

In 2017, our addressable TV business embarked on a journey driven by the belief that technology, data, and media could revolutionize advertising for both brands and viewers. This belief was not unique in the adtech industry, but it inspired us to pioneer the first proprietary TV addressable audience platform, allowing advertisers to target more meaningful audiences with multi-dimensional attributes. At this early stage of our innovation journey, our proprietary platform had a significant impact. It provided advertisers with optimized media placement, increased media efficiency, improved viewer experiences, and boosted performance.

Curiosity led us to explore the role of attention in the effectiveness of TV addressability. We suspected that attention played a vital role in driving better results since we were delivering addressable ads on TV screens during high-quality content. To investigate this, we conducted a study in the UK. The study aimed to measure audience attention levels across TV content and establish a baseline for advertising.

We sought to answer questions like: What factors influence advertising attention? What can advertisers do to capture more attention? Armed with this stimulus, we engaged our agencies and advertising clients to help shape the scope of our work and to encourage participation. Our study involved 250 households and 7,503 OTT and linear TV ads from 18 brands in various sectors. We used eye-tracking technology to gather attention data and examined variables such as age, gender, affluence, life stage, and more. We also conducted a concurrent study on broadcast linear TV attention. To assess the impact of attention on brand choice, we employed short-term advertising strength (STAS) measurement, which involved discrete choice modeling to measure brand uplift.

Our findings were enlightening:

1. The platform had the most significant impact on ad attention, surpassing audience, creative, and branding.
2. Longer OTT ads garnered more active attention, with a 30-second ad gaining 15 seconds of active attention (60-second ads gained 30 seconds). This trend did not hold for online formats.
3. OTT outperformed linear TV in capturing active attention, with viewers giving about 20% more attention per second to OTT ads.

4. Active attention positively correlated with increased sales for advertisers, demonstrating a significant impact on brand performance.
5. Audience relevance significantly influenced active attention, particularly in addressable audiences, where relevant ads generated higher attention. We continued our exploration by partnering with University College London to delve into how attention influenced cognitive response and memory structures.

More recently, Inspired by the work of industry experts like Karen Nelson-Field, Orlando Wood, and Peter Field, we commissioned research and developed solutions to help advertisers and agencies make more effective decisions to maximize addressable TV's potential by leveraging our unrivaled understanding of addressability x attention and creative effectiveness. What began as a simple belief has led to a series of innovations that benefit brands and viewers alike.

We now strive to create fewer, but better, ads that enhance the overall advertising experience.

TAKE IT TO WORK

The most significant learning here is the transformative power of innovation and data-driven insights in advertising. This journey highlights how technology, data, and audience attention can be harnessed to create more effective and relevant ads. It underscores the importance of continuously exploring and adapting to new insights, collaborating with experts, and prioritizing quality over quantity to enhance the advertising experience for both brands and viewers.

Angelina Eng, Interactive Advertising Bureau (IAB)

Icebreaker Question: If you could time travel to any era just for the fashion, where would you go, and what outfit would you rock?
Icebreaker Answer: If I could time-travel for fashion, I'd whisk myself back to the vibrant 1980s, a decade that resonates with my youth in Queens, New York/Channeling my inner Madonna and Janet Jackson, my ensemble would feature acid-washed skinny jeans, high-top sneakers, and vivid leg warmers, topped with a graphic tee and a patch-adorned denim or leather jacket. Big, silver, long-hanging earrings and a stack of bangles would accessorize my look, while my hair would be styled in a bold perm, reminiscent of the glamorous styles I adored on shows like Dynasty. Drawing inspiration from the pages

of Cosmopolitan and Vogue, my makeup would be as daring and colorful as the era itself, encapsulating the eclectic and rebellious spirit of the 80s.

In the ever-evolving landscape of digital advertising, my journey into the realm of attention metrics was not a sudden turn but rather a culmination of experiences and a deep-seated passion for industry standards. Long before I assumed the role of Vice President of Measurement, Addressability, and Data Center at the Interactive Advertising Bureau (IAB), I had been an advocate for the measurement standards within the digital advertising sphere. Over the course of my career, I have held a variety of positions in account management, media planning and buying, ad operations, and data analytics. These roles provided me with a holistic understanding of the industry and the pressing need for reliable measurement standards.

At IAB, my primary responsibility was to identify the challenges and trends stemming from the rapidly evolving data landscape. My role involved providing insights and guidance to the industry, and developing industry standards and guidelines. In this dynamic environment, data-driven decision-making is paramount, and measurement standards are the cornerstone. Historically, the industry relied on metrics such as Opportunity To See (OTS), reach, frequency, and GRPs (Gross Rating Points). While these metrics provided valuable insights, they often provided a surface-level under-standing of the audience's interaction with the content.

In 2022, attention metrics emerged as a promising next step in this measurement evolution. The allure lay in its potential to offer insights into advertisement effectiveness, a missing puzzle piece. As the market for atten-tion metrics grew, IAB organized our first IAB Measurement Leadership Summit in early 2023, focusing on attention metrics. This event gath-ered executives from advertising agencies, brands, publishers, ad tech, and measurement companies in an interactive event aimed at sharing perspectives and ideas for the future of attention. The summit's key takeaways illuminated our next steps for attention metrics. Foremost among them was the stark absence of consensus on what constituted "attention." This lack of accord was due to the inherent subjectivity of attention, the disparities across media channels and devices, and the array of methodologies employed to measure it. It became abundantly clear that attention metrics needed to account for these diverse factors. Moreover, it was evident that attention metrics were still in their infancy, requiring further development and education.

However, both buyers and solution providers expressed a desire for atten-tion metrics to evolve into a transactable metric, signaling its potential significance in the industry's future. We realized attention could impact revenue, inventory, and user experience. Publishers wanted to understand this impact as advertisers relied on metrics to assess effectiveness. Furthermore, evaluating attention should consider ad creative, separate from device, channel, or format.

We quickly launched the IAB Attention Task Force in March 2023. The plan included gathering input, facilitating discussions and developing guides. We took a bottom-up approach, recognizing that the definition of attention for advertising differed from academic research. Our goal was to work with the Media Rating Council (MRC) on a set of guidelines for attention measurement. Leading IAB's journey into attention metrics, I realized its immense potential to revolutionize digital advertising.

While attention is just one metric among many, from OTS to business outcomes, it's pivotal. I'm honored to spearhead the establishment of measurement standards that the industry can adopt, reshaping digital advertising's core foundation. One can achieve and fulfill transformation with a vision, enthusiasm, and openness to new experiences. In this book, visionaries and pioneers of attention economics describe how they have overcome innovation hurdles, generating value for themselves, their organizations, and their clients. They have showcased that attention economics extends beyond being a mere catchy phrase, serving as an influential method of connecting with audiences in an oversaturated and clamorous environment. They have also inspired others to explore the potentials of attention economics individually. Their knowledge and perspectives have played a pivotal role in progressing this area and setting benchmarks for future developments.

TAKE IT TO WORK

While attention is just one metric among many, from OTS to business outcomes, it's pivotal. One can achieve and fulfill transformation with a vision, enthusiasm, and openness to new experiences.

Jean Paul Edwards, OMD Worldwide

Icebreaker Question: If you could only eat one food for the rest of your life, what would it be, and why?

Icebreaker Answer: It would have to be sushi both healthy and delicious (I assume someone else is funding this long-term dietary experiment). The first time I bought sushi was with the express intention of proving to myself I would hate it, I could not have been more wrong. Illustrating we should always challenge our priors.

First a bit of context; the word advertising is derived from the Latin 'advertere'—to direct one's attention to, give heed. Attention is not a new concept, it has always been a key consideration in media planning and activation, however, there is a modern interpretation. We see the importance of attention being based on two key shifts:

1. The proliferation of media experiences, especially since the advent of digital media in terms of both the quantity of content available and the diversity of experiences from unviewable ads through immersive 3d.
2. The ability to measure physiological proxies of attention such as gaze and emotional response.

We came to reappraise attention in the 2010s through the lens of empathy; our ability to better understand the consumer's situation and their experience of advertising messages.

It soon became clear to us that the existing metrics based around reach, frequency and viewability only told part of the story. The industry's understanding of the attentive experience had little empirical evidence and was defined through the supply and demand of impacts, i.e., this is why cinema impacts are more expensive than TV impacts. The new capabilities to measure the attentive experience of advertising meant that we could now provide that empirical evidence. We had attention measurement capabilities in several local markets operational for some time. This experience expanded to global studies with a wide range of media partners and clients to measure to initially benchmark attention delivery across channels.

Crucially we also studied the various levers that impacted the delivery of attention and that attentions impact on brand and sales metrics across 6Cs:

- The **content** of the ad—its various attributes colours, sounds, tone etc.
- The **culture** of the audience targeted demos, markets
- The **context** in which the message is delivered
- The **communications** imperative of the brand across different objectives and brand attributes
- The **contacts** of the plan describing its budget level, effective frequencies and reach
- The **constructs** of the messages, the different formats used in display, video, social feeds and more.

The more we looked, the more nuance we found. Discovering the market had not adequately priced-in attention or optimised the outcomes derived.

This is essentially because different brands or campaigns have different attention requirements, for example:

- Salient, market leading brands with simple messages and famous logos do not need a large amount of attention, so more expensive, high attention formats may be wasteful.
- Campaigns with more complex messages or brands with less familiarity have higher attention requirements.

If those requirements are not met the impacts are not just ineffective, they are negatively effective, driving awareness and intent to a more dominant competitor. We found dozens of dependencies like this which enable us to calculate attention requirements for different briefs.

Our global planning tools now contain measures of the attention delivery across all channels in the form of the proportion of impacts that will deliver those requirements. This means we can more precisely allocate budgets across channels that most cost effectively deliver the attention required. These principles also apply in placement and activation as we bid for impacts based on specific attention requirements. Local panels and measurement initiatives measure and model attention delivery across placements in numerous environments. Enabling the impact of attention optimisation to fully scale.

Our clients Intuitively understand that attention is crucial to success, but it is evidence that really shifts the needle from innovation experiment to change in approach. A library of cases illustrates these attention optimisations deliver not just uplift in brand metrics but also sales impact, increasing sales volumes whilst also delivering lower CPAs.

We believe that thinking of attention as range of different requirements, rather than as a single dimension or fungible currency has number of positive implications for industry as a whole;

- They enable brands to more effectively leverage their unique assets and attributes meaning their optimal attention solution is unique to them and less liable to commoditization.
- Content can be monetised better, it is not just the high attention channels that have value, low attention media has its place when used correctly.
- This aligns the incentives of buy and sell side reducing the impulse to force more seconds of attention.
- Perhaps most importantly it better respects consumer attention, only utilizing the time required to get the message across.
- There are also positive climate impacts as fewer impressions are wasted.

We originally thought that attention might be a six-month project to recalibrate our tools with improved measures. What we found instead was a deeper understanding of the experience which has led to many optimisations and approaches that shift strategy, planning, buying measurement and creative alike. The 'attention mine' is by no means exhausted.

TAKE IT TO WORK

Different brands and campaigns have unique attention requirements. Understanding these requirements allows for more precise budget allocation, optimizing attention delivery across channels, and enhancing brand metrics.

Erez Levin: Attention Evangelist and Media Quality Specialist

Icebreaker Question: What would you put on a billboard for the world to read?

Icebreaker Answer: Quality and Quantity.

Dreaming of, and fighting for, a more equitable Ad-Supported internet—the internet isn't fair, and it never will be. But that doesn't mean we shouldn't strive for a fairer ecosystem, the one we were promised that can self-sustain itself with at least an approximate balance between users, publishers, and advertisers.

From a very young age, I had a keen sense of fairness and justice. This often manifested itself as perceived injustices to me by my older brother, so much so that everyone was convinced I'd be a lawyer one day. And while my appetite for vocally proving my arguments tempered, I never lost that sixth sense to spot injustices and the instinct to try to correct them (I was touting "see something, say something" before it was mainstream). My love of and deep curiosity about the power of advertising similarly goes back as far as I can remember, and so it was no surprise that I ended up in the field. Though all my informal and formal education about advertising was in the pre-Internet era (i.e. "marketing fundamentals"), my first job was in digital ads, and I fell in love, hard. It truly felt like we were the pioneers that would break John Wanamaker's truism, bringing full accountability to media spend and effectiveness through precise and granular tracking.

Then over my first decade in ads, and increasingly so through my second, I started to notice the cracks in the narrative. Cognitive dissonance can only be ignored so often and for so long, especially if you're born with the unlucky gene of natural curiosity. After enough evidence piled up, patterns of inequitable outcomes for advertisers, quality publishers, and users, I could no longer deny what I knew to be true. At that point, a switch flipped, and I had a clear view of the severity and scale of the singular root cause of what ails this industry: bad measurement.

In the early days, I pointed fingers at all the bad actors I saw, and there were too many to count. But soon enough I realized this was a systems and incentives problem, which allowed me to take a much more dispassionate and thoughtful approach: "don't hate the player, change the game." And thus began my strategic crusade, aligning with numerous other industry allies focused on adjacent areas or similarly possessing deeply held beliefs that by fixing measurement we could restore balance and fairness to the internet ecosystem and make marketing effective again. By fixing the ad-supported model, we would create incentives for high quality content and remove the incentives for low quality content, including misinformation and disinformation and the ugly corners of the web that hide behind a veneer of legitimacy but are simultaneously hosting some of the worst outright and borderline fraud that are poisoning our society.

Fortunately, despite the industry's deeply entrenched systems, standards, and incentives, in a relatively short period of time we've been able to create a multi-front wedge where a flood of market players have created narratives and solutions that make these issues impossible for buyers to ignore, and usually profitable to embrace.

The balance of incentives will soon tip over. But even with all the success we've seen, I believe we are still in the early innings of the Attention economy. It's only a matter of time before we no longer need to answer the first question: "Why should we focus on Attention?" and shift entirely to the more important and challenging one: "How do we solve for Attention?." I've never pretended that this was a simple challenge, but the importance of solving this problem to restore desperately-needed balance in the internet ecosystem is far too important, not just for the ad industry, but for all of society, to let complexity stop us. Let's get to work.

> **TAKE IT TO WORK**
>
> The industry is now at an inflection point where those that challenge the status quo will be rewarded, until the incentives become realigned. It is inevitable, so the best time to get on board is right now.

Joanne Leong, dentsu

Icebreaker Question: If you could only eat one food for the rest of your life, what would it be, and why?

Icebreaker Answer: Japanese food! I love all the styles of Japanese cuisine—whether it's cooked, raw, fried, fermented—all done impeccably and with the utmost levels of conscientiousness, and the desserts are divine.

I currently lead, and have shaped, dentsu's Attention Economy initiative since its onset 6 years ago. At the time, we saw an opportunity for change; we felt that the value system used in media planning and buying hasn't kept pace with the complexity of the media landscape and the change in consumer attention. It was still considering all impressions equally, and therefore conversations with clients were always about the trade-offs between reach and cost, vs the true value of that exposure.

We wanted, and needed, a more human-centric metric that will hopefully create a better ecosystem for advertisers, clients, and agencies. In order to do so, we embarked on a multi-year research program to understand and apply consumer attention. We felt that in order for this to be impactful, we needed to collaborate with the industry. As such, we involved clients, researchers and media owners from the very beginning and got feedback from them along the way to shape and design the approach of our initiative.

This was a big win, as it eventually helped with the adoption and buy-in of attention metrics internally and helped us think about it from different perspectives across the industry. We then took the data/models from our research and incorporated that into the way that we plan, buy, and measure media. We've made incredible and amazing progress but as with anything, the devil is always in the details.

As an industry, we still face operational challenges ahead of us, in terms of agreeing on the definitions around attention and how it is scaled and applied across different channels. Ultimately, the only way we can get there is through collective efforts and collaboration, research, and dialogue.

> **TAKE IT TO WORK**
>
> We are in a currency crisis! It's been illuminating to see the real gaps between what impressions and viewability tell us (i.e., what's served) vs. what is actually being consumed by people. Up to 85% of desktop display ads that are technically "viewable" aren't seen! It's wild. There is a real disconnect between cost and attention (and therefore the value) of ads.

Paolo Provinciali, LinkedIn

Icebreaker Question: What's your weirdest talent or skill that not many people know?

Icebreaker Answer: I am a coffee geek and I have been roasting my own coffee for the past 10 years. When I'm done geeking out about marketing, you'll find me running my own coffee roastery somewhere in the Adriatic coast of Italy.

As a marketing and advertising professional (and son of two neurologists), I love finding ways to best deliver the right message to the right person at the right time to create awareness, change perception, and drive behavior. I'm a big advocate for the Attention Economy because it allows me to be more efficient and effective at it—but more importantly—I believe it can play a critical role in improving the lousy reputation advertising has. Let me explain. Most metrics used to transact on advertising are based on media delivery and interaction rather than its ability to influence the human element of our target audiences. Many efforts have been made to drive accountability in media by creating pay-for-performance incentives based on business outcomes. Nevertheless, such measures are incredibly complex and often unfair because they lump together many factors that are outside of the control of a single group or agent (e.g., product positioning, price, competition, creative messaging, macroeconomics, and others). Moreover, with the proliferation of content driven by the growth of digital media—which will accelerate dramatically with the expansion of generative AI tools—people have developed the ability to tune out messaging that they deem irrelevant.

This poses an increased challenge for marketers to break through and create resonance. In this context, measuring and optimizing for human attention offers two key advantages:

1. It drives audience centricity and aligns incentives between marketers, publishers, and consumers: high-attention environments often provide a

positive audience experience (good for consumers), which in turn attracts audiences that publishers can monetize at premium pricing (good for publishers) because advertisers know their message will not be ignored (good for marketers).

2. It drives the right level of accountability to all the stakeholders involved: media sellers can be held responsible for providing high-quality attentive environments, and it puts pressure on the marketers to develop a creative that can capture and retain attention, drive resonance, and ultimately influence behavior.

Over the past few years, thanks to academic research and the validation of many field studies, it has become unquestionable that capturing human attention is a prerequisite for marketing impact. While it is not the sole requirement to guarantee success, it offers sophisticated professionals the ability to better diagnose and optimize the variables influencing the outcomes of their efforts. Although much of this sounds intuitive and a positive step forward, introducing another metric in established businesses and industries was incredibly challenging. Much of the skepticism and resistance was driven by the comfort of a suboptimal status quo and sometimes by some hidden incentives to maintain an imperfect system. However, being an early mover in this space allowed me (and my brands) to capitalize on the information asymmetry created by the fact that the vast majority of media inventory is not priced based on its ability to capture attention.

By taking an arbitrage approach in my media buying strategies, I could maximize the ROI of my campaigns by securing high-attention inventory priced at a low cost and avoiding low-attention inventory at high prices. In the long term, an arbitrage approach is not sustainable to guarantee consistent outcomes, but more importantly, aligning the incentives of the buy and sell side of the advertising marketplace towards metrics that ensure audience-centricity and a positive audience experience, will allow us to raise the bar for the industry as a whole. This is the reason why I believe the Attention Economy can play a critical role in the betterment of the advertising industry's reputation: from being considered a tax on your content that people tune out or even pay to avoid, to becoming a positive experience that allows people of all means to access high-quality content and information, while connecting consumers to the brands and products that they'll want and love.

While measuring human attention is not new, applying the Attention Economy notions to marketing and advertising is still nascent. There's still little consensus between well-renowned practitioners on basic concepts such as defining attention, measuring it, and whether it can ever become a trading currency. Yet, this should not deter us from further exploring and investing in this science. The ability to capture human attention is the advertising industry's foundation. Finding solutions to complex problems and breaking down the many variables influencing our desired outcome makes us experts at what we do.

TAKE IT TO WORK

The Attention Economy can play a critical role in the betterment of the advertising industry's reputation: from being considered a tax on your content that people tune out or even pay to avoid, to becoming a positive experience that allows people of all means to access high-quality content and information, while connecting consumers to the brands and products that they'll want and love.

Jon Waite, Havas Media Group

Icebreaker Question: What's the most random and useless fact you know, but can't resist sharing it with people?

Icebreaker Answer: Haribo, the German sweet brand. Stands for HAns RIegel BOnn, The name of its founder and the city in Germany from which it was founded. Totally useless… but always so little known. Plus I can't resist a Haribo… my weakness!

Media is broken'. A colleague said this to me upon seeing a media plan being presented to a client. The client pushed back on the value of TV, of OOH and of Cinema and requested more social media and more programmatic display ads, media with cheap CPMs to which they could 'easily assign value'. How was it that some of the best media experiences for consumers were being so overlooked by brands? Media was broken, a culmination of years and years of competition between agencies vying for client's business, ever decreasing discounts on media, ever decreasing resources being allocated to strategy and planning roles whilst the focus became 'media procurement'. Buy media, buy it cheap.

The problem is the media experiences that consumers have within different media are so incredibly different, and the currencies and metrics we use to trade units of media say nothing about the propensity of certain media to deliver effectiveness for brands. 'Impressions' are almost infinite, new websites with ad placements for sale pop up every single day, mostly designed to drive 'clicks' and sell advertising impressions without providing any value to the viewer i.e. good quality entertaining content.

So what to do about this huge divide between media experiences that are valuable to consumers and the broken media trading ecosystem? That was the question we asked ourselves when the 'Attention Economy' was conceived. Impressions are infinite, but it's consumer attention that is a valuable and scarce commodity. But changing an entire media trading economy would never be an easy thing. Billions of advertising dollars every single year are traded on these 'legacy currencies' and the number of stakeholders from media owners, agencies, brands, auditors and more make meaningful change incredibly difficult. We knew it would take time, arguments, a lot of money and patience.

Most people said we'd be 'wasting our time', there was 'a way things are done' and some people had even tried similar things in the past, they said that was unlikely to ever change. But a group of colleagues and I found that hard to swallow. We set about finding others who thought like us, others who saw a broken value exchange between brands and consumers and who could help us prove this concept of an 'Attention Economy'. We launched a programme consisting of forward-thinking media owners, rigorous and respected researchers and brands with the aim of highlighting the nature and differences of attention across select media channels and formats, to see if there was a different way to evaluate the differing media experiences consumers were having and how that could affect the results of a campaign for brands.

What resulted was the first industry whitepaper on 'The Attention Economy', from which a huge body of work has since grown. The paper showed that 'Attention' could be measured in a meaningful way, that it changed dramatically across media choices and that indeed when people pay attention to ads, this ultimately can lead to better results for brands in terms of measures like Brand Consideration, STAS and Recall. What we learnt from this was that existing measures of media quality were deeply flawed, especially in the 'digital' (Online) space and that if we were going to create a more equitable ecosystem between advertisers, content owners/producers and audiences, things needed to change. We needed to incorporate these measures into how we decide where to spend money, to reward content creators who ultimately deliver better experiences for audiences and in turn greater results for brands.

A lot has changed in this time, in my role I've been actively working to ensure we incorporate attention metrics into our media planning, buying and optimisation processes and practices. But there's still a long way to go in producing a larger body of real world evidence of effectiveness and potentially working towards a standardization of 'Attention Metrics' with industry bodies.

> **TAKE IT TO WORK**
>
> Don't accept what 'is' just because that is how it has always been done. We work in a constantly and possibly endlessly evolving space that does not stand still, at the whim of cultural and technological change. Think about real people, real experiences and how they (and you) interact with the world around you, don't accept something as truth just because the 'numbers' tell you it's right. If something doesn't feel right, question it and seek to understand why.

Sorin Patilinet, Mars

Icebreaker Question: What would you put on a billboard for the world to read?

Icebreaker Answer: Don't forget how badly you once wanted what you have now.

I was born in communist Romania during a time when global brands were forbidden, and advertising was purely state propaganda. I learned to love advertising after the fall of communism, discovering a brand-new world full of color, opportunities, and new brands. That was the golden age of advertising when we watched ads for fun and education—when attention to advertising was not a challenge but a given.

Fast forward 20 years, as I experienced the ups and downs of a big advertiser in my Marketing Science role at Mars, attention to advertising became a problem. Without a clear culprit, there are many ways in which the ad industry inflicted self-harm. By focusing more on the HOW of advertising, we forgot about the WHY. We fell in love with technology and the opportunity it offers, forgetting what our role is: to bring value to consumers. As consumers moved to digital, we simply ignored early signals and unleashed an avalanche of brand messages without any attention to quality context, purely hunting attention without politeness. Consumers responded by ad-blocking, skipping our messages, and ignoring our attempts to talk to them.

I got interested in the Attention Economy early, understanding that managing attention doesn't mean squeezing every second of brutal attention but listening deeply to consumer behaviors to improve. I understood that paying attention to what people pay attention to helps us, as marketers, repair our lost communication with consumers.

For me, creative or content was the priority focus for understanding the impact of attention. Signals that show us the presence of attention, confusion, and even boredom are goldmines for marketers to dig into. Using second-by-second tracking of real research respondents' behaviors, we understood what drives attention, how we lose attention, and how our communication can be even more consumer-friendly and effective.

While the industry was mostly focused on becoming digital, at Mars, we embarked on a journey to prove the link between attention and sales impact irrespective of digital or non-digital formats. And we proved it. It's not if attention drives business impact; it's what kind of creative construct triggers the attention that drives business impact. The question of quality of attention is what we care about now.

We learned to make better advertising. We learned about the importance of human presence, familiar situations, humor, audio, and the constant need to "keep it simple." Nothing new, just the basics.

Mutually, I've shared the Mars story on numerous stages, and I've brought peer companies further on the attention economy thinking by joining the board of the Attention Council and being an advocate for behavioral research for the good of consumers.

TAKE IT TO WORK

To make better advertising, "keep it simple." Nothing new, just the basics. Human presence, familiar situations, humor, audio—all very important triggers of attention that drive business impact.

7.2   The Early Adopters

The Early Adopter Brief:
The **'what'** they were trying to achieve when testing attention measurement
The **'plan'** they took
The **'outcome'** achieved

Scott Luther, TRG

Icebreaker Question: If you could time travel to any era just for the fashion, where would you go, and what outfit would you rock?

Icebreaker Answer: 1920s for sure—who doesn't feel more confident in a three-piece suit?

Case Study Category: Strategy, Creative, Planning

Objective: what did you want to achieve in your case study and why?

In our industry people always take sides. When it comes to advising clients on how to best engineer growth, our organization had leaders in two camps emerge: some that would dive deep into the marketing science, building clear statistical models to logic our way into an answer; and in the other camp, the those who are comfortable with alchemy, willing to take leaps in search of something evocative. We needed a unifying philosophy that could help explain—and be relied upon, again and again—how those in each camp were right. Attention became our answer.

Method: what was the plan you took to achieve this and how did you execute?

Attention is a simple concept that contains multitudes. Attention can be studied, tracked, verified, quantified, and compared. It also must be earned, it can never be guaranteed. Attention is not binary, it's on a spectrum, and it can be additive. Using attention as a concept creates a unified language for how we help advise our clients. We can engineer opportunities for higher attention, we can optimize and make improvements to the media strategies that create this space, and we can also work to deliver the magic—crafting compelling creative that earns a disproportionate amount of attention.

Outcome: what did you achieve and/or learn for your business?

Bringing this philosophy into the organization removed friction in the process and helped different disciplines work better together, more fully recognizing how each could help the other succeed. This has led to new—and more successful—projects with existing clients, and attracted new like minded clients to our agency.

TAKE IT TO WORK

Attention is a simple, but not simplistic concept. Because it feels so common sense, it is in more danger of becoming jargon—and therefore, losing the true meaning—as people within the industry try to advance their own attention-agendas. Maintaining a wide view of the concept of attention is essential to realizing its full value.

Stephen Cleary, The National Lottery

Icebreaker Question: What's your weirdest talent or skill that not many people know?

Icebreaker Answer: I'm quite proud of my Kermit The Frog impression.

Case Study Category: Strategy, Creative, Measurement

Objective: what did you want to achieve in your case study and why?

I was brought into the office of a senior manager to show off our latest work. It was a beautifully shot three minute documentary video. Everyone internally was delighted with what was produced. I was really proud of it too. It was heartbreaking when our empirical research showed it was likely to be watched for only a couple of seconds. At The National Lottery we now believe advertising works through memories, and we know the importance of getting people's attention if we want them to buy our brand. When they are dreaming of a life-changing win, or they pop into their local shop to get some lunch, will our brand come to mind? We wanted to make our digital brand building advertising more effective. With our digital spend on the rise year on year, we were questioning if we were really getting what we paid for. We wanted to know how long people are actually looking at our ads, and if our brand is even getting noticed.

Method: what was the plan you took to achieve this and how did you execute?

We took part in an Attention Study for the Irish market. This was a first-of-its-kind study in the market. This research would measure how much real attention people pay to ads on Facebook, Instagram, Twitter and YouTube. By 'real attention' we mean human Irish adult eyes on our ads rather than the data that the social media platforms were telling us. A panel of 400 Irish adults was sourced to participate in the study. They would download an app from Amplified Intelligence, accept the privacy permissions, and then scroll through their digital feeds as they usually would do in their everyday lives. The phone's camera would track their attention to advertising through eye gaze.

Outcome: what did you achieve and/or learn for your business?

We learned a couple of seconds of attention is all you might get on social media. It was a harsh reality but one that was hard to deny as it aligned with the global data we had seen. If we have a short window to get your brand noticed, we figured our ads have to be really well branded. The results from the study have transformed our digital advertising strategy. We see our role for brand advertising on social media as a gentle reinforcement of our distinctive brand assets. We're fortunate at The National Lottery that we have a strong set of distinctive brand assets which we've worked hard to grow over the last couple of years. If we need our brand to get noticed in a couple of seconds, we make sure to use these assets rigorously. We like to say "big, early and often." The beautiful long form storytelling pieces are no more, sadly. It's hard to justify spending hundreds of thousands of euros on producing ads like this if we know they wouldn't be watched beyond a couple of seconds. We're focused on short form and visual ads that don't contain long story arcs and can be understood with and without audio. Now I am able to show that senior manager how effective our ads really are.

> **TAKE IT TO WORK**
>
> Just because you can advertise online with long videos, doesn't mean you should. Social media advertising is a gentle reinforcement of your distinctive brand assets. With attention being so short, it is very helpful to have a strong list of assets you can rely on to get your brand noticed. The more effective ads are likely to be short and well branded.

Phil Jackson, Haleon

Icebreaker Question: If you could only eat one food for the rest of your life, what would it be, and why?

Icebreaker Answer: Italian food, as they have by far the broadest cuisine that's both delicious and healthy. I'm also a big fan of Italian wine!

Case Study Category: Buying, Measurement

Objective: what did you want to achieve in your case study and why?

We have a Global Media learning agenda made up of five strategic pillars that are linked to levers of growth, one of which is 'Media Attention'. The objectives of this pillar are twofold: (1) Demonstrate that higher attention media placements/inventory drives incremental business outcomes versus historical norms and (2) Identify the most cost-efficient approach(es) for achieving higher attention media placements/inventory Since early 2022, we have been testing in markets around the world, to build a repository of evidence to inform both objectives, and this latest test in the US for Sensodyne was set up to deliver learning's towards both. For this programmatic open-exchange Video campaign we sought out to test four different in-flight bidding strategies, to compare their respective performance. The bidding strategies selected are outlined in the 'method' section, however for further context, we wanted to compare the performance of a 3P algorithm provided by a leading attention vendor versus the native bidding algorithms available in our preferred DSP; DV360. The overall objective of this campaign was to achieve awareness and recall of Sensodyne messaging amongst a broad target audience, so the following metrics were measured; CPM, VCR, CPCV, Attention and Ad-Recall Lift, with the primary success KPI across the four test cells being Ad-Recall Lift.

Method: what was the plan you took to achieve this and how did you execute?

A four-cell control vs. exposed experiment was activated within DV360 with all variables including frequency, CPM cap, creative, etc. kept consistent across all cells, with the test variable being the bidding algorithm used. The bidding algorithms used across the four cells were: (1) Attention custom algorithm (3P attention vendor), (2) AVOC (DV360 native), (3) Max Viewability 10s (DV360 native), and (4) vCPM (DV360 native—historical BAU tactic). The campaign was live for around two weeks (late June to early July 2023) with periodic checks to ensure daily pacing was in line with minimum requirements to achieve the necessary amount of reach to achieve enough survey respondents by test cell. As previously mentioned, the question selected in the brand lift survey focused on Ad-Recall as the business outcome. The same 3P attention vendor who provided the attention custom algorithm for bidding, also appended their pixel tracking to all live placements across the campaign to be able to measure and report on attention achieved by each cell, based on their propriety attention metric.

Outcome: what did you achieve and/or learn for your business?

The campaign successfully delivered statistically significant Ad-Recall Lift results across all four cells, which we considered to be extremely positive as previous tests in some other smaller markets had run into difficulties in achieving the required reach to deliver the necessary number of survey responses in all test cells. Based solely on attention and Ad-Recall Lift, the AVOC cell was the winner, however it's also the cell with the highest CPM. The 3P attention custom algorithm cell unexpectedly finished the campaign with the lowest average CPM, over 3X lower than the AVOC cell, and it also delivered an attention score that was comparable with AVOC, however the Ad-Recall Lift it achieved was much lower than AVOC and very similar to both vCPM and Max Viewability 10s. Overall, the test has further reinforced the belief that certain types of 'higher' attention can drive incremental business outcomes; however, we need to continue to test what the most cost and time efficient way of achieving that higher attention is. E.g., Upfront planning versus in-flight optimization and if we are optimizing in-flight, which bidding type is preferable.

> **TAKE IT TO WORK**
>
> Attention as a metric is a great step forward because it forces us, as marketers, to look outwards to the people we're trying to communicate with and influence, whereas other metrics were perhaps leading to too much introspection. Whilst that is undoubtedly a positive thing, it means we need to show patience around how we all establish a common understanding of the various ways this new metric is not only measured, but also the levers we can influence to affect it. Ultimately, it's something that will require a lot of nuance and consumer understanding in its application.

Baptiste Amar, GetYourGuide

Icebreaker Question: If you could time travel to any era just for fashion, where and when would you go, and what outfit would you rock?

Icebreaker Answer: Okay I would definitely go early days of the Roman Empire—toga era. Something comfy, cozy, flowy—yet quite sexy as well. As I think about it, that's actually how I would qualify most of my current closet (comfy, cozy, flowy, sexy).

Case Study Category: Strategy, Planning, Buying

Objective: what did you want to achieve in your case study and why?

Our initial objective was to complement our creative qualification framework. We pre-qualify every ad with a pretesting approach—which is in the conditions of a panel survey; aka not in situ. We wanted to generate additional data to ensure our creatives were doing the job in getting the necessary attention to lift awareness and brand health metrics, especially on social platforms. Ultimately, the objective of this first batch was to prove the criticality of curating for attention—we proved that!

Method: what was the plan you took to achieve this and how did you execute?

In order to achieve the objective above, we used gaze tracking in real-time formats in two cities in the USA. It qualified the attention second-by-second for 6 creatives in 3 social platforms. The initial goal was to understand which creative performed better by platform/format… but that's not the outcome we got; it was way more ground breaking.

Outcome: what did you achieve and/or learn for your business?

The results generated super valuable outcomes. Here are the top 3:

(Strategic) Drivers of attention: We had this hypothesis that creativity was the main driver of attention. The results were clearly invalidating it: Within the platform, all creatives delivered similar attention patterns; Across platform though, the same creatives drove very different attention. This got us to reorder priorities, and think about the platform first.

(Tactical) Optimisations: Upon the results, we massively optimized our media and creative mix. For e.g., one platform did not generate enough attention to create impact; we had the feeling it didn't, but it was a bold decision and being able to scientifically confirm the hypothesis drove alignment and action. This generated savings as we removed layers of vastly ineffective creatives; and it helped us pivot our creative strategy for next year, expecting large uplift YoY.

(Tooling) Measurement stack: As we prove the value of the tool we used from the first round, we now have it included in our measurement framework—and it's part of our creative qualification stack.

TAKE IT TO WORK

My biggest learning was the hierarchy of the attention drivers. Being able to *scientifically* invalidate the hypothesis that creativity is the main driver of attention independently from media buying was critical to drive alignment internally. This reflected in (1) a step change of our media x creative strategy with extra focus on catering for platform specificities, (2) a more relevant set of metrics to assess the quality of our delivery, and (3) clear roadmap to optimize our digital distribution ongoingly towards high attention, driver-by-driver!

Ollivier Monferran, Essity

Icebreaker Question: If you could put a message in a bottle and send it to your past self, what would it say?
Icebreaker Answer: Choose the red pill!
Case Study Category: Creative, Planning, Buying, Measurement
Objective: what did you want to achieve in your case study and why?
As a brand builder selling FMCG products, my main objective is to build mental availability. In order to succeed in the digital landscape, capturing attention is a must have. Working in a big corporation, our colleagues in charge of media guidelines are always pushing us to use social platforms (META) for building awareness. As a consumer, my level of attention on such platforms is so low that I was questioning the interest of doing so.

Having attention data is now providing me concrete evidence that inventories in META feed only generate "low attention" which has to be taken into consideration when we build our strategies.

Method: what was the plan you took to achieve this and how did you execute?

As Media & Digital Director, I have the opportunity to pilot between 15 and 20 digital campaigns per year for 7 different brands. We decided to plug our solution capturing attention on all of them since January 2023. We did use "attention" data for optimizing, in real time, our campaign performance generating massive improvement (+225% of attention in average VS benchmark in France). In addition, after a strong 8 months of tests, we have now a quite reliable dataset for using "attention" data in all our 2024 strategies (planning, buying, content production).

Outcome: what did you achieve and/or learn for your business?

Our main learning is that all digital inventories are not equal. In France, 25% of digital inventory is generating 0 attention. 25% is generating "high attention" (more than 7") and the 50% remaining generates low attention (between 1.5" and 2"). This raises a big question. Should we invest all our media money on high attention inventories (mainly catch up TV + Youtube)? Or, should we try to maximize our reach (by diversifying our media mix) including "low attention" inventories? We are more keen to follow the 2nd option. That said, we will need to learn how to create content which is distinctive and impactful enough for building memory (and not only add recall) in "low attention" context. This also means our media buying will take the lead VS our content production process. Significant change in our current WoW… Never easy to implement in big corporations like us:)

> **TAKE IT TO WORK**
>
> Relying only on "old" and "classical" digital metrics such as visibility, VTR, CPM… could be misleading. These metrics do not give you the right understanding about how your digital media is performing. Open your eyes, stop following lobby recommendations, test by yourself, learn and optimize.

James McDonald, Audience Group

Icebreaker Question: If you could put a message in a bottle and send it to your past self, what would it say?

Icebreaker Answer: Dear Young James, While old age gives you wisdom, it also regrets all of the parties you didn't have. Hugs and hangovers are all you need. Lots of Love, Old James.

Case Study Category: Buying

Objective: what did you want to achieve in your case study and why?

Our client's year on year budget was stable in an inflationary environment, so we needed to do more with what was effectively less. We knew from previous results that when our client's share of voice was high, sales followed (five to seven months later). Our objective was to disproportionately win Extra Share of Memory without spending on Extra Share of Voice.

Method: what was the plan you took to achieve this and how did you execute?

If our ad is not seen, it can't be noted. If it is not noted, it can't be remembered. If it isn't remembered, it won't serve any value in building brand salience and allowing the brand to be recalled as people enter the category to purchase. Our approach was to start treating brand salience and ad recall as though it were a direct response campaign. Working with Chalice AI, we developed a custom bidding algorithm that linked to an online brand study. This algorithm analyzed any uplift on brand or ad recall, found the auction conditions that related to this uplift and then selected (and won) auctions that were likely to also aid in brand and ad recall. With this method, alone, an uplift of 14% in our client's ad recall was observed. Once this was established, we partnered with a 3Party attention vendor to build a pre bid score to better inform and guide the custom-bidding algorithm. This pre-bidding score was based on the attention level of the ad placement being auctioned. In essence we were able to confidently bid higher amounts for ad placements with more seconds of attention. This enhancement ensured that our budget was invested into placements that both had a high likelihood of having high attention and a high chance of delivering brand and ad recall in the quantitative study.

Outcome: what did you achieve and/or learn for your business?

The results showed a 74% uplift in brand recall after the attention-data-fed algorithm was pushed. It resulted in higher recall without spending any extra budget delivering the client a higher share of memory without lifting ESOV. While this one tactic can't be isolated in the broader business results, it was a key change to the year-on-year media strategy in a year that netted that client their largest ever number of leads and appointments.

TAKE IT TO WORK

There is little doubt in my mind that optimizing your media buy for attention delivers better brand recall which leads to higher mental availability of your brand come purchase occasion. This leads to a consideration of what is an optimal frequency and can you afford to advertise less often when you are maximizing the impact of each impression.

Lisa Hale, Specsavers and Anna Wilson, Tangerine

Icebreaker Question: If you could put a message in a bottle and send it to your past self, what would it say?

Icebreaker Answer: Relax and trust yourself, no matter how loud opposing voices are, trust in your evidence and your voice and in time you'll be heard.

Case Study Category: Strategy, Creative, Planning, Buying, Measurement.

Objective: what did you want to achieve in your case study and why?

Our objective was to clearly prove a hypothesis that we've seen pieces of evidence to support over the last five years: Brand storytelling content in social media and online news keeps people's attention longer than other types of content or ads. This deep attention approach builds salience which builds effective long- term outcomes and 'primes' audiences to improve short-term results.

Method: what was the plan you took to achieve this and how did you execute?

Tangerine and Specsavers partnered with an attention vendor to conduct a study of 2,200 nationally represented people in the UK. The respondents were shown real world social media feeds and online news pages with different types of brand storytelling content, adverts, and all the other things people would see when genuinely spending time in social media/online. We used eye tracking technology to measure how much attention different types of content received and post-exposure analysis to understand the impact of this attention on delivering brand outcomes:

- **Awareness** (recall)
- **Consideration** (salience factors (message understanding, favourability, sentiment and trust))
- **Action** (intent to book).

Outcome: what did you achieve and/or learn for your business?

We successfully proved the hypothesis, results showed:

1. Brand storytelling content generated more attention than other forms of content—social media (+130%) and open web (+600%).
2. Deep attention on brand storytelling content builds salience. Non-customers exposed to brand storytelling content in both social and news showed significant increases in salience factors, such as brand trust (+35%), brand talkability (+42%), and brand favorability (+57%).
3. Deep attention on brand storytelling content builds understanding of messages. Non-customers exposed to brand storytelling content also showed a better understanding of brand consideration messages, such as seeing the brand as more caring (+48%) and feeling better about the brand (+35%).
4. Combining brand storytelling, deep attention strategies with brand ads improved brand outcomes. Using brand storytelling to prime audiences generated a 41% uplift in spontaneous brand recall and a 42% increase in intent to book.

Applying these learnings to real-world campaigns has shown to increase conversion volumes and reduce CPA. In summary, deep attention (brand storytelling) strategies are a powerful tool for capturing and holding attention, improving salience factors and brand consideration messages, and priming audiences for conversion ads.

Take It to Work

When brands combine the strength of deep attention strategies, which deliver a different shape of attention, with traditional advertising models, brands can be both more effective at building efficient and effective outcomes. To allow this to happen, media platforms (particularly in social) need to change and allow brands to buy ads against deep attention objectives (e.g. retention rates, attention in feed or longer watch times).

7.3   The Wrap Up: Think the Same Campaign 2024

Where would the world be without dreamers like Kristian, Angelina and Erez? Where would we be without early adopters like Scott, James and Phil? Where would we be without Steve Jobs urging us to "Think Different"? In such a world, we would lack vision, imagination, passion, and leadership. We wouldn't propel progress, nor would we drive change. We would think the same.

Perhaps this might be the campaign Steve Jobs would have launched if he weren't a dreamer and if he hadn't been supported by those enthusiastic early adopters who eagerly lined up for the first desktop iMac G3 slot-loading CD ROM in Bondi Blue:

> Here's to the conventional ones. The conformers. The compliant. The rule followers. The square pegs in the square holes. The ones who see things just like everyone else. They strictly adhere to rules. And they have great respect for the status quo. You can't quote them, you can't disagree with them, you can't glorify or vilify them. The only thing you can do is overlook them. Because they maintain things as they are. They keep the human race in place. And while some may see them as the stable ones, we see them as ordinary. Because the people who are sane enough to know they can't change the world, are the ones who don't
>
> Think The Same Campaign. 2024

7.4   List of Contributors

Baptiste Amar. Head of Media Science, GetYourGuide

Baptiste Amar is the Head of Media Science at GetYourGuide, the world's leading platform to find and discover travel experiences. In his role, he's coordinating with teams of marketers, researchers and analysts to build innovative measurement and experimentation platforms for Brand marketing.

Baptiste has a background in statistics and econometrics, and spent most of his career as a data analyst/scientist in various industries in France and Germany (telecoms, hospitality, travel). Before his current position, Baptiste worked for 3+ years in the Marketing Analytics team at GetYourGuide, where he was in charge of building critical analytics enablers for the marketing organization (e.g. attribution & media mix modeling, Brand analytics framework).

Kristian Claxton: Managing Partner Emerging Innovation, GroupM

Kristian is an accomplished senior business executive known for driving growth and innovation in complex global organizations. With a proven track record of successful innovation and transformation, he currently serves as Managing Partner, Emerging Solutions at GroupM Nexus. In this role, he strategically evaluates and prioritizes emerging innovations with a focus on both local and global initiatives with substantial global growth potential. His approach emphasizes optimizing for quality over quantity and fostering scalable, repeatable enhancements to future and existing solutions.

Stephen Cleary: Brand Manager, Irish National Lottery

Stephen Cleary, 34 year old marketer from Derry, Northern Ireland. 10 years professional experience including global football brand marketing at adidas, and currently brand manager for the Irish National Lottery.

Jean Paul Edwards: Managing Director Product, OMG WW

Jean-Paul has been with OMD for over 25 years. He founded Manning Gottlieb OMD's Digital team in 1997, and then led the agency Media Futures offering. He now works at OMD Worldwide to drive development of the network's offering in a digitally led, data centric media environment. This role is currently focused on a range of development areas, such as the measurement, delivery and optimisation of attention to deliver differentiated brand experiences, as well as the leverage of AI tools for analytics and consumer engagement, global consumer research programmes.

Angelina Eng. VP Measurement, Addressability and Data Center, Interactive Advertising Bureau (IAB)

Having started her career in advertising in 1994, Angelina Eng went on to achieve executive leadership positions making substantial contributions to the evolution of digital media, marketing, ad operations, and analytics. As a Vice President of the Measurement, Addressability and Data Center at the IAB, Angelina has played a critical role in creating industry standards and guidelines, shaping the digital advertising landscape as we know it today.

Throughout her leadership roles at esteemed firms such as Morgan Stanley, Merkle, dentsu, and Publicis, she assisted over 150 marketers in various advertising aspects and has contributed substantially to the development of industry standards, leading the industry in areas of addressability, measurement and media.

Lisa Hale. Head of Social Media, Consumer PR and Brand Activation, Specsavers UK, Spain and Republic of Ireland

Lisa Hale is Head of Social Media, Consumer PR and Brand Activation at Specsavers UK, Spain and Republic of Ireland. Lisa joined Specsavers in 2019, setting up the brand's first ever social media team, working with the business to introduce its first integrated earned media approach, initially via social media and then consumer PR, focusing on how these channels can bring the brand's core messages to life by capturing and holding attention through cultural relevance and audience first thinking. She joined from PR and Social Media agency, Tangerine, where she was Associate Director. Her 16 years experience in the industry comprises B2C and B2B marketing campaigns, stakeholder relations and public affairs activity for brands including Pizza Hut, Vimto, M&S Bank, Reebok, Specsavers, National Grid, John Lewis, Tesco and Sainsburys. Lisa has led multiple award winning campaigns, all born out of attention strategies.

Phil Jackson. Global Digital Marketing Effectiveness Innovation Director, Haleon

Phil is Global Digital Marketing Effectiveness Innovation Director for Haleon. He is based in London, within the Global Consumer Business Insights & Analytics team, where he is responsible for driving a Globally consistent approach to how Haleon marketers hold their investments in Digital Marketing accountable, both in terms of building brand equity and contributing to incremental, profitable sales growth. His recent focus has been in support of Haleon's holistic marketing effectiveness programme; including the standardization of the metrics and tools that are used to measure the effectiveness of Digital Marketing, CBIA governance of Global learning agendas and the piloting of emerging measurement innovations such as attention measurement and 'cookie-less' cross-media reach and frequency solutions.

Joanne Leong. Global Head of Planning, dentsu

As the Global Head of Planning, Joanne's role is to drive consistency, best practice, innovation and inspiration around the craft of planning across our agency brands and markets. She is also the lead for dentsu's Attention Economy program, where she spearheads a market-leading research program with forward-thinking researchers, tech companies, media owners, and dentsu clients that is aimed at developing attention-based capabilities and metrics to revolutionize the way the industry plans, measures, and buys media. Joanne has 16 years of experience in the media industry with a strong focus on strategy, consumer insights, and communications planning, across various verticals including CPG, Telecom, and Finance.

Scott Luther. Head of Connections and Brand Performance Marketing, TRG

Thank goodness there's a job market for people who like "thinking about stuff" and "asking good questions" because, put simply, that's what Scott really does. For the past decade, Scott has been instrumental in growing the "figure it out group" at TRG, helping clients make sense of new and emerging opportunities to grow. In that time he's helped bring attention and a shelf full of awards to clients like The Home Depot, MD Anderson Cancer Center, the Cayman Islands Department of Tourism and Firehouse Subs.

James McDonald, Audience Group

With over 30 years of experience in the advertising industry, James McDonald worked with some of the largest global agencies before co-founding Audience Group. His company has rapidly grown into a leading media and advertising services agency, known for its application of advanced marketing technologies that drive business growth.

James is dedicated to applying data science to advertising, marketing, and media strategy. He believes that much of current performance advertising is ineffective, which drives his evidence-based approach. This methodology helps clients invest their media dollars with confidence, ensuring their strategies are grounded in solid data and analytics.

Ollivier Monferran. South West Media & Digital Director, Essity

Ollivier Monferran is a seasoned professional in digital transformation and media efficiency, with a 15-year track record in sectors including B2C, Automotive, and E-commerce. His tenure at Essity was marked by significant advancements in digital and media strategies, notably enhancing D2C business growth and shaping data-driven marketing approaches. Ollivier's pragmatic approach to strategy and implementation reflects his commitment to continuous learning and improvement. His expertise in optimizing consumer attention on digital platforms has contributed substantially to improving media efficiency, aligning well with current industry trends.

Sorin Patilinet. Global Marketing Sciences Sr Director, Mars. 'The Marketing Engineer'

As the leader of the Global Marketing Effectiveness team at Mars, I have the privilege of helping some of the world's most beloved brands, including M&M's, Snickers, Skittles, Pedigree, Extra Gum, and Royal Canin, to get better at marketing. My team crafts cutting-edge consumer insight-generation solutions using the latest advancements in social sciences and tech while staying grounded in our deep understanding of human and pet behaviors. For over seven years, I've pioneered the use of Attention and Emotion behavioral datasets for creative excellence and become a leading advocate in the exciting Attention Economy space. I'm always ready to engage in lively debates about the future of brands and consumer relationships with them. As a Marketing Science enthusiast, I love sharing my insights and perspectives with the community. Whether you catch me at industry events or follow my "Engineering Marketing" blog online: https://www.sorinp.com

I am happily married to Felicia and the proud father of Sebastian and Emma. I love airplanes, Japan, and Liverpool FC.

Paolo Provinciali. Vice President of Marketing, Growth Performance and Operations, LinkedIn

Paolo Provinciali is LinkedIn's Marketing Vice President of Growth, Performance, and Operations. He oversees Media, Web, Analytics, MarTech, and Business Platforms strategy and operations to ensure the growth of LinkedIn's business. Before this role, he led the owned and paid media across LinkedIn's

B2B and B2C businesses. Prior to LinkedIn, Paolo was the VP of Media and Data for Anheuser Busch InBev (ABI). He ran advertising for the brewer's iconic brands in the US and led the efforts to build the Marketing Data organization to collect, enrich, and utilize first, second, and third-party data. Paolo also established the Global E-commerce Marketing team at ZX Ventures. Before ABI, Paolo was at Google for nearly ten years, where he helped establish the internal Media team, and developed the digital and programmatic best practices to advertise Google's B2B and B2C products worldwide.

Jon Waite. Global Managing Director—Head of Media Experience Development, Havas Media Group

Currently responsible for global planning and activation strategy and agency product and capability development across all media channels. Over 15 years' experience in media agencies, in planning, trading, product development and global partnerships roles. A special interest in cross media measurement and planning approaches having designed and built agency tools to meet this challenge.

Major champion of 'Attention' for media planning and buying, managing global research programs, and co-authoring the 2019 and 2021 Dentsu whitepapers with Professor Karen Nelson-Field and Lumen Research.

Dad to two boys Jacob (5) and Aiden (3), lives in Kent and enjoys running and playing golf in my spare time plus a part time Horological enthusiast.

Anna Wilson. Chief Digital Innovation Officer, Tangerine

Anna is passionate about helping brands build and grow their market share by improving brand understanding and consideration, as well as being experienced in crisis comms and reputation management. She has worked with a variety of brands, including Specsavers, Bodyform, Pizza Hut, Iceland Foods, and Reebok.

Anna is proud to be part of an award-winning team known for its strategic insight, clever and nimble activations, and industry-leading campaigns. She is also committed to meaningful measurement that demonstrates return on investment for clients.

Most recently, Anna has been involved in bringing the Shapes of Attention research to market. This research provides clear evidence of how the communications industry is delivering brand fame, changing perceptions, and increasing market share for clients.

8

Attention to Ethics

I began to wonder why the verb that goes with 'attention' is 'to pay'.

Is it a debt? A duty? A tax? An outlay of energy?

Work seems to be involved in the phrase, or perhaps sacrifice. And what do
we get back, if we pay it?
Helen Garner. Author

In constructing an outline for this chapter, it became quickly apparent that
the topic has the potential to expand endlessly. There's an abundance of official principles released by various organizations, covering a wide array of
subjects, from genAI and Third Party Data to sustainability, mental health
impacts, programmatic supply chains, cross-media measurement, and the list
goes on.

The primary objective here was to condense this extensive pool of information into a more focused and manageable collection, with a specific emphasis
on a particular area of value. This value encompasses not only ethical considerations relating to respect, reciprocity, quality, and transparency within
the context of attention and attention measurement but also extends to
addressing the fundamental question Helen Garner poses.

Garner encourages us to explore the curious relationship between attention
and the act of 'paying', prompting us to reflect on a single, pivotal question:

What is the nature and cost of attention in our lives, and what do we, as humans, gain in return for our investment?

While this chapter may only skim the surface of ethical considerations, its aim is to provide comprehensive guidelines and principles within the areas it does cover.

So, thank you for your valuable attention, we hope you feel rewarded for your investment. And welcome to the #positiveattentioneconomy.

8.1   The Viewer Value Exchange

Changing the Language for an Advertiser-Consumer Value Exchange

Section by Dr Anna R. McAlister, Director of Curriculum and Assessment, Institute for Advertising Ethics.

Companies in the commercial space (including retailers, advertisers, and the brands they represent) need to be mindful of their impact on society. Understandably, all commercial entities are motivated to make profit. However, the quest for success should not leave consumers feeling stressed, confused, angry, or inadequate. Unfortunately, any reader of this book can probably relate to times when their experiences as consumers have led to such feelings.

Stress and confusion can arise when there is an abundance of information that overwhelms a consumer. Likewise, a lack of access to pertinent information can lead a consumer to feel nervous about their potential purchase. Pestering consumers with too-frequent communications (e.g. daily emails) or disruptive communications (e.g. poorly-timed text messages that arrive outside of typical waking hours) can likewise cause stress. Anger and frustration are common when a consumer is unable to easily pause or avoid communications from commercial entities (e.g. when a password is required to unsubscribe from advertising emails).

Simple solutions to such problems exist for advertisers who are motivated to enhance the consumer experience. For example, side-by-side comparison charts and knowledgeable salespeople can help a consumer navigate an otherwise overwhelming purchase decision. Such solutions typically come with a price, though. Companies that do not prioritize consumer well being may be tempted to take the cheaper route.

Why should a company spend more to ensure consumers feel comfortable? Although companies can achieve short term success using subversive tactics, long term success is related to customer loyalty. According to Colin Angle—chairman, CEO, and founder of iRobot—the most loyal customers are those who have experienced upset with a company and been treated well. These folks are even more loyal than customers who have never experienced an upset with a company. Being treated well means the company engages in behaviors that are sustainable (e.g. offering after-sale service). Underhanded tactics may be effective in the short term. However, long term, these tactics fail. Once the consumer realizes they have been duped or manipulated, they become skeptical (perhaps even resentful) and are more likely to engage their defense mechanisms in future. As a result, the use of sneaky tactics becomes less effective over time.

Modern marketing is highly tailored and often referred to as 'targeted marketing'. Through STP analysis (i.e., segmentation, targeting, and positioning), the advertiser establishes their target market segment, tailors their message to target that audience, and positions the offering such that it holds a unique representation in the mind of the consumer. While 'targeted marketing' is considered a normal modern practice, we challenge the reader to consider the analogy of targeting as reminiscent of hunting. Hunting suggests the existence of a predator/prey relationship. Rather than hunting, marketers should perhaps focus on an approach that better resembles fishing. That is, they should tailor their messaging to lure in folks who would naturally feel inclined to be interested in the offering. Consumers should not have to feel that they are constantly on guard for fear of being taken advantage of or trapped.

Institute for Advertising Ethics

Founded in the United States, the Institute for Advertising Ethics (IAE) is a 501(c)3 nonprofit organization that espouses the value of commercial entities behaving ethically as they go about their business. According to the IAE, there are 9 principles of ethical advertising that serve to ensure advertisers are successful while also respecting consumers whom they influence. These nine principles are as follow:

Principle 1: Advertising, public relations, marketing communications, news, and editorial all share a common objective of truth and high ethical standards in serving the public.

Principle 2: Advertising public relations, and all marketing communications professionals have an obligation to exercise the highest personal ethics in the creation and dissemination of commercial information to consumers.

Principle 3: Advertisers should clearly distinguish advertising, public relations and corporate communications from news and editorial content and entertainment, both online and offline.

Principle 4: Advertisers should clearly disclose all material conditions, such as payment or receipt of a free product, affecting endorsements in social and traditional channels, as well as the identity of endorsers, all in the interest of full disclosure and transparency.

Principle 5: Advertisers should treat consumers fairly based on the nature of the audience to whom the ads are directed and the nature of the product or service advertised.

Principle 6: Advertisers should never compromise consumers' personal privacy in marketing communications, and their choices as to whether to participate in providing their information should be transparent and easily made.

Principle 7: Advertisers should follow federal, state and local advertising laws, and cooperate with industry self-regulatory programs for the resolution of advertising practices.

Principle 8: Advertisers and their agencies, and online and offline media, should privately discuss potential ethical concerns, and members of the team creating ads should be given permission to express internally their ethical concerns.

Principle 9: Trust between advertising and public relations business partners, including clients, and their agencies, media vendors, and third party suppliers, should be built upon transparency and full disclosure of business ownership and arrangements, agency remuneration and rebates, and media incentives.

QUICK EXPLAINER

Who Are They: Institute for Advertising Ethics. Washington, DC, New York, London

The Institute for Advertising Ethics (IAE) is a 501c3 non-profit built to address the urgent and complex issues of ethical standards and practices across all aspects of advertising communications. It incorporates the vision of Wally Snyder, a member of the Advertising Hall of Fame, Andrew Susman, an entrepreneurial advertising executive and Linda Thomas Brooks, the CEO of the Public Relations Society of America.

It aims to address ethical standards in advertising across all areas. The IAE launched the Certified Ethical Advertising Executive (CEAE) program in 2022 with the University of Texas at Austin. This program empowers ethical advertising executives to identify and mitigate ethical risks and promote ethics in their careers. Less than two years after launching the first-ever advertising ethics certification program in the U.S., the Institute for Advertising Ethics (IAE) launched a version in the U.K. in 2023. The U.K. program, which was co-designed by U.K. advisor Geraint Lloyd-Taylor of Lewis Silkin, is similar in format to the U.S. version, but features individual contributions from leading U.K. thinkers.

The history began with the work of Wally Snyder who joined with the University of Missouri 's Reynolds Journalism Institute and the American Advertising Federation (AAF) to incubate a collaboration. This collaboration yielded a comprehensive body of knowledge on advertising ethics including the codification of Practices and Principles and the publication of the principal textbook in the field: "Ethics in Advertising: Making the Case for Doing the Right Thing."

In March 2017, Susman and Michael Donahue co-founded The Advertising Trust & Transparency Forum, concentrating on ethical concerns within the advertising industry. This forum complemented the IAE's consumer-oriented focus. Susman and Donahue aimed to merge the work of the Advertising Contract Exchange by Ken Zinn, CMO of the American Bar Association, with the Advertising Trust & Transparency Forum and the Institute for Advertising Ethics, forming the Institute for Advertising Ethics.

The United Nations Sustainable Development Goals and The Conscious Attention Economy

Section by Kristofer Doerfler, Director of Innovation, CMI Media Group.

Your attention is being exploited and since your attention is key to what you focus on in a given moment, and your life is a totality of moments, the exploitation of your attention is therefore the exploitation of your life. Every second thousands of businesses, organizations, governments and individuals are vying to spread their message to you by capturing your attention to encourage you to take their desired action, which may or may not be in your best interest. The constant exposure to these messages, coupled with the profit-driven objectives of platforms aiming to gather data and retain users' attention for extended online periods, has resulted in an era marked by information overload, emotional fatigue, and widespread misinformation. You, your family, friends, and the society you live in are all feeling the repercussions of the exploitative sides of the current attention economy. These consequences are contributing to the breakdown of institutions, individual autonomy, and human well-being.

In addition to direct human impact, the environment and societies are also being negatively affected by the current attention economy. Healthy natural ecosystems have a human impact problem, humans have a misinformation problem, and misinformation has an attention economy problem as it is the financial model behind the flow of most media and information in society. We therefore need to evolve the current attention economy, not only to protect online businesses and vulnerable people, but civil society and nature as well.

The United Nations Sustainable Development Goals (SDGs) were formed in 2015 by the global community to "end poverty, protect the planet, and ensure that by 2030 all people enjoy peace and prosperity." The truth is the world is woefully off target from achieving these goals and the misaligned incentives of the current attention economy to extract human attention for the lowest cost is contributing to poor outcomes. In the name of driving more attention to online spaces, people in our societies are being pushed further into ideological corners and our anger, fear, and outrage are being fueled to drive more views and clicks on content. Many businesses, organizations and governments are leveraging the attention economy to drive over-consumption of natural resources, oppress vulnerable groups, drive inaction for important causes, and in some cases even promote genocide. If we want to achieve a world where there is no poverty, increased climate action, clean water, good health, well-being, responsible consumption, reduced inequalities and other key areas of the UN SDGs, then we need to re-imagine the attention economy to be less exploitative of people and instead focus on human well-being and the flourishing of the natural world.

The re-imagined attention economy—The Conscious Attention Economy

For all its shortcomings, the attention economy certainly does have its positive aspects as it enables quality journalism, the democratization of access to information, the creation of wonderful content such as movies and shows, and when done right, the connection of brands to people who could benefit from their products and services. The favorable attributes within the existing attention economy provide a basis for reimagining its extractive aspects, aiming to improve human consciousness, foster human connection, and contribute to the attainment of the UN Sustainable Development Goals (SDGs) (Fig. 8.1).

Fig. 8.1 United Nations sustainable development goals

When people have greater control and awareness over what they are exposed to and its purpose, they are better able to exercise agency over directing their attention. This improves the likelihood of them being better informed, happier, and empowered to take action on what matters to them rather than be influenced by the will of bad actors. In a scenario where businesses vie for the creation of trusting, impactful, and enduring relationships with people, as opposed to merely navigating the diminishing returns of low-cost media and advertising saturation, they stand to become more profitable. This is because their messaging is likely to resonate more effectively with their core audiences while fostering long-term sustainable consumption. For example, a 2023 report by The Telegraph found that almost 50% of "online internet traffic is fake" and "nearly $100 billion is wasted annually on displaying ads to an audience that does not exist" (source). This not only means trillions of dollars in advertising is lost to fraud as businesses compete for cheap impressions, but also the energy required to serve those ads to fake audiences is wasted and drives a large carbon footprint of at least 352.8 k megatons of emitted CO_2 for display advertising in the U.S alone—this is the equivalent of the emissions from electricity use of 163,837 U.S. homes (source for calculation). To change this, the advertising industry will need to make significant changes to promote greater transparency and accountability.

Some examples of how businesses can correct the issue of online ad fraud are as follows: eliminate made-for-advertising sites (MFAs) that are deceptive and bombard people with ads, increase consumer control over data so they can validate their identities themselves, add greater transparency into the quality of programmatic advertising inventory such as through attention and trust based metrics, and incorporate CO2 and nature preservation goals into media campaigns. These changes, amongst others, will create higher quality media and online experiences for people that will improve business outcomes, the environment, and empower individuals with more control over what they are exposed to. When organizations and governments promote more ethical online and offline spaces by supporting attention-based systems that encourage well-being we will have stronger institutions and healthier societies too. Our collective future depends on our shared ability to grow the positive qualities of the attention economy, reduce the harms and invent new systems of connection based on quality of life rather than maximizing short-term profits.

So what are the steps to achieving this attention economy that focuses on quality of life and well-being? The roadmap is the "conscious attention economy", which is a system defined by respect and reciprocity, where all stakeholders benefit and business models are generative rather than extractive, meaning that, as business is accomplished more effectively, value continuously increases for all entities—businesses, governments, society, nature and individuals alike. It is a system that engages peoples' attention with respect, acknowledging their right to informed choice, while supporting that health and well-being should be designed into algorithms, social engagement models, digital environments and business models. It is an attention economy which achieves the UN SDGs by creating positive feedback loops, both online and offline, which empower and educate people with more agency over how they can use their own attention to take action over what matters most to them. It encourages positive emotions such as awe, love, hope, and joy without exploiting our fears. It helps guide us to a more sustainable and regenerative future where online spaces feel supportive rather than toxic.

This conscious attention economy can be a reality. You can find an outline of the conscious attention economy roadmap at https://consciousattention economy.org that was developed in partnership with the United Nations to provide a new economic model for sustainable development in the attention economy and plant seeds for people to take action for a better future. Similarly to how the UN SDGs are broken into goals, the conscious attention economy roadmap is broken out into principles which can be used to achieve the UN Sustainable Development Goals by building the principles into spaces designed to capture attention.

1. Individual Sovereignty
2. Harmlessness
3. Privacy & Data Protection

4. Transparency
5. Accountability
6. Fairness & Inclusivity
7. Freedom from Exploitation
8. Harmony with Nature
9. Attention Literacy
10. Adaptive Systems (Fig. 8.2)

To help visualize a world impacted by the conscious attention economy, here are some examples of the effects it will have:

Promoting fairness & inclusivity online helps achieve gender equality (SDG 5) and reduced inequalities (SDG 10) by supporting diverse voices, content and data practices.

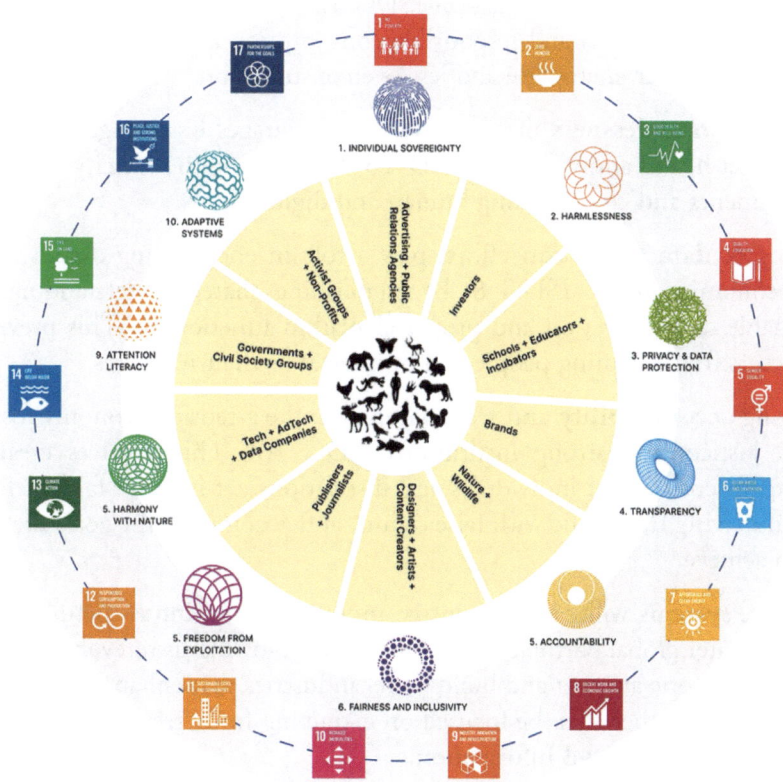

Fig. 8.2 Conscious attention economy ecosystem

Attention literacy encompassing the knowledge and education on how to assert control over one's and others' attention, supports quality education (SDG 4) and sustainable cities and communities (SDG 11). It achieves this by diminishing the influence of disinformation and online fraud while increasing awareness about positive causes.

Individual sovereignty and freedom from exploitation promotes less poverty (SDG 1) and reduced inequality (SDG 10) by giving people greater power over their online experiences and the generated profits while supporting better business outcomes through more long-term trust-based interactions.

Additionally, global advertising and the internet has a carbon footprint larger than the airline industry (sources below), while data use and storage can reach 21% of global carbon emissions by 2030 (source: World Wide Waste Book). This indicates that an attention economy that is more **harmonious with nature** will support affordable and clean energy (SDG 7), clean water & sanitation (SDG 6), climate action (SDG 13), life on land (SDG 14), life below water (SDG 15) and responsible consumption and production (SDG 12) through lower energy use and less overconsumption.

Embracing **harmlessness** in online spaces encourages less hunger (SDG 2) and greater health and well-being (SDG 3) by reducing the toxicity of online environments and championing human and digital rights.

Privacy & data protection efforts play a role in encouraging decent work and economic growth (SDG 8) by establishing shared understandings of reasonable data collection and proper algorithm functioning. This prevents bad actors from draining people and businesses of their resources.

Ensuring **accountability and transparency** in the attention economy fosters peace, justice, and strong institutions (SDG 16). This involves creating systems to ensure that individuals and institutions act in good faith, refrain from deceiving the public with false claims, and accomplish the goals they set out to achieve.

Adaptive systems will lead to industry, innovation, and infrastructure (SDG 9) and greater global partnerships (SDG 17) by allowing us to evolve how we interact with one another and build better industries that enhance the quality of human life rather than be focused on extracting finite resources.

Important Additional Information:

1. Modok, A. (2023). Role of Social Media in Inciting the Genocidal Acts: A Case Study on Myanmar's Rohingya. Contemporary Challenges: The Global Crime, Justice and Security Journal, 4.
2. Scope3 State of Sustainability Report—December 2023
3. Shelley, L. (2023). The internet is worse for the environment than airlines. Performance Marketing World. https://www.performancemarketingworld.com/article/1799142/the-internet-worse-environment-airlines
4. https://consciousattentioneconomy.org/
5. https://gerrymcgovern.com/world-wide-waste/
6. https://www.epa.gov/energy/greenhouse-gas-equivalencies-calculator#results
7. https://www.thedrum.com/news/2022/11/07/advertising-adds-extra-32-annual-carbon-footprint-every-person-the-uk

---

QUICK EXPLAINER

Who are 'The Conscious Attention Economy Working Group'?

The Conscious Attention Economy (CAE) Initiative working group was launched in 2021 as a collaboration between Future Capital https://futureofcapital.org/ and the United Nations New Economics for Sustainable Development (NESD) https://www.un.org/en/desa/unen/policy-briefs. The CAE Initiative is currently active as a project under the SDG Impact Fund https://www.sdgimpactfund.org/.

The core working group is a diverse collaboration of professionals from technology, advertising, academic, civil society, finance, non-profit and creative sectors who are passionate about creating a world that works for all life. The group works collaboratively with the United Nations and is funded by Future Capital. Future Capital's mission is to convene individuals and organizations to manifest conscious economic models that can deliver health, well-being, and prosperity in support of mutual interdependence for all beings including the Earth.

MISSION: to develop an ethical and value-based shared framework that puts individual well-being, personal sovereignty and a verdant natural world at the center of attention. To enable all stakeholders, those who create, collaborate, contribute, design, teach and engage in attention-based systems, to work, live and thrive in a world that is supported by an ecosystem based on these shared values.

How Do We Move at the Speed of Safety? The Three Rules of Humane Technology

The Center for Humane Technology is a highly respected non-profit organization in the USA who focus on addressing the ethical and societal challenges posed by technology and digital platforms. They have helped over 100 million people globally understand the harms of extractive technology through the documentary film The Social Dilemma, the podcast Your Undivided Attention and many other initiatives.

Aza Raskin, Co-Founder at the Center, recently said on their podcast 'Your Undivided Attention', "If I was Sam Altman of OpenAI or Demis Hassabis from DeepMind or Sundar from Google, and I understood these three rules, the things that I would be trying to do is to host a convening of all of the actors in the space to figure out how do we do this right? How do we move at the speed of safety?".

What does this even mean? It signifies that those who operate online media platforms bear a crucial responsibility, one that requires them to refrain from rushing to be the first and instead, carefully consider the profound impact the technology we create has on people's lives. They outline three ethical principles that should be taken into account during the development of technology. These rules were written with a focus on online media, but are now being used. The Three Rules of Humane Technology are:

- **Rule 1: When we invent a new technology, we uncover a new class of responsibility.**

    We didn't need the right to be forgotten until computers could remember us forever, and we didn't need the right to privacy in our laws until cameras were mass-produced. As we move into an age where technology could destroy the world so much faster than our responsibilities could catch up, it's no longer okay to say it's someone else's job to define what responsibility means.

- **Rule 2: If that new technology confers power, it will start a race.**

    Humane technologists are aware of the arms races their creations could set off before those creations run away from them—and they notice and think about the ways their new work could confer power.

- **Rule 3: If we don't coordinate, the race will end in tragedy.**

    No one company or actor can solve these systemic problems alone. When it comes to AI, developers wrongly believe it would be impossible to sit down with cohorts at different companies to work on hammering out how to move at the pace of getting this right—for all our sakes.

In summary, "How do we move at the speed of safety?" is a call for tech industry leaders and organizations to prioritize safety, ethics, and responsible development over speed and innovation. It urges them to consider the broader impact of their technology and collaborate to ensure that advancements benefit society as a whole without causing harm or tragedy. These rules provide a good baseline for vendors and engineers to abide by.

The Evolution of Three Rules Rules

Notably, the concept of 'the rule of three' appears to be a recurring pattern in the domain of technology. This tendency of three rules or laws can be traced back to the fundamental principles that underpin both mathematics and technology design, with Newton's laws serving as a relevant reference point. The choice of three rules is said to enhance memorability, which is particularly valuable when dealing with complex concepts. The following examples, mostly scientific and one fictional but influential, underscore this recurring trend.

Newton's Three Laws of Motion (1687, Philosophiae Naturalis Principia Mathematica)

Newton's Three Laws of Motion, formulated by Sir Isaac Newton in the late seventeenth century, are the bedrock of physics and have broader implications in science and engineering. The laws describe the relationship between the motion of an object and the forces acting on it. By applying these laws, scientists and engineers can predict the motion of objects accurately including trajectories, velocities, and forces involved in various physical scenarios. This predictive power is essential for designing everything from vehicles and bridges to space missions. To this day these three fundamental laws remain an essential component of our comprehension of the physical universe. Newton's Three Laws of Motion are:

- **Rule 1 Inertia:** A body remains at rest, or in motion at a constant speed in a straight line, unless acted upon by a force.
- **Rule 2 Momentum:** The net force on a body is equal to the body's acceleration multiplied by its mass or, equivalently, the rate at which the body's momentum changes with time.
- **Rule 3 Reaction:** If two bodies exert forces on each other, these forces have the same magnitude but opposite directions.

Isaac Asimov's Three Laws of Robotics (fiction 1942, but later published in Nature)

Isaac Asimov's 'Three Laws of Robotics' are a set of fictional rules that the science fiction author introduced in his stories and novels involving robots. While fiction, these rules have since been influential in discussions about artificial intelligence, robotics, and the ethics that arise when machines possess the capability to interact with humans in various ways. Asimov's three Laws of Robotics are:

- **Rule 1 Inaction:** A robot may not injure a human being or, through inaction, allow a human being to come to harm.
- **Rule 2 Obedience:** A robot must obey orders given it by human beings except where such orders would conflict with the First Law.
- **Rule 3 Protection:** A robot must protect its own existence as long as such protection does not conflict with the First or Second Law.

Isaac Asimov's Addendum: The Three Laws (1981, Compute Magazine)

Some forty years later Asimov wrote an article suggesting that he should not be praised for creating the Laws, because they are 'obvious'. He suggests the laws apply as a matter of course, to every tool that human beings use, whether robotic or not. His initial laws all boil down to three simple things—Is the tool safe? Does it do what it is supposed to do? and, Will it last? It is a pretty simple concept. Here are three extended rules Asimov gives as applied to 'tools':

- **Rule 1 Safety:** A tool must not be unsafe to use. Consider a knife. The first law of 'knifedom' is that it be used safely. No one would use a knife if it meant cutting one's fingers off.
- **Rule 2 Effective:** A tool must perform its function effectively. Therefore a knife must be given a sharp edge (provided it is safe as per Law 1), for no one is interested in hacking away uselessly with a dull blade.
- **Rule 3 Integrity:** A tool must uphold integrity during cutting. Of what use would a knife be if it broke or dulled while cutting?

Asimov writes, I have my answer ready whenever someone asks me if I think that my Three Laws of Robotics will actually be used to govern the behavior of robots. Once they become versatile and flexible enough to be able to choose among different courses of behavior. My answer is. "Yes. The

Three Laws are the only way in which rational human beings can deal with robots—or with anything else.

—But when I say that, I always remember (sadly) that human beings are not always rational."

Murphy's Three Laws of Responsible Robotics (2009)

Several decades later Asimov's three laws had become so ingrained in popular culture through entertainment that they now appear to influence society's expectations regarding the behavior of robots around humans. As such, in 2009 Professor Robin Murphy (Computer Science and Engineering at Texas A&M) and David D. Woods (director of the Cognitive Systems Engineering Laboratory at Ohio State) published 'The Three Laws of Responsible Robotics' to replace them with a more scientific approach about the role of responsibility and authority when designing not only a single robotic platform but the larger system in which the platform operates. Woods said, "Our laws are a little more realistic, and therefore a little more boring" and that "We wanted to write three new laws to get people thinking about the human–robot relationship in more realistic, grounded ways."

- **Rule 1 Safety:** A human may not deploy a robot without the human–robot work system meeting the highest legal and professional standards of safety and ethics.
- **Rule 2 Obedience:** A robot must respond to humans as appropriate for their roles.
- **Rule 3 Autonomy:** A robot must be endowed with sufficient situated autonomy to protect its own existence as long as such protection provides smooth transfer of control which does not conflict with the First and Second Laws.

The Biometric Institute's Three Rules of Biometrics (2020, Compute Magazine)

With the rise of surveillance based technologies, The Biometrics Institute recently introduced the 'Three Laws of Biometrics' to serve as a guiding framework for individuals and organizations utilizing biometric technology, emphasizing responsible and ethical practices. Formulated in 2020, these laws underwent a meticulous review process to ensure their validity and relevance. On their official website, the Institute articulates its mission, stating, "We want our members to ask with every application, Just because we can, should we?—Thoroughly assessing each use case and the impact on its users. We are calling on the biometrics community to ensure the technology continues to serve us responsibly and ethically, not exploit us."

- **Rule 1 Policy:** Policy comes first. Any use of biometrics is proportionate, with basic human rights, ethics and privacy at its heart.
- **Rule 2 Process:** Process follows policy. Safeguards are in place to ensure decisions are rigorously reviewed, operations are fair and operators are accountable.
- **Rule 3 Technology:** Technology guided by policy and process. Know your algorithm, biometric system, data quality and operating environment and mitigate vulnerabilities, limitations and risks (Fig. 8.3).

TAKE IT TO WORK

The Three Rules are pretty obvious. Make product that is safe, does what it claims, and lasts.

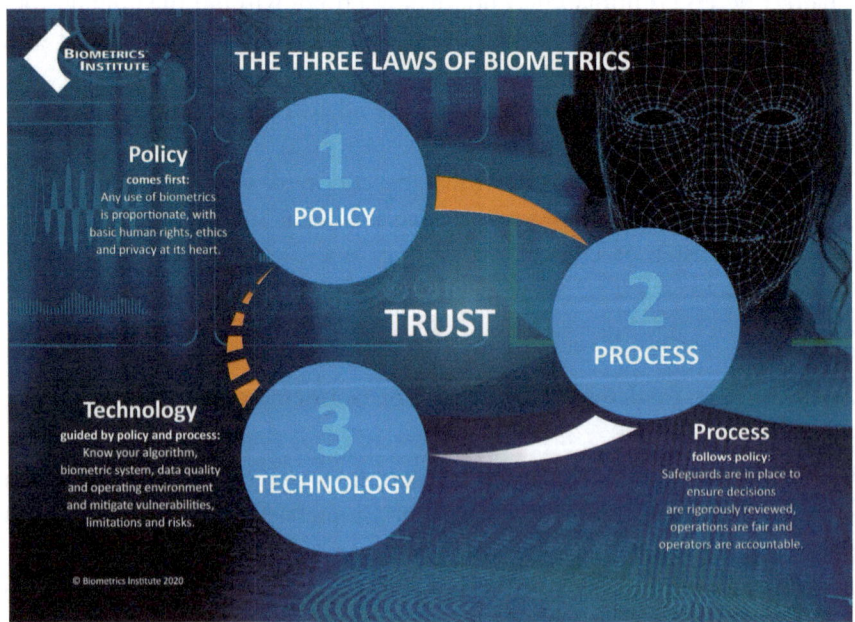

Fig. 8.3 Three laws of biometrics

QUICK EXPLAINER

Who is 'The Biometrics Institute'?

The Biometrics Institute was founded in 2001 and represents a unique multi-stakeholder community spreading across the globe including a large number of government agencies, banks, airlines, airports, biometric experts, privacy experts, regulators, suppliers and academics as well as international observers such as United Nations agencies, EU institutions and IGOs. They provide an unbiased and independent platform for discussion bringing together different perspectives to provide a balanced viewpoint on biometrics.

MISSION: The mission of the Institute is to promote the responsible, ethical and effective use of Biometrics and related technologies that respect the Institute's ethical guidance as an independent and impartial international forum for biometric users and other interested parties.

In order to achieve this mission, the goals of the Biometrics Institute are:

1. To develop thought leadership and guidance for the responsible use of biometrics, using the input of experts.
2. To facilitate knowledge transfer to members, prospects, key stakeholders and the public.
3. To act as a connector for the global Biometrics industry including users, suppliers, academics, regulators and privacy advocates
   https://www.biometricsinstitute.org

8.2 Considerations of Attention Data Collection, Quality and Use

Three Rules of Attention Measurement (2024)

Striving for excellence and longevity is a significant departure from the metrics that have dominated our industry over the past two decades, where metrics proved ineffective, and the dominance of surveillance capitalism prevailed. If as an industry we embrace a set of guiding principles for designing high-quality attention products while safeguarding user interests, we can ensure the long-term sustainability of an attention-driven economy. Then attention at least has a chance to be an appropriate reinvention of an invention.

Considering all the elements discussed in this chapter by all the experts in advertising ethics, biometrics, humane technology and a conscious attention economy and we apply the 'Three Rules' approach to attention (safety, function, integrity), here is a set of three rules to get the conversation started:

- **Rule 1 Safe:** Attention measurement vendors should prioritize privacy rights, engage in a fair value exchange, obtain meaningful consent, compensate individuals for their data, minimize essential data collection, and prevent biases in models.
- **Rule 2 Effective:** The data collected and models created should accurately represent the intended phenomenon (human attention), leading to more consistent and improved advertising practices and greater data utility.
- **Rule 3 Longevity:** Attention measurement vendors must prioritize model predictability and generalizability, as these factors foster longevity, stability, and value in the attention economy.

WHERE ARE THEY NOW

In Attention Economy Book 1 we reported that Jon Mandel broke the ad agency model in the mid-2000s.

Jon Mandel was a heavy hitting agency CEO who lifted the lid on agency rebates, kickbacks and all things transparency and trust. What followed from his whistleblowing speech was nothing short of a category 5 hurricane. Firstly, approximately US$50 billion of accounts were put up for review, then a second wave of disintermediation is said to have occurred when advertisers started going direct to online publishers. The online publishers readily embraced this by ramping up operations to focus on direct relationships with advertisers (and their data). It was perfect timing for the growth and commercialisation of online targeting. As a consequence, Google and Facebook are now said to bank some of the richest first and second party data in the world.

1. **An Update:** In a recent interview, Jon Mandel discussed key points related to media rebates and transparency, reflecting on his historic speech at the ANA Media Conference five years ago. Here are the main takeaways from the interview:
2. **Progress Since the Speech**
   Mandel said that The ANA provided a contract template, but not all advertisers are taking full advantage of it. A few clients have been diligent in auditing and ensuring compliance with contracts, which has contributed to healthier relationships.
3. **Things still needing work**

   (a) Clarity and consistency in relationship contracts and agreements. Many issues arose due to different interpretations of contract terms.

(b) A multidisciplinary approach across the organization to KPIs. Advertisers can then ensure that everyone in the organization and its advertising supply chain is rewarded for desired outcomes, rather than reward for unintended negative actions.

(c) Appoint a chief media officer responsible for internal media management and governance of their media investments including performance delivery, media accountability and transparency.

(d) Advertisers should be aware of issues related to data consolidation and portability, as these can impact switching costs and flexibility in marketing and media. This should extend to technology, platforms, data ownership, and rights.

4. **Regrets**

The impact of the issue was not fully understood by all. He highlighted that not only were dollars being redirected away from working media, but suboptimal media recommendations were also a significant problem, which might have been missed by some.

https://www.ana.net/blogs/show/id/mm-blog-2020-03-jon-mandel-qanda

How Much Attention is Enough?

Section by Daniel Lyas, Amplified Intelligence.

As a society, we are obsessed with 'optimizing'. Our culture tells us that we should always be doing it, inside and outside of the business world. The notion of continuous improvement, driving us forward, is a hallmark of so-called success. I believe we've forgotten that *to* optimize doesn't always have to mean *more*.

This book clearly illustrates that in the business world (and our society), human attention is one of the most valuable and lucrative commodities on the planet. Who is remembering that it is finite and precious—and human?

When we think about human attention, more isn't always more. In fact, we see instances in our data where there's surplus attention for the given objective. Put another way, if we can meet our commercial objectives with 3–4 seconds of a human's time, why would we take 8 or 10?

This is not an idealistic fantasy, and we are seeing real-world approaches to attention adoption that are born from this idea. Various industry organizations that are working with attention think this way, however what we observe as a best practice is a product from Omnicom Media Group's largest agency, OMD.

In 2022 they launched an **Attention Requirement Calculator** (ARC) built with Omnicom's data strategy arm, Annalect. Their tool automates attention-informed planning to make clients' media spend more efficient and effective. Firstly, it calculates how much attention would be required to achieve a desired brand, campaign or commercial outcome. If the tool recommends the ad should engage consumers for 3 seconds, "then you need to consider what channel and platform will provide that amount of mental availability to the audience" said Philip Lincoln, Managing Director of Communications Planning at OMD.

"When we think about attention, it came from our original desire to show an improvement in the way we harness our clients' dollars to do better outcomes," Chrissie Hanson, OMD USA CEO said in an interview with Jonathan Steuer, cofounder and chief executive of Anonymous Media Research.

Some kinds of products such as pharmaceuticals have detailed explanations about symptoms and side effects that require longer viewer attention to be more effective. "We begin by understanding not only the brief, but then what is the attention requirement," Hanson said, "and then we from there construct what is the right contact, what's the frequency, what's the right construct, the size and shape of the ad. What's the right context and frankly, how much attention is required for the plan?".

I believe the adoption of attention in our industry should be approached from this mindset. One where 'users' of attention data consciously make decisions to give back time to consumers. After all, surplus attention is surplus reach. Such a mindset would ultimately propel us towards a less-cluttered digital experience, where the viewer value-exchange is equal. A world where digital experiences enhance, not extract from our lives. Humanity deserves it, and I think that is a world in which I want to live in.

Quality Attention Data, an Ode to Vitruvius

This absence of standardized scientific integrity amplifies our responsibility to be vigilant and principled. Let's rally together, ensuring our industry's research compass is both precise and trustworthy. When billions are in play, trust isn't a luxury; it's essential. Institute for Advertising Ethics.

In the first century BC, Marcus Vitruvius Pollio, a Roman civil engineer and architect who lived from 80–70 BC to after c.15 BC, possessed a deep understanding of what constituted effective research. His most renowned work, "de Architectura libri decem," which translates to "Ten Books on Architecture," has made him famous. Vitruvius is recognized as the original authority in classical architecture based on rule-based systems, and his writings even served as inspiration for Leonardo da Vinci's famous drawing of the Vitruvian Man, illustrating the ideal proportions and structural stability of the male body. Vitruvius advocated that the field of architecture should be grounded in guiding principles, both theoretical and practical. He emphasized adherence to principles of Order, Arrangement, Eurythmy, Symmetry, Propriety, and Economy, believing that following these rules would prevent buildings from deteriorating over time. He held the expectation that architects who diligently followed these principles would ensure the longevity and durability of their structures. Vitruvius's primary aim was to share this knowledge and translate these principles from abstract concepts into practical application. His work, "de Architectura," achieved significant success, and his advice has continued to influence architectural practice for centuries. To this day, his writings are incorporated into the curriculum of introductory architecture courses at universities worldwide.

Structures worldwide stand firm today, owing their strength to the extensive implementation of Vitruvius's guiding principles. Engineering, in general, follows this pattern: building something robust ensures its endurance, whereas subpar construction not only shortens its lifespan but also exposes risks to users and the systems it serves. Our attention measurement ecosystem should adhere to similar principles.

In keeping with the rules of three, here are three rules that are specifically related to data quality as it relates to the collection of attention data and the models constructed upon it.

Human Precedent Data that powers an attention model should predominantly be sourced from deterministic human interactions.
Data quality is of paramount importance when constructing machine learning models aimed at understanding and replicating human behavior, especially in complex domains like human attention. These models heavily rely on human-provided data for training, making quality assurance and validation processes critical. These processes should specifically address potential errors and biases, focusing on accuracy, especially when dealing with small, non-dynamic datasets.

Natural Attention data should be collected in a natural manner to ensure higher accuracy.
Humans tend to exhibit more natural behavior in familiar environments, and they may behave unnaturally or concentrate more in unfamiliar settings. Achieving better measurement precision requires exposing viewers to advertising in entirely natural settings, such as those collected from real platforms rather than just realistic simulations. This can be accomplished

using passive cameras instead of gaze-tracking goggles, minimizing the need for frequent calibration interruptions, and conducting observations in real-world settings as opposed to controlled laboratory environments.

Accurate The data collected and the resulting models should accurately represent the intended phenomenon—human attention.

In the context of gaze estimation, achieving high accuracy relies on having a robust, individual-level training dataset gathered from natural settings and subject to continuous improvement and cross-validation practices. Similarly, for tag-based solutions, accuracy depends on maintaining continuous access to the type of high-quality human data, as mentioned. Consistency is essential to validate accuracy. When attention via gaze or models of attention hold over a range of conditions, it can then be used predictively with confidence. Accuracy is a crucial component of data quality, as inaccurate data and unreliable models can result in poor recommendations, biased results, and a loss of user confidence in the data's usefulness and meaning for interpretation or further analysis.

TAKE IT TO WORK

Question vast differences in results. When results are vastly different than expected, and they cannot be explained, it usually means they are not right.

Revisiting Goodhart's Law

Section By Dave Goodfellow, Head of Measurement, Asia–Pacific @ Pinterest

As new metrics surface for understanding media effectiveness, I'm constantly reminded of Goodhart's law—when a measure becomes a target, it ceases to be a good measure.

Goodhart's law comes from British Economist and namesake, Charles Goodhart, who first posited the idea in the 1970s and has since been proven true many times, across many disciplines. The law carries a primal truth. When there's an incentive to hit a metric (i.e. a target), people instinctively try to game the system to hit that metric and in doing so alter the context in which it exists. Viewability is a clear example of this, and its evolution provides foreshadowing of the pitfalls for attention metrics and the wider potential impact of the media industry gaming human attention.

When the concept for viewability was introduced in the early 2010s, viewability performance across the media ecosystem was much worse than it is today. On average, less than half of all Display or Video ads were viewable. That was shocking to many sides of the media ecosystem at the time, but was also somewhat to be expected. Until that point, no media owner had built or designed their ad products with the explicit goal of them being "viewable." Moreover, an ad's opportunity to be seen had not been quantified so precisely before. Viewability standards, the most widely used one coming from the Media Ratings Council, asserted that to be considered viewable, 50% of an ad's creative must be on-screen for a minimum of 1 continuous second for display ads or 2 seconds for video ads. Once that measure became a target, the user experience and design around advertising started to evolve rapidly and significantly.

People quickly began to understand the mechanics impacting viewability performance. Media owners began enhancing their ad products to perform for viewability and media buyers invested heavily in inventory that hit the metric. The incentive was there and in many cases, performance thresholds for viewability were mandated as part of media buying terms. In a few short years, major design shifts took place to service this incentive.

Lazy loading—where content is loaded gradually as a user scrolls, rather than all at the same time—became the norm. Perpetual autoplay video disappeared, especially on desktop where a video ads playing in a browser tab you weren't looking at could run up non-viewable impressions for days, pushing down viewability for that media owner. And the idea of a forced view and non-skippable ads experience became commonplace (and showed positive results for viewability in the process). The user experience (UX) of the internet fundamentally changed to meet the new target.

Quality of attention

While the dynamics of viewability and its impact on internet design and media consumption is clear, Goodharts Law could be equally applicable to other common metrics like CPMs, Clicks and more. So it stands to reason that as attention metrics become an increased focus for the media industry, that a similar fate is probable. The important distinction with attention metrics is that the downstream impact of gaming human attention may have a far larger potential impact on humanity than any metric that has come before it.

Today, the majority of discussions and optimisations around attention metrics are geared towards driving a quantity of attention. This is partly because it's the simplest and most universal way to measure attention (i.e.

in seconds), but also because there's a common sense logic that the more of someone's attention an ad receives the more likely it will drive an awareness, consideration or conversion outcome. And so, optimizing towards a greater quantity of attention seems like a healthy marketing strategy at face value.

Optimizing toward a greater quantity of attention means driving up total time spent with advertising. And while there are several ways this can be gamed already, the clearest and most effective is UX and ad design. The placements that generally drive the highest quantity of attention force the viewing experience or heavily incentivise it. This increases the total time spent with advertising and puts a greater distance between the consumer and the end content they're after.

If we draw on the learnings from viewability and anticipate UX and Design shifts that target increased time spent metrics, it's easy to project an internet with a much larger number of forced view placements in future. Not only would this create a poorer user experience for the internet overall, but it also raises an important ethical question "How much of any one person's time should be consumed by advertising?." A person who sleeps 8 hours on average has less than 1000 waking minutes each day. The more that advertising optimizes toward the quantity of attention, the more time will be eroded from the individual and the greater potential there is for detrimental impact on individuals and society at large. So as an industry, we need to carefully consider the downstream consequences before making quantity of attention a target for effectiveness.

As the media industry's ability to measure attention has developed in recent years, there's no doubt that it will continue to be an important and valuable measure of effectiveness. However, if we're to do that in a humane and productive way, it's most likely that the quality of attention is where we should be focusing our efforts.

MEANWHILE IN THE REAL WORLD

Here is a book excerpt by Gerry McGovern on what he calls World Wide Waste (2020).

Digital is physical. Digital is not green. Digital costs the Earth. Every time I download an email I contribute to global warming. Every time I tweet, do a search, check a webpage, I create pollution. Digital is physical. Those data centers are not in the Cloud. They're on land in massive physical buildings packed full of computers hungry for energy. It seems invisible. It seems cheap and free. It's not. Digital costs the Earth.

One of the most difficult challenges with digital is to truly grasp what it is, its form, its impact on the physical world. I want to help give you a feel for digital. I'm going to analyze how many trees would need to be planted to offset a particular digital activity. For example:

- 1.6 billion trees would have to be planted to offset the pollution caused by email spam.
- 1.5 billion trees would need to be planted to deal with annual e-commerce returns in the US alone.
- 231 million trees would need to be planted to deal with the pollution caused as a result of the data US citizens consumed in 2019.
- 16 million trees would need to be planted to offset the pollution caused by the estimated 1.9 trillion yearly searches on Google.

We don't have an energy production crisis. We do have an energy consumption crisis. We consume far too much of everything the Earth produces and in the last 40 years our appetites for everything have exploded, driven and enabled by advances in digital technology. Recycling and renewables are often a form of greenwashing for big corporations. To go 100% renewable would not be without its costs, as the machines that make wind and solar technology need to be manufactured, consuming energy, the batteries in our electric cars need precious raw materials. We consume too much energy, that's the problem, and like our waistlines, these habits have gone out of control.
https://gerrymcgovern.com/

8.3   The Wrap Up—The Shonkys as a Force for Change

'CHOICE' is an independent consumer advocacy group in Australia with a rich history spanning over 60 years. It was founded by consumers, for consumers, and boasts a substantial membership base comprising hundreds of thousands of individuals. The organization is deeply committed to various consumer rights including product safety, unfair consumer practices, addressing price gouging, privacy laws and more. Their mission is to fight to make markets fair, safe and just for Australian consumers.

One of their prominent initiatives over the past 18 years has been the annual 'Shonky Awards,' during which they publicly expose and condemn products and services that have caused significant distress, disappointment, and inconvenience in consumers' lives. This event serves as a powerful and public platform and over the years, and 128 Shonky's awarded, CHOICE's diligent efforts have yielded substantial outcomes including government inquiries, regulatory reforms, and organizational transformations.

Here are some of CHOICE's most celebrated Shonky Awards based on the positive changes initiated:

In 2011 a Shonky was awarded to: **The Whole Home Insurance Industry** for using confusing language or 'legalese'. After a major weather event that left half the country submerged underwater, homeowners were shocked to find out that their insurance policies did not cover flood damage, mainly due to the unclear standard definition of the term 'flood.' In response the federal government took action and amended the Insurance Contracts Regulations 1985 to introduce a standard definition and settlements to home owners were reached.

In 2014 a Shonky was awarded to: **The Commonwealth Bank** for calculated deceit putting clients into risky and inappropriate investments to meet bonus goals, costing consumers millions of dollars and leading to lost life savings. This uncovered a string of issues that would ultimately lead to an initial Senate inquiry, followed by a full Royal Commission on the entire Australian banking industry.

In 2017 a Shonky was awarded to: **Takata Airbags** for a critical safety risk with the potential to cause death. This led to the government initiating one of the largest mandatory product recalls in Australian history. Tens of thousands of vehicles, across many makes and models were held to account in the recall.

In 2022 a Shonky was awarded to: **Qantas** for deteriorating service and complicated and unfair rules around COVID travel credits. This led to the early departure of a CEO, a commitment to board turnover, a back down on travel credits and legal proceedings for the recovery of travel credits.

Public shaming has emerged with the advent of digital media. Maybe it's time for our industry to reverse the roles and establish its own Shonky Awards to spotlight questionable practices.

8.4   List of Contributors

Kristofer Doerfler. Co-founder of the Conscious Attention Economy (CAE), Innovation Director and Regenerative Media Lead at CMI Media Group

The CAE initiative is a working group in partnership with Future Capital and the United Nations for New Economics of Sustainable Development (NESD).

Born and raised in New York City, Kris is an advertising professional and director of innovation at CMI Media Group, where he has helped lead efforts to re-imagine the marketing ecosystem to be more ethical and sustainable. He is a passionate environmentalist who understands we are at a crossroads in our physical, mental, and digital realms where a new ethos and new metrics are needed to judge success. He brings this passion and understanding into the advertising world to help combat attention exploitation issues such as misinformation, fraud, and information overload in order to bring to life a healthier internet culture. As the co-founder of the Conscious Attention Economy Working Group in connection with Future Capital, Kris has partnered with the United Nations to develop the principles and action points for The New Economics For Sustainable Development: Attention Economy alongside a diverse team to achieve a more regenerative future.

Dave Goodfellow. Head of Measurement Asia–Pacific, Pinterest

Dave Goodfellow is Head of Measurement, Asia–Pacific, at Pinterest, leading a team that partners with advertisers to measure and maximize their impact on Pinterest, as well as develop strategies and research to drive forward the evolution of Measurement in the media industry.

Dave has spent the better part of two decades working as a marketer and measurement leader across paid, owned and earned aspects of the media ecosystem. His career started in Public Relations, where his earliest roles were working agency-side managing communications for tech and lifestyle brands.

As the industry became increasingly social and digital, so did Dave's skill set and mindset. He's held digital communications and social media strategist roles at leading integrated marketing agencies. He transitioned from agencies to vendor-side roles, including over five years at Oracle, leading product and partnerships development for customer analytics, viewability measurement and contextual marketing technologies.

Dave lives in Sydney, Australia and is a proud dad to two kids. When he's not thinking about media and measurement, you'll typically find him tinkering with electronics, refining his woodworking skills or playing D&D with friends and family.

Daniel Lyas. Amplified Intelligence, Senior Manager Revenue Operations

Daniel Lyas is a media professional and an early employee at Amplified Intelligence. He has a deep understanding of attention measurement best practices and has helped a host of global brands and agencies adopt both methodologies and solutions into their strategies. With expertise in customer partnerships, project management and process building, Daniel has helped accelerate business growth and scale customer acquisition to drive adoption of attention across the globe. Daniel is deeply passionate about the broader outcomes the work and goals of Amplified Intelligence has on the end user and the role attention can play in driving meaningful change for media measurement.

Dr Anna McAlister. Professor of Marketing, Endicott College

Dr. Anna R. McAlister is Professor of Marketing at Endicott College, where she teaches courses in Research Methods, Consumer Behavior, and Marketing. She also teaches courses at Michigan State University in online Strategic Communication Master's program and their undergraduate Advertising Management program. Dr. McAlister's research focuses on the effects of advertising targeted to children, with a particular focus on public policy matters. She has published in Journal of Public Policy & Marketing, Journal of Advertising, Child Development, Psychology and Marketing, and various other journals, and has won multiple awards for her teaching and research.

McAlister serves as the Director of Curriculum and Assessment for the Institute for Advertising Ethics. She also serves as Deputy Editor at Journal of Marketing Communications, and is on the editorial review board for Journal of Advertising and Journal of Interactive Advertising.

References

Asimov, Isaac. (1950). *Runaround*. I, Robot (The Isaac Asimov Collection ed., p. 40). Doubleday. ISBN 978–0–385–42304–5.

Asimov, Isaac (1981, November). The Three Laws. *Compute!* (p. 18). Retrieved October 26, 2013, https://archive.org/details/1981-11-compute-magazine/page/n19/mode/2up?view=theater

Bhargava, V., & Velasquez, M. (2021). Ethics of the Attention Economy: The Problem of Social Media Addiction. *Business Ethics Quarterly, 31*(3), 321–359. https://doi.org/10.1017/beq.2020.32

Biometrics Institute. *Three Laws of Biometrics*. Retrieved from https://www.biometricsinstitute.org/the-three-laws-of-biometrics/

Centre for Humane Technology. *Three Laws of Humane Technology*. Retrieved from https://www.humanetech.com/podcast/the-three-rules-of-humane-tech

Elmahmudi, A., & Ugail, H. (2021). A Framework for Facial Age Progression and Regression Using Exemplar Face Templates. *The Visual Computer., 37*. https://doi.org/10.1007/s00371-020-01960-z

Modok, A. (2023). Role of Social Media in Inciting the Genocidal Acts: A Case Study on Myanmar's Rohingya. *Contemporary Challenges: The Global Crime, Justice and Security Journal, 4*. https://doi.org/10.2218/ccj.v4.9123

Morley, O. (2022). How OMD's Attention Planning Tool Transforms Campaign Strategy. *AdWeek*. https://www.adweek.com/agencies/how-omds-attention-planning-tool-transforms-campaign-strategy/

Murphy, R. R., & Woods, D. D. (2017). Beyond Asimov: The Three Laws of Responsible Robotics. In *Machine Ethics and Robot Ethics*. Routledge.

Newton, I. (1687) *Philosophiae Naturalis Principia Mathematica*. Londini, Jussu Societatis Regiæ ac Typis Josephi Streater. Prostat apud plures Bibliopolas.

Williams, R. (2023). Operationalizing Attention to Drive Better Outcomes: OMD USA's Chrissie Hanson. *Beet TV*. https://www.beet.tv/2023/07/attention-metrics-move-beyond-ad-viewability-to-help-track-outcomes-omd-usas-chrissie-hanson.html

Zhan, J. (2022). Three Laws of Technology Rise or Fall. *BenchCouncil Transactions on Benchmarks, Standards and Evaluations, 2*(1), 100034.

9

Back to the Future Gazing

"Your future hasn't been written yet. No one's has. Your future is whatever you make it. So make it a good one."
Dr. Emmett Brown, Back to the Future: Part III (1990)

Doc Brown, while quirky, was undeniably brilliant particularly when it comes to understanding the future (and his DeLorean). And in light of the content within this book, Doc Brown's quote is on point. We do have the opportunity to write the next chapter in the history of measurement and we owe it to our industry to make it a good one. But just what might this next chapter look like? George Orwell said, "People can foresee the future only when it coincides with their own wishes, and the most grossly obvious facts can be ignored when they are unwelcome." So will personal biases influence our perception and judgment? Perhaps more to the point, will we as an industry ignore the obvious truths due to their lack of commercial appeal? Only time will tell.

This chapter is a look back into the future, we are shaking the Magic 8 ball once more.

We asked a small and distinguished panel of future-thinking researchers, practitioners and commentators what the next 5 to 10 years might look like in marketing, advertising and measurement—much like our approach in the original Attention Economy book. The brief was for 'no boundaries', to be candid and express this future how you see it.

© The Author(s), under exclusive license to Springer Nature
Singapore Pte Ltd. 2024
K. Nelson-Field, *The Attention Economy*, https://doi.org/10.1007/978-981-97-0084-4_9

But first, just like Professor Scott Galloway who every December checks in on the provocative predictions he makes the year prior, we are also holding ourselves accountable by reviewing some of the most controversial predictions of the past.

So the first section of this chapter returns to the future and score-checks predictions from book 1 (written 2019), while the second section goes back to the future of the future, where our new set of big thinkers unleash.

9.1   Futurists Past: Predictions Hit and Missed

Dr Wolfgang Henseler

This future position kicked off at a point where HAL 9000 meets The Truman Story. A place called Internet 4.0. By a Professor of Digital Media and Managing Director of Sensory Minds GMBH.

Prediction 1. People will not be able to distinguish between real and artificial

RIGHT: Advancements in AI, especially in 2023 in deep learning and computer vision along with the widespread accessibility of AI tools, have made creating convincing deepfake content easy. This blurs the line between real and artificially generated images and videos. This might be all fun and games when it's an impersonation of Tom Cruise on TikTok; Barack Obama on Buzzfeed or even the Catholic Pontiff wearing Balenciaga, but it can be life changing when deepfake evidence starts to creep into courtrooms. In 2021 A paper by Daniel Seng and Stephen Mason reports that "courts and lawyers alike will increasingly have to contend with the issues associated with the admissibility of evidence generated and produced by AI systems."

Prediction 2. Regulatory institutions will (sometimes belatedly) try to control the social, moral and ethical borders of big tech

RIGHT: On tracking: $5billion class action against illegal internet tracking in private mode (Chasom Brown et al versus Google LLC).

On data breaches: Amazon: $877 million USD related to GDPR 2021. Instagram: $403 million USD related to GDPR 2022. TikTok: $370 million USD related to DPC 2023. And the list goes on.

On generative AI: Class Action vs GitHub Copilot 2022 for copyright infringement. Hood versus ChatGPT for defamation. Getty Images versus Stability AI 2022 for copyright infringement.

Prediction 3. The value of data will be less about the raw commodity and more about how it is processed and used

RIGHT: The rise of genAI has transformed raw data processing, with System 3 thinking, as advocated by Sofie Pires, accelerating and deepening this transformation. Unlike in the past, where advanced data analysis was limited to university labs and tech giants, today, businesses of all sizes can access and utilize AI tools to enhance their data analytics, uncovering patterns that once required expert coding. This accessibility levels the playing field, enabling businesses to make more informed decisions, better mine the raw data they have, and gain a competitive edge.

Bob Hoffman

This dystopian future was equal parts entertaining and scary which largely revolved around Facebook and Google. Bob Hoffman, known as the Ad Contrarian.

Prediction 1. There will be deep political polarization resulting in societal disruption

RIGHT: You just have to look at the fallout from former President Donald Trump's remarks on the Ellipse on Jan. 6 2021 to know this was a correct prediction. Since then Anti-Defamation League (ADL) continues to run the award winning #stophateforprofits campaign to hold social media companies accountable for hate, racism and extremism on their platforms. Facebook was also under fire from the Wall Street Journal in 2020 as being a "conduit for conspiracy theories and partisan sparring about the coronavirus pandemic. In essence, Facebook is under fire for making the world more divided."

Prediction 2. The government will intervene and confiscate extensive data from Facebook, Google and other marketing companies

NOT YET: The FBI were unsuccessful in 2015 when it filed a case against Apple with a federal court judge to access data on an iPhone owned by the San Bernardino Health Department, and it looks like no data has been confiscated yet. With that said, in 2021 The Federal Trade Commission (FTC) started considering new rules to address harmful commercial surveillance and weak data security. Commercial surveillance involves collecting and profiting from people's information, and mass surveillance has increased the risks of data breaches and manipulation. The FTC is still seeking public input to determine what measures might be taken. Although things have started in the USA where in April 2024, US president Joe Biden signed into law to protect Americans from Foreign Adversary Controlled Applications Act, which is an effective ban or forced sale of TikTok from its parent company ByteDance.

Prediction 3. I will be imprisoned by Facebook or Google executives

WRONG: Last we checked, Bob Hoffman is not in prison, but you never know what is to come. His new book, Adscam, is particularly scathing while his March 2023 address to the EU parliament, is particularly accusatory of the surveillance techniques employed by the big socials. This might tip them over.

Dr Augustine Fou

This future position takes us through the fall and rise of AdTech and hot potatoes by one of the most vocal Ad Fraud researchers.

Prediction 1. A crash is coming for AdTech

RIGHT: 2023 has left our industry in a perfect storm for change (see Chapter 4). In 2022 Forbes said "The future of digital advertising is said to be at a crossroads where the shift to 'zero-party data' is imminent." This perfect storm is driving a new era of measurement after 30 years of mess.

Prediction 2. AdTech companies that were based on illegal/unethical surveillance marketing will blow up and go away

NOT YET: But TikTok is under increasing scrutiny. Between January and March 2023, TikTok faced 15 lawsuits for violating the Federal Wiretap Act through its in-app browser's unauthorized user tracking. Throughout 2023, multiple countries, including the United States, have considered banning TikTok due to security concerns. India banned the platform in mid-2020, resulting in significant losses for ByteDance. Several other countries and government bodies, including Britain, Australia, Canada, the European Union's executive arm, France, and New Zealand's Parliament, have also prohibited TikTok on official government devices.

Dr Karen Nelson-Field

This future position questions the relative value of traditional laws of brand growth given the opaque pipes of adtech and mismeasured impression delivery. It questioned how 'will' brands grow?

Prediction 1. Within 10 years we will be forced to reconsider the laws of brand growth

RIGHT: The seemingly irreparable and mismeasured condition of impression delivery in digital media means that reach based planning, which underpins many of the traditional laws of brand growth, are broken. Until attention data is applied as a hygiene data input to reach planning workflows, we need to reconsider how these laws can work under the current conditions that impact advertising delivery.

Prediction 2. A very large part of our future buying will be restricted to a few players and a very large part of our advertising dollars will be assigned to them. Bricks and mortar sites will significantly diminish

NOT YET: While buying from only a selected few is not quite here yet, it is coming. JD.com, Alibaba, Amazon and others are only years away from being the majority holders of our advertising dollars. The 2023 acquisition of Flywheel, the largest ever by Omnicom Global, suggests at least some of their >$14bn ad dollars are heading that way. Flywheel offers services designed to help brands sell on digital marketplaces operated by companies including. Amazon. In preparation for this change, yes, bricks and mortar sites significantly diminished. This was fast tracked by the pandemic.

9.2   Futurists Present: Another Shake of the Magic 8 Ball

The Swinging Pendulum. Nick Manning

It's easy to see why Attention has received so much, well, attention in recent years.

The explosion in channel choice for consumers has produced a massive expansion in ways to theoretically reach and influence them, with a vast and overwhelming increase in commercial messaging. While overall time spent with media has increased, people are skipping from channel to channel in the blink of an eye, second-screening and scrolling through our carefully-crafted ad content. Unsurprisingly, studies show that advertising impact and effectiveness has declined and people feel bombarded and have switched off from advertising as a result.

Vast sums of money are wasted on advertising that no-one notices and often only reaches an artificial audience, or none at all. Without the measurement of attention it is virtually impossible to measure true ad exposure. Impressions as a currency are pretty useless without the right audience overlay supplemented by attention metrics, even before cost applies. The move to attention as an essential element of audience measurement is hugely welcome and especially so as part of the overall shift to the measurement of marketing effectiveness.

We are fortunate to have new statistical techniques and Artificial Intelligence to help us parse gargantuan amounts of data, even if a lot of it is incompatible and we have to use probability and good old-fashioned judgment to bridge the data gap. We will see Attention metrics being added to the marketing (not just media) mix in a world of infinite choice for brand-building, product selling and influence on behavior and attitudes.

We will get better at measuring the effect of different kinds of content and creative messaging and, hopefully, starting to differentiate between good and less good when it comes to media, answering some key questions, for example:

1. Why do Primetime GRPs perform better than other daypart GRPs?
2. Why do some impressions grab people's attention more than others?
3. What roles do context, intention, location and attention play in driving business results?

Transparency in marketing and media will eventually arrive when our industry moves to impact and effectiveness measurement as the base principle for strategy, planning and execution. This is almost the polar opposite of today, where "because we can" is the dominant theme. Market mix modeling can only work properly if the right data goes in, and today that is not fully possible. We're missing pieces of the jigsaw and only marketing and media transparency can help us complete the picture.

One key to transparency of data and money is for our industry to finally emulate others and take commercial contracts seriously, rather than as a cat and mouse game. Compliance should not be optional. We do not yet have all of the data we need to achieve complete impact and effectiveness measurement but we can and should use what we have and seek further progress. We certainly have better tools.

One reason for the current roaring success of Commerce Media is the ability to pull different levers in the various component channels and watch the results come in, with a virtuous circle of optimisation (the 'flywheel effect'). Other marketing channels will need to catch up or lose money to a channel that is more measurable.

An industry based on the measurement of impact and effectiveness would see a welcome return to the base principles that were taken for granted in former times. Advertisers advertised for growth and they knew that big messages in big media did this best, often supplemented by targeted product messages.

These days we have plenty of targeted product messages without the 'air cover'.

To borrow a cricketing term, brands should have the confidence to score in 6s and 4s, while taking the odd single. It's riskier and can go wrong, but the results can be spectacular. We've been down the road of trying to build an innings through only scoring singles (person by person) and it is harder, takes longer and is less successful.

The right kind of impact and effectiveness is the key to marketing success and attention will sit at the heart of the new way to achieve it as long as our industry shakes off its aversion to new methods and the supply-side evolves to accommodate it.

This may be 'back to the future' but it's the right, and perhaps only, answer.

When Tech Becomes Truly Invisible, Communication Becomes Screenless. Sofia Pires

If there's one thing we can all rally against, is that screens are stealing our attention. The Luddites might argue that we need to return to analogue and reclaim our experiences in the real world.

But I think there is another option. One that is not going back to the past, but it's fast-forwarding us into the future. Where technology is invisible, where it augments our intelligence without distracting us from our surroundings.

In the future, attention won't be about who shouts the loudest, but who whispers the closest to you.

And that is the tech that Imran Chaudhri and Bethany Bongiorno have built with Hu.ma.ne, taking their years of experience at Apple to design their so-called AI pin, which provides us information not through a device, but through tech that is no longer visible. Screenless. Seamless. Sensing.

This is the opposite of a computer stuck in front of our eyes like Apple's Vision Pro and Metas' Q VR sets.

It was back in 2017 when the American journalist Walt Mossberg raised the idea of the disappearing computer.

As he wrote in his last article before retirement: "I expect that one end result of all this work will be that the technology, the computer inside all these things, will fade into the background. In some cases, it may entirely disappear, waiting to be activated by a voice command, a person entering the room, a change in blood chemistry, a shift in temperature, a motion. Maybe even just a thought."

Mossberg called this Ambient computing, the transformation of the environment that surrounds us through artificial intelligence and capabilities that don't seem to be there at all.

This was the same year when Facebook was also working on systems that use the brain to type, and also when Neuralink was first publicly reported as a new neurotechnology company, and has since been developing implantable brain–computer interfaces.

In my work on System 3 and how technology could impact decision-making, I use Neuralink as an example of how we'll merge with machines. In it, I explored the hypothesis of a future where humans and machines merge fully and what happens in that symbiotic intelligence. It's a future where technology will enable us to experience the world with more of our senses and less of our screens.

Similarly, Max Tegmark is calling this new evolution of us the Homo Sentiens, emphasizing what makes us humans is less and less about intelligence, but about our ability to have wonderful experiences and feel love and joy.

And that's what happens when technology increases and devices disappear, experiences will come forward. Augmenting our ability to be present, instead of blocking us from the physical reality, no screens between us.

As we stare at the end of the traditional media platforms as we know them today, a new opportunity emerges for brands, media companies, government, or other institutions to connect with audiences more naturally, where attention is not connected to the screens, but to our natural surroundings.

I have no answers yet, but I leave you with the provocation: As these companies are re-imagining the human-tech relationship, how do we re-imagine new forms of communication that live beyond screens?

Sources:

Imran Chaudhri—Ted talk 2023 https://www.youtube.com/watch?v=gMs QO5u7-NQ

Walt Mossberg 2017 https://www.theverge.com/2017/5/25/15686870/
walt-mossberg-final-column-the-disappearing-computer

System 3 IPA essay 2022 https://ipa.co.uk/knowledge/ipa-blog/system-3-
will-bring-us-to-our-senses/

Portable Identity will be the New Pixel. Michael Bürgi

In 10 years, almost all "content" will be sponsored, in the sense that there will
be no more interruptive ad breaks in content—rather, much like The Truman
Show, all advertisements will be baked into the content. This development
will slowly and steadily grow out of the world's fascination with influencers
and creators. Shoppable video will be so ubiquitous that retail and fashion
advertising will have morphed into an agent-controlled business that works
to get products into programs.

The public will have the choice of creating their own consumer ID—
much like a social security number for all purchases. It will obviate the need
for companies to figure out who their consumers are, or what their shopping habits are. The appeal to create a consumer ID will be the extensive
discounts and savings participating companies can offer in exchange for this
vital data that consumers will throw off. Whether these consumer IDs will
be government-controlled or accessed is still unclear. But it will be universal,
originating in Asia and eventually migrating west, as with so many other tech
innovations. By 2034, 65% of the world will have a consumer ID (available
to anyone over 12 years of age—any younger will be controlled by parent or
guardian).

This portability of identity will enable an explosion in screens everywhere.
Close a public bathroom stall, and a screen will entertain you while you sit
on the proverbial throne. Not only on your car's dashboard, screens will also
be in the back of headrests so that all passengers can enjoy content of their
own choosing. Much like modern airplanes, public transportation will have
screens in every seat—bluetooth-accessible and able to be personalized. Home
video screens will double as information portals, where virtual keyboards will
be accessible through VR wear. There will be no more distinction between
your TV set and your computer/laptop—they are the same.

All content will be offered a la carte, as the streaming services continue to
dominate the distribution of content. Linear TV will pretty much be gone,
and even sports and awards shows will be available on demand as opposed to
via mass-viewing opportunities.

Finally, to enable the marketing opportunities all these changes usher in,
agencies will again rebundle into creative entities bristling with the above data

(from consumer IDs) that informs how and where they place their clients' marketing messages. Media and creative can no longer stay separate—in fact, creative and media even together will take a backseat to the negotiating that will have to take place for each marketer to fold its message into content as described at the beginning of this prediction.

Five major agency groups will control 90% of all marketing messaging. None of the existing holding companies will be one of them.

The Future of a More Balanced & Fair Ad-Supported Internet Ecosystem. Erez Levin

An incorporation of media quality measures into digital advertising always felt like an inevitability, and thus it was a bet that could be made confidently if one could afford the unclear time horizon and the inherent reputational risks. Now that we are on the precipice of seeing this destiny begin to manifest, it is critical that we prepare ourselves for the many direct and indirect changes that will be felt from this massive realignment of incentives, not just in the advertising industry, but across all of society.

Below are three vignettes that explore the impact of these changes through different lenses. While the brief descriptions of these changes may currently appear to be relatively benign, and most occuring gradually enough that they will be perceived as a disruptive but standard evolution, I believe we will look back in 5 years and find it impossible to call this time anything short of a revolution.

The Evolving Ecosystem of the Ad-Supported Internet

The health of the web is directly related to the ratio between the cost of content production, and the monetization of that content (primarily via advertising today). Currently this ratio is off kilter, mostly because of low quality content over-monetized and high quality content under-monetized by poorly measured advertising, and the consequences are far-ranging from decreased effectiveness for marketers, to the incentivization of lower and lower quality content.

These challenges will be further exacerbated with the proliferation of GenAI and an exponential increase in even more low quality content. Fortunately, some tectonic industry changes currently underway will force a renewed focus on media quality and begin a long-overdue and much-needed rebalancing of the ecosystem. This will lead to very important dynamics that will affect the 3 constituent groups of the ad-supported internet.

1. Users—A rise of "The Rewarded Web", where new walls will gate previously "free" premium content that can only be unlocked with money (subscriptions, micro-payment), time/attention (forced view video ads, surveys, etc.) or data use consent. This will feel like an unwelcome change for many, and will come with second-order effects that cause some negative societal outcomes, but it will be critical to restore a fair value exchange to incentivize the production of quality content.
2. Marketers—A shift away from avg. CPMs that distort everyone's understanding of the value of ads, especially as they fluctuate with dynamic ratios between high, medium, and low quality/attention ads. Customizable AI leveraging human insights and media quality measures will play a large role here. Creative will become a priority again.
3. Publishers—Ad-supported publishers that have unique and high quality or attention-generating content, or 1st party data, will command high CPMs. Others will look for other ways to differentiate & justify median (not avg.) CPMs, while the long-tail will receive minimal budget allocation with the lowest CPMs.

These changes will start to gradually be felt over the next few months and years until we see this major overhaul of the internet, and all the media we consume, as we currently know it. And despite the expected and yet-to-be-discovered negative consequences that will surely surface as a result, I strongly believe the fairness and balance achieved will be a net positive change to the world (Fig. 9.1).

Ad Inventory Landscape of the Future

The demise of 3P cookies and the rise of quality-based ad measurement & buying will lead to an ad landscape that looks completely different from the one we know today.

Rather than using audience identifiers as the primary vector by which to value media, with budget and pricing allocations happening effectively downstream, I believe we will see media begin to get valued based on two criteria. This will create 4 distinct buckets of ad inventory in the future distinguished based on formats (unique vs. commoditized) & data (enhanced vs. absent), each with unique relative value, pricing, and transaction types determined largely by their supply & demand imbalances.

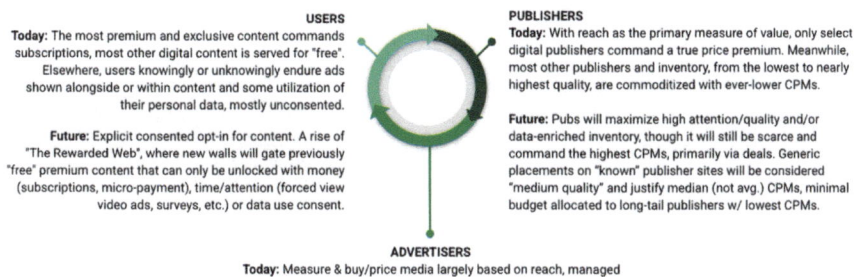

Fig. 9.1 The evolving ecosystem of the ad-supported internet. Erez Levin. 2023

The below diagram (Fig. 9.2) is a rough and oversimplified framing of how I see this playing out, which can be summed up like this:

1. Every publisher and content-creator will want to get into the top right quadrant, though very few will be able to enter this rarified space.
2. Nearly every other publisher needs to do everything in their power to get out of the bottom left quadrant, differentiating with formats or data. This will also be very difficult for most.
3. What excites me most about this change is that it will force marketers to truly factor media quality measures into their advertising practices, moving away from averages that are completely unrepresentative of the media that they buy and have led to a rapid race to the bottom.

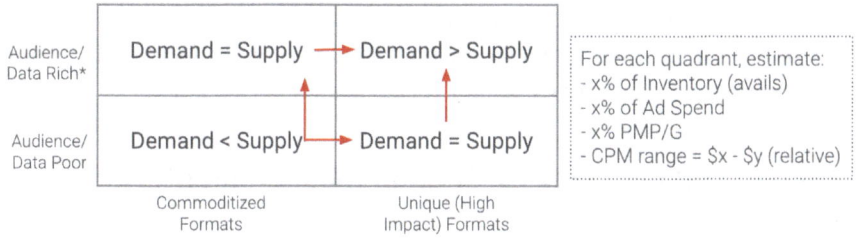

Fig. 9.2 Ad Inventory of the Future. Erez Levin. 2023

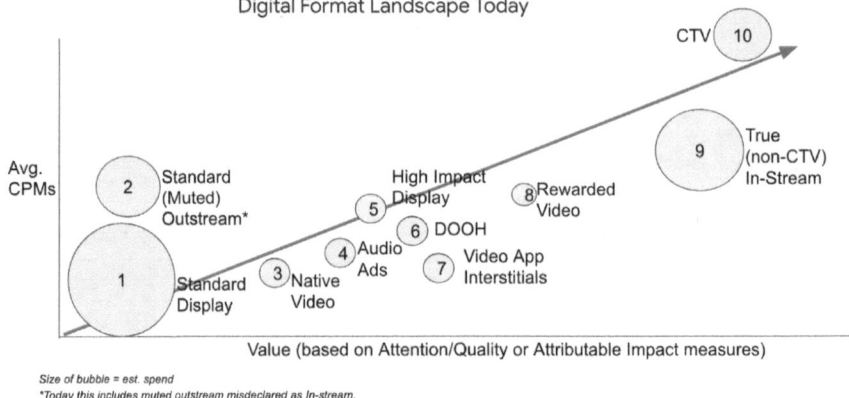

Size of bubble = est. spend
*Today this includes muted outstream misdeclared as In-stream.

Fig. 9.3 Digital Format Landscape Today. Erez Levin. 2023

Formats in Flux

As the digital media landscape evolved and fragmented, new ad formats and placements were created. Those formats that drove increased yield for publishers expanded. Because the buy side of the market did not evolve their measurement standards & buying practices in tandem, this led to a misalignment between monetization and value largely based on formats. As the industry shifts away from primarily deterministic user-based targeting & measurement, and begins to strongly weigh media quality and attention measures, we will see a realignment of spend and CPMs by formats.

Here I've charted a very rough & imperfect view of the current format landscape. Though the relative sizes and positions of these bubbles can be debated, what is more important is to consider how these will shift when quality becomes a primary factor in buying and measurement. Though a perfectly optimized market is impossible to achieve, we will nonetheless see these bubbles move up and down so each sits closer to the green line, and while bubbles 1 & 2 are likely to shrink, that spend is likely to shift towards and grow many of the other bubbles (Fig. 9.3).

A Human-Led Currency for Human Measurement. Andy Brown

There has been much discussion around whether attention metrics can be used as an audience measurement currency. There is a lot of debate about what constitutes a currency. A quick internet search gives the following:

1. General estimation: the rate at which anything is generally valued.
2. Transmission from person to person as a medium of exchange; circulation.

I think here is where some of the differences of opinion lie, because at one level currency is defined as a widespread agreed valuation (in this case the value of a media opportunity) perhaps part of a syndicated research audience measurement service; or something at a micro level for an individual transaction, that a buyer and seller can agree a financial price and provision.

As a media researcher, I feel that there necessarily needs to be compromise in any measurement (a balance between relevance, accuracy, practical implementation and cost). I do think human-based attention metrics (alongside other indicators perhaps directly linked to other behavioral and performance variables), will become an integral part of a currency providing net opportunity to see (OTS) and the ability to value video advertising (c.-85% of ad spend). As with much media audience measurement going forward, it is likely to be integrated/calibrated with "big data sources" e.g. set top box/server data. As bodies such as the advertiser group ISBA develop solutions such as Origin for cross media measurement, attention metrics can provide a lens through which a value can be assigned to the deduplicated reach and the associated impressions. Ie. What is the value of a TV impression versus that of a native digital video platform?

I think the challenge to all of this, is the sell side (perhaps more in traditional media) signing up for lower scale, higher quality audiences. I would argue it breaks one of the "primary rules" of audience measurement…big numbers trump small! In other words, any attempt to segment a gross audience whether by visual attention, effectiveness graded inventory or even use of GSR or neuroscience will end up delivering a lower audience count than the typical gross impressions or rating points from a typical audience measurement solution or native digital platform.

Do I envisage a single-source attention measurement solution adopted across all media channels? I think that will be challenging e.g. If we assume visual attention with or without big (behavioral) data is adopted for "TV" and native digital video (and all stops in between), there is a challenge to have a common methodology that would handle radio alongside the various video channels. So as already mentioned there will necessarily need to be a compromise in approach. That said, perhaps there could be some common principles of measurement of attention across channels. E.g. A gross to net audience calculation approach.

All of this change will necessarily create (in the short-term) a group of vendors who might win or lose from such a change. It is therefore important in my view to have standards set and validated by an independent measurement body, whether that may be a Joint Industry body for audience measurement or an independent auditor such as the Media Ratings Council (MRC).

As recent audience measurement history has shown in the US, we are living in a multi-currency world and that trend is likely to spread beyond the confines of the US. This means that a single supplier of attention metrics is unlikely to prevail, but there could be a range of suppliers operating within industry standards as audited by MRC, CESP or some equivalent body.

9.3   The Wrap Up: The Industry's Reply Letter To Bob Hoffman

To wrap up this 'chapter of big thinking', it might be time to reply to a big thinker from the last book, a past futurist. Bob Hoffman is a highly accomplished writer and speaker in the advertising field, but perhaps most known these days for his 'heads should roll' approach to his commentary and speeches on big tech that he considers 'divisive and toxic'. He is the author of six Amazon #1 best-selling books on advertising. He is also one of the most sought-after international speakers on advertising and marketing. In 2012 he was selected "Ad Person of the Year" by the San Francisco Advertising Club. He addressed the British Parliament in 2021 and the European Parliament in 2023 on matters of national interest related to ad fraud and threats to democracy.

While Bob wasn't a futurist in this book, his dark humor, with a touch of scary reality, needed to resurface. So here we paraphrase his original open letter to the industry, then we 'pen' a cautious reply hoping to improve his mood.

Bob's Letter

To whoever finds this,

It's been six years since I was arrested and held in this camp. I often wonder what my wife and daughter think. I don't know how many people there are here but it seems like thousands. I've been told that there are dozens of these camps here in California and hundreds throughout the country. I never expected to be imprisoned. I had always been a rules-following, tax-paying type. But problems began in the early 2020s when deep political polarization started to appear, and a second, seemingly unrelated issue, when the rise of what was called 'data-driven marketing'.

In those days the marketing industry believed that by having more information about us they could communicate with us in a more persuasive fashion. To get more information, they developed technology to follow us in our everyday activities. It was called 'tracking'. They tracked what we read, who we corresponded with, what we said in our correspondence, where we went, and what we did. At the time we didn't think much of it because in return for tracking they provided us with some very useful and, frankly, fun and interesting stuff. We didn't really foresee how this could go wrong.

There were several companies back then that were particularly good at tracking and had collected a very large amount of information about people. Two of them were Google and Facebook. Now for the most part they kept their information private and it didn't seem to have much effect on our everyday lives. But there must have been something I wrote or something someone wrote about me that raised a red flag. Maybe it was my injudicious musings about all the data that was being collected falling into the wrong hands. And here I am.

I'm going to bury this now in the hope that someday it will be found. If you find this, please try to locate my family and tell them I'm okay and I love them.

Bob Hoffman. Spring (I think) 2027

The Industry Replies

Dear Bob,

Wow, six years in a camp? That's quite the ordeal. Your message did reach us, and in 2026 things are ok, we think.

First things first, we found your wife and daughter, they are well. We know because we checked their IP addresses and found them surfing all sorts of websites only yesterday. We are happy to send you, and 5 million others, the list of sites, time of day, physical location, social comments, shopping transactions and their new bank account details if you want. I also see they have been on Tik Tok, but I can't seem to get access to what they are up to there.

Look, the good news is this, since you left the world is changing. The industry is trying hard to fix its problems, we know we need to change and the cookie did eventually crumble, even after several false starts and it still needs work (clearly because I know your daughter just bought some baby clothes on Amazon if that means anything to you). Oh and perhaps of interest, Mark

Zuckerberg retired for a career in wrestling last year. Not that many heard about that though, as he decided to release that PR only in the Metaverse.

Look, you never know, maybe in the future, politicians will win elections by promising not to send us spam emails! We didn't quite get there though for the 2024 US election, but let's not talk about that.

But for now, hang in there, Bob. Perhaps you could update us on your progress with your pen and paper. Or, even better, perhaps you could send us some data so we can find you and break you out. And who knows, maybe by the time someone reads your next message, the world will be a much different place.

In the meantime, take care and keep the faith,

Kind Regards,

The Industry. Summer 2026

9.4   List of Contributors

Andy Brown. Andrew Brown and Associates & CEO of The Attention Council

Following a degree in Marketing, Andy started his career at Anglia Television, now part of the UK commercial network ITV. He then joined BMRB, now part of Kantar; where responsibilities included the international expansion of the company's single-source consumer TGI survey into Europe and Latin America, an initiative which led to the formation of the KMR Group and his subsequent appointment as CEO in 2001.

After the acquisition of TNS in 2008 and a number of high-profile acquisitions and strategic partnerships in North America, Latin America and Asia, Andy formed the board of Kantar Media and was named CEO of the combined business, a position he has held from 2013 till 2020 (whilst also being on the Kantar Executive Committee). That business managed Kantar's global interest in Audience Measurement, Reputation Intelligence, TGI and Advertising Intelligence. He left Kantar after the successful sale of the business to Bain Capital.

Since leaving Kantar and with over 30 years of research experience, Andy has taken on a number of consulting and advisory roles: They range from posts with Dynata (market research), Ipsos (media measurement), The One Partnership (talent/brand partnerships), Digital I (SVOD audience research), TVision to The Attention Council (specialist measurement of the attention economy).

Michael Bürgi. Senior Editor Media Buying & Planning, Digiday

Michael Bürgi is a veteran journalist and Senior Editor at Digiday, based in New York/New Jersey. He specializes in marketing, media, and content, and his extensive career has made him a respected figure in these fields. Michael's expertise is sought after for his ability to tell compelling stories that capture attention, whether in writing, in person, or onstage. Michael's journey in the media world began as a reporter for Channels magazine (backed by the late Norman Lear) in the 1980s. But the majority of his career was spent at Adweek sibling Mediaweek, where he steadily progressed from reporter to News Editor and eventually served as Editor-in-Chief for nearly a decade. He briefly transitioned to the agency world as Senior Vice President and Director of Global Communications at Starcom MediaVest Group before returning to his passion of journalism. At Adweek, he took on the role of Director of Editorial Partnerships and later became Senior Vice President of Content and News at DiGennaro Communications. Outside of his professional life, Michael is a devoted fan of the New York Knicks, an amateur marine biologist and an avid foodie.

Erez Levin. Attention Evangelist & Media Quality Specialist

Though my professional career has existed entirely in the digital advertising era, I am an old soul when it comes to marketing fundamentals. Having spent nearly a full decade focused on the media supply landscape at a time of rapid fragmentation, I witnessed the health of the ad-supported web degrading due to what I diagnosed as an industry-wide, single-minded pursuit of quantity measures at the expense of quality measures. As a result, I have committed myself to one important career goal above all others; to reintroduce & reintegrate the concepts of media quality into the digital & cross-channel advertising ecosystems, paired with modern technologies that can achieve unprecedented effectiveness together.

Nick Manning. Founder at Encyclomedia International (ex CEO Ebiquity)

Nick Manning is an independent consultant, commentator, investor and author. His career spans over 40 years, including 27 years in the media agency world.

Nick co-founded Manning Gottlieb Media, now re-named MG OMD and the largest of Omnicom's UK media agencies. Nick was CEO of OMD's UK media agencies prior to entering the world of independent media consulting. This has included 10 years at Ebiquity, a year at Medialink and since 2019 within his own media consulting business, Encyclomedia International.

Nick's client work includes extensive involvement with the ANA on their media transparency initiatives and he is a frequent commentator on advertising and media matters.

Sofia Pires. AI & Society Strategist, Winner of the President's Prize for Outstanding Body of Work in the 2022 IPA Excellence Diploma in Brands

Sofia Pires is a unique thinker with a strong comms background having led strategy for HSBC, HP, Unilever and Diageo at WPP and Omnicom media agencies. Beyond corporate, she has spoken at forums such as Ignite London and lectured at the University of Greenwich.

Over the past 5 years, she delved into Artificial Intelligence at the University of Cambridge, the LSE and the Singularity Group, exploring its intersection with society and its impact on work across industries.

Sofia won the President's Prize for Outstanding Work in the 2022 IPA Excellence Diploma, for her novel approach to what she coined System 3, when AI and human cognition converge.

References

Federal Trade Commision USA. (2022). FTC explores rules cracking down on commercial surveillance and Lax data security practices. https://www.ftc.gov/news-events/news/press-releases/2022/08/ftc-explores-rules-cracking-down-commercial-surveillance-lax-data-security-practices

Gozman, V. (2022). The slow death of third-party cookies. *Forbes*. https://www.forbes.com/sites/theyec/2022/09/12/the-slow-death-of-third-party-cookies/?sh=5cbf38ff4026

Hill, M. (2023). The biggest data breach fines, penalties, and settlements so far. CSO online. https://www.csoonline.com/article/567531/the-biggest-data-breach-fines-penalties-and-settlements-so-far.html

Hoffman, B. (2022). Adscam. Type A Group LLC.

Hoffman, B. (2023). My talk at the EU parliament. https://typeagroup.createsend.com/campaigns/reports/viewCampaign.aspx?d=d&c=FC142680CDB9311A&ID=386E63F648DA11042540EF23F30FEDED&temp=False&tx=0&source=Report

Seng, D., & Mason, S. (2021). Artificial intelligence and evidence. *Singapore Academy of Law Journal, 33*, 241–279. https://doi.org/10.3316/informit.856086196428655

Stempel, J. (2023). Google fails to end $5 billion consumer privacy. *Reuters*. https://www.reuters.com/technology/google-fails-end-5-billion-consumer-privacy-lawsuit-2023-08-08

Walsh, D. (2023). The legal issues presented by generative AI. MIT Sloan School of Management. https://mitsloan.mit.edu/ideas-made-to-matter/legal-issues-presented-generative-ai